The *Illustrated* Stuart Dictionary

Dodo. About three feet tall, this flightless bird from Mauritius was last sighted in 1662. Its lack of fear of human hunters and the arrival of dogs and pigs led to its extinction. (*Artist: J. Le Keux, early nineteenth century. Wellcome Images*)

The *Illustrated* Stuart Dictionary

An A to Z of Notable Characters, Themes and Events from 1603 to 1714

Simon Sandys-Winsch

PEN & SWORD
HISTORY

First published in Great Britain in 2026 by
Pen & Sword History
An imprint of Pen & Sword Books Limited
Yorkshire – Philadelphia

ISBN 978 1 03619 975 3

A CIP catalogue record for this book is available from the British Library.

Typeset by Mac Style
Printed in the UK by CPI Group (UK) Ltd, Croydon, CR0 4YY.

FSC
www.fsc.org
MIX
Paper | Supporting responsible forestry
FSC® C013604

The Publisher's authorised representative in the EU for product safety is Authorised Rep Compliance Ltd., Ground Floor, 71 Lower Baggot Street, Dublin D02 P593, Ireland.
www.arccompliance.com

For a complete list of Pen & Sword titles please contact:

PEN & SWORD BOOKS LIMITED
47 Church Street, Barnsley, South Yorkshire, S70 2AS, England
E-mail: enquiries@pen-and-sword.co.uk
Website: www.pen-and-sword.co.uk
or
PEN AND SWORD BOOKS
1950 Lawrence Road, Havertown, PA 19083, USA
E-mail: uspen-and-sword@casematepublishers.com
Website: www.penandswordbooks.com

To

Sam, Hannah and Isabel

In memory of Rich Hayward (1965–2026)

Contents

SCOTLAND
Aberdeen
Killiecrankie
Glencoe
Dundee
Edinburgh
Dunbar
Wigtown
Newcastle
IRELAND
Derry
Ulster
Belfast
Boyne
Drogheda
Galway
Aughrim
Dublin
Limerick
Wexford
Marston Moor
York
Preston
Hull
Liverpool
Manchester
Nantwich
Leicester
WALES
Norwich
Naseby
Cambridge
Worcester
Edgehill
Oxford
The Gabbard
London
Bristol
Newbury
Chatham
Sedgemoor
Portsmouth
Lostwithiel
Torbay
Plymouth
Isle of Wight
Scilly Isles
Areas under royalist control in Dec. 1643

THE STUARTS (1603–1714)

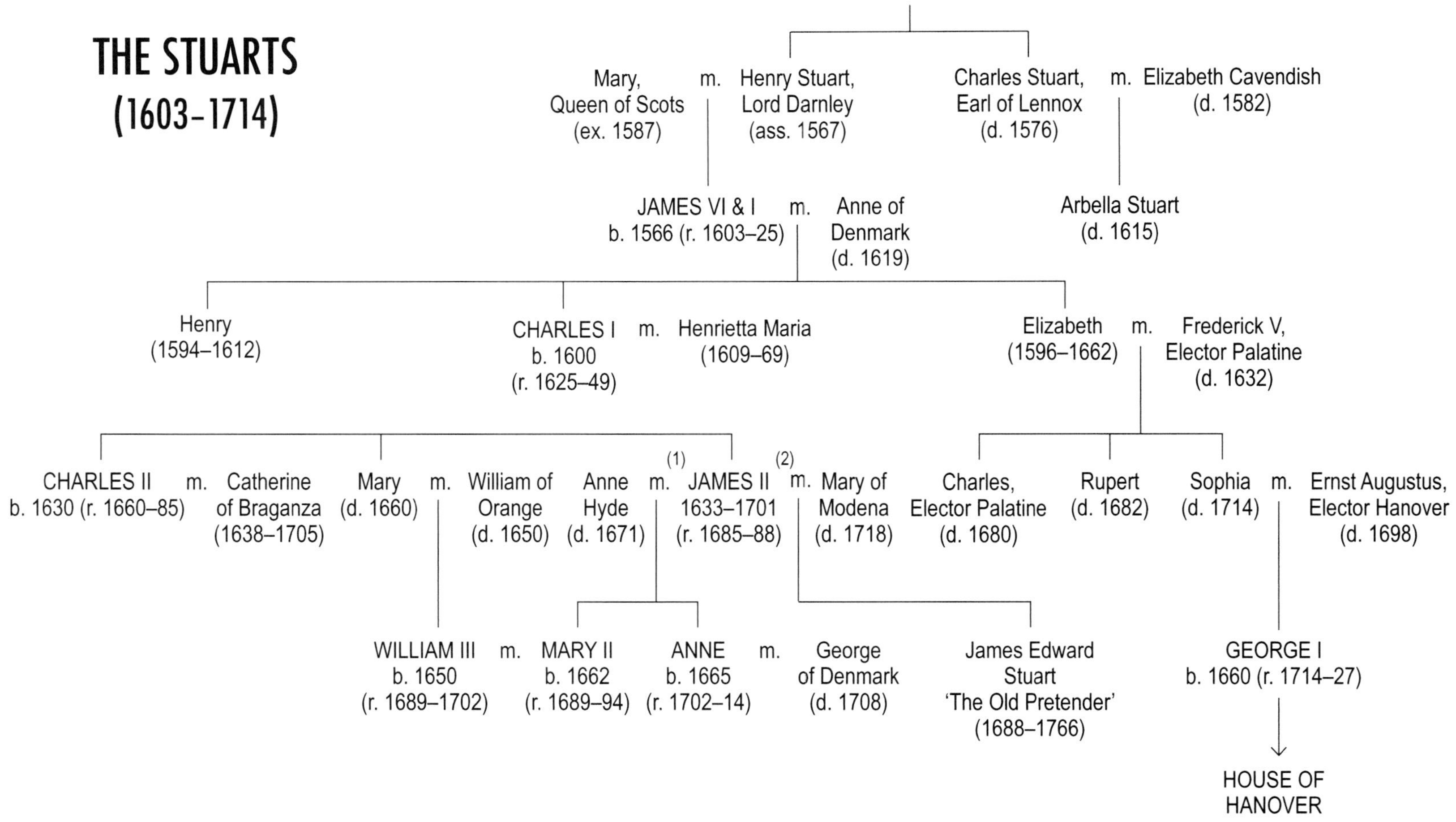

Preface

Another age, another signpost.

The Stuart era, however, comes across as having more gravitas than its predecessor. While the Reformation and development of the English state in the Tudor period are critically important, the seventeenth century behaves as the more serious of the two Early Modern Age siblings. The complexities of its political, scientific and literary developments are such that they had me scratching my head at times. I can only hope that I have successfully put them down on paper in a succinct and understandable fashion. Furthermore, there are two key strands that thread their way through the century: royal prerogative vs parliamentary privilege and an irrational fear of Catholicism. The major crisis points occurred when these two strands became intertwined in 1641–42, 1678–81 and 1688.

Again, I was faced with the excruciating problem of what to include and, again, I apologise for my omissions. Why not Prince Henry, Godolphin or the Duchess of Portsmouth? I hear you cry. Or Exclusion Crisis, Petition of Right or the Boyne? The line, of course, must be drawn somewhere but fortunately, such omissions are often referred to in other entries.

As alluded to, the Stuart Age is an incredibly important transitional period. Imagine, if you can, a person born in 1600 and, near the end of his/her incredibly long life, looking back from 1710. The noticeable changes would have been startling: the beginnings of a constitutional monarchy and a two-party political system, England's union with Scotland, scientific breakthroughs and the growth of towns and industries, greater involvement in politics by the masses, the first high-street shops alongside coffee and tea houses, buildings made of bricks and glass windows with chimneys, overseas colonies and exotic fruits, people being entertained by female actors, cricket and newspapers, primitive street lamps and piped water and the beginnings of religious tolerance and independence for women. Our 1710 supercentenarian's mind would have boggled at what the future held.

Welcome to the Stuart Age.

Timeline

JAMES I

1603	Death of Elizabeth I; accession of James VI of Scotland. Witchcraft Act. English population around four million.
1604	Peace treaty with Spain. Hampton Court Conference.
1605	Gunpowder Plot.
1606	First Union Jack flag.
1607	Founding of Virginia. Flight of the Earls.
1609	Statutes of Iona.
1610	Jonson's *The Alchemist* premieres. Failure of the Great Contract.
1611	King James Bible first published.
1612	Death of Robert Cecil. Death of Prince Henry.
1615	Completion of Coke's *Reports*.
1616	Death of William Shakespeare.
1617	Start of Buckingham's rise to power.
1618	Articles of Perth. James I's *The King's Book of Sports*.
1618–48	Thirty Years' War on the continent.
1619	Death of Anne of Denmark.
1620	Bacon's *Great Instauration*. Pilgrim Fathers sail to America. Hapsburg invasions of Palatinate and Bohemia. First successful submarine.
1623	Expedition to Spain by Prince Charles and Buckingham.

CHARLES I

1625	Death of James I; accession of Charles. Great Plague. Charles marries Henrietta Maria. War declared against Spain. Cadiz expedition. Bacon's *Essayes*.
1627	Five Knights' case. War against France. La Rochelle expedition.
1628	Petition of Right. Assassination of Buckingham. Harvey's *De Motu Cordis*.
1629	Parliament dissolved. Start of Charles's eleven years' personal rule.
1632	Death of John Eliot in the Tower. Wentworth appointed Lord Deputy of Ireland. Van Dyck settles in England.
1633	Laud appointed Archbishop of Canterbury. First sale of bananas in England.

1637	Prynne, Burton and Bastwicke pilloried. Prayer Book Riots in Scotland.
1637–38	John Hampden vs Ship Money case.
1639–40	Bishops' Wars with Scotland.
1640	Short and Long Parliaments summoned.
1641	Execution of Strafford. Erosion of royal prerogative by Parliament. Irish Rebellion. Grand Remonstrance.
1642	Charles attempts to arrest five MPs. Outbreak of the Civil Wars. Battle of Edgehill.
1643	Royalists capture Bristol. First Battle of Newbury. Solemn League and Covenant. Death of Pym.
1644	Battles of Marston Moor, Nantwich, Lostwithiel and Second Newbury.
1645	Self-Denying and New Model ordinances. Execution of Laud. Battle of Naseby.
1645–47	'Witch Fever' in East Anglia.
1646	Charles surrenders to Scots and end of First Civil War. Newcastle Proposals.
1647	Heads of Proposals. Putney Debates
1648	Second Civil War. Battle of Preston. Pride's Purge of Parliament

INTERREGNUM

1649	Execution of Charles I. Scots proclaim Charles II as king. Publication of *Eikon Basilike*. Outbreak of Third Civil War. House of Lords abolished. England invades Ireland. Massacres at Drogheda and Wexford. Banbury Mutiny.
1650	First coffee house opens. Battle of Dunbar. English population around five million.
1651	Battle of Worcester. End of the Civil Wars. First Navigation Act. Hobbes's *Leviathan*.
1652	Completion of conquest of Scotland.
1652–54	First Anglo-Dutch War.
1653	Completion of conquest of Ireland. Dismissal of Rump Parliament and Cromwell proclaimed Lord Protector. Battle of the Gabbard.
1655	Rule of the major-generals. Capture of Jamaica.
1657	Battle of Santa Cruz de Tenerife.
1658	Death of Cromwell.
1660	Restoration of the monarchy.

CHARLES II

1660	Declaration of Breda. Charles II returns and is crowned. Founding of the Royal Society. May's *The Accomplish't Cook*.

1660–69	Pepys's diary.
1661	Boyle's *The Sceptical Chymist.* Rescissory Act in Scotland. First race-based slavery law in Virginia.
1661–65	Enacting of the Clarendon Code.
1662	Charles marries Catherine of Braganza. Champagne invented in England.
1664	English capture New Amsterdam (New York).
1665–67	Second Anglo-Dutch War.
1665	Great Plague. Hooke's *Micrographia.* First newspaper – *The London Gazette.*
1666	Fire of London.
1667	Dutch raid on the Medway. First insurance company. Milton's *Paradise Lost.*
1667–74	Government dominated by the Cabal.
1668	Newton's reflecting telescope.
1669	Penn's *No Cross, No Crown.*
1670	Treaty of Dover. Bushel's case.
1672–74	Third Anglo-Dutch War.
1673	First Test Act.
1674–78	Government dominated by Earl of Danby.
1675	First effective microscope. Work begins on Wren's St. Paul's Cathedral.
1676–77	Bacon's Rebellion in Virginia.
1677	Behn's *The Rover* premieres.
1678	Second Test Act. Bunyan's *The Pilgrim's Progress.* Dryden's *All for Love* premieres.
1678–81	Popish Plot
1679	Habeas Corpus Act.
1679–81	Exclusion Crisis.
1679–88	'The Killing Time' in Scotland.
1681	Founding of Pennsylvania.
1683	Rye House Plot.
1684	Frost Fair.

JAMES II

1685	Death of Charles II and accession of James, Duke of York. Monmouth's Rebellion. Parliament prorogued. Matchlocks largely replaced by flintlocks.
1686	Godden vs Hales case.
1687	Declaration of Indulgence. Newton's *Principia.*
1688	Imprisonment of seven bishops. Birth of James Edward Stuart. Glorious Revolution. James flees the country.

WILLIAM III and MARY II

1688–97	War of the League of Augsburg.
1689	Accession of William of Orange and Mary. Bill of Rights. Battle of Killiecrankie. Toleration Act. Locke's *An Essay Concerning Human Understanding* and *Two Treatises of Government*. Purcell's *Dido and Aeneas* premieres.
1690	Battle of the Boyne.
1692	Massacre at Glencoe.
1692–93	Salem witchcraft trials.
1694	Bank of England founded. Death of Mary II. Triennial Act.
1694–1700	The 'Seven Ill Years' in Scotland.
1695	Licensing Act expires.
1695–97	Currency crisis.
1700	Darien Scheme abandoned. English population just over five million.
1701–14	War of the Spanish Succession.
1701	Act of Settlement. Death of James II.

ANNE

1702	Death of William III and accession of Anne.
1703	Great Storm.
1704	Battle of Blenheim.
1707	Act of Union.
1708	Breakdown of Anne's relationship with Sarah Churchill. Newcomen's steam engine.
1709	Darby uses coking coal for smelting iron. First county cricket match.
1710	Tories replace Whigs in power.
1711	Marlborough dismissed.
1713	Treaty of Utrecht.
1714	Death of Anne and succession of George I. End of the Stuart Age.

A

Anglican

A follower of the Church of England

After his break from Rome in the 1530s, Henry VIII had set himself up as the Supreme Head of the English Church and broken the power of the pope in England. He had also destroyed all monastic power to increase his revenues. Over the next twenty years the country had vacillated between adopting the new Protestant religion or maintaining the old **Catholic** ways. Finally, in 1559, Elizabeth I created the Church Settlement which adopted a compromising position in the hope of reconciling both sides. This was backed up by the 39 Articles of Religion (1563) which laid out the faith and practice of this new Church of England. These Articles were then incorporated into the Protestant *Book of Common Prayer*.

Broadly Protestant in nature, the new Church rejected the key Catholic belief in transubstantiation (bread and wine turning into the body and blood of Christ during the Eucharist), stated that services should be in English, priests could marry and that faith, rather than good works, led to salvation. Catholics, however, could take comfort from the non-prescriptive nature of the Articles and the retention of bishops' authority and two of the seven sacraments – baptism and the Eucharist. Priests could also continue to wear vestments and Elizabeth's title, 'Supreme Governor of the English Church', was more palatable than Henry VIII's 'Supreme Head'.

This 'middle way' was vigorously defended by the queen and her archbishops in the face of strong attacks by **Puritan** elements within the Church. Puritans believed that the Settlement was merely a halfway house and wanted a much more extreme version of Protestantism. Wrangles within the Church even spilled over into occasional parliamentary outbursts but Elizabeth held firm. It was the theologian, Richard Hooker, who gave Anglicanism a theological basis. His *Of the Lawes of Ecclesiastical Politie* (1594–97) rebutted both Catholic and Puritan standpoints and argued that human reason was as important as the Bible and Church tradition.

The Anglican Church was very much tied to the authority of the monarch. Therefore, any criticism of the Church was construed as criticism of the Crown. This meant that religion and politics were inextricably linked and would lead to devastating consequences in the first half of the seventeenth century when the **Civil Wars** erupted. As a backlash to the Puritan republic a more militant Anglican Church emerged after 1660, and it was only after the **Glorious Revolution** that it began to assume a more tolerant and stable character.

First Anglo-Dutch War
(1652–54)

In the early 1650s, it appeared that England and the United Provinces (Dutch Republic) should be natural allies. Both countries were similarly Calvinistic in religion and fiercely anti-**Catholic** and neither had a monarchy. Fifty years previously, England had been helping the Dutch in their war of independence against Spain. However, political and economic differences had come to the fore.

In 1649, the Dutch, like other nations, had been shocked by the execution of **Charles I** and supported the claim to the English throne of his son, Charles, giving him asylum. Charles's sister had married into the ruling Orange family and it was an English monarchist who assassinated the English ambassador later that year. At the same time, English merchants were becoming increasingly bitter about Dutch domination of their trade routes and their expulsion from the Dutch East Indies. The Dutch merchant fleet was considerably larger due to the relative cheapness of ship-building in the Provinces – just over £4 per ton of ship compared to £7 per ton in England. This was due to cheaper timber floated down the Rhine, lower wages and use of mass-production methods. The Dutch had also initiated a joint-stock company which provided a mass of capital for ship-building and overseas ventures.

Such advantages meant cheaper transportation costs and so it was usually Dutch ships which carried resources to England from its colonies in North America. Dutch traders were also able to buy cheap English cloth, dye it and sell it back in England at great profit. Adding insult to injury, the huge Dutch fishing fleet was also netting vast quantities of fish in home waters.

In 1651, England's Lord Protector, **Oliver Cromwell**, attempted to solve the problem by proposing a joint English-Dutch commonwealth that could dominate world trade. However, the Dutch, having spent the past eighty years fighting for their freedoms were not prepared to surrender their independence to England.

Allegory of Dutch prosperity. Merchant ships fill the foreground with wealthy Amsterdam in the distance. (*Artist: poss. R. de Baudous, c. 1614. Royal Library of Belgium*)

From this point on, matters escalated. The English **Parliament** then passed the Navigation Act, which banned any middlemen (mainly the Dutch) from carrying goods into England. This act of mercantilism had little effect on the Provinces as English goods were only a small percentage of their trade. Far more damaging were the acts of English privateers who used the new law as an excuse to capture Dutch merchant ships. In response, the Dutch brought more armed merchantmen into their fleet. The English then revived what they perceived as an ancient right of theirs – to be recognised as 'lords of the seas'. This meant that all foreign ships had to strike their flags, i.e. show submission, when encountering an English ship in the Channel or North Sea.

Near Dover in May 1652, the first shots were fired in anger between admirals Tromp and **Blake** when the former refused to strike his flags. The battle was inconclusive, but war was officially declared by England straight afterwards. An English victory at Kentish Knock (October 1652) was followed by a sobering defeat off Dungeness several weeks later and the English were also swept out of the Mediterranean after a defeat near Leghorn. In 1653, the Dutch were driven out of the Channel and then suffered a catastrophic defeat at the **Battle of the Gabbard**, an encounter that highlighted the superior English ships and tactics. The English now controlled the North Sea and started to blockade the Dutch coast. The subsequent collapse in trade and economic misery forced Tromp to try and break the stranglehold. Off the Dutch coast at Scheveningen, the Provinces suffered a final defeat and Tromp was killed.

With little hope of victory, the Dutch sued for peace, but Cromwell was also keen to end this damaging war with fellow Protestants. As a result, the Provinces were given surprisingly lenient peace terms at the Treaty of Westminster (April 1654). The main concessions were the retention of the Navigation Act and the promise not to allow the young **William of Orange** to become Stadtholder (he later did become king of England!). Dutch ships had to strike their flags in the Channel, too, but the main prize, the wealth of the East Indies, remained in Dutch hands. Cromwell's attempts to unite the two countries were again rejected and the underlying commercial rivalry was not addressed.

Second Anglo-Dutch War

(1665–67)

The driving force behind this conflict was, again, commercial rivalry. English merchants were jealous of Dutch control of the lucrative East Indies and their supremacy in the Baltic. They were also contesting domination of the Atlantic **slave trade** and in the Mediterranean. Dutch success was founded on a huge ship-building industry and availability of cheap capital based on its innovative banking system. This, in turn, allowed the Dutch merchants to undercut all competitors and to dominate world trade.

The Navigation Acts of 1660 and 1663 tightened up the 1651 Act by banning English colonies from exporting various named raw materials to foreign countries – an act of mercantilism aimed at protecting English trade. This was not enough for the merchant class, however, who were convinced that success in the **First Anglo-Dutch War** had led to economic prosperity. Their continued complaints about confiscations of English ships in the East Indies pressurised the government into distributing bellicose literature that likened their rivals to fat, slippery 'two-legged cheese worms'. In 1664, a squadron of English frigates easily captured New Amsterdam (renamed New York, in honour of James, the Duke of York), which only served to galvanise the jingoistic mood in England. By now, according to the diarist, **Samuel Pepys**, the country was 'mad for war'.

A 38-gun frigate. (*Artist: P. Puget, seventeenth century. Metropolitan Museum of Art*)

The Dutch, led by De Witt, reluctantly accepted the loss of New Amsterdam – it was not of great significance to them – but sent a fleet to protect their trading stations in West Africa. The English responded by attacking Dutch merchant ships and, amid great joy, **Charles II** declared war in March 1665.

The Lord High Admiral – **James, Duke of York** – immediately ordered a blockade of the Dutch coast to prevent enemy squadrons from uniting and to strangle the Dutch economy. However, a lack of provisions temporarily forced his ships back to port. The Dutch gathered their forces and, in June, met the English fleet 40 miles east of Lowestoft. There, the stronger and more powerful English ships used line of battle, as opposed to the Dutch melee approach, and shattered their opponents. A poor chain of command and ill-discipline added to Dutch difficulties, and it was only the desultory English pursuit that allowed most of their ships to return to port. The defeat, however, greatly angered the Dutch people; some even threw one of their admirals into the sea and hurled stones at him.

The following year, the Dutch managed to amass more capital ships (those of the greatest size and armament) although the shallow waters around the Netherlands meant that they could never match the largest of the English capital ships. In June, the two fleets met in one of the longest naval battles in history – the Four Days' Fight. Around eighty ships faced each other, both using line of battle for the first time. The result was inconclusive although the English came off worse, suffering 25 per cent casualties and the loss of twenty ships (Dutch losses were 10 per cent casualties and four ships). These figures are partly a reflection of the more aggressive and risky tactics adopted by the English commanders, **Prince Rupert** and **George Monck**, and partly because a French declaration of war had diverted some English ships away in the initial stages of the battle.

By the end of the year, the spiralling costs and damage to trade meant that both sides were keen to open peace talks. The negotiations were stalling, however, and De Witt, aware of King Charles's peace talks with France, decided to launch a daring attack which would force the English to sue for peace. The subsequent **Raid on the Medway** in June 1667, led by Admiral De Ruyter, was one of the worst disasters in the history of the Royal Navy. The defeat had a huge psychological effect on the English population, many of whom had just suffered the **Plague** and **Fire of London**. The unhappy mood of the country, combined with his dire financial circumstances, forced Charles to agree to the Treaty of Breda in July.

In terms favouring the Dutch, England recognised that any goods being imported from Germany could be transported in Dutch ships and that, in times of war, neutral ships could not be attacked. All captured islands in the West Indies were returned too. Oddly enough, perhaps, the Dutch preferred to keep the colony of Suriname, which they had captured, in exchange for the loss of New Amsterdam (New York). The sugar plantations in the former were considered far more valuable. Therefore, for the first time, the eastern seaboard of America, from Canada to Florida, was recognised as being under English control.

Third Anglo-Dutch War

(1672–74)

The origins of this conflict lay in the terms of the Secret Treaty of Dover (1670) between **Charles II** and the French king, Louis XIV. Louis' objectives were to defeat the United Provinces so that he could conquer the Spanish Netherlands. To achieve this, he needed to isolate the Dutch, hence the need for an alliance with England. Among the terms was a promise by Charles to provide sixty warships and 4,000 troops to assist Louis. In return, Louis would provide him with £230,000 per year and the control of some lucrative Dutch ports once the Provinces were conquered. The money would give Charles a fair degree of financial independence from **Parliament** and the war would offer a chance of revenge after the humiliations of 1667.

War broke out in 1672 – a disastrous year for the Dutch – when the French conquered huge swathes of the country and an Anglo-French fleet threatened to land troops on the coast. The opening of dykes to flood their lands prevented annihilation on land and aggressive action by De Ruyter at the Battle of Solebay deterred a seaborne invasion. Fearful of a French-dominated Europe, Spain and the Holy Roman Empire intervened and forced France back. At the same time, the lower draught of De Ruyter's ships allowed them to hide behind the Dutch sandbanks and launch damaging hit-and-run attacks upon the allied fleet.

Charles's money was rapidly drying up, and public opinion turned against the war. The general feeling that France was using England for its own gain was even voiced by **Prince Rupert** himself who accused the French fleet of not pulling its weight. Despite the Treaty of Dover, the king was forced to seek peace. At the Treaty of Westminster (1674), the Provinces paid England a small indemnity and recognised it as 'lord of the sea' in the Channel and North Sea. It also returned New York which it had recaptured in the previous year. From a personal point of view, Charles was pleased that the war had cost De Witt his position (and life – an angry mob hanged his body by the feet, ripped it apart and ate it!) and elevated his nephew, **William of Orange**, to Stadtholder of the Provinces.

* * *

The three wars had profound effects. Despite winning two of them, the 1670s mark the beginning of the end of the Dutch Republic's Golden Age. With its shipping routes so close to England, Dutch commerce had been badly hurt, and the government became burdened with crippling war loans and interest payments. At the same time, as France grew stronger, it had to divert more resources to its land defences. Meanwhile, England developed a stronger economy and started to replace Dutch hegemony in world trade. Within fifteen years, the Dutch had become reliant upon English strength to protect it from French aggression. In the end, it was a victim of its own success as its neighbours sought to copy and surpass its achievements.

The wars brought technical improvements to the English navy. In its arms race with the Dutch, it built bigger ships with greater armaments (over 2,000 tons, 100 guns and 800 crew). It also copied the Dutch design which was wider and had its lowest tier of guns higher above the water. This allowed for more storage space which meant there were enough provisions to be out at sea for six months instead of just ten weeks. Additionally, the English successfully developed the line of battle tactic, a signalling system to improve communications and improved discipline. In effect, the wars sowed the seeds for English domination of the high seas.

Anne

(1665–1714)

Queen of England, **Scotland** and **Ireland** from 1702 and Queen of Great Britain and Ireland from 1707 to 1714

Anne was the younger daughter of **James, Duke of York** (and niece of King **Charles II)** and his first wife, Anne Hyde. Her mother died when she was 6 and two years later (1673), James married an Italian princess, Mary of Modena, and publicly declared his **Catholic** faith. Subsequently, the king ordered that she and her elder sister, Mary, were to be brought up as **Anglican**s. Anne's **education** was typical of an aristocratic girl of the time with the focus being on making her as marriageable as possible. Learned women were not considered desirable and so her knowledge on a range of subjects such as history, politics, law and philosophy was therefore very limited.

In 1677, Anne's sister married the Dutch leader, **William of Orange**, and moved to Holland. Charles finally chose a husband for his second niece in 1683 – Prince George of Denmark – a Protestant, which would appeal to his subjects. The choice was also designed to please his ally, Louis XIV of France, who sought an alliance with Denmark to isolate his Dutch enemies. The **marriage** turned out to be a very loving one despite the accusations of George being a vacuous and drunken dullard. Charles once said of him, 'I have tried him drunk, and I have tried him sober and there is nothing in him!' It is true that he was docile and lacked ambition; in his later position as Lord High Admiral he showed little interest other than building model ships. He was a good-natured, loyal and loving husband, however, and Anne became increasingly dependent on him.

Charles II died, childless, in 1685 and so Anne's father became King **James II**. Three years later, leading politicians asked William of Orange and Mary to rescue England from James's increasingly autocratic and pro-Catholic rule. In the ensuing **Glorious Revolution** (1688), Anne, being an Anglican, threw in her lot behind her sister and brother-in-law. Before fleeing the country, James was heard to lament, 'God help me. Even my children have forsaken me!' In the following year, the **Bill of Rights**, outlined the royal succession. After **William III** and **Mary II**, the throne would go to Mary's children. Failing that, Anne and her children would inherit.

In the early 1690s, Anne fell out with the new monarchs. They tried to prevent her from having a parliamentary income and blocked George from military office. Possibly, they feared an opposition group coalescing around her. Matters were made worse when they clashed over Anne's friendship with **Sarah Churchill**. Her husband, the general, **John Churchill**, had been sacked and they had to have Sarah physically removed from Anne's household. Soon after, Mary paid her a visit but instead of commiserating over the death of Anne's newborn baby, she berated her for her friendship with Sarah. It was the last time the sisters ever saw each other. After the Churchills were rehabilitated in 1698, Anne and William were publicly reconciled although she still referred to him as 'the Dutch monster'.

When Mary died, childless, in 1694, Anne became first in line to the throne. She was, however, in the middle of a long series of personal tragedies. She fell pregnant seventeen times in the same number of years. Twelve times, she either miscarried or gave birth to stillborn children. On four other occasions, the infants died before the age of two. The only survivor, Prince Henry, was a sickly child and he too passed away, aged 11, in 1700. Anne and George were overcome with grief and ordered a day of mourning for each anniversary of Henry's death. By now, it was clear that neither William nor Anne would create heirs. To prevent the chance of another Catholic monarch, **Parliament** passed the Act of Settlement (1701) which offered the British throne to the Protestant granddaughter of **James I** – Sophia, the Electress of Hanover and her heirs.

As Queen

Anne was proclaimed queen straight after William's sudden death in March 1702 but, in some respects, she was not a natural choice for such a position. She was naturally shy, depended on well-scripted speeches and impromptu conversations were embarrassingly awkward, especially given her limited education. On occasions, she was seen to move her lips to pretend that she had contributed to a discussion. This was all a far cry from the monarch she most admired and dressed like – Elizabeth I. She had also suffered from poor **health** for most of her life partly due to her continual pregnancies and, from the 1690s, developed incapacitating gout. The subsequent lack of exercise made her put on much weight and led to

A specially designed sedan chair to take Queen Anne to her coronation. It was lower to the ground and with an open back to allow her coronation robes to flow behind. (*Author: Thornbury and Walford's 'Old and New London', 1870s via historicalmedallions.com*)

further health problems. For her coronation ceremony, she had to be carried in a sedan chair, and, around court, she used a wheelchair or was seen speeding around in a chariot-like chaise.

Despite the encumbrance of her ill-health, Anne was able to rule, not just reign. The Crown was still the centre of government, and she had the right to appoint and dismiss ministers. Her approval for new policies was always sought although, through non-cooperation, ministers could sometimes force her hand. Anne would display a great deal of interest in politics and regularly attended cabinet meetings and the House of Lords. Technically, she could support parliamentary bills but that did not guarantee their success. The Tories, for instance, brought forward the Occasional Conformity Bill which aimed to disqualify non-Anglicans from public office. Despite the queen's support, it failed three times to pass through Parliament. She did, however, veto the Scottish Militia Bill in 1708 – she feared that the proposed Scottish militia would support a threatened invasion by her half-brother, James Edward Stuart. This was the last time a British monarch vetoed a parliamentary bill.

Anne's natural sympathies lay with the **Tories** as both saw themselves as defenders of the Anglican Church. However, from the start, she declared that her two main aims were to reduce French power and ensure the Protestant succession. The Tories were, at best, half-hearted on these issues though so it was to the **Whigs** that Anne turned for most of her reign. With Churchill leading her armies in the War of the Spanish Succession (1701–14) and Sidney Godolphin skilfully raising the funds, the country saw unprecedented success on the continent. By 1709, however, the public (and Anne) wanted peace. Heavy taxation, the Whigs' rejection of generous French peace terms and horrendous allied casualties at the Battle of Malplaquet all led to Tory domination of government from 1710. Separate peace negotiations damaged Britain's reputation in the eyes of her allies but the eventual Treaty of Utrecht (1713) successfully established long-lasting peace and gained Britain trade concessions, several overseas possessions such as Gibraltar and Newfoundland and France's recognition of the Act of Settlement.

The greatest influence over Anne in the first half of her reign was her childhood friend, Sarah Churchill. So close were they that Anne was happy for Sarah to treat her as an equal. When writing to each other, for instance, they addressed each other as 'Mrs Morley' (Anne) and 'Mrs Freeman' (Sarah). Sarah's power and influence increased as her husband won a string of victories, most famously the **Battle of Blenheim**. The more Sarah dominated however, the more Anne resented her subordinate role. Politically, they clashed over the appointment of ministers. Preferring an end to the war, Anne turned to the Tories, while Sarah tried to force her to appoint Whigs who supported her husband's war effort. Added to this was Anne's growing resentment of Sarah's high-handed and insensitive

Embroidered picture showing Anne presenting Marlborough with a laurel wreath. (*Artist: unknown, 1710. Metropolitan Museum of Art*)

behaviour towards her. In 1708. For example, she publicly told the queen to be quiet outside St Paul's Cathedral. Later that year, George died and Anne was completely grief-stricken. Sarah, however, merely told her to get over it and took down his portrait from the wall.

As Sarah became increasingly absent, Anne took the opportunity to turn to a servant of a far gentler nature – Abigail Hill, later Lady Masham. Abigail then moved into Sarah's rooms at Kensington Palace and, in 1711, officially replaced Sarah when Anne appointed her Keeper of the Privy Purse. Afterwards, Sarah published Anne's private letters and unfairly accused her of being weak and ignorant as well as being a lesbian. It is true that Anne had had several romantic relationships with females in her life but such 'passionate affairs' between women were quite normal at that time and did not necessarily mean anything sexual. Abigail, meanwhile, had connections with the Tory party and, partly because of her new position of influence, Tories replaced several Whig ministers in key positions. This, in turn, led to Churchill's dismissal and the war's conclusion.

Despite feeling a sense of guilt over betraying her father in 1688, Anne never faced any serious threats from those who supported his cause – the Jacobites. James died in 1701 but his son's claim to the throne was supported by most Catholic countries. The issue became more serious when the Scottish Parliament insisted on the right to ignore England's Act of Settlement and choose its own monarch after Anne's death. Alarmed at the prospect of a Franco-Jacobite, hostile neighbour on its northern border, the English government threatened to impose trade sanctions. Already struggling economically, the Scots backed down and, aided by a few well-aimed bribes, agreed to the Acts of Union (1707). By this, **Scotland** would retain its Church and legal system, but it agreed to the Act of Settlement and the English and Scottish parliaments became one, sitting in Westminster. The Kingdom of Great Britain thereby came into existence – a concept that had been eagerly supported by Anne ever since her accession.

The queen's health had been deteriorating for months but it was a series of strokes that finally killed her in August 1714. So overweight had she become that, at her funeral, it took twelve pallbearers to carry her almost square-shaped coffin. Two months earlier, Sophia of Hanover had died and so it was her son, George, who inherited the British throne. One of Anne's doctors wrote, 'I believe sleep was never more welcome to a weary traveller than death was to her.' It is true that Anne had suffered for a great deal of her life, both physically and mentally, and she had continually battled those who had tried to manipulate her. The publicly acrimonious split with Sarah Churchill had been particularly painful and had damaged her popularity.

On balance, it is probably fair to say that the crown had never sat easily upon Queen Anne's head. She had taken her role seriously, spoken passionately in defence of her country and Church and was a great patron of music, poetry and theatre. However, she had never sought the limelight and her insecurities meant that she was always dependant on others for comfort and advice. It should be remembered, too, that she was Britain's first constitutional monarch and, as such, her power was curtailed by the development of party politics. All things considered, though, Anne's reign can also be remembered for its military successes, foreign acquisitions and union with Scotland, all of which facilitated Britain's path towards a global empire.

Anne of Denmark

(1574–1619)

Wife of **James I** (and VI). Queen of **Scotland** from 1589 and of England from 1603

Anne, pronounced 'Anna', was the daughter of King Frederick II of Denmark and Sophie of Mecklenburg. She was brought up in a caring and loving household and probably received an excellent **education**. She was a particularly skilled linguist and could speak, German, French, English and Scots.

Marriage contract between Anne of Denmark and James VI of Scotland. The seals of all the witnesses are attached. (*Author: unknown, 1589. Danish National Archives*)

Aged 14, she was married by proxy to James VI of Scotland and, soon after, set sail to meet her 23-year-old husband. Storms, however, forced her to disembark in Oslo. James, concerned about Anne's welfare and impatient with waiting, displayed a rare romantic impulse by sailing across the North Sea to rescue her. Upon meeting his tall, blonde and blue-eyed bride, he shocked Anne's entourage by kissing her in public! The wedding took place in Oslo, they honeymooned around Denmark, and she finally arrived in Scotland in May 1590. Soon after, Anne was crowned in the first Protestant coronation in Scotland's history. At this stage, by all accounts, the **marriage** was a happy and loving one.

Relations between the two started to strain, however, over a dispute about the lands around the former abbey of Dunfermline which Anne had been promised in the marriage settlement. The lands, with their accompanying income, were vital for her if she was to be able to fund her own court and servants. James had granted wardship of these lands to his chancellor three years earlier and it was only through her determination that she finally won ownership. Matters deteriorated further after the royal couple had their first child, Henry (1594). As was the Scottish tradition, he was sent away to a lord's household to be raised but Anne was devastated and fought hard for custody of her son. Public rows and tears ensued but James refused to budge. In 1600, Anne was even accused of supporting a conspiracy against James – but with no evidence. Despite all this and James's clear preference for the company of men, they had six more children – **Elizabeth**, **Charles** and four who died in infancy.

In 1603, Elizabeth I of England died, and James travelled south to claim the throne that he had been offered. Anne, while pregnant, took the opportunity to try and reclaim her son but her failure to do so caused such anger that she suffered another one of her miscarriages. After refusing to travel to London until she had custody of Henry, James finally acquiesced. By now, however, religious differences had arisen. It was becoming clear that Anne, despite her Protestant upbringing, had discreetly adopted **Catholic**ism and her refusal to take the **Anglican** communion during the Westminster coronation was a source of much embarrassment for the new English king.

The more relaxed social scene in London was much more to Anne's liking and she received a generous income from estates that had once belonged to Catherine of Aragon as well as her Scottish lands. Meanwhile, she and her husband continued to drift further apart. While James preferred to stay in hunting lodges outside the capital, Anne enjoyed the comforts of Greenwich Palace and Somerset House (she renamed it Denmark House). After narrowly surviving the birth and death of her last child in 1607, she refused to have any more children and she and James spent the rest of her life apart. Every so often arguments would continue to flare up, such as when Anne accidentally shot and killed James's favourite hunting dog, but matters were always resolved. James would even seek her approval of his male favourites (she detested Robert Carr but liked **George Villiers**).

Anne's court became a cultural hub of Jacobean England. The production of masques (disguisings), which had been popular in Tudor England, reached its zenith. Based on mythological themes, masques were danced rather than acted and the final dance would usually include the, sometimes drunken, audience. With witty scripts written by **Ben Jonson** and elaborate sets and costumes designed by **Inigo Jones**, Anne's masques at Whitehall Palace were as good as any being performed on the continent. The queen, an elegant dancer herself, would sometimes perform on the stage and occasionally draw criticism such as when she revealed her lower legs or, while six months pregnant, she blackened her skin to pretend she was an African. Interestingly, some of the masque ideas came from Anne herself and possibly reveal her true character. In one performance, being the queen, she was expected to play the role of Juno but, instead, she demanded the part of Athena, the goddess of war and wisdom. These masques, some with all-female casts, are also seen as an important stage in female performance.

Anne was a great patron of other art forms too. She commissioned Jones to design Banqueting House in Whitehall and the Queen's House at Greenwich and watched many of Shakespeare's plays. She collected books, too, and employed several musicians, composers and painters. The ensuing cultural vibrancy in early seventeenth-century England drew much admiration from abroad but, at home, Anne's extravagance received much criticism in some quarters. Politically, Anne had little access to power, but she was not without influence. She helped to arrange her children's marriages, intervened on behalf of the Elizabethan favourite, Walter Ralegh, and aided in the dismissal of Robert Carr.

Prince Henry hunting. Would events have unfolded differently had he succeeded his father? (*Artist: R. Peake the elder, 1603. Metropolitan Museum of Art*)

From 1612, though, Anne started to withdraw from public life. The death of Prince Henry that year was a terrible blow to her, and, in the following year, Elizabeth departed for Bohemia with her new husband. At about the same time, Anne started to suffer attacks of gout, which restricted her movements. From 1616, she began showing symptoms of dropsy (oedema) and chose a more solitary existence. Moments of recovery allowed her to go hunting and she even attempted an incognito trip to the shopping centre at the Royal Exchange. She eventually died in March 1619 at Hampton Court Palace in the same room as Henry VIII's wife, Jane Seymour, had in 1537. Due to his superstitions regarding illness and death, James rarely visited Anne during her final illness and was absent at both her death and her funeral. Despite this and their distant relationship, it appears he was genuinely saddened by her passing and wrote melancholic poetry in her memory.

As recently as the late twentieth century, historians have regarded Anne as an insignificant, unintelligent extravagance in the Jacobean court. If one digs deeper, however, one finds a woman of much intelligence and strength of character who made a significant contribution to England's cultural development.

Ashley Cooper, Anthony (1st Earl of Shaftesbury)

(1621–83)

Politician

Ashley Cooper came from a wealthy, landowning family in southern England. Aged 10 when his parents died, he was sent to live with the trustees of his inheritance. At 15, he enrolled at Oxford University but left within a year after instigating a minor riot. He then studied law at Lincoln's Inn and, in 1639, married Margaret Coventry, daughter of the Lord Keeper of the Great Seal for **Charles I**. She died after ten years; he had two more **marriage**s but only one of his children reached adulthood. Using his family connections, he became MP for Tewkesbury during the Short **Parliament** of 1640, despite still being a minor aged 19 and joined the king's side upon the outbreak of the **Civil Wars** in 1642. This was short-lived, however, as he believed that Charles was heavily under the influence of **Catholic**s and he switched to the Parliamentarian cause.

It is unknown whether he supported the king's execution, but he became an official of **Oliver Cromwell**'s republican Commonwealth, first as a justice of the peace and later as a member of the Council of State. Ashley Cooper was also elected to the Barebones Parliament of 1653 and, in the following year, voted in favour of Cromwell becoming king. However, in 1655, he disagreed with the Lord Protector's decision to allow the army to rule the country instead of Parliament and fell from favour. For the rest of the decade, he continued to fight for parliamentary rule and had to deny accusations that he was a secret monarchist. At one point he was even involved in plots to initiate uprisings against the army.

By 1660, he realised that the country needed to restore the monarchy and, as a member of the Convention Parliament, voted in favour of this. He, along with eleven others, travelled to The Hague to invite **Charles II** to take his throne. Ashley Cooper was pardoned for working with the Commonwealth regime and joined the king's privy council and, in the following year, Charles made him Lord Ashley. Further advancement, however, was prevented by his opposition to the policies of the **Earl of Clarendon**, the Lord Chancellor. In Parliament, he campaigned for religious toleration and argued, successfully, that only those directly involved in Charles I's death should face charges of treason. This led to him, as a member of the regicide commission, having to sentence former colleagues to death.

During the 1660s, Ashley Cooper became a proprietor of the province of Carolina in North America (named after Charles I). He took a great interest in its governance and asked the philosopher, **John Locke**, to help draw up the colony's constitution. Locke had been a medical student when they met in 1666 and treated a cyst on Ashley Cooper's liver by inserting a tube attached to a permanent external tap. His royalist enemies later nicknamed him 'Tapski' (a reference, also, to his support for Poland's elected monarchy). With Ashley Cooper's input, Locke created a constitution which was feudal and aristocratic in nature but did allow for religious toleration and secret ballots during elections.

After the fall of Clarendon in 1667, Ashley Cooper became a member of the Cabal that dominated the government for the next seven years (his was the second 'a' in Cabal). During this period, he campaigned for leniency for Protestant opponents to the **Anglican** Church, customs duties reform and union with **Scotland**. He also supported the outbreak of the **Third Anglo-Dutch War** and had agreed to the Treaty of Dover (1670), unaware of its secret clauses. Despite his suspicions of French motives, he had previously been a sugar plantation owner in Barbados and saw Dutch commercial power as being a major threat to English trade. In 1672, Charles rewarded Ashley Cooper by appointing him Lord Chancellor and making him Earl of Shaftesbury.

This represented the zenith of his career, however, because Shaftesbury became increasingly concerned about the royal succession. With the king having no legitimate heirs and refusing to remarry, the heir to the throne was his brother, **James, Duke of York**, a suspected Catholic. He therefore supported the Test Act (1673) which forced all holders of public office to take the Anglican communion. Shaftesbury's fears grew when York refused to do so and married the Catholic Mary of Modena, which raised the prospect of the couple producing a Catholic heir. Shaftesbury now threw his energies into having James barred from the succession and making the king's illegitimate son, the Duke of Monmouth, first in line to the throne. Charles, in support of his brother, sacked Shaftesbury at the end of the year.

Lord Shaftesbury. (*Artist: R. Cooper from Duchess of Dorset collection at Knole, 1859 via Wikimedia Commons*)

Shaftesbury now worked tirelessly in opposition to the monarchy and to James's succession. Whipping up anti-Catholic fervour in Parliament, he supported a range of bills which attacked the Duke of York. To defend his brother, Charles prorogued Parliament and ordered Shaftesbury to leave London. In 1675, Shaftesbury anonymously wrote his *A Letter from a Person of Quality to his Friend in the Country* in which he attacked absolutist government and divine right and argued that Protestantism and the rule of law had to be defended. After publication, this book became a bestseller partly because, for the first time, it revealed debates within the House of Lords. Ignoring his ban from London, he made eloquent speeches in Parliament denouncing royal power for which he was temporarily lodged in the Tower of London (1677).

By now, Shaftesbury's supporters were coalescing into a political faction which became known as the **Whig** Party. Shaftesbury and the Whigs were quick to take advantage of the **Popish Plot** in 1678 by forcing another Test Act through Parliament which forced Catholic peers to resign from the Lords. They also demanded, in vain, the removal of York and the king's Catholic wife, **Catherine de Braganza**, from the royal court. Shaftesbury had now become very popular, especially with Londoners who saw him as a guardian of their religion and liberties. Fearing for his life, they even provided armed escorts to protect him. Shaftesbury also directed his attacks against the king's royalist chief minister, the Earl of Danby, by trying to impeach him. However, this, along with a bill to exclude York from the throne was thwarted by Charles proroguing Parliament again. He did succeed, though, in passing the Habeas Corpus Act (1679) with the aim of preventing any future unlawful imprisonments by a tyrannical monarch.

By 1681, it was becoming clear that the Popish Plot had just been a sham. This discredited the Whigs and enabled their political opponents, the **Tories**, to take the ascendancy. That year, Shaftesbury was sent to the Tower again, for high treason. Using *habeas corpus*, he was eventually brought to court and the lack of any reliable evidence led to his release. This led to great celebrations on the streets of London with crowds shouting, 'No Popish successor, no York, a Monmouth' and 'God bless the Earl of Shaftesbury!' In the following year, Charles fell ill. Parliament had been dissolved so Shaftesbury, fearful of York's imminent accession, felt that the only course of action left to him was open rebellion. He even considered assassination of the king and York. However, he lacked enough support and, fearing a return to the Tower, he decided to flee the country. His health deteriorated on the journey to Amsterdam where he died in February 1683.

Despite being permanently crippled and having to use a walking stick, Shaftesbury was a huge political figure with great energy and intelligence. Many of his contemporaries derided him for the number of times that he switched his loyalties. This, however, was only due to the consistency of his beliefs. He fought hard for constitutional government and the prevention of absolutism, either by the monarch or by the army. In the process, he became the first political leader of England – the central figure behind the Whig party. Ultimately, Shaftesbury failed in preventing the accession of James, Duke of York but the events of that reign vindicated him and his principles triumphed in the **Glorious Revolution**.

B

Bacon, Sir Francis

(1561–1626)

Politician, philosopher, author and lawyer

Bacon was born in York House, the son of the Lord Keeper of the Seal and his mother was sister-in-law to Elizabeth I's chief advisor, Lord Burghley. He attended Cambridge University aged 12 and then, three years later, studied law at the Inns of Court. He continued his studies while touring abroad and began his parliamentary career soon after. Being constantly in debt, he frequently sought political advancement but, despite his closeness to the queen's favourite, the Earl of Essex, Bacon was constantly thwarted by Elizabeth's evident dislike for him. After Essex's attempted revolt (1601) he gained some favour in his role as state prosecutor at the subsequent trial, but it was not until the accession of **James I** that he gained the promotions he sought.

Bacon was knighted in 1603 and then attained the posts of Solicitor General (1607), Attorney General (1613), privy councillor (1616) and finally the top position of Lord Chancellor in 1618. His rise to power was eased by his support for the royal prerogative and some of James's aims, such as a political union with Scotland but he was also a skilled mediator and managed to gain **Parliament**'s trust too. Bacon's rise was facilitated by the death of his cousin and chief minister, **Robert Cecil**, in 1612 and his close friendship with the king's favourite, **George Villiers**, but he also revealed a Machiavellian side to his character in the way that he removed his main rival, **Sir Edward Coke**, from positions of influence.

In early 1621 Bacon was made Viscount St Alban but, soon after, spectacularly fell from power. After being accused of taking bribes to influence court cases, he admitted to taking money from litigants, a common practice then, but never to manipulating any trials. However, the damage was done and he had to resign from all his posts and was even briefly imprisoned in the Tower. James abandoned him, possibly to divert attention from similar accusations being laid against Villiers, and Bacon may have stepped down willingly anyway. Certainly, he was suffering ill-health at the time, and he may have wanted to avoid accusations of sodomy. In 1606, he had married the 13-year-old Alice Barnham but his constant debts and possible preference for men along with her later adultery made the marriage a childless and unhappy one.

His forced retirement enabled Bacon to complete the huge body of written work for which he is best known. Perhaps most famous of all were his *Essayes* (completed in 1625) in which he philosophised on fifty-eight topics ranging from truth, death, love and friendship to atheism, architecture, deformity and travel. The work was widely praised by contemporaries for its eloquence, witty analogies, vivid imagery and richness of language. Many phrases that he created are currently in the *Oxford Book of Quotations* such as 'knowledge itself is power', 'hostages to fortune' and 'if the hill will not come to Mohammed, Mohammed will go to the hill'. Such is the quality of Bacon's writing that there are even those who claim that he edited the **King James Bible** and was the true author of Shakespeare's works. A year later, *New Atlantis* was published in which he laid out his vision of utopia on the island of Bensalem.

Even more important is Bacon's contribution to the field of science. He believed that human progress was being limited by reliance on knowledge from the scriptures and the ancient Greeks such as Aristotle. In his *Great Instauration* (1620) he conceived a plan to enable a golden age for mankind, facilitated by a whole new approach to natural philosophy (science). Instead of creating hypotheses and finding evidence to prove them, as was currently practised, Bacon insisted on doing away with all human preconceptions and, instead, using methodical examination of what could be observed, repeatedly, to arrive at conclusions. This radically new approach, known as scientific method, became the cornerstone for all future scientific progress, enabled the Scientific Revolution later that century and made Bacon a hero in the eyes of those like **Boyle** and **Hooke**.

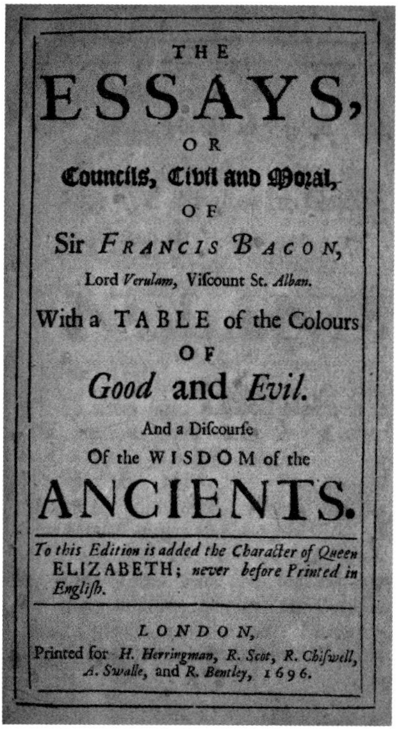
THE
ESSAYS,
OR
Councils, Civil and Moral,
OF
Sir FRANCIS BACON,
Lord Verulam, Viſcount St. Alban.
With a TABLE of the Colours
OF
Good and Evil.
And a Diſcourſe
Of the WISDOM of the
ANCIENTS.
To this Edition is added the Character of Queen ELIZABETH; never before Printed in Engliſh.
LONDON,
Printed for H. Herringman, R. Scot, R. Chiſwell, A. Swalle, and R. Bentley, 1696.

Title page of *Essayes*. (*Author: F. Bacon, 1696 edition via Wikimedia Commons*)

He died in Highgate from pneumonia after stuffing a dead chicken with snow to see if the ice would preserve it. Lauded by the likes of Descartes, **Ben Jonson**, Jefferson and Kant, Bacon is probably the single biggest influence on Western philosophy in the modern age. His restless, massive intellect attempted to address every issue in **society** – from government, law and colonies to science, gardening and health – in his hope that humans would eventually reach their Bensalem.

Behn, Aphra

(1640–89)

Writer, poet and playwright

The first thirty years of Behn's life is shrouded in mystery possibly because she, herself, wanted to cover up her own tracks. It seems that she was born in Kent, the daughter of a barber called Johnson and a wet-nurse. Being a girl, a formal **education** was not open to her, so it is assumed that she taught herself by reading the works of various authors. Behn possibly had a **Catholic** upbringing although she later stated that she only attended church to spy on the young men there.

Either by being fostered or betrothed, she became connected to minor gentry and, in 1663, her 'family' travelled to Suriname (then an English colony) to serve the governor. While there, she claimed to have met an African slave leader who later became the inspiration for her most famous book – *Oroonoko*. A few months later, she returned to England and married a Dutch (or German) merchant named Johan Behn. He died soon after, in 1664, but she kept his name then, somehow, she came to the attention of the royal court who employed her as a spy on behalf of **Charles II**. In this role, she was sent to Antwerp during the **Second Anglo-Dutch War** to try and turn a Dutch spy into a double agent. We do not know if she succeeded but the government's failure to pay her forced her to borrow money to return home and her inability to pay her debts may have landed her in a debtors' prison. Whatever the truth, it was financial problems that forced her to turn to writing.

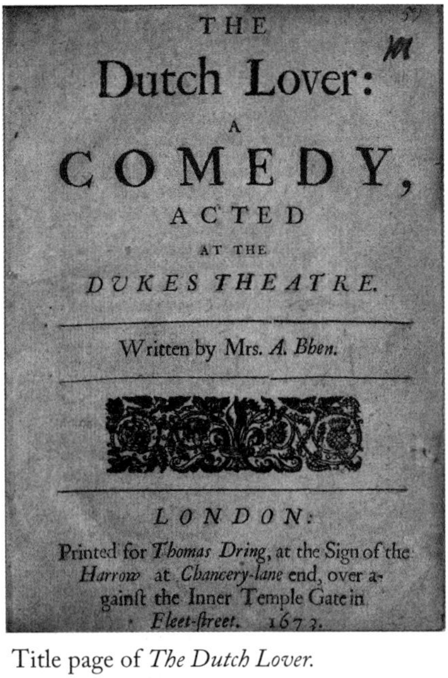
THE

Dutch Lover:

A

COMEDY,

ACTED

AT THE

DUKES THEATRE.

Written by Mrs. A. Bhen.

LONDON:

Printed for Thomas Dring, at the Sign of the Harrow at Chancery-lane end, over againſt the Inner Temple Gate in Fleet-ſtreet. 1673.

Title page of *The Dutch Lover*. (*Author: unknown, 1673. Boston Public Library*)

Behn had already written some poetry, but it was employment by the King's Company and the Duke's Company that was to sustain her living. Under her nom de plume of Astrea (her codename as a spy), she wrote – *The Forc'd Marriage* (1670) and *The Amorous Prince* (1671) – tragicomedies that promoted sexual equality and were very popular. The anti-Dutch comedy, *The Dutch Lover* (1673), failed after being panned by the critics on the basis that it was written by a woman. Her cause was not helped by her tumultuous relationship with a bisexual lawyer named John Hoyle. Not only was sodomy a crime then but he also had a history of violence. Behn responded by stating that it was the lack of educational opportunities that prevented more women from achieving success.

The height of her commercial success came in 1676–78. *Abdelazer* was her only tragedy but far more successful was the comedy, *The Rover*, an adaptation of an earlier play, which the king loved. The story revolves around the amorous adventures of a group of young English men and women during a Naples carnival and was a typical Restoration comedy that was probably Behn's most successful work. *Sir Patient Fancy*, starring **Nell Gwyn**, is the story of a young woman's love affair during her **marriage** to a rich, old man. Again, it was a success despite the critics' attacks for being too bawdy. Behn retorted by stating that such criticism would never have been levelled at a male playwright. During the hysteria surrounding the Popish Plot, Behn wrote more political plays. As a supporter of the **Tories**, she lambasted the **Whigs** but was threatened with arrest for attacking the king's illegitimate son, the Duke of Monmouth.

Theatre audience numbers dropped off in the early 1680s and so Behn turned to writing prose. The first – *Love-Letters Between a Nobleman and His Sister* – was inspired by a contemporary scandal and lays claim to being the first English novel. Her most famous, however, was *Oroonoko* (1688), one of the earliest philosophical novels that questioned the morality of **slavery**, and many see it as the start of the abolitionist movement. In the same period, she also translated pieces of French and Latin literature.

Behn predominantly saw herself as a poet and the 1680s saw the publications of three anthologies of her work. Usually writing in couplets, her verses had a fresh energy with a satirical edge, were often tinged with erotic elements and based upon the relationships of people she knew. Her most famous, *The Disappointment*, touched upon the theme of rape and mocked male impotence while *The Willing Mistress* celebrated female sexual desire. In *Selinda and Cloris*, two women unite against a faithless male lover and develop a physical and intellectual attraction for each other.

The demise of the theatres meant that Behn died in poverty and debt but, nevertheless, was buried in Westminster Abbey. A writer of great versatility and skill, her output was second only to **Dryden** but, for many, she was the vanguard in the fight for gender equality. Determined not to be reliant upon a husband, she was the first Englishwoman to earn a living through writing and was happy to break conventions and push against a patriarchal **society**. Behn later faded into obscurity as the Victorians shunned a woman who wrote about eroticism, sex and relationships from a female's perspective and regarded her writings as morally depraved. Since the 1970s, however, a reevaluation of her work has been so successful that a statue of her was erected in Canterbury (February 2025). The last word on this pioneer should probably go to the author, Virginia Woolf, who, in 1928, wrote, 'All women together, ought to let flowers fall upon the grave of Aphra Behn … for it was she who earned them the right to speak their minds.'

Bill of Rights

(1689)

An Act of **Parliament** that limited the power of the monarchy

After King **James II**'s flight from England in 1688, Parliament drew up a Declaration of Right in February of the following year. This was read to the country's new monarchs, **William III** and **Mary II**, who, during their coronation speeches, agreed to govern according to Parliament's laws. In November 1689, the Declaration became the Bill of Rights which Parliament enacted into law. The relatively quick and peaceful change from absolutist to constitutional monarchy became known as the Bloodless or **Glorious Revolution**.

The Bill of Rights starts by listing James II's misdeeds and then, heavily influenced by the ideas of **John Locke**, it lists the rules by which England had to be governed. The main points are listed below:

1. The monarch cannot suspend or impose laws without Parliament's approval.
2. The monarch cannot control the Church of England.
3. Taxes cannot be raised without Parliament's approval.
4. The raising of an army in peacetime, without Parliament's consent, is illegal.
5. There must be no interference in the election of members of Parliament.
6. There must be freedom of speech within Parliament with no fear of prosecution.
7. Parliament needs to be summoned frequently.
8. Prisoners shall not suffer cruel punishments or excessive payments of bail or fines.
9. Fines and seizure of property before conviction is illegal.
10. People have the right to trial by jury.

The Bill then barred any Catholics from the throne and outlined the order of succession – after William and Mary, the crown would first pass to Mary's heirs and then the heirs of her sister, **Anne**.

The Bill of Rights reinforced the 1628 Petition of Right and 1679 Habeas Corpus Act, but it also marked a monumental shift from absolutist monarchy to constitutional government. By limiting the monarch's powers, even to the point of nominating royal successors, it established the fact that, after sixty years of conflict, Parliament had finally won the fight for control of England. It has had a great impact abroad, too, by being a model for other statements of rights. These include the Declaration of the Rights of Man and of the Citizen in France (1789), the United States Bill of Rights (1791) and United Nations Universal Declaration of Human Rights (1948).

Blake, Robert

(1598–1657)

Admiral

Admiral Blake. (*From the Works of Thomas Carlyle, 1896 via Wikimedia Commons*)

Blake was born in Bridgwater, Somerset, and his father was a wealthy merchant. After attending Oxford university, he hoped to become a don at Merton College, but his application failed because its warden disliked short men (Blake was five feet, five inches tall)! After his father died in 1625, he returned home to look after the family estate as he was the eldest son. It has been suggested that this kept him so busy that he found no time for **marriage**.

In 1640, Blake represented Bridgwater in the Short **Parliament** but defeat to the royalist candidate later that year denied him entry to the Long Parliament. The **Civil Wars** broke out in 1642 and being a **Puritan**, he joined the Parliamentarian army in the West Country. After distinguishing himself during the fall of Bristol (1643) he successfully defended Lyme Regis and then captured the key town of Taunton. There, he fought off three royalist sieges before capturing Barnstaple. By the end of the war Blake had been promoted to colonel, his courage and determination having earned him widespread respect.

In 1649, he was appointed as one of the three 'Generals-at-Sea'. His priority was to destroy the small royalist fleet, led by **Prince Rupert**, which had been harassing English merchant ships. After being driven away from **Ireland**, Rupert sailed to Lisbon, where he received the backing of the Portuguese king. Blake, however, defeated the Portuguese fleet and then chased Rupert into the Mediterranean, where he drove the remaining royalist ships ashore in their attempt to escape. Later, in 1651, he captured the last royalist naval base on the Isles of Scilly. For these achievements, Parliament awarded him £1,000 (equivalent of £100,000 in 2025) and he joined the Council of State – **Oliver Cromwell**'s 'privy council'.

Blake faced far more daunting challenges during the **First Anglo-Dutch War** (1652–54) when he came up against large enemy fleets led by his able rival, Admiral Tromp. After an indecisive skirmish off Dover and victory at Kentish Knock, he suffered a bruising defeat near Dungeness (December 1652). Blake gained his revenge in February the following year when, off Portland Bill, he encountered Tromp escorting a merchant fleet home. Blake's squadron had become separated from the other two and, as a result, was outnumbered and outgunned for several hours. His ship, *The Triumph*, suffered terrible damage and casualties (over 100 killed) and he, himself, was badly wounded in the thigh but his stubborn tenacity forced the Dutch to back off and make a fighting retreat. After recuperating from his injury, Blake's late arrival at the **Battle of the Gabbard**, in June 1653, ensured another English victory and, ultimately, Dutch defeat in the war.

He followed this up with a string of further successes. To avenge acts of pirates operating out of North Africa, Blake attacked Tunis in 1655. Aided by the wind blowing smoke from his guns toward the defenders, he not only destroyed the shore batteries but also set ablaze the enemy ships. It was the first time that land defences had been overcome by ships and Blake only suffered sixty-five dead and wounded. His greatest victory, perhaps, came against the Spanish in 1657 when he attacked the port at Santa Cruz de Tenerife. Many thought this harbour was impregnable, but Blake destroyed the fort as well as the Spanish treasure fleet and its escort for the loss of one ship. An impressed Cromwell gave him a valuable diamond ring.

Blake's success came not only from his determination and bold tactics. After his defeat at Dungeness, he demanded an overhaul of the English navy. The subsequent Articles of War (1653) enforced a strict chain of command and disciplinary code upon the navy. Now, all offences from swearing and sodomy to disobedience and desertion, were to be heavily punished. Sailors were now expected to fight out of duty, not for profit. He also issued the 'Fighting Instructions' that introduced the line of battle, a tactic which allowed all ships to fire broadsides simultaneously. A clear signalling system, using flags, was also outlined.

Returning from the Canary Islands, Blake died within sight of Plymouth. He may have been suffering from oedema and scurvy. After his bowels were buried in a Plymouth church, his body was embalmed and sent to London where Cromwell and his leading generals attended the funeral at Westminster Abbey. After the Restoration, his body, along with others, was disinterred and thrown into a lime pit outside St Margaret's Church. Blake's achievements probably cannot be overstated. He engendered a respect for the English navy which had not been seen since the 1580s and placed it on a path towards global superiority. To many, he is a peer of Nelson and Drake although, prior to his failed attack on Santa Cruz in 1797, Nelson himself said, 'I do not reckon myself equal to Blake.'

Blenheim, Battle of

(1704)

A significant clash of arms during the War of the Spanish Succession

In 1701, a war broke out that was to engulf most of Europe for the next twelve years. As he lay on his deathbed, Carlos II – the last of the Spanish Hapsburgs – nominated as his heir the grandson of Louis XIV of France instead of the Austrian candidate. The Spanish Empire extended from South America and Florida to northern Italy and the Spanish Netherlands and the thought of an already-powerful France acquiring these territories caused much alarm among European leaders. Louis XIV provoked further animosity when he publicly recognised the son of **James II** as King James III of England and announced that French merchants would have exclusive rights to the trading of **slaves** with the Spanish colonies in America. A Grand Alliance, consisting of the Austrian Holy Roman Emperor, several German states, such as Prussia, and **William III** – king of England and Stadtholder of the Dutch Republic – was formed to prevent French domination of the continent.

In charge of the Anglo-Dutch forces in the Netherlands was **John Churchill** and, in 1704, he recognised a major threat to the Alliance: French forces were starting to combine with their Bavarian allies to march on Vienna and knock Austria out of the war. To prevent this, he aimed to disobey his Dutch masters by marching his army south to the Danube where he would join forces with the Austrian general, Prince Eugene of Savoy, and defeat the Franco-Bavarian army. By constantly deceiving the French army that was shadowing him and ensuring that his men were well supplied, he managed to march them 250 miles in five weeks and rendezvous with Eugene on the Danube in August. On the 13th, the two armies faced each other near the village of Blindheim (Blenheim).

The French took up a defensive position from Blenheim, on the Danube, to Lutzingen which lay 3½ miles away among some wooded hills. In charge of the 56,000 men and ninety guns was Marshal Tallard. Marshal Marsin and Maximilian, Elector of Bavaria, controlled the forces near Lutzingen while General Clerambault fortified Blenheim itself. In front, was the marshy Nebel stream. Opposing him were the 52,000 men of Churchill's international force – English, Austrians, Dutch, Germans and Danes – and sixty-six guns. Eugene took up position opposite Lutzingen while General Cutts faced Blenheim.

From about 8 am, the allied troops had to endure hours of French artillery fire while waiting for their army to become fully deployed, suffering 2,000 casualties in the process. One cannon ball brushed perilously past Churchill, himself, covering him with dust. Finally, at 2 pm, Cutts launched an assault on Blenheim's defences. Nicknamed 'Salamander' as he was always found where the fire was hottest, he maintained a series of bloody assaults on the well-fortified French lines. Meanwhile, on Churchill's right, Eugene launched several attacks, on very difficult terrain, against well-entrenched positions. In the centre, allied troops crossed the Nebel in an unusual formation. Churchill had ordered large gaps between his infantry brigades to allow cavalry through.

Cutts directs the attack on Blenheim village. (*Artist: W. Turner, c. 1832 via Wikimedia Commons*)

In Blenheim, Clerambault panicked and ordered reserves to reinforce his defences. The effect was to weaken the centre and overcrowd the village with soldiers who could not even reach their own front lines. Soon after 5 pm, Churchill saw his opportunity and launched a frontal assault in the centre where the French formations were composed largely of cavalry units with little infantry support. Tallard desperately asked for support from Marsin and Clerambault but both replied that all their men were tied down. Subsequently, his centre collapsed with several thousand horsemen drowning in the Danube during their escape. His remaining infantry battalions formed a defiant square in which every man was killed by cannon fire and musket shot.

To avoid encirclement, Marsin and Maximilian fled west pursued by Eugene and, by dusk, the troops in Blenheim were surrounded. Clerambault had drowned while attempting to cross the river and his subordinates, seeing the futility of further resistance, laid down their arms. The Franco-Bavarians had suffered 13,000 casualties and 14,000 captured with many officers taken including Tallard himself. The marshal spent the remainder of the war as a prisoner in comfortable lodgings in Nottingham where he apparently introduced celery to his English captors. The allies had suffered a similar number of casualties but had won a crushing victory.

The news of Blenheim reverberated around Europe and had significant consequences. Austria had been saved, the Grand Alliance had been secured, the myth of French invincibility had been destroyed and Churchill's reputation and his successful partnership with Eugene had been established. It also stands, shoulder to shoulder, with the likes of Waterloo and Agincourt in the annals of the British army. More immediately, Bavaria surrendered and was occupied by imperial troops, and the French were forced onto the back foot. At the Treaty of Utrecht (1713), Louis' grandson was recognised as the king of Spain, but he renounced any claim to the French throne and so the feared union of the two major powers was averted.

Boy

(c. 1638–44)

Dog

During **Prince Rupert**'s imprisonment in Linz, the Earl of Arundel gifted him two rare hunting poodles, one black and one white, to raise his spirits. The black one died early on, but Rupert immediately became very attached to the other and named it Boy (even though it was probably a female!); such was their companionship that even the Ottoman sultan, Murad IV, sought one for himself. Upon his release in late 1641, Rupert, with Boy in tow, travelled to England where he aided his uncle, **Charles I**, during the **Civil Wars**.

In the early stages of the war, Rupert became the iconic, dashing, royalist cavalry commander whose burgeoning reputation made him **Parliament**'s prime enemy. Boy followed her master into every battle and skirmish and soon became a source of propaganda for Rupert's enemies. They claimed she had supernatural powers derived from **witchcraft** and was the Devil's familiar. Royalist satirists then jumped on this and enhanced Boy's powers by stating that the dog had shape-shifting capabilities, was a reincarnated 'Lapland lady', could find hidden treasure and catch in her mouth bullets aimed at her master. Royalist soldiers adopted her as their mascot (she is the first official British Army Dog) and promoted her to Sergeant-Major-General. Boy also played with Charles I's children and was hand-fed capon breast by the king himself. She was even said to cock her leg and urinate every time **John Pym**'s name was mentioned.

During the battle of Marston Moor (1644), Boy was tied up in the royalist camp, but she managed to get loose and, while looking for her master, was killed in the battle. Such had been her cult status, that Parliament claimed that her killer had been 'a Valiant Souldier, who had skill in Necromancy' and celebrated her death in various woodcuts and pamphlets.

Death of Boy. A witch looks on as Boy is shot and turns black. (*Artist: unknown, c. 1644. BBC History Magazine*)

Boyle, Robert

(1626–91)

Scientist, philosopher and theologian

Boyle was born in county Waterford in Ireland, his father having acquired land there during the Tudor plantations of the 1580s. His mother died, after the birth of her fifteenth child, when he was three. After being raised by a wet nurse, he spent three years at Eton College then, in 1639, he embarked on a tour of Europe with a brother and his French tutor. He returned in 1644 and settled at a family estate in Dorset. By this time, the serious young man had become a devout **Anglican**, and his first books concerned ethics and theology.

By 1649, Boyle had become very interested in scientific research and set up a laboratory at his home. He then attempted to continue his work in Ireland while keeping an eye on his deceased father's lands. Local scepticism about his work, however, along with a lack of materials led him to accept an invitation to work in Oxford. By this time, he was a member of the 'Invisible College' – a discussion group of natural philosophers that included **Christopher Wren** and **John Locke**. With **Robert Hooke**, he created a portable air pump with which to conduct experiments with vacuums and air pressure. His most famous discovery, published in 1662, is now known as Boyle's Law – given a fixed temperature, a gas will exert more pressure when squeezed into a small space and the inverse is true.

In 1660, with eleven others, Boyle became a founder member of the Royal Society, an academy aimed at the promotion of science. He then went on to produce over forty books on a wide range of subjects that included chemistry, alchemy, philosophy, theology and medicine. His most famous, *The Sceptical Chymist* (1661), outlined the belief that all matter is made up of particles. He also discovered the role that air played in combustion, respiration and the movement of sound. It is, therefore, little wonder that some refer to him as the 'Father of Chemistry'.

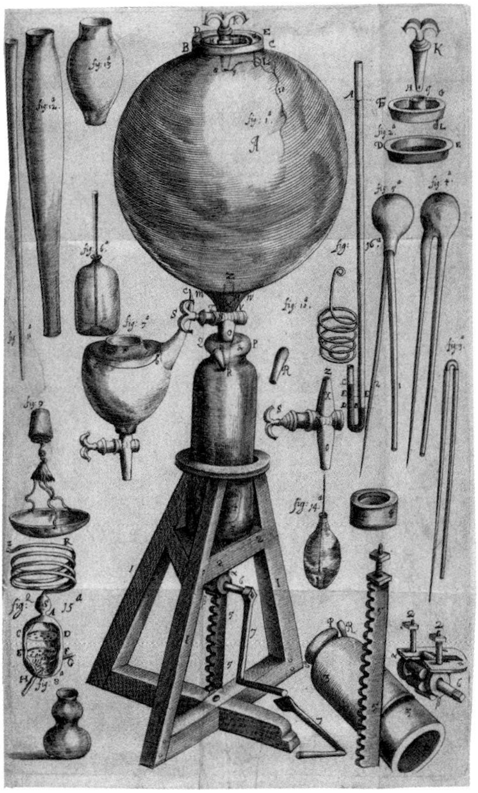

Boyle's air pump. With images showing several experiments (*Author: R. Boyle, 1660. Science History Institute*)

Boyle moved into his sister's house in London in 1668. Katherine Jones, Viscountess Ranelagh, was a remarkable woman who was already renowned for her intellect and wielded some influence in politics, theology and philosophy. She was also an expert physician and conducted experiments, such as distillation, to create new medicines. When her brother moved in, she set up a new laboratory for him and, apparently, worked alongside him. Such work was unique for a woman of the seventeenth century.

Boyle was also a devout Christian and donated much money to missionaries and translations of the Bible. He advocated the compatibility of God and science, believing that a better understanding of natural laws would bring people closer to God. In studying science, he hoped to benefit **society** in other ways too. His wish list of twenty-four inventions included the extension of people's lives, the ability to fly, medicines that dulled pain, unsinkable ships and a way of calculating longitude. Most of his wishes have since come true. Along with his discoveries, Boyle should be remembered as a pioneer of scientific method. As such, he would create a hypothesis based on an observation which he would then test by experiment and come up with a measurable analysis. He considered it just as important for an experiment to disprove a hypothesis, too, to dismiss speculative theorising.

Never a healthy person, suffering from weak hands and eyes and periodic illnesses, he gradually retired from public life from 1669. After a series of strokes, he died a week after Katherine and was buried at St Martin-in-the-Fields.

Buckingham, First Duke of

see Villiers, George

Bunyan, John

(1628–88)

Preacher and writer

Bunyan was born into relatively humble surroundings in a village near Bedford where his father was a tinker who owned a small plot of land. Little is known of his **education** and in 1644, at the age of 16, he joined the Parliamentary army during the **Civil Wars**. After three years, he left the army and returned to his home village where he took up his father's trade and married.

Up to this point, Bunyan's life had been carefree, fun-loving and, in his own words, full of 'vice and ungodliness'. This included a debauched life in the army and ignoring **Puritan** rules in the 1650s such as the ban on bellringing and dancing on Sundays. He underwent a spiritual conversion, however, after claiming to hear a voice from Heaven warning him to change his ways. Bunyan then became a regular Puritan preacher at the Bedford Meeting house and in the surrounding countryside.

After the Restoration in 1660, though, non-**Anglican**s were banned from preaching. Bunyan refused to comply and was sentenced to three months in Bedford prison. This turned into twelve years as he repeatedly refused to give up preaching despite the hardship this entailed for his family – they survived on donations from his supporters and the sale of shoelaces that Bunyan made in prison. It was only in 1672, after the Declaration of Indulgence created more religious toleration, that he was freed.

It was during his imprisonment that Bunyan wrote the most famous of his many books – *The Pilgrim's Progress* (first published, 1678). The book is an allegory written in two parts; the first can be considered autobiographical and is set in surroundings inspired by those close to his home. The story follows a man called Christian who is trying to make his way in life from 'The City of Destruction' (this world) to 'The Celestial City' (Heaven). Along the way, he meets all sorts of dangers and temptations – characters and places such as Mr Legality, Obstinate, the Hill of Difficulty and Vanity Fair – and is helped by Goodwill, Faithful and Hopeful. The second part deals with Christian's wife and children embarking on the same journey.

After his release, Bunyan spent his time preaching and writing. Visiting numerous parishes around the county on horseback, he became affectionately known as 'Bishop Bunyan'. He suffered another, short, imprisonment in 1677 for refusing to attend

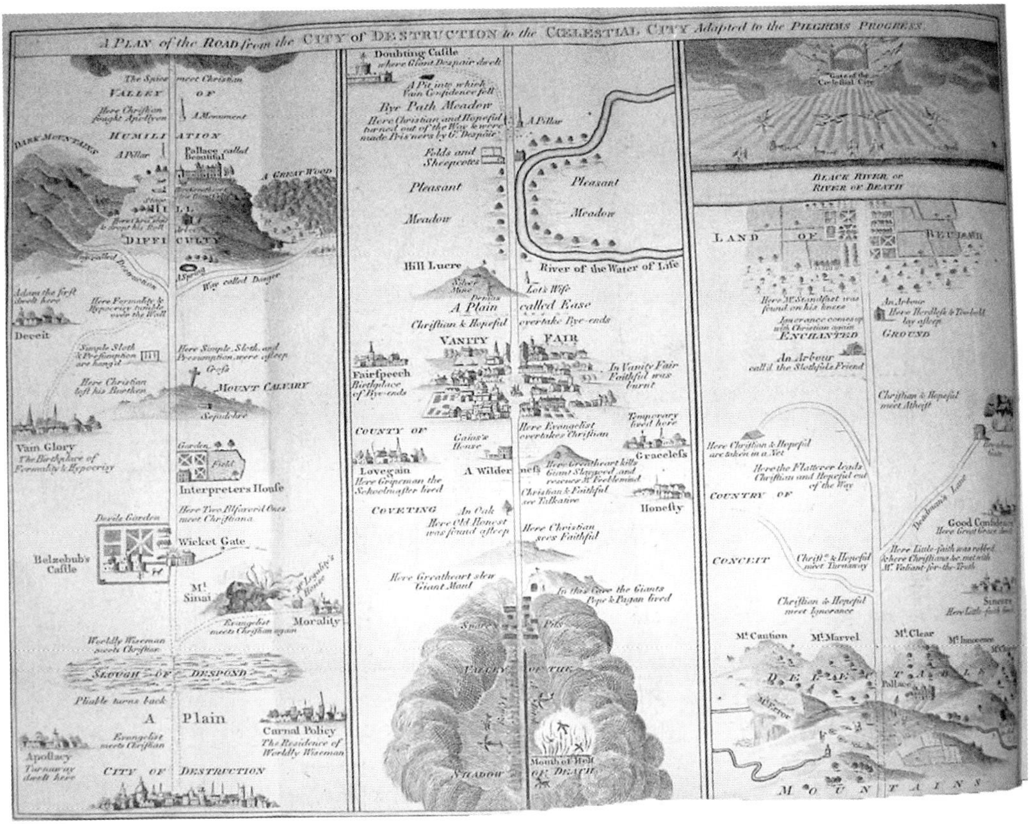

Fold-out map showing Christian's journey. (*Artist: T Conder, c. 1778 via Wikimedia Commons*)

Anglican services but, soon after, the publication of *The Pilgrim's Progress* brought him a degree of fame. Becoming a bestseller very quickly, it has a claim to being one of the ten most published books of all time. Its plain language, written in the style of a folktale, provided a greater understanding of abstract theology but, at the same time, it was a simple story that included adventure and humour. By the nineteenth century it had become essential family reading and a way of instilling godliness into children; it influenced many writers, too, such as Charles Dickens, Louisa May Alcott, C. S. Lewis, John Steinbeck, Enid Blyton and Charlotte Bronte.

In 1688, Bunyan caught pneumonia after riding through heavy rain to visit some friends and died soon after. Decrying pride and worldly goods, most of the money from *The Pilgrim's Progress* went to his publisher and so his estate, at the time of his death, was only worth £42 (£5,500 in 2025). Still, it would have been enough for his family to have bought ten cows or seven horses!

C

Castlemaine, Countess of

see Palmer, Barbara

Catherine of Braganza

(1638–1705)

Wife of **Charles II** and queen of England, **Scotland** and **Ireland** from 1662 to 1685

Catherine was the second daughter of King John IV of Portugal who, in 1640, had regained Portuguese independence from Spain. Keen to gain allies as well as recognition for his country's independence, John agreed to a one-sided **marriage** settlement with Charles II. In return for English military support, England acquired Tangier (too expensive to maintain so handed to Morocco in 1684), Bombay (an important root of Britain's future empire in India) and trading rights in Brazil and the East Indies along with £330,000.

Catherine arrived in Portsmouth in May 1662, where she and the king married before travelling on to London. However, having been brought up in a sheltered nunnery, nothing prepared her for the excesses of Charles II's court. While she was shy, modest, innocent and devoutly **Catholic**, the English court was dazzling, frivolous and fashionable with Charles and his courtiers surrounded by sexually promiscuous women. Her mother-in-law, **Henrietta Maria**, praised her for her saintliness but the ladies of the court mocked her and her entourage for their hairstyles and outdated clothes.

The language barrier made matters difficult but worst of all for Catherine was having to tolerate her husband's mistresses, particularly the **Countess of Castlemaine**. Castlemaine showed nothing but dislike for the new queen and insisted on residing and giving birth to the king's son in Hampton Court Palace while the royal couple were honeymooning there. Even worse, Charles gave her the most senior position in Catherine's household – Lady of the Bedchamber. The queen fainted when she heard this and later refused to accept her. Rows ensued, Charles dismissed Catherine's Portuguese servants, ignored her and publicly paraded around with Castlemaine. Eventually, the humiliated queen gave in and took in the royal mistress although feuding between the two continued.

The difficulty of her position was deepened by her inability to produce an heir for the kingdom. While Charles's mistresses produced at least twelve illegitimate

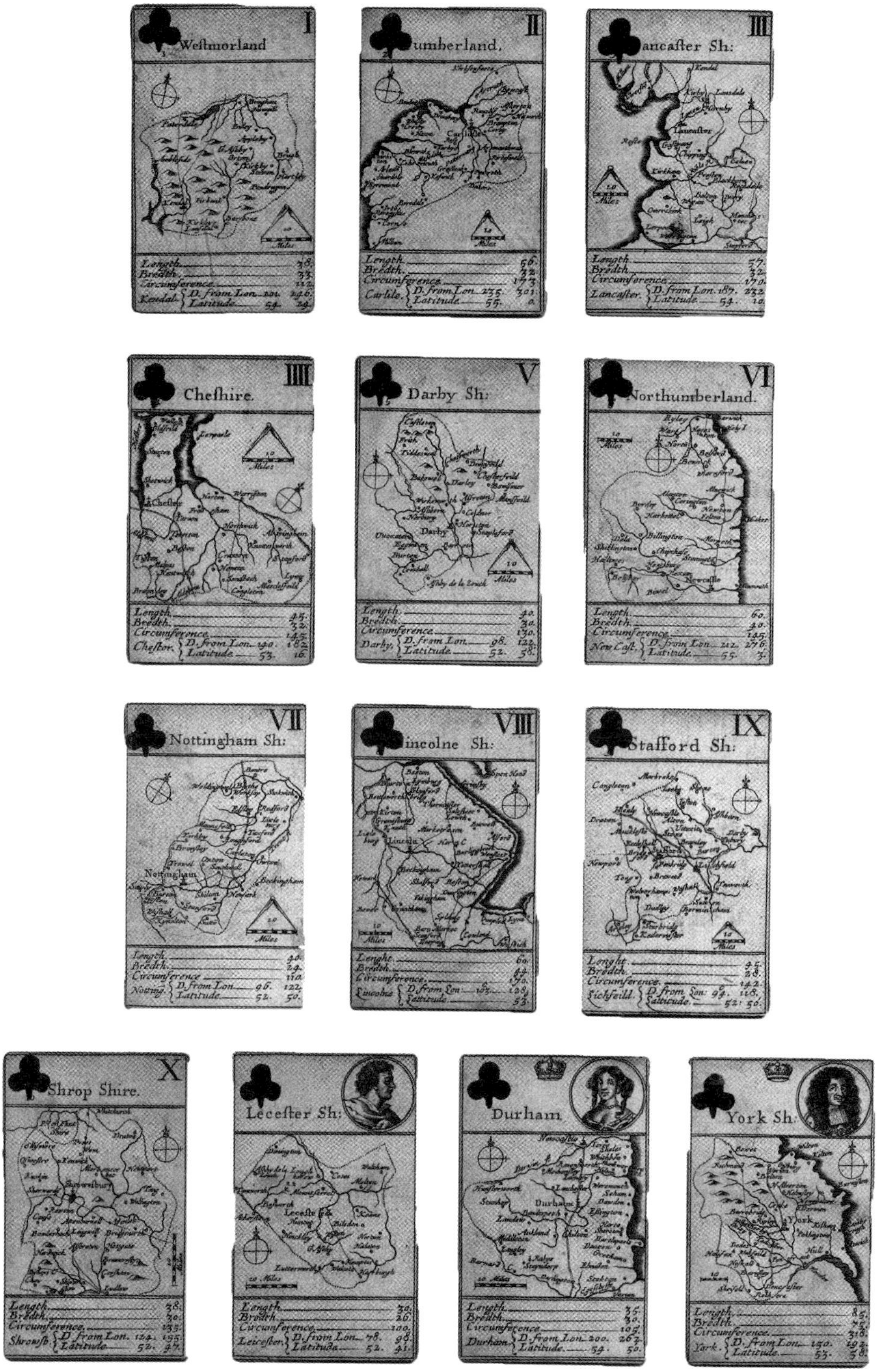

Playing cards. Catherine is depicted on the queens with Charles II on the kings. The cards have information about each county. (*Artist: unknown, c. 1675. British Museum*)

children, Catherine could only manage three miscarriages. This only heightened calls from both the king's advisers and opponents to divorce the Catholic queen and marry a Protestant who could provide an heir which would block the accession of the king's Catholic brother, **James, Duke of York**. To his credit, Charles refused to consider the proposal and loyally, if not ironically, remained loyal to his marriage vows. Her position was particularly threatened during the hysteria of the **Popish Plot**, but the king steadfastly defended her. Catherine's Catholic religion, although it barred her from ever being crowned, was probably the one thing that protected her mental **health**. In a private chapel, with up to six priests, she showed daily devotion to her faith. Such devoutness even impressed the king, and he allowed her to have a Catholic Lord Chamberlain to run her household.

Catherine always accompanied Charles during his royal duties, and the public started to respect their loyal, good-natured and pious queen who provided a sharp contrast with her licentious husband. At the same time, she began to relax into court life. Playing cards, hosting masques, dancing, archery and country picnics were her favourite pastimes. She also hosted the Queen's Circle, a daily social event held in her bedchamber. It became increasingly popular with time and was the place to be seen and to hear news.

As King Charles lay dying in 1685, Catherine was too upset to stay by his bed and begged for his forgiveness. The king replied, 'Alas poor woman! She asks for my pardon? I beg hers with all my heart; take her back that answer.' Afterwards, she stayed in England partly because of a lawsuit in which she claimed money from a former Lord Chamberlain. She was present during the **Glorious Revolution**, but her religion made her increasingly mistrusted, so she returned to Portugal in 1692 where she became a respected political figure. Twice, in fact, she acted as regent for the new king, her brother.

One can feel nothing but sympathy for Catherine of Braganza. Various parallels can be drawn between her and the more famous Iberian princess, Catherine of Aragon, first wife of Henry VIII. For the Portuguese princess, however, the contrast between her upbringing and English court life was probably far more shocking. Catherine deserves great admiration for her strength of character too. Despite all the personal pain and sadness she must have felt, she continued in her duties as a loyal queen and was a model of decorum.

Catholic

A follower of the Catholic religion

The people of England had followed the Catholic faith for many hundreds of years until the English Reformation in the sixteenth century. When King Henry VIII broke away from the authority of Rome in the 1530s, Protestant ideas rapidly infiltrated the country from Europe. After Elizabeth I came to the throne in 1558, a church settlement was finally produced which established a mild form of Protestantism in England – the **Anglican** Church.

By 1603, few people were still alive who remembered being part of a Catholic Church; for the vast majority, the Anglican Church was all that they had known. It is estimated, therefore, that only about 20 per cent of England's four million people (800,000) were Catholics when **James I** started his reign. By 1700, their numbers had dropped to no more than 4 per cent of a population of 5.5 million (220,000). Most of these Catholics tended to live in the rural areas of the north and west and had a higher representation in the upper class.

Despite their relatively low numbers, the seventeenth century witnessed a continual undercurrent of anti-Catholicism. This was partly due to Protestant propaganda, such as Foxe's *Book of Martyrs*, which kept alive the memories of Mary I's burning of Protestants in the 1550s. Also, events such as the **Gunpowder Plot**, the Thirty Years' War on the continent and the **Popish Plot** produced fears of a Catholic takeover. These fears even worked themselves into the causes of the **Civil Wars**. At such times, anti-Catholic laws would be more rigorously enforced but most Catholics were loyal to the Crown and, for the most part, coexisted happily with their Protestant neighbours. Nevertheless, social pressure to conform, as well as the penal laws, led to the reduction in Catholic numbers over the course of the century.

Key Catholic beliefs included:

1. The infallibility and leadership of the pope.
2. The sacred authority of ordained bishops and priests.
3. The importance of the seven sacraments to receive salvation. These included baptism, marriage and penance for one's sins.
4. Transubstantiation: the belief that the bread and wine really do turn into the Body and Blood of Christ during the Eucharist.
5. The use of images, crucifixes, candles, music and vestments during services.
6. Salvation is gained through good works, such as pilgrimages, as well as faith.

Cecil, Robert (First Earl of Salisbury)

(1563–1612)

Politician and chief advisor to **James I**

Cecil was the younger son of William Cecil, Lord Burghley, and Mildred Cooke. His father was Elizabeth I's chief minister and, recognising his son's talents, trained him in the art of statecraft from an early age. Unfortunately for Cecil he was born with scoliosis which gave him a curved spine, hunched back and an eventual height of five feet, four inches. This exposed him to mockery throughout his life, even by his monarchs; Elizabeth referred to him as her 'pygmy' and James I called him his 'little beagle'.

He became a member of **Parliament** in 1584 and, from 1590, started to take on the duties of Secretary of State with his father as his constant guide. In the following year, he joined the Privy Council as its youngest member but, as he accrued more power, he came into conflict with the queen's flamboyant favourite – the Earl of Essex. The rivalry intensified after Burghley's death in 1598, and Cecil only triumphed after the failure of Essex's Rebellion and his subsequent execution in 1601. Despite Cecil's calls to treat the rebels with clemency, the affair turned public opinion against him as Essex had been a popular figure.

Although he had initially supported the Spanish Infanta's claim to the throne, after Essex's removal he campaigned for James VI of Scotland to succeed the ageing queen. From 1601, Cecil was engaged in secret, coded correspondence with James in which he offered advice and assurances. When Elizabeth died in 1603, he stayed in London to arrange her funeral and ensure there was no outbreak of trouble. Afterwards, James rewarded him for facilitating the smooth transfer of power by keeping him as Secretary of State and, in 1605, granted him the earldom of Salisbury.

For the first nine years of James I's reign, Cecil was a loyal servant who worked hard to protect and strengthen the monarchy. His first job was to end the ruinously expensive war with Spain that had started nineteen years previously. In the Treaty of London (1604), he negotiated Spanish recognition of the Protestant monarchy of England in return for the cessation of English aid to Dutch rebels fighting for their independence. The deal greatly benefited English merchants as they were now free to trade within the Spanish empire. Afterwards, Cecil promoted James's desire to be a peacemaker and helped to ensure that his reign was a peaceful one.

In 1605, he successfully uncovered the **Gunpowder Plot** – an attempt to murder the king, overthrow the government and install a **Catholic**-friendly regime. Various conspiracy theories have since arisen accusing Cecil of encouraging the conspirators in order to gain favour with the king or provide an excuse for the subsequent persecution of Catholics. This is unlikely though given both the lack of evidence and his lenient attitude towards law-abiding Catholics.

After becoming Lord Treasurer in 1608, Cecil had more power concentrated in his hands than even his father had ever had. His new position, however, introduced him to an alarming budget deficit. Increased Crown expenditure under James, added to the considerable debt from the previous reign, meant that royal debts amounted to £1.4 million (equivalent of £190 million in 2025). He successfully reduced this by increasing duties on imports and exports, but this was still not enough. So, in 1610, he devised the innovative Great Contract – a deal by which Parliament would award James a regular, annual income in return for the king waiving certain feudal dues such as wardship. Cecil's plan nearly worked but Parliament's dislike of James's extravagance and the king's reluctance to give up his traditional rights meant that the deal fell through. Thereafter, he was forced to squeeze more money out of royal feudal rights such as the granting of titles.

Robert Cecil. The motto 'Late but in earnest' means good works may require delays. (*Artist: after J. de Fritz the elder, c. 1600. National Trust*)

Overworked and suffering from pain and exhaustion, Cecil travelled to Bath to take the waters in early 1612 but stomach cancer killed him on his return journey. His power and acquisition of immense wealth were epitomised by his lavish reconstruction of Hatfield House, but he had also become a figure of hate, as revealed by the crude satire that emerged after his death. He was blamed, primarily, for stringent fiscal policies while being accused of tax evasion. It is certainly true that Cecil ensured his own financial prosperity but there can be no questioning his hard work, loyalty and administrative and political skills. Nor was it any coincidence that his death was followed by a general malaise and inefficiency in James's government.

Charles I

(1600–49)

King of England, **Scotland** and **Ireland** from 1625 to 1649

Charles was the second son and youngest surviving child of James VI of Scotland (later, **James I** of England) and **Anne of Denmark**. A weak and sickly child, he had to be left behind in Scotland when his father journeyed south to claim the English throne in 1603. Possibly suffering from rickets, special boots had to be designed to strengthen his ankles, but he overcame this infirmity as he later took up fencing and dancing as well as horse riding. He also had a stammer, something which stayed with him for the rest of his life. For quite a while, he remained in the shadow of his older brother, Prince Henry, who was far taller and more confident (Charles would become the shortest-ever English king, measuring five feet, four inches). Charles would try to emulate him but Henry's sudden death in 1612 threw him into the limelight as the heir apparent.

He had a sheltered upbringing and came across as a quiet and reserved man who appeared proud but awkward on social occasions. In the early 1620s, he came under the influence of his father's favourite, the **Duke of Buckingham**. In 1623, they both travelled incognito to Spain to try and negotiate James's wish for a **marriage** between Charles and the Spanish Infanta. The mission was a fiasco, though, as the Infanta refused to marry a heretic and, back home, **Parliament** was dead set against the idea of the prince marrying a **Catholic** anyway. They returned home eight months later with nothing to show for their failure except for a few jewels, a pair of gloves, four camels and an elephant (which became very expensive to maintain). The public celebrated his failure, but a vengeful Charles declared war on Spain straight after his accession.

1625–29

Charles ascended to the throne after his father's death in March 1625 amid rumours (unfounded) that Buckingham had poisoned James. The first four years of his reign can be considered a microcosm of the king's relationship with Parliament and a reflection of their respective characters.

On the continent, the Thirty Years' War had broken out and his sister (**Elizabeth**) and brother-in-law, the Elector Palatine, had lost their lands in Germany to Austrian Hapsburg forces. Charles wanted to regain these lands for Elizabeth and so joined the anti-Hapsburg orbit by marrying the French princess, **Henrietta Maria**, in 1625. He followed this up by sending an expeditionary force to Germany, but his undersupplied troops achieved nothing. He also put Buckingham in charge of a raid on Cadiz, which became a costly failure due to its poor organisation. In 1627, Buckingham led another, more disastrous, expedition to the west coast of France to support French Protestant rebels but lost 80 per cent of his troops in the process.

The summoning and dissolution of three parliaments within four years reflects the degree of domestic opposition to the king's policies. Most MPs, now led by **John Eliot**, were alarmed by Charles's marriage to a Catholic and feared Henrietta Maria's influence, a concern not helped by her refusal to attend her husband's Protestant coronation ceremony. Indeed, in the marriage treaty, Charles had secretly agreed to lift restrictions on English Catholics. However, their main target at this stage was Buckingham whom they blamed for the foreign policy fiascos although their own lack of funding had contributed to the failures.

Parliament also attacked the billeting of troops in people's homes, the raising of taxes without its permission and the imprisonment of those who refused to pay them. The king, however, was emboldened by the Five Knights case (1627) when judges upheld his decision to imprison five knights for refusing to pay forced loans. Undeterred, Parliament's demands coalesced into the Petition of Right the following year. Charles initially agreed to these but then prorogued Parliament and carried on as before.

Later that year, Buckingham was assassinated. As wild celebrations among the public ensued, an isolated and anguished king blamed Parliament and increasingly turned to Henrietta Maria for support. A few months later, he decided to dissolve

The Speaker held down in his chair. (*Artist: H. Paget from Cassell's History of England, c. 1909 via Wikimedia Commons*)

Parliament once and for all and rule by himself but not before imprisoning nine MPs, including Eliot, for holding down the Speaker in his chair so that a defiant resolution could be passed before Parliament's closure. The tone, however, had been set. Arrogant and aloof, Charles had eschewed the drunkenness and informality of James I's court but had clearly inherited his father's belief in divine right with all the deferential hierarchy that came with it. Any duplicity on his part was merely the wish of God. As for Parliament, it had revealed a combative, surly nature never seen before, one that would not simply lie down and go away.

1629–40

Although known by his enemies as the 'Eleven Years' Tyranny', the 1630s was a decade of peace and relative prosperity. Without Parliament, Charles was unable to fund wars so resorted to diplomatic means to win back the Palatinate for his sister. At home, he was happy indulging in his love of the arts. He enjoyed masques, theatre and poetry but it was the visual arts that he especially adored. He amassed some of the finest paintings in Europe, hired the Flemish artist, **Anthony Van Dyck**, to be his court painter and his compatriot, Rubens, to decorate the Banqueting Hall in Whitehall Palace. He also employed the architect, **Inigo Jones**, to work on various grandiose projects such as Covent Garden Square. By the end of his reign, Charles had acquired a staggering 1,760 paintings, most of which were sold off by Parliament after the **Civil Wars**. He also enjoyed the pleasures of a happy, loving and indolent family life with Henrietta Maria producing nine children (five of whom survived childhood).

Money, however, was still needed to finance this lavish lifestyle. For this, the king resorted to old feudal levies, some of which had not been raised for centuries. These included fines for those people earning more than £40 per year for not attending his coronation, the selling of monopolies whereby a trader could buy complete control of certain commodities such as soap (this had the effect of raising prices), restoring the ancient boundaries of forests and fining those now farming within 'forest lands' (this caused riots in the west). Charles also resorted to seizing merchants' money and goods but most notorious of all was Ship Money. This was an old tax raised in coastal counties with the aim of building ships in times of war. The king, however, raised the amount and charged inland counties too. In 1637, the Buckinghamshire MP, John Hampden, refused to pay on the grounds that the tax had not been approved by Parliament. The court case became a national platform for resistance to Charles's taxes and the fact that five of the twelve judges voted in favour of Hampden made the result a hollow victory for the king.

During this period, Charles was also keen to impose religious uniformity on his kingdom, and he favoured the High Church form of **Anglican**ism (known as Arminianism at the time). This involved a greater degree of ritual and decoration and authority for priests and bishops. To enforce this, he appointed **William**

Laud as Archbishop of Canterbury in 1633. Such reforms were anathema to **Puritans** who regarded them as a step towards Catholicism. Those who protested, however, were strictly dealt with by the Court of High Commission and the Star Chamber. The most famous case was that of the three Puritans – William Prynne, Henry Burton and John Bastwick – who published arguments against the reforms. After being convicted in the Star Chamber, they were pilloried, whipped and had their ears removed.

William Prynne in the pillory. (*Artist: unknown, from Cassell's History of England, c. 1865 via Wikimedia Commons*)

Possibly, Charles could have continued in this vein for many more years but he committed a serious blunder in Scotland, a realm he had only visited once since his birth, and set off a chain of events that led to the Civil Wars. In the name of uniformity, he ordered the imposition of the English Prayer Book upon the **Presbyterian** Scots in 1637. At St Giles' Cathedral, Edinburgh, stools were thrown at the minister, and riots broke out in protest. Charles attempted to deal with the insubordination militarily (the Bishops' Wars), but the Scots' army contained far more experienced and motivated troops. The king, on the advice of Laud and his Lord Deputy of **Ireland**, the **Earl of Strafford**, recalled Parliament to gain funding for a better army. The Short Parliament (April–May 1640), however, would only address royal abuses of power before providing taxes and so Charles dissolved it after only three weeks. The Scots then occupied Durham and Northumberland and demanded payment of their soldiers' expenses before returning home. Cornered, the king was forced, in November, to summon what became known as the Long Parliament.

1640–49

Parliament had now become dominated by a junto of Puritans, led by **John Pym**, which was determined to curb royal power. Fearing Strafford's plans to have them impeached for supporting the Scots, they struck first with a bill of attainder that stated he was guilty of treason. Despite the accusation that he was conspiring to crush Parliament with his army from Ireland being unsubstantiated, he was imprisoned in the Tower in November. Laud followed him in December.

1641 saw a steady deterioration in relations between Crown and Parliament. Charles made a series of concessions which, privately, he viewed as being temporary. He agreed to the abolition of 'illegal' taxes such as Ship Money, the abolition of the courts of Star Chamber and High Commission, the execution of Strafford (not exactly temporary!) and an act stating that Parliament could only be dissolved by its members. Many MPs, however, now thought that the reforms had gone too far and started accusing 'King Pym' of wanting to seize power especially when, in November, he put forward the **Grand Remonstrance** – a long list of grievances against the king.

Matters began to spiral out of control when news came through of a rebellion in Ireland in which Protestants were being massacred by Catholics. Politics and religion, always close bedfellows in the seventeenth century, now merged into one. Through pamphlets and preachers, Pym whipped up anti-Catholic hysteria among the Puritan communities in the city of London. Bishops in the Lords, accused of blocking reform, were intimidated by mobs and forced away from Parliament. Malevolent rumours started to circulate about the 'papist-in-chief' – the queen. Was she in cahoots with the Irish rebels? Had she deceived the king by producing illegitimate children? Calls began for her impeachment. Added to this dangerous atmosphere was the publication of the Grand Remonstrance. The king's 'wrongdoings' had now been shared with the public. The final straw for Charles was Parliament insisting that it, not the king, should take control of an army to subdue the Irish rebels.

Charles could no longer stand by and let his family be threatened and allow himself to become a mere 'puppet king'. So, he resolved to take drastic action. On 4 January 1642, he took an armed escort and broke protocol by entering the Commons to arrest his five main opponents, including Pym. Forewarned by a palace insider, the five had already fled to the city. Asked where they were, the Speaker of the House bravely replied, 'I have neither eyes to see nor tongue to speak' unless commanded by the chamber. Charles uttered, 'I see my birds are flown' and beat a humiliating retreat to cries of 'Privilege!'

The king had now made the mistake of acting like a tyrant trying to trample on parliamentary liberty and this was compounded the following day when the same happened in London's Guild Hall where the city's leaders refused to hand over the five MPs. London was in uproar and, suspecting a royalist assault, called up its 20,000 armed militia. Fearing for their safety, the royal family fled by boat from Westminster on the 10th. Henrietta Maria fled abroad to raise money by pawning the crown jewels while Charles attempted to seize the royal arsenal at Hull but was rebuffed. Prolonged attempts were made to prevent war, but he found Parliament's demands intolerable so, on 22 August, the king raised his standard at Nottingham, thereby signalling the outbreak of the Civil Wars.

Charles had no military training but assumed strategic control of the royalist armies and set up his headquarters in Christ Church College, Oxford. He was present at several of the battles such as Edgehill and both of those fought near Newbury despite showing much dislike of the slaughter. At **Naseby**, he had to be dragged away to avoid being captured. It is hard to assess his capability as a commander as it is not clear how much advice he took on board from his subordinates. With hindsight, perhaps, he should have pressed on to London straight after Edgehill, but his delay enabled the parliamentarians to strengthen its defences at Turnham Green. After Turnham Green, he could have joined up with supporters in Kent and threatened the capital again but decided to retreat to Oxford instead. Too cautious at the start of the war, in the hope of avoiding further bloodshed, he was too impulsive in 1645 when he decided to confront a superior army at Naseby. He also badly damaged his popular standing by summoning Irish forces to his aid in 1643.

In 1646, with his forces disintegrating and Oxford surrounded, Charles disguised himself as a servant and fled north. He surrendered to Scottish forces (allied to Parliament) at Newark, hoping to broker a deal which would split his enemies. After nine months, however, the Scots handed him over to Parliament for £100,000 in January 1647.

By now, arguments were breaking out between Parliament and its army which encouraged Charles to procrastinate during the negotiations. If he could escape, then he could watch his enemies fall apart and wait for either side to seek his support and put him back in power. In November 1647, he escaped through a private garden at Hampton Court Palace and fled south to the Isle of Wight where he believed the governor was a royalist. Parliament, however, was informed and the governor ordered to confine him in Carisbrooke Castle. Postwar negotiations restarted but Charles made a secret deal with a faction of the Scottish Parliament by which he agreed to make England Presbyterian in return for a Scots' invasion of England. This 'Engagement' was wrapped in lead and buried in the castle's garden. The resulting Second Civil War saw the Scottish army crushed at Preston (August 1648).

Parliament agreed to continue negotiations but the army, led by **Oliver Cromwell**, had had enough. It was clear to them that the king could not be trusted, and peace could not be attained while he was alive. After staging a military coup, the army ordered Charles to London where he was put on trial for carrying out 'wicked designs, wars, and evil practices' against his country. The indictment included accusations of 'all the treasons, murders, rapines, burnings, spoils, desolations, damages and mischiefs to this nation, acted and committed in the said wars'. Over the first three days, Charles made dignified refusals to plead, stating that no earthly court could try a king and that he represented 'the liberty of the people of England'. God had given him authority and so only God could punish him. After a further two days of hearing witnesses, the court declared, 'Charles Stuart, as a tyrant, traitor, murderer, and public enemy to the good people of this nation shall be put to death by the severing of his head from his body.'

Execution of Charles I. Note the soldiers surrounding the scaffold. Fairfax and Cromwell occupy the top corners. (*Artist: unknown, from 1649 German print via Wikimedia Commons*)

After a tearful farewell to two of his children, Charles stepped out of a window of the Banqueting House at Whitehall Palace onto a scaffold. He had put on extra clothing as it was a freezing day, and he did not want the crowd to think he was shivering with fear. His last speech could not be heard by the crowd – fearing unrest, the army had placed several ranks of soldiers around the scaffold. Those beside him heard him talk of his regret over Strafford's execution, his desire for the people's liberty and that only a king could protect them from illegal government, and he described himself as 'a martyr of the people'. He laid his head upon the block and, after giving a signal, was decapitated with one blow by the disguised executioner. When the king's head was held up, one witness described 'such a groan … as I never heard before and I desire I may never hear again'. Members of the crowd and guards surged forward to dip handkerchiefs in his blood and cut off locks of his hair before a troop of cavalry drove the crowd away from the scene. Afterwards, Charles's head was sewn back onto his body but the army refused to allow a burial in Westminster Abbey and so he was laid to rest in St George's Chapel at Windsor Castle.

The execution of Charles I initially caused much celebration, but this was soon followed by a sense of shock and anxiety partly caused by the publication of *Eikon Basilike* (1649) – royalist propaganda that portrayed the king as a martyr. Never had an anointed king been executed. The established order had been rocked, it felt like the world had been turned upside down and many feared for the future. England became isolated as foreign leaders, horrified at the precedent that had been set, treated it as a pariah state. In the long run, it can be rightly described as a seismic event in English history, a key turning point in the country's transformation from absolutist monarchy to parliamentary democracy. In the shorter term, however, the king's trial and execution had been the actions of a small, radical minority which ultimately meant that the country's experiment with republicanism was doomed to failure.

As for Charles himself, assessments have generally not been favourable. At best, he was a dignified and loving family man who fought and died for his beliefs. It is also fair to say, however, that his unswerving belief in divine right and lack of understanding of the world outside his palace led him to making calamitous blunders from which he was too stubborn to back down. Any compromise was seen as expedient, and he created a reputation for duplicity and unreliability. Arguably, the clash between royal and parliamentary authority was inevitable and Charles was merely the catalyst. The violence of this clash, however, can be attributed to the fact that he was the wrong man for the wrong time.

Charles II

(1630–85)

King of **Scotland** (1649–51) and king of England, Scotland and **Ireland** (1660–85)

Charles was born at St James's Palace, Westminster, under an auspicious bright, daytime star – probably a supernova. He was the eldest surviving son of **Charles I** and **Henrietta Maria** and spent most of his childhood at Richmond Palace with his younger siblings. His upbringing was a happy and loving one, but this was curtailed by the outbreak of the **Civil Wars** in 1642 when the family fled from the dangerous mobs of London. While his mother went abroad to raise money for the king, Charles and his brother, James, stayed with their father. After witnessing the Battle of Edgehill (1642) from a safe distance, the two boys spent the next three years at the royalist headquarters in Oxford. At the tender age of 15, Charles was given nominal command of the royalist forces in the south-west. The victorious Parliamentary forces, however, forced him to flee to France where he rejoined his mother in 1646.

In Exile

From France, the family moved to the Dutch Republic where they tried to drum up support for their captive father. It was in vain, though, as Charles I was executed in early 1649 although, straight afterwards, Scotland proclaimed him 'King Charles II'. In him, they saw a man who could safeguard their **Presbyterian** religion in the face of the victorious **New Model Army** in England. Charles agreed to make all three of his kingdoms Presbyterian in return for Scottish military support, but the deal was done with much bitterness especially after he was forced to dismiss most of his 'unholy' retinue and denounce his own and his parents' sins. He had, after all, been brought up an **Anglican** and neither did the deal go down well with his Anglican supporters in England. It was all for nothing anyway. **Oliver Cromwell** defeated the Scots at Dunbar (1650) and again at Worcester (1651) where Charles fought bravely and had two horses killed underneath him. Afterwards, he was a fugitive within England for six weeks. **Parliament** put out a reward of £1,000 (about forty years' worth of wages for a skilled craftsman) for his capture. Protected by a few loyal supporters and having to disguise himself as a servant, he had a few narrow escapes, once hiding in a priest hole and later up an oak tree. In October, he finally boarded a ship to safety in France.

'The Scots holding their young king's nose to the grindstone'. A satirical image showing Prince Charles bowing to the Scots' demands. (*Artist: unknown, c. 1650 via Wikimedia Commons*)

For most of the 1650s, Charles and his family had to move from one country to another as Cromwell made treaties with their hosts. At each court, they sought funds to help reclaim their kingdom, but they were never enough. An agreement with Spain did provide them with a small force but this was decimated at the Battle of the Dunes (1658) by an Anglo-French army. A few months later, Charles had reason to hope when news came through of Cromwell's death and chaos ensued in the subsequent power vacuum as various groups jostled to hold sway. To impose order, General **George Monck** took military control of the situation and ordered the return of a parliament which favoured the Restoration of the monarchy.

To encourage an invitation to accept the throne, Charles drew up the Declaration of Breda (April 1660) in which he promised religious toleration, a general pardon for most of his father's enemies, back pay for Monck's soldiers and not to take back lands of royalists seized after 1649. Throughout the Declaration he also stated that he would cooperate with Parliament and a few days later, a formal invitation was received. Charles landed at Dover on 25 May and entered London to cheering crowds on 29 May, the date of his thirtieth birthday. 29 May was declared a public holiday – Oak Apple Day (in memory of the oak tree in which he once hid) – and remained so until 1859. Some places still celebrate it today.

As King

A new crown had to be made for Charles's coronation as the old one had been melted down by his father's enemies. Many of these, he kept on in government and allowed them to retain their titles and lands much to the chagrin of some loyal royalists who remained destitute. Many supporters who had suffered were compensated though. Katherine de Luke, for instance, had lost her husband in battle and a son to indentured slavery. Acting as a courier of secret royalist messages, she had been caught and thereafter whipped daily and tortured with lit matches. Of the regicides, thirteen were executed, most being hanged, drawn and quartered while the majority were given life imprisonment. Even death did not prevent their executions – several, including Cromwell, were disinterred, beheaded and had their heads displayed on spikes facing the spot where Charles I had been executed.

The executions of Cromwell, Bradshaw and Ireton. Their skulls on the roof of Westminster Hall are labelled 1, 2 and 3. (*Artist: unknown, c. 1661 via Biometrika*)

Despite this grisly start, the beginning of Charles's reign was marked by a blossoming of culture that had been forced underground during the Puritan republic. Theatres reopened, for instance, **coffee houses** and gambling became popular and there was a blossoming of **sport**, literature, science and semi-opera. Charles, himself, was the embodiment of this sense of fun and freedom. At six feet, two inches and with a swarthy complexion, confident, outgoing, quick-witted and promiscuous, he provided a sharp contrast to his father. Such was his sexual appetite that he was nicknamed 'Old Rowley' after the most virile stallion in his stables. In total, he had an estimated thirteen mistresses which he happily flaunted in public. These included the domineering **Countess of Castlemaine**, the unpopular Duchess of Portsmouth and the orange-seller-turned-actress, **Nell Gwyn**. He also fathered at least fourteen illegitimate children to whom he bestowed various titles. When today's Prince William becomes king, he will be the first direct royal descendant of Charles II, his mother (Princess Diana) being descended from two of Charles's children. He also enjoyed two vigorous daily walks with his dozen spaniels in St. James's Park where he would feed the ducks. He loved sport too, with tennis, sailing and riding horses being his favourites; twice, he even won races at Newmarket – the only monarch to do so.

Another of his interests was science. As a child, his tutors included the physician, **William Harvey** and the philosopher, **Thomas Hobbes**, but Charles was fascinated by a very broad range of subjects – medicine, botany, chemistry, alchemy, anatomy, astrology, navigation, gardening and clock mechanisms. The latter caused him to put clocks all around Whitehall including seven in his own bedroom! He had his own laboratory, a thirty-six-inch telescope in the palace gardens and loved to converse with the top scientists of his day such as **Robert Boyle** and **Christopher Wren**. More importantly, in 1662, he granted a charter to the Royal Society with the aim of encouraging scientific exploration and, later, founded the Royal Observatory at Greenwich.

Administrative detail, however, bored him and so he earned a reputation for laziness. He much preferred playing with his toy spaniels and would bring them to important meetings to provide a welcome distraction (the toy spaniel was renamed King Charles spaniel). His marriage, in 1662, to **Catherine of Braganza**, brought a very advantageous dowry but no children. Her miserable existence among his mistresses did not seem to affect him although, later, he did stand by her when her position was threatened due to her devout **Catholic**ism.

Despite Charles's declaration for religious toleration, the first half of the 1660s saw the enactment of the Clarendon Code, named after his chief minister, the **Earl of Clarendon** (unfairly so, as he was against most of it). These laws were aimed at persecuting non-Anglicans. For instance, the Corporation Act required all town officials to take Anglican communion, and the Five Mile Act banned non-conformist ministers from teaching or being within 5 miles of where they used to work.

The honeymoon period of the Restoration, certainly within London, was ended by a series of disasters – the **Plague** (1665), the **Fire of London** (1666) and the Dutch **Raid on the Medway** (1667). The **Second Anglo-Dutch War** had been going well but this latter event was seen as a national disaster. It was caused by financial negligence of the navy and Charles quite unfairly diverted the blame onto Clarendon who was sacked and sent into exile. He then had to settle for unfavourable peace terms with the Dutch.

The disaster highlighted a major problem for Charles. In 1660, Parliament had voted him an annual income, but it was never enough for a spendthrift king who desired financial independence. Hence, in 1670, he signed the Treaty of Dover with his cousin, King Louis XIV of France. The public 'cover' treaty stated that Charles promised to send soldiers and warships to aid France in its planned war against the Dutch in return for the control of various Dutch ports. In the secret deal, however, the English king vowed to declare himself a Catholic at some appropriate time, Louis would pay him an annual sum of £160,000 and provide troops, if necessary, to assist in restoring Catholicism to England. Had the details been revealed during his reign, the consequences would have been catastrophic for Charles, but they did not become known until historical research unveiled them in 1771. More immediately, the subsequent **Third Anglo-Dutch War** (1672–74) became an expensive and unpopular stalemate. French subsidies dried up after peace was made and Charles, unsurprisingly, kept any religious opinions he had to himself.

He did, however, attempt to allow religious toleration, for non-conformists as well as Catholics, with his 1672 Declaration of Indulgence but Parliament responded by compelling him to retract the declaration and accept the Test Act (1673). This forced anyone in public office to regularly take Anglican communion. These events caused the fracturing of the Cabal – a disparate group of five ministers who had run the country since Clarendon's fall. This group (their initials spelt C.A.B.A.L.) neither trusted each other nor the king and their power made them unpopular with Parliament. However, they do represent the first attempt at government by cabinet rather than a single favourite.

Following their split, one of its members, Lord **Ashley** (now the **Earl of Shaftesbury**) became the focal point of opposition to the king's brother – **James, Duke of York**. James had revealed himself to be a Catholic after the Test Act and yet, with Charles having no legitimate children, was the heir to the throne. The group that coalesced around Shaftesbury became known as the **Whigs** and they campaigned to exclude James from the throne. Charles stood by his brother, however, and refused their demands to divorce Catherine and remarry or to nominate his eldest illegitimate son, the Duke of Monmouth, as his heir. In this, he held firm, strengthened as he was by his new chief minister, Lord Danby, and his supporters known as **Tories**.

Matters seriously came to a head in 1678. The **Popish Plot** was brought to light, in which claims were made of Catholic plans to assassinate the king and place James on the throne. Even Catherine was accused of planning to poison him. The king greatly doubted the veracity of the accusations, but it led to a wave of anti-Catholic hysteria. At the same time, details leaked about him asking for secret subsidies from Catholic France. In Scotland, attempts to repress non-conformists had led to a Presbyterian uprising and, with little money to suppress the trouble, there was a real danger of a repetition of the events that had led to the Civil Wars. To help defuse the crisis, he sent his brother abroad and dispatched a force to defeat the Scottish rebels. By repeatedly dissolving Parliament, he also prevented the passing of an exclusion bill against James, and, at the same time, his Tory supporters used the fear of anarchy to drum up support for the king. This, along with the discrediting of witnesses in the Popish Plot, meant defeat for the Whigs and Shaftesbury had to flee abroad in 1681. Victory for Charles and the Tories was confirmed in 1683 after the discovery of the **Rye House Plot** – an attempt by Whigs to murder both James and the king.

Charles II in a wig. Charles brought the fashion from France, partly to cover his prematurely greying hair. Wigs were made from human hair although the cheaper ones used horse and goat hair. Heavy, uncomfortable and often lice-ridden, owners dusted them with scented powder to mask odours. (*Artist: J van der Vaart, between 1682 and 1721. Rijksmuseum*)

Only now, in the last years of his reign, was Charles able to act like an absolutist monarch, confirming Whig fears that he wanted to attain powers like Louis XIV. Buoyed by popular support, Tory loyalists and new subsidies from France, Charles was able to rule without Parliament. He lacked the money to get involved in continental wars, but he did bolster his power at home. James's influence in government increased, many Whig estates were seized, municipal charters were interfered with so that only Tory officials were appointed and judges and juries were handpicked to produce favourable court verdicts.

In February 1685, Charles suffered a stroke and then endured four days of medical torture. His 'expert' physicians bled him, cauterised him, induced him to vomit, squirted a laxative up his rectum and burned the membranes in his nostrils. Shocked by what she saw, the queen had to flee the room. Typical of the man's humour, however, he apologised for taking so long in dying then, after asking to see the sun rise one more time, he passed away. Some contemporaries thought he had been poisoned but the symptoms match kidney failure. This, in turn, may have been caused by his numerous scientific experiments with mercury. In his final moments, he was received into the Catholic Church by a priest who had aided him during his escape in 1651. Whether he was conscious enough to be aware of this 'conversion' or if he was already a Catholic can never be known. Straight afterwards, James was proclaimed king.

The reign of Charles II saw a flourishing of science, culture and the arts and it occupies a unique period of English history. In the period 1649–88, absolutist monarchy had been defeated but no one had worked out a system to replace it. The 'Merry Monarch' further muddies the waters by not appearing to have had any long-term policies other than financial independence and survival (he refused to 'go on his travels again'). In religion, it is not clear if he genuinely wanted tolerance and, in foreign affairs, his guiding principle seemed to be acquiring French subsidies. Only near the end of his reign did he have the courage and ability to seek absolutism, but it is hard to assess whether this had been an aim of his from the start. Charles has had many detractors, but he does seem to have been a master of political expediency. He showed skill in surviving the crisis of 1678 while, at the same time, holding firmly to his belief in the royal succession. On other matters, he was willing to bow to the holders of his purse strings – Parliament. The reign of his brother would probably have turned out differently had he been willing to do likewise.

Churchill, John (Duke of Marlborough)

(1650–1722)

General and statesman

Churchill's father, Winston Churchill, had been a Dorset landowner who had joined the royalist side during the **Civil Wars**. After **Parliament**'s victory, he was heavily fined, and the family had to relocate to his mother-in-law's humbler surroundings in Devon. John Churchill attended St Paul's School in London, but his career was only able to take off after his sister, Arabella, started an affair with **James, Duke of York**, brother of **Charles II**. Consequently, Churchill became a page to James and then a junior officer in the army (1667). It seems that he also shared one of the king's mistresses – the **Countess of Castlemaine** – which benefited him financially.

Churchill's first taste of action was in 1672 at the Battle of Solebay during the **Third Anglo-Dutch War**. Two years later, on the continent, he commanded an English regiment fighting alongside French forces led by the renowned Turenne and perhaps learned much from this great commander. Soon after his return to England, he met the 15-year-old Sarah Jennings, a maid of honour to James's second wife, Mary of Modena. Despite his father's insistence on a more lucrative match, Churchill married Sarah in 1678, and their loving **marriage** produced seven children, five of whom reached adulthood.

Churchill remained loyal to James during the exclusion crisis of Charles II's reign and was rewarded with a peerage. In 1685, James acceded to the throne, and, in the same year, Churchill jointly led the infantry forces which destroyed **Monmouth's Rebellion** at Sedgemoor. He did, however, become increasingly concerned with the king's pro-**Catholic** policies and, with some reluctance, deserted him in 1688 during the **Glorious Revolution**.

The new king, **William III**, initially rewarded him with more titles and a place on the privy council. Churchill was also given his first independent command when he successfully defeated Jacobite forces in southern **Ireland**. However, William and Queen **Mary** never fully trusted him. He publicly complained about positions being given to William's Dutch followers and they were fully aware that he was still in contact with James in France. Like several others, Churchill was seeking forgiveness from the former king just in case he made a successful return. Also, Sarah's influence with Princess **Anne** rankled the joint monarchs, especially as she was next in line to the throne if they remained childless. In 1691, Churchill was suddenly fired from all his positions and, in the following year was accused of high treason and sent to the Tower of London for five weeks. After his release, he remained out of favour for several years and was even accused, unfairly, of forewarning the French of an imminent English attack on Brest. Churchill was only reconciled to William in 1698 when he was restored to his positions and, when the War of the Spanish Succession broke out in 1701, William appointed him as commander of the English forces. Churchill's position was further enhanced the following year when William died, and Anne became queen because he now had two supporters at the highest levels of power – Sarah (close friend to Anne) and the Earl of Godolphin (Lord Treasurer).

As commander of the Anglo-Dutch forces against France, Churchill achieved some degree of success at the start of the war for which a grateful queen proclaimed him Duke of Marlborough. Success, however, was tempered by intense grief at the death, from smallpox, of his only son and heir in Cambridge. The demands of war soon forced him to return to the Spanish Netherlands though and the events of 1704 would soon catapult him to fame. Marlborough anticipated a fatal Franco-Bavarian march on Vienna which would have defeated Austria, a key member of the Grand Alliance and so decided to march his army south to the Danube to block this planned attack.

The march itself was a display of brilliant planning and deceit. The Dutch government would have forbidden it for fear of being exposed to Villeroi's French army in the north. However, Marlborough convinced them (and Villeroi!) that he was merely advancing down the Moselle valley into France. Villeroi tried to shadow him down the Rhine, but further ruses allowed Marlborough to steal several marches on him so that when the key battle was fought, Villeroi was unable to assist. He rendezvoused, as planned, with German and Danish reinforcements along the way and showed meticulous attention to detail. Prearranged supply depots prevented his men and horses from going hungry, two transit hospitals were set up in advance and paid German cobblers ensured his soldiers always had fresh boots. Such was the care that he showed for his men that they affectionately called him 'Corporal John'. After completing a 260-mile march in a mere five weeks, Marlborough combined with his key ally, Prince Eugene, near the Danube and inflicted a crucial and devastating defeat on the Franco-Bavarian forces at **Blenheim**. As a result, not only was Austria saved but it destroyed the myth of French invincibility and strengthened the Grand Alliance's resolve. Back home, Anne rewarded Marlborough with Woodstock Park in Oxfordshire and the money to build Blenheim Palace, the largest private house in the country.

Duke of Marlborough. Holding a marshal's baton with a battle being fought in the background. (*Artist: after A. van der Werff, between 1701 and 1731. Rijksmuseum*)

This was the just the first in a string of victories – Ramillies (1706), Oudenarde (1708) and Malplaquet (1709). The greatest of all, possibly, was the capture of Bouchain (1711) after penetrating French defensive lines with no casualties. The historian, David Chandler, remarked, 'The pure military artistry with which he repeatedly deceived Villars [French commander] during the first part of the campaign has few equals in the annals of military history.' Marlborough's successes were due to his attention to detail, anticipation based on knowledge of opposing generals, his ability to maximise the lie of the land and the ability to deceive his enemies and alter a plan as a battle developed. He was also more decisive than his opponents in seeking battle and more aggressive in his use of artillery, cavalry and infantry. The latter, for example, he arranged in three rows to maximise their firepower. At the same time, the French were using outdated tactics that had succeeded in the past.

By now, the allies had reconquered most of the Spanish Netherlands, occupied parts of northern France and 'Malbrouck', as he was known to the French, was ready to strike at Paris itself. His deadliest foes, however, lay at home. There had been much political in-fighting between the **Tories**, who favoured a naval war, and the **Whigs**, who supported the continental war. The pyrrhic nature of the victory at Malplaquet allowed the Tories to wrest control of government from the Whigs

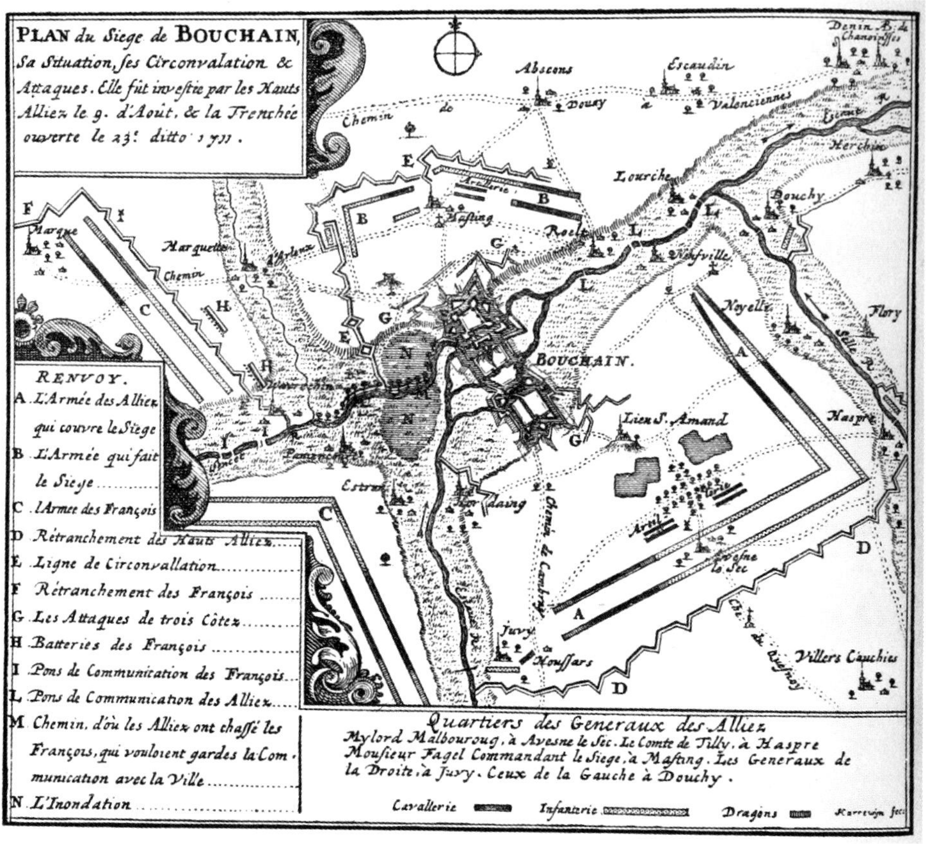

Siege of Bouchain. Possibly Marlborough's greatest victory. By being previously outmanoeuvred, French forces (left) were unable to lift the allied siege of Bouchain (centre). After its fall, only the fortress of Cambrai stood between the allies and Paris. (*Artist: unknown, from Histoire d'Iwuy, 1887. British Library*)

and led to Godolphin's dismissal. At the same time, the queen, who favoured an end to the war, had tired of Sarah's high-handed behaviour and dismissed her. Marlborough, now isolated, came under personal attack. He was accused of siphoning off money meant for payment of supplies and soldiers' wages and of deliberately prolonging the war for his own gain. The former may have contained some truth (he was known to be very cautious about money), but the latter was very unlikely. He did not help himself, though, when he demanded from Anne the Captain-Generalship of the army for life. With public opinion also against the long and draining war, the queen felt able to dismiss Marlborough in late 1711. Tory representatives had already started secret peace talks with the French and, in 1713, the Treaty of Utrecht ended the conflict.

Attacked in Parliament and by the press, the Duke and Duchess left Britain for Holland and Germany where he was feted as a saviour in various courts. Two years later, on the day of Anne's death in 1714, they returned and he was restored as Captain-General by George I. He directed operations against the 1715 Jacobite uprising in **Scotland** but suffered two strokes in the following year. Afterwards, he made a steady recovery, regained most of his speech and was able to ride a horse. In 1719, he and Sarah moved into the east wing of the unfinished Blenheim Palace but he died a few years later after another stroke. Initially, he was interred in Westminster Abbey, but, as per Sarah's instructions, he was reburied beside her body at Blenheim when she died in 1744.

Many historians and military experts regard Marlborough to be Britain's greatest general of all time – a view that was supported by the Duke of Wellington one hundred years later. There is certainly a good argument for this as his victories raised the country's prestige and turned Britain into a major power. It should also be remembered that he was a very able diplomat too. A disparate alliance in which each country had different war aims was successfully held together by his powers of negotiation and ability to see the wider picture. Any accusations of greed and corruption, whatever the truth in them, seem to pale in comparison.

Churchill, Sarah (Duchess of Marlborough)

(1660–1744)

Courtier and royal favourite

Sarah was a daughter of Richard Jennings, a Hertfordshire landowner who fought for **Parliament** during the **Civil Wars** and became an MP. Her elder sister, Frances, was a maid of honour to Anne Hyde, first wife of **James, Duke of York** and she, in turn, became a maid of honour to his second wife, Mary of Modena, in 1673. Two years later, she met **John Churchill**, an army officer and member of James's court. The couple fell in love but both of their families disapproved of the match for financial reasons. Sarah refused Churchill's offer to become his mistress and so they secretly married in 1678. Only when she became pregnant, later that year, was the **marriage** announced.

Before this, Sarah had developed a close friendship with James's younger daughter, **Anne**. The shy and impressionable 10-year-old princess was in awe of the confident, vivacious and beautiful teenager and the two began a close and long-standing relationship. During the **Glorious Revolution** of 1688, Sarah helped to persuade Anne to betray her father and arranged their escape from house arrest to Nottingham.

Life for the Churchills became difficult in the 1690s. The new king, **William III**, distrusted John due to his continued correspondence with the exiled James II and even imprisoned him for a few weeks. Meanwhile, the bond between Sarah and Anne had strengthened to the point where they now treated each other as equals. In correspondence they used the pet names they had given each other – Mrs Freeman

(Sarah) and Mrs Morley (Anne). However, the king's wife and Anne's older sister, **Mary II**, greatly disliked the power and influence that Sarah wielded in Anne's household. She repeatedly ordered Anne to dismiss her, but she refused. When Mary eventually evicted Sarah from Whitehall Palace, Anne left with her, and the sisters were never reconciled.

The Churchills had become largely rehabilitated by the end of the decade, but it was only when Anne became queen in 1702 that their respective careers reached their peaks. John was appointed Captain-General of the Anglo-Dutch forces in the War of the Spanish Succession while Sarah was bestowed with the highest titles in Anne's court – Mistress of the Robes, Groom of the Stool, Keeper of the Privy Purse (one of only two women to hold that post) and Ranger of Windsor Great Park (the only woman to hold that title). Sarah's dominance of the queen was unassailable as she controlled her visitors as well as her finances. Later that year, she became the Duchess of Marlborough following John's elevation to a dukedom. His successes on the battlefield augmented her influence and she, in turn, worked incessantly to maintain support for him in the government.

Anne and Sarah's relationship, however, soured as the reign progressed. The very frankness which had endeared Sarah to the princess had now become hurtful and disrespectful for the queen. Anne preferred a **Tory**-dominated government, but Sarah tried to force her to choose **Whig** ministers as they supported her husband's war effort. In addition, Sarah spent more time away overseeing the construction of her new home at Blenheim Palace in Oxfordshire. During these absences, the queen turned increasingly to her new Lady of the Bedchamber, Abigail Masham. Abigail, a cousin of Sarah's, had been brought into the queen's household by the Duchess to help her out of poverty. She was everything that Sarah was not – gentle, compassionate, kind and flattering – and Sarah became furious when she eventually discovered that Abigail had replaced her as Anne's closest confidante. Rows between the two former friends grew worse. In 1708, Sarah publicly told the queen to be quiet at a service in St Paul's Cathedral and, later that year, was brutally unsympathetic when Anne's beloved husband died. She even helped to spread rumours that the queen and Abigail were having a lesbian relationship.

By 1710, the Tories had assumed control of government and the public had tired of the war, so Anne no longer felt the need to keep the Marlboroughs in employment. At a final meeting, she reduced Sarah to tears by icily refusing to answer her questions and then dismissed her. The Duke, too, was sacked after accusations of embezzlement and the state funding for Blenheim Palace was removed. Under a cloud of unpopularity, the couple lived abroad for a couple of years, mainly in Holland and Germany. Sarah, however, found life there tiring and dull and longed to return to England. This they did in 1714 on the same day that Queen Anne died.

The Duke and Duchess were rehabilitated by the new king, George I, and Sarah now spent much time trying to arrange favourable marriages for her daughters.

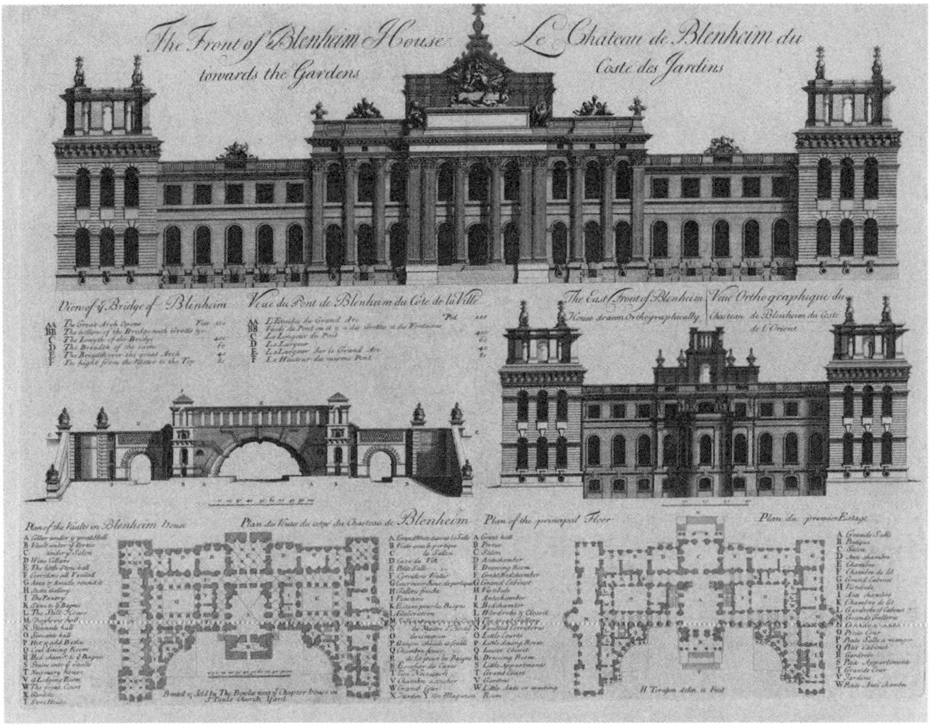

Blenheim Palace. Plans showing the front façade, east side and bridge. (*Artist: Sir J. Vanbrugh, c. 1724. Rijksmuseum*)

She also cared for her husband after he suffered two strokes in 1716 and helped him to recover. Meanwhile, work on Blenheim Palace had recommenced and she enjoyed acting as a business manager for its construction and design although she later disliked it as a home, describing it as 'that great heap of stones'. After John's death in 1722, Sarah refused all offers of marriage as she preferred to retain her independence. She then made several shrewd property investments, her twenty-seven estates making her the richest woman in Europe with a fortune estimated to have been £4 million.

Sarah seemed to become more formidable and outspoken as she grew older. She became estranged from most of her daughters and her arguments with eminent people were well known. She fell out with Robert Walpole (Britain's first prime minister) for blocking the marriage of her granddaughter, Lady Diana Spencer, to the Prince of Wales, she harassed the renowned architect, Sir John Vanbrugh for being extravagant, she was rude to George II by saying he was 'too much of a German' and angered his wife by refusing her access to her estate in Wimbledon. Neither did she make herself popular with the public by fighting in court to have the construction of Blenheim Palace funded by the state even though she could easily have afforded it herself. Sarah's final assault, however, was upon her old friend. In 1742, she wrote a memoir which detailed her relationship with Queen Anne. Not surprisingly, perhaps, she portrayed herself in a much more favourable light than the queen. Upon her death, aged 84, her will left very little money to charity but she was extremely generous to her servants.

Queen Anne's biographer, E Gregg, states that the Duchess had 'an almost pathological inability to admit the validity of anyone else's point of view' and even the Marlboroughs' friend, the Earl of Godolphin, considered her bossy and interfering. It seems evident that Sarah Churchill was indeed a difficult person to get on with. Her bad temper was renowned; she did not suffer fools gladly and much of what she did was out of self-interest. At the same time, though, people found her charming, witty and intelligent and it is very hard not to admire such a strong-willed, outspoken and capable woman living in a male-dominated world.

Civil Wars

(1642–51)

Also known as the British Civil Wars, Wars of the Three Kingdoms or the English Revolution

The violence that convulsed the British Isles in the mid-seventeenth century was largely a culmination of rising political and religious tensions. King **Charles I** was a strong believer in divine right and favoured a High **Anglican** Church. A growing number of members of **Parliament**, however, were concerned by Charles's absolutist behaviour and wanted to protect Parliamentary liberties. At the same time, the Commons had become dominated by **Puritan**s who viewed the king's religious reforms as a return to **Catholic**ism. Events spiralled out of control in 1641 as a junto of Parliamentarians attacked royal powers and Charles struggled to preserve them. The tipping point probably came in November when news filtered through of a Catholic rebellion in **Ireland**. The junto, motivated by self-preservation, stirred up the London mob with news of massacres of Protestants and rumours that the king and queen had arranged the uprising. Charles's disastrous attempt to restore his authority by trying to arrest five key MPs only inflamed the situation, and, in January 1642, he and his family fled the capital to seek safety.

First Civil War (1642–46)

Over the next several months, negotiations failed as the king refused to agree to demands which would have seriously curtailed his power. At the same time, leaders from both sides sought control of the country's towns and cities. Brawls began to break out and in one such disturbance in Manchester the first fatality occurred. In

August, Charles raised his standard outside Nottingham around which he began to rally an army and then marched west to gather more supporters. Simultaneously, Parliament appointed the Earl of Essex to raise an army of volunteers with which to 'rescue his Majesty's person' from his ill-intentioned advisors (very few at this stage considered the drastic step of abolishing the monarchy). By now, Parliamentary soldiers had become known as 'Roundheads' due to the short hairstyles of the apprentices who had dominated the London mob at the beginning of the troubles. Royalist soldiers, in turn, were called 'Cavaliers', a derogatory term referring to brutal Spanish *caballeros* or horsemen. Many districts wanted nothing to do with the quarrel and formed bands of 'clubmen' to defend their localities. This task, however, became impossible as the war progressed.

A true and exact Relation of the manner of his Maiesties setting up of His Standard at *Nottingham*, on Munday the 22. of August 1642.

First, The forme of the Standard, as it is here figured, and who were present at the advancing of it

Secondly, The danger of setting up of former Standards, and the damage which ensued thereon.

Thirdly, A relation of all the Standards that ever were set up by any King.

Fourthly, the names of those Knights who are appointed to be the Kings Standard-bearers. With the forces that are appoynted to guard it.

Fifthly, The manner of the Kings comming first to *Coventry*.

Sixtly, The *Cavalieres* resolution and dangerous threats which they have uttered, if the King concludes a peace without them, or hearkens unto his great Councell the Parliament; Moreover how they have shared and divided *London* amongst themselves already.

London, printed for *F. Coles*, 1642.

Charles I raising his standard at Nottingham. From a parliamentary pamphlet (*Artist: unknown, 1642 via Wikimedia Commons*)

The first skirmish was fought at Powick Bridge, near Worcester, where Charles's nephew, **Prince Rupert**, drove off a small detachment of Roundhead cavalry. The first major battle, however, took place in October 1642 when Essex attempted to block Charles's advance on London. The ensuing Battle of Edgehill was indecisive though and both sides claimed victory. However, Charles's delay after the battle proved costly as Essex was given time to organise London's defences. At Turnham Green, in November, the Royalist forces faced poorly trained and poorly armed civilians. The royalists were short of ammunition and outnumbered though and Charles was reluctant to bring bloodshed upon his own capital and so he ordered a withdrawal to Oxford where he set up his headquarters for the rest of the war. He was never to get as close to London again.

By the end of 1642, the south-east of England had been secured for Parliament as well as most of the navy. All ports, bar Newcastle, were under Roundhead control too. The king's support was strongest in the north, west Midlands, Wales and Cornwall. For many, choosing sides was straightforward. A Puritan merchant, for instance, would almost certainly have taken Parliament's side due to his opposition to Charles's religious and taxation policies. A wealthy Anglican landowner, however, would more likely have stayed loyal to the monarchy from which his ancestors had been granted land. Most Welshmen, too, were staunchly royalist and disliked Parliament's perceived pro-Englishness. It is not for no reason that

Wales became known as 'the nursery of the King's infantry'. Most tenants and apprentices fought, willingly or not, for whichever side their lord or master chose. Some joined the first army that appeared, looking for money and adventure, while others were pressganged. There were also hundreds of foreign mercenaries such as the Croat, Captain Fantom, who declared, 'I care not for your Cause, I …fight for your halfe-crowne[s], and your handsome woemen.' Finally, there were large numbers of those with split loyalties the best-known example being the Verneys of Buckinghamshire, father and son fighting on opposing sides despite the anguish it brought to the family.

1643 was largely a year of Royalist successes. Cavalier armies advanced from Cornwall, the west Midlands and the north and, by the winter, controlled two-thirds of the country. In July, Prince Rupert captured Bristol – a major port and England's second largest city but the drawn battle of Newbury (September) was a missed opportunity to destroy Parliament's main field army. Both sides now realised that support was needed from elsewhere if victory was to be attained. Charles made a peace deal with the Irish rebels which freed up Crown troops who had been fighting there. This, however, upset many of his supporters, some of whom deserted his cause. For its part, Parliament made an agreement with **Scotland** – the Solemn League and Covenant – by which the Scots would provide military support in return for England adopting a **Presbyterian** form of Church government. This arrangement caused some Roundheads to desert too and divisions in Parliament were further deepened by the death of its leader, **John Pym**. He had managed to unite Anglicans, Presbyterians (both wanted some form of Church hierarchy and sought a peace settlement) and Independents (wanted no hierarchy and sought the complete military defeat of the king).

Early 1644 saw **Thomas Fairfax** defeat a Royalist relief force from Ireland at Nantwich, Cheshire. The advent of Scottish troops put further pressure upon Royalist forces in the north, forcing their leader, the Earl of Newcastle, to take refuge in York. Prince Rupert made a lightning dash north to relieve the siege, capturing Liverpool and Bolton en route. He succeeded in rescuing Newcastle, but their joint forces were smashed at Marston Moor (July 1644). This was the largest battle of the war with approximately 20,000 men on each side (although quite small in comparison to those armies fighting in the Thirty Years' War on the continent). The defeat effectively ended the Royalist cause in northern England but, elsewhere, the Roundheads could make no progress. In fact, they suffered a heavy defeat at Lostwithiel in Cornwall (August) and failed to defeat a weaker enemy at the Second Battle of Newbury. At the same time, Royalist forces in Scotland, led by the Earl of Montrose, won a string of victories and prevented large numbers of Scottish troops from playing any further part in England.

Early 1645 saw the Self-Denying Ordinance passed through Parliament. This was an attempt by hard-line Independents, such as **Oliver Cromwell**, to wrest control of the armed forces away from the traditional leadership of the lords. Many

The Whitecoats' last stand at Marston Moor. The Earl of Newcastle's infantry regiment famously refused to surrender and was almost completely wiped out. (*Artist: unknown, from T. Roosevelt's Oliver Cromwell, 1900 via Project Gutenberg*)

suspected that Parliamentarian generals such as the earls of Essex and Manchester were too half-hearted in their campaigns against the king and preferred a negotiated peace. The Self-Denying Ordinance forbade anyone from being an MP and a military leader at the same time. As hereditary lords could not resign their titles, Essex and Manchester had to give up their commands. Cromwell, too, was an MP but was given special dispensation. This was followed by the creation of the **New Model Army** – England's first full-time, professional army – led by Thomas Fairfax, with Cromwell commanding its cavalry. This was the force that destroyed Charles's largest field army at **Naseby** (June). During the battle, the royal baggage was captured among which were found letters asking for Catholic troops from Ireland, France and the pope. The publication of these further damaged Charles's reputation and strengthened the position of the Independents in Parliament. After Naseby, the king made futile attempts to link up with Montrose in Scotland as his forces elsewhere were beaten by Fairfax and Cromwell. The worst loss was that of Bristol in September and, in the same month, Montrose was finally defeated. By the end of the year, the Royalists only held Devon, Cornwall, north Wales and a few isolated outposts such as Oxford, Exeter and Newark.

1646 consisted mainly of mopping-up operations by Parliament's forces, the last pitched battle being at Stow-on-the-Wold (March). The defeated Royalist commander, Lord Astley, presciently said to his captors, 'You have done your work, boys, and may go play, unless you will fall out among yourselves.' Charles managed to escape from the encircled city of Oxford and, in May, surrendered to Scottish troops besieging Newark in the hope of driving a wedge between the allies. They eventually surrendered him to Parliament though after he rejected their Newcastle Propositions and the First Civil War was over.

With hindsight, we can say that defeat for the king was inevitable after 1643. Initially, he had the most money and the best commanders, but he failed to press home this early advantage. Parliament controlled the wealthier and more populous south-east. It had an established tax base and, with its control of the ports, could tax all trade too. Charles's economic base was far more agrarian and he could never have afforded a Cavalier equivalent of the New Model Army. Parliament's control of the navy also prevented the Royalists from receiving much support from sympathetic countries abroad although their involvement in the Thirty Years' War would have made this unlikely anyway. So, the longer the war went on, the less likely that Charles could win it. Parliament's alliance with Scotland and the reforming of its army merely hastened Charles's defeat.

Second Civil War (1648)

For the first half of 1647, Charles was the prisoner of a Parliament which had become dominated by Presbyterians who wanted him to accept the Newcastle Propositions which would have reduced monarchical power and introduced Presbyterianism to England. Independents within the New Model Army feared such a deal being done behind their backs and were angry about the unpaid wages which Parliament owed its soldiers. So, in June, officers seized Charles and offered him the remarkably conciliatory Heads of Proposals, which even allowed the retention of bishops (though with less power). Soon after, the army occupied London and forcibly purged Parliament of its leading Presbyterians.

The king, for his part, played for time and waited for his enemies to come to blows with each other. In November, he escaped but was recaptured and imprisoned on the Isle of Wight. There, he made a secret deal with a Scottish delegation in which he accepted Presbyterianism in return for military support. In the summer of 1648, coordinated Royalist uprisings broke out around the country, the most serious being in south Wales, Essex and Kent where elements of the navy went over to the king. Too late to take advantage of these revolts before they were crushed, a large Scottish force marched into Lancashire where it was defeated by Cromwell at Preston (August). This ended the Second Civil War.

Third Civil War (or Anglo-Scottish War of 1650–51)

The events of 1648 vindicated the Independents' view that Charles could not be trusted and would never agree to a deal. So, after a further purge of moderate MPs (Pride's Purge), Parliament voted to bring Charles to trial for treason and he was beheaded in January 1649. The army then sailed to Ireland and brutally restored English authority which had been missing from the island since 1641.

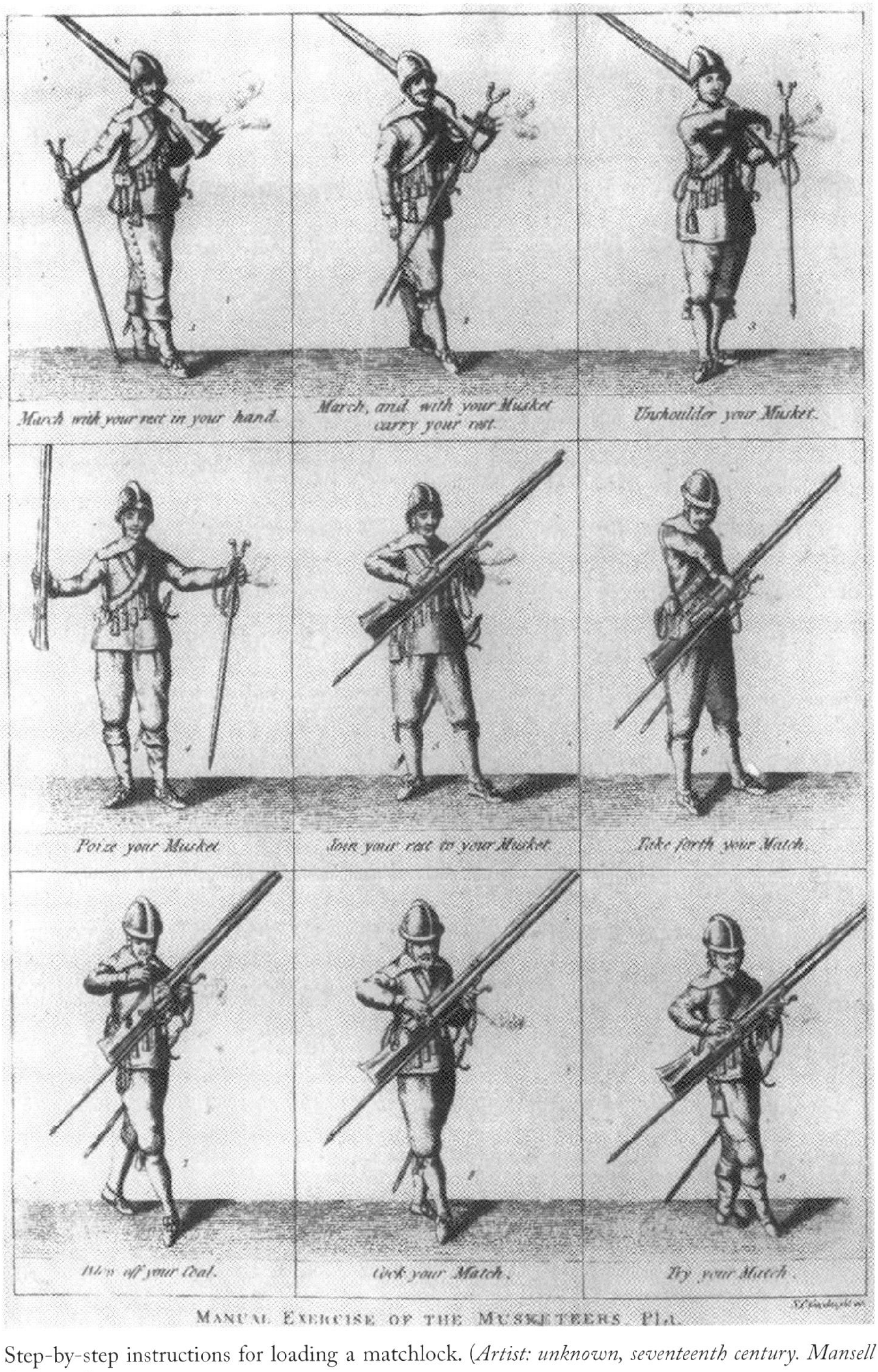

Step-by-step instructions for loading a matchlock. (*Artist: unknown, seventeenth century. Mansell Collection*)

In the meantime, the Scots, horrified by the execution of their king, proclaimed his son **Charles II** in return for enforcing the Presbyterian Church across Britain. Cromwell returned from Ireland and launched a preemptive attack on Scotland (June 1650). This started off badly as the Scottish commander, David Leslie, refused to be drawn into battle and the English had to make a bedraggled retreat southward. Outside Dunbar, in early September, Leslie came under political pressure to attack and left his advantageous hilltop position. Cromwell then counterattacked and smashed his opponents.

He then advanced further into Scotland to inflict a decisive defeat. Charles persuaded Leslie that their only chance was to take what was left of their army, march into England and gather royalists to their cause. Cromwell gave chase after leaving behind enough troops for General **Monck** to mop up all remaining resistance. After a three-week march, the exhausted Scottish force reached Worcester where it was hoped that royalist supporters from Wales and the west Midlands would join them. Only sixty did; most did not want to endorse Scottish Presbyterianism. Hugely outnumbered and poorly equipped, the Scots were routed in the streets of Worcester (September 1651). Prisoners went into forced labour either in the Fens or **Virginia**. Leslie was sent to the Tower of London and Scotland became fully integrated into the English republican government. Charles, himself, just managed to escape to France but the battle ended the Civil Wars.

* * *

The Civil Wars and the execution of Charles I had a huge impact on British history. In the short term, there was the sheer cost of a conflict which involved around 600 battles and sieges. Most of these took place in a large swathe of territory across the contested Midlands while some areas, such as the south-east, saw very little fighting. An estimated 100,000 soldiers died in the wars and about the same number of civilians resulting from starvation, due to requisitioned food supplies and the diseases that accompanied itinerant soldiers. Atrocities were commonplace, too, such as those inflicted upon Catholic civilians by Puritan troops. These figures amount to about 4.5 per cent of the population which make the conflict the bloodiest in English history. In Ireland, possibly as much as 20 per cent of the population died in the 1641–52 period.

As well as the threat of hunger and violence, civilians had to put up with billeting, forced labour, the breakdown of law and order and the destruction of much property. Many castles, manor houses and churches were vandalised or destroyed and about 10 per cent of all urban homes were ruined. Moreover, people suffered increased taxes to pay for the war. In the absence of royal power and bishops, who had overseen censorship, there was a proliferation of radical religious and social groups too. Many of these were considered to have dangerous proposals such as the **Levellers**, Diggers and Ranters whose ideas spread rapidly by way of pamphlets and public speakers. It is no wonder that many people felt that the world had turned upside down.

In the long term, the conflict had important repercussions. Heads of state abroad were horrified by the king's death and, for a while, England became isolated. Cromwell's experiments with republicanism ultimately failed and the monarchy was restored in 1660. However, Charles's defeat and subsequent trial and execution showed that a king was not above the law and could be held accountable for his actions. Charles II understood this principle and **James II**, to his own cost, chose to ignore it. Only after the **Glorious Revolution** of 1688 was the framework of a constitutional monarchy finally established.

Clarendon, First Earl of

see Hyde, Edward

Coffee Houses

The cultivation and use of coffee originated in Ethiopia and from there it spread to Arabia, Egypt and Turkey where it became immensely popular as a stimulant. Traders then brought it to Europe where it was initially viewed with suspicion due to its bitter flavour and popularity with Muslims. Coffee first arrived in England in the late sixteenth century and was first used by physicians as a possible cure for scurvy, smallpox and drunkenness. In 1637, the diarist, John Evelyn, saw it being drunk in Oxford by a Greek scholar stating that he was, 'the first I ever saw drink coffee'.

Oxford, too, saw the first coffee house – The Angel – open in 1650. London followed suit two years later when an eccentric Greek opened his doors off Cornhill (now called the Jamaica Wine House). The number of establishments grew slowly but the sense of liberation that followed the Restoration saw an explosion in numbers so that, by 1675, there were over 3,000 in England, the majority being in London.

The coffee houses were sometimes called 'penny universities' because entry was one penny (equivalent to around 50 pence in 2025) and people went there to exchange knowledge as well as to gossip and socialise. **Isaac Newton** even claimed that his *principia mathematica* was conceived in a coffee house. An unusual feature of these establishments was the diversity of their customers. Anyone, from any sector of **society**, could rub shoulders and exchange views with anyone else if they were civil. Rich and poor were able to give their views at the same table, so some historians view the coffee house as an early democratic institution. Some also state that they were a driving force of the Enlightenment, where coffee-fuelled debate saw reason reign over superstition, religion and tradition.

Interior of a coffee house. A large coffee cauldron hangs over the fire with tall coffee pots in front. (*Artist: unknown, late seventeenth century via Wikimedia Commons*)

Certain places attracted certain types of clientele. For example, the Grecian attracted lawyers, artists met at Old Slaughter's and Garraway's was frequented by scientists. Stockbrokers were considered too uncouth for the Royal Exchange and so met at Jonathan's. Merchants conducted their deals at Lloyd's which later became a major insurance company. One went to the coffee house to discover and debate, and poor behaviour was frowned upon: swearing, for instance, carried a fine of 12 pence. The attraction of the coffee house was its civilised and intellectual atmosphere unlike the rowdier taverns. There were one or two exceptions though. Moll King's had an unusually wide, diverse clientele ranging from courtiers and traders to pimps and drunkards. As for the coffee itself, it tended to be quite thick and gritty, never with milk but sometimes with sugar.

The coffee houses also acted as hubs for news. Every table would have the latest newspapers and pamphlets (included in the entry price) and 'runners' would spread news from one establishment to another. The most popular literature were *The Spectator* and *Tatler* which simply regurgitated the news and gossip that had been heard in the coffee houses. Political news was always popular. The failures of the **Third Anglo-Dutch War**, for example, caused much anti-government discussion for which Lord Danby, **Charles II**'s chief minister, tried to close them down in the mid-1670s. The resulting uproar forced him to back down, however.

For women, such a closure may well have been most welcome. They could serve at the coffee houses but could not enter as customers. Male-centred discussions about business, literature and politics, for example, were not supposed to concern women and entering a coffee house would have damaged their respectability, especially as some became the haunts of prostitutes. Most complaints about the new fashion did, in fact, come from women. The *Women's Petition Against Coffee* (1674) argued that the 'nauseous puddle water' was rendering their husbands impotent and preventing them from carrying out their domestic duties.

By the late eighteenth century, coffee-house culture had disappeared although it continued on the continent. They had become the reserves of elitist intelligentsia, and some transformed into gentlemen's clubs. Moreover, tea overtook coffee in popularity – it could easily be prepared at home and teashops tended to welcome both genders. In fact, the first teashop was opened by Twinings in 1717 for ladies of fashion. It was not until the 1990s that coffeehouse chains brought back social coffee drinking.

Coke, Sir Edward

(1552–1634)

Jurist and parliamentarian

Coke was born into Norfolk gentry, his father being a wealthy barrister who had acquired land and attended Norwich Grammar School. After three years at Cambridge university, he attended London's Inns of Court where he impressed with his detailed knowledge of the law. A barrister at the mere age of 26, Coke's remarkable memory and industry earned him the patronage of those in power and allowed him to rise rapidly through the legal ranks. By 1594, he was the Attorney-General as well as Speaker of the Commons in **Parliament**.

Early in the reign of **James I**, Coke vigorously led the prosecution in cases against Walter Ralegh and survivors of the **Gunpowder Plot**. His brutal attacks against the former, based on the flimsiest of evidence, tarnished his reputation but gained him much favour with the king. As a result, he was promoted to Chief Justice of the Court of Common Pleas in 1606. Coke considered this court to be 'the lock and key of the common law', which he regarded as the overriding law of the land, law that was based on the precedent of legal cases since the Middle Ages rather than any statutes of Parliament. It was inevitable, therefore, that he would clash with James's attempts to assert the royal prerogative.

Coke first attacked the power of the Church's Court of High Commission by attempting to block many of its cases, insisting that they had aspects that meant they should be judged by the common law. When brought before James, Coke refused to be intimidated and even insisted that the king himself was subject to the law and could not alter it. Only the intervention of **Robert Cecil**, his friend and James's chief minister, saved Coke from imprisonment.

Coke could not simply be removed; he was far too popular and widely respected for that. His position was weakened, however, by Cecil's death in 1612. This allowed his main rival, **Francis Bacon**, to persuade James to promote Coke to the Court of King's Bench where, as chief defender of the king's rights, he could hardly cause any trouble. However, he continued to promote the common law by blocking the king's wishes (most famously in the case of the **Puritan** preacher, Edmund Peacham, who Coke said was not guilty of treason after he wrote a sermon predicting rebellion). By 1616, James had lost all patience and dismissed him from his posts. With support from the queen (**Anne of Denmark**), Coke regained some favour though and was allowed to seek ways of improving revenue in the Exchequer.

1621 saw the start of the final phase of Coke's career. As MP for Liskeard in Cornwall, he became the unofficial leader of the opposition in Parliament. There, he led the impeachment of Bacon for corruption, attacked plans for Prince Charles to marry the Spanish Infanta and defended Parliament's right to free speech. For these, Coke was imprisoned in the Tower for seven months but in 1624 he succeeded in pushing through the Statute of Monopolies. Monopolies on everyday goods such as salt and starch had become increasingly unpopular as they drove up prices. James had granted many to courtiers as a way of raising revenue, but the statute now eliminated most of them. Some historians even regard it as one of the first steps towards the **Civil War**s.

After the accession of **Charles I** (1625), Coke spoke out against the king's favourite, **Buckingham**, and the perceived increep of **Catholic**ism but his finest hour was yet to come. At the age of 76, in response to perceived monarchical attacks on people's rights, he masterminded the Petition of Right (1628) in which Parliament demanded:

- no taxation without Parliament's consent
- no imprisonment without a fair trial
- no billeting of troops on people's homes
- no martial law in peacetime

Charles dismissed Parliament but the petition has since become a cornerstone of the British and American democracies. Coke then went into retirement and died aged 82 at the same time as troops were ransacking his home looking for incriminating documents.

As a person, Coke was arrogant and pedantic as well as fearless and driven. He saw little need for winning friends to assist in his court struggles and was accused of using his detailed knowledge of the law to profit from land sales. His second marriage, to Elizabeth Hatton, was a disaster. Their arguments over her property became public knowledge but more scandalous was his forced abduction of their daughter to thwart Elizabeth's choice of husband. Nevertheless, Coke stands

To the Kings most Excellent Maiestie

Petition of Right. (*Author: English Parliament, 1628. National Archives*)

as the champion of English common law and his written works – *Reports* and *Institutes of the Laws of England* – provide much of the framework and precedent for the law today.

Crime and Punishment

Deterrence and retribution were the key driving forces behind law and order in Stuart **society**. With there being no police force, it was hoped that the brutality of punishments would make people think twice before committing a crime. The only form of security was a night watchman patrolling the streets, announcing the time and chanting,

Look well to your locks,
Fire and your light,
And God give you good night
For now the bell ringeth

Four times a year, criminal cases were dealt with at quarter sessions by justices of the peace at the county town's courtroom. More serious offences, that carried the death penalty, were tried at the biannual assizes, which were overseen by a pair of travelling judges responsible for an area of the country.

Capital punishment could be applied to any felony, of which there were 300 types, and non-capital offences were known as 'trespass'. The law also recognised six classes of people to help decide what type of crime had been committed and the severity of the punishment: nobility, yeomen (small freeholder of land), peasants, tradesmen, labourers and women. Offences committed against people of a 'higher' class would usually carry a heavier penalty. Despite the high number of capital offences, it seems that judges and juries often preferred to show clemency. For instance, in cases where was some doubt or it was a first offence, defendants could claim benefit of the clergy by proving that they could read (some illiterate felons tried memorising passages from the Bible!). This usually led to a branding on the thumb instead of a hanging and **Ben Jonson** avoided the gallows this way. Women could also 'plead the belly' by claiming they were pregnant. If backed up by a jury of matrons, then justice could be postponed for up to nine months in which time new evidence could hopefully be found. A plea of temporary insanity, or a fit of madness, would avert an execution too although full insanity would lead to a stay in a notorious lunatic asylum, such as Bedlam, where cruel 'correctional' methods

Execution of Anne Green. A servant accused of infanticide, Anne was hanged in Oxford in 1650. Despite friends pulling on her and soldiers clubbing her to expedite her death, Anne recovered before physicians could dissect her. She was then pardoned and later married and had three children. (*Author: W. Burdet from A Wonder of Wonders, 1651 via Wikimedia Commons*)

were used. Transportation also became increasingly used whereby a criminal would carry out slave labour in the new colonies of **Virginia** and the West Indies.

Unsurprisingly, perhaps, the most common offence was stealing; a capital offence if the stolen item was worth more than a shilling (12 pence) which was a day's wage for a London labourer. The underworld of thieves even developed its own cant, or slang, for different types of stealing. 'Figging law' was pickpocketing or cutting purse strings, 'Barnard's law' was cheating in cards, 'curbing law' was stealing goods through an open window with a long hook and the 'black art' was lock-picking. The 'high law' (highway robbery) seemed to peak in the fifty years following the Restoration with many highwaymen being ex-soldiers from the **Civil Wars**.

Homicide was obviously a capital offence peaking in the early seventeenth century to around 150 per million per year (currently, it is 11.7 although a direct comparison should bear in mind that the lives of many seventeenth-century victims would have been saved with modern medical care). The probable reason was the high unemployment and inflation caused by the population surge at the time combined with the demobilisation of soldiers after the long war with Spain in 1604 (15 per cent of able-bodied men had been conscripted). These men, now trained in the art of combat, often returned home and found themselves destitute. With both larceny and homicide rates peaking at this time, it is no wonder that contemporaries were fearing a complete breakdown in law and order despite the rates being significantly higher on the continent. Murder was usually of a member of the community, unpremeditated and with a blunt instrument or fists. The domestic homicide rate seemed to remain steady at around 6.8 (0.00023 today).

Other capital offences included **witchcraft**, rape, sodomy and bestiality – very low conviction rates due to lack of evidence – and bigamy. With husbands often away for many years, bigamy must have been quite common and hard to detect. The kidnapping of children and selling them into forced labour was also common. Suicide was a capital offence too(!) and the deceased's property would be confiscated, and the body would not receive a religious burial.

Most serious of all were crimes against the state. For high treason, women were burned at the stake, commoners were hanged, drawn and quartered (hanged until almost dead, insides drawn out and body cut into quarters) and noblemen were beheaded. Executioners often showed mercy by strangulating a woman first or ensuring that a victim was dead before being disembowelled but had to be aware of the mood of the watching crowd. An unpopular victim was expected to receive the full force of justice. For petty treason (servant killing a master or woman killing her husband), women would be burned and men hanged.

There was a multitude of trespass offences, too, such as:

Begging/Vagrancy	– Whipped, put in stocks or branded with a 'V'.
Assault	– Fined. Wife-beating was allowed but excessive violence was increasingly frowned upon in the seventeenth century. Only in 1976 did domestic violence become illegal.
Petty Larceny	– Whipped, branded with a 'T' or possible amputation of hand.
Brawling/Swearing	– Stocks.
Poaching	– Whipped (hanged if caught at night).
Scolding/gossiping	– Scold's bridle around head or ducked in water.
Debt/Perjury/Libel	– Pillory.

Imprisonment was used but jails were usually holding places for suspects awaiting trial. A prisoner was expected to pay for his accommodation; families provided food and conditions could be improved by bribing the gaolers. Some gaolers were so corrupt that they even allowed convicts to continue their illegal activities. The prostitutes in Bridewell prison, London, for instance, continued to ply their trade behind bars with their guards receiving a cut of the profits.

Woman wearing a scold's bridle in New England. (*Artists: J. & E. Steele from A Brief History of the United States, 1885 via Wikimedia Commons*)

Cromwell, Oliver

(1599–1658)

Soldier and statesman

Cromwell was the only surviving son of a moderately wealthy Huntingdon landowner. His great-great-grandfather had married the sister of Henry VIII's chief minister, Thomas Cromwell, had adopted his surname and benefited from the Dissolution of the Monasteries. Oliver attended Cambridge university but returned home, without a degree, upon his father's death in 1617 to run the family estate. Three years later, he married Elizabeth Bourchier, the daughter of a London leather merchant. The **marriage** seems have been a caring one and the couple had nine children, eight of whom reached adulthood.

For the next twenty years Cromwell was of little significance outside his locality. As an MP for Huntingdon he witnessed the dramatic closure of **Parliament** in 1629 and, as a justice of the peace, he defended the rights of commoners affected by the drainage of the Fens that began in 1630. At around the same time, debt forced him to sell his lands, rent a farm near St Ives and live off the sale of wool and eggs. It may have been the accompanying stress that triggered a period of mental depression and physical illness. It may also have been the catalyst for his spiritual conversion – convinced that he had been 'the chief of sinners', he now believed that he was one of God's Chosen and adopted **Puritan**ism. In 1634, Cromwell attempted to emigrate to seek a better life in America but was prevented from doing so by the government. Two years later, though, his status and finances recovered when he inherited his uncle's properties in Ely.

1640–49

In 1640, Cromwell represented Cambridge in the Short and Long Parliaments and asked his family to join him in London. As a volatile and outspoken MP he demanded regular meetings of Parliament, the abolition of bishops and taking control of the army away from King **Charles I**. During the debate on the **Grand Remonstrance**, he threatened to emigrate immediately if it did not pass through the Commons. Then, when war seemed inevitable, in the summer of 1642, he returned to Cambridge to organise its defences and raise companies of soldiers.

Cromwell's fame and reputation was established during the **Civil Wars**. He raised a troop of cavalry from his home county but arrived too late to take part in the first major engagement of the war (Edgehill) in October 1642. The poor performance of Parliament's cavalry made him see the need to create a regiment that was innovative in its discipline and organisation – the 'Ironsides'. Regularly paid and highly trained, these troopers rode into battle knee-to-knee as a solid, powerful block that could wheel on command instead of making wild and uncontrollable dashes. Cromwell also preferred men of loyalty, no matter how low-born, and officers of the Puritan faith who could motivate them. Discipline was strict too – swearing was fined and deserters were whipped. It was the actions of these 'Ironsides' that proved decisive at Marston Moor (1644) by which time, Cromwell had been promoted to lieutenant-general.

Early the following year, the Self-Denying Ordinance led to the sacking of Parliamentarian generals such as the earls of Manchester and Essex whom Cromwell believed to be too half-hearted in their attempts to win the war. The subsequent **New Model Army** was led by Sir **Thomas Fairfax**, but Cromwell commanded its cavalry and put much energy into its organisation. This was the force that then destroyed the king's army at **Naseby** (1645) and defeated all remaining royalist forces to end the First Civil War.

During the prolonged negotiations regarding a post-war settlement, Cromwell started to become an opponent of Parliament. Always concerned about his soldiers' welfare, he demanded the months of back pay that they were owed. He was also alarmed about Charles and Parliament making a deal which would create a **Presbyterian** Church in England as, by this time, he was in a group known as the Independents who wanted relative freedom of worship and no Church hierarchy. The army, too, was dominated by Independents and refused to disband when ordered to do so by Parliament. Matters escalated when senior officers seized the king from parliamentary control and offered him a more generous deal – the Heads of Proposals. Even at this stage, Cromwell believed in having a monarchy and rejected the demands of **Levellers** within the army to introduce a 'one man, one vote' democracy.

However, Charles's secret deal with the Presbyterian Scots and the subsequent outbreak of the Second Civil War had a radicalising effect upon him. He defeated a superior Scots' army at Preston (1648) and crushed royalist uprisings elsewhere, but the events compelled him to believe that the king could never be trusted and 'to call Charles Stuart, that man of blood, to an account for that blood he had shed, and mischief he had done'. At the same time, Cromwell began to use much Biblical imagery in his speeches and letters, convinced as he was that he had been chosen to carry out God's will and that the army was God's chosen instrument, not the king or Parliament.

Far from putting the king on trial, Parliament was still trying to negotiate with him and so, although absent from London at the time, Cromwell later gave his approval of Pride's Purge (December 1648). Under orders from Generals Fairfax and **Ireton**, army troops occupied key positions in London and Colonel Pride blocked 231 moderate and Presbyterian MPs from entering the Commons. This left around 200 MPs who became known as the 'Rump Parliament'. Angered by this military coup, even the majority of these refused to attend the vote which ordered the king's trial. After the court found Charles guilty (January 1649), John Bradshaw, the court's president, and Lord Grey signed the death warrant, but the army's officers were reluctant to commit regicide. It was Cromwell, however, who apparently seized the pen, scribbled his signature and cajoled the others to do likewise.

1649–53

He now became a member of the Council of State – the executive body that established a republican 'Commonwealth of England' – and one of its first actions was to abolish the House of Lords. Soon after, Cromwell had to deal with disaffected units within the army. Many soldiers had still not been paid and still demanded male universal suffrage. Cromwell would only release money for payment, however, and had to brutally suppress a couple of mutinies. The Leveller movement was thereby crushed although, since 1975, Levellers' Day is still commemorated in Burford where three of the ringleaders were executed.

Massacre at Drogheda. (*Author: M. O'Reilly from Lives of Irish Martyrs and Confessors, 1880. Duquesne University*)

Most of **Ireland** had been a **Catholic**, self-governing state since 1642 and Cromwell was sent to bring the island to heel and prevent it from being used as a royalist base. In August 1649, the New Model Army landed at Dublin and went on to seize the ports of Drogheda and Wexford. Cromwell held a known hatred of Catholics and referred to the Irish as 'barbarous wretches' and, in both towns, terrible massacres ensued of both soldiers and civilians. He believed the slaughter would prevent future bloodshed and, indeed, most other towns did quickly surrender afterwards, and terms of surrender were adhered to, but many people today have still not forgiven him for his brutality. In May 1650, he was ordered back to London and Ireton was left to complete the conquest which was finally achieved in 1653.

Cromwell had been summoned to lead an army against the Scots who had proclaimed Charles's son as King **Charles II**. His pre-emptive invasion of **Scotland** almost ended in an ignominious retreat but, after the Scots made a tactical error, his decisiveness led to possibly his greatest victory, at Dunbar (September 1650). Before the battle, such was Cromwell's anxiety that he was seen chewing his lips causing blood to drip from his chin. Afterwards, he described it as 'a high act of the Lord's Providence to us [and] one of the most signal mercies God hath done for England and His people', In the following year, another Scottish force invaded England. Leaving General **Monck** behind to capture the remaining royalist strongholds, Cromwell pursued it southwards as far as Worcester. There, he skilfully coordinated a multipronged attack to crush the opposing forces and capture the city (September 1651) although Charles himself managed to elude capture.

The Rump Parliament, meanwhile, had been doing some good work in protecting England's commercial interests but its MPs appeared to be self-serving and reluctant to draw up a new constitution which would have led Parliament to dissolve itself. Cromwell wanted reform that would provide a permanent alternative to monarchy and by 1653 had lost all patience. On 20 April, he stood up and threw insults at various MPs before declaring, 'You have sat too long for any good you have been doing lately ... Depart, I say; and let us have done with you. In the name of God, go! ... you are no Parliament!' He then ordered soldiers to clear the chamber and lock the doors behind them. A month later, he agreed to an assembly of 'godly men' chosen by the council of army officers. They met at Whitehall but became known as the 'Barebones Parliament', named after one of its members – Praise-God Barebones. Constant bickering and lack of progress, however, led it to dissolve itself after a mere five months.

Cromwell dismisses the Rump Parliament. On the walls is written, 'This House is to let'. (*Artist: unknown, 1653. British Museum*)

1653–58

The rule by Parliament experiment had failed and so Cromwell accepted the position of Lord Protector to bring about more a stable and efficient government. His rule was constrained by the Council of State and a new British Parliament in which, for the first time, Scottish and Irish MPs sat. This was set out in England's only written constitution in history. However, with the support of a loyal standing army, it could be argued that his power surpassed that of previous monarchs, certainly that of Charles I in 1641. His head appeared on coins, he signed documents *Oliver P* (same style as *Charles R* for 'Rex'), was addressed 'Your Highness' and received an annual salary of £100,000 (equivalent of £15 million in 2025).

As part of his efforts to bring about a 'godly' nation of Independent worshippers he sought religious liberty for most Protestant groups. The **Anglican** Church had effectively been disestablished in 1645, and churches were encouraged to adopt Puritan practices but there were no fines for non-attendance, even for Catholics. He also encouraged the immigration of Jews (banned for the past 350 years) to boost commerce although some religious sects such as the Quakers were considered too radical and were banned. Cromwell opposed capital punishment for minor **crimes**, allowed civil marriages and wanted to reform the law. However, he often found himself thwarted by his parliaments which resented the influence of the army upon which his power rested and feared any radical reforms which they believed would destabilise **society**.

Most controversial, perhaps, was Cromwell's experiment with military rule. After a minor royalist uprising in March 1655, he decided to split England and Wales into eleven administrative areas, each ruled by a major-general and aided by security commissioners. It was also hoped that the local taxes that paid for each area's militia would reduce the huge government debt and that the new administrators would promote a 'reformation of manners' and assert Puritan morals. This led to some over-zealous commissioners attempting to ban 'pointless' entertainments like theatre, sport and inns. Working on Sundays was not allowed; even going for a walk on that day could result in a 50-pence fine (£20 in 2025). Women could find their faces being scrubbed if caught wearing makeup and feast days were replaced by monthly fast days. Most famous was the banning of Christmas festivities (an initiative of Parliament's, not Cromwell's). These measures were met with widespread passive resistance and created greater antipathy towards the government. It is probable that Cromwell thought the major-generals and commissioners had gone too far; he, himself, enjoyed music, hunting and playing bowls and allowed dancing at his daughter's wedding. So, after ten months, he ended the experiment (September 1656).

Regarding foreign policy, Cromwell soon finished the **First Anglo-Dutch War** in 1654 and focused on prolonging an ongoing war between France and Spain to prevent a coalition of the two most powerful Catholic nations. After much dithering, he finally decided to support France, the main reason being financial. The standing army and navy were a huge drain on government expenses but the capture of Spanish treasure ships and islands in the West Indies could prove extremely lucrative. It was also hoped that a larger island than Barbados (taken in 1625) would be a better dumping ground for Scottish royalists and so reduce the need to maintain troops in Scotland.

An expedition to Hispaniola was repulsed but then captured Jamaica after a six-day campaign (May 1655). Closer to home, Admiral **Blake** harassed Spanish shipping and won a major victory in the Canaries (April 1657), and an Anglo-French army defeated a Spanish/Royalist force at the Battle of the Dunes (June 1658) for which France gave England the port of Dunkirk. Cromwell also sent Blake into the Mediterranean to enforce protection of British commercial interests and made trade treaties with Sweden and Portugal. The overall effect was to end England's isolation after Charles I's execution and give it its highest diplomatic standing of the seventeenth century. Many historians point to these events as being the start of England's path towards becoming a global power built on commercial foundations.

To find a stable solution to the governance of the country, Parliament offered Cromwell the crown in the spring of 1657. He agonised for weeks over what to do but finally declined, stating, 'I would not seek to set up that which Providence hath destroyed and laid in the dust, and I would not build Jericho again.' However, anyone watching the ceremony in which he was reinstalled as Lord Protector could be forgiven for thinking he was a king. Although he had no crown, he still wore a purple ermine-lined robe and bore a sword of justice and a sceptre. He was also allowed to nominate his successor and create peers for the restored House of Lords, now known as the Other House.

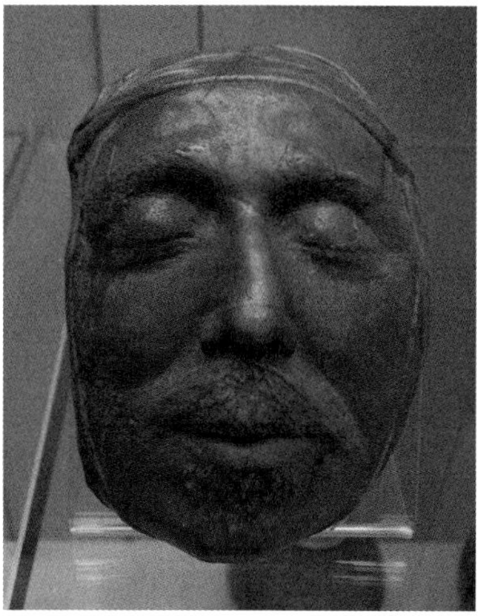

Oliver Cromwell's death mask. Made from the original wax impression from his face soon after his death. Later to be used as a model for his funeral effigy. (*Artist: from T. Simon's wax mould, 1658. British Museum*)

In the following year, he contracted a kidney disease which was complicated by a serious bout of malaria (originally contracted in the Fens). For the latter, he refused quinine as it had been discovered by Catholic missionaries and he rapidly went downhill after hearing of the death of his favourite daughter, Elizabeth. On 3 September 1658 – the anniversaries of Dunbar and Worcester – he died during a great storm at Whitehall Palace. He had nominated his son, Richard, to be his successor but he possibly knew that the English Republic would die with him for he had become its essential pillar. Sure enough, eight months later, Richard ('Tumbledown Dick') abdicated as he lacked authority in both parliament and the Army and the Stuart monarchy was restored in 1660. Soon afterwards, Cromwell's body was disinterred from Westminster Abbey, decapitated, hanged in chains at Tyburn then thrown into a pit. His head, along with those of Ireton and Bradshaw, was put on a spike and placed on the roof of Westminster Hall (the site of Charles I's trial). There it stayed for around thirty years until the wind blew it down and a guard took it home. It then became a grisly collectors' item until finally being buried under the chapel of Sidney Sussex College, Cambridge, in 1960. Some doubt its authenticity, though, and claim that his body was secretly reburied before 1660 to protect it from vengeful royalists.

Oliver Cromwell is one of the most contentious figures in British history and is impossible to pigeon-hole. For many years after his death, he was vilified as a moralistic, hypocritical failure and then swept under the carpet. His rehabilitation only began under the Victorians who started to see him as a man of pious sincerity who only wanted the best for his country. They even erected the famous statue of him, holding a sword and Bible, outside Parliament. Today, except in Ireland, he is generally seen in a positive light. In 1999, he came third in Radio Four's search for the greatest Briton, and, in 2002, he was in the top ten in a similar poll for BBC TV. Cromwell was, in many respects, ahead of his time but he could not balance his desire for a godly revolution with the majority's fear of social upheaval; a problem accentuated by the public's mistrust of the army which was his main pillar of support. He ultimately succeeded in destroying absolutist monarchy but failed to create a permanent republican solution. He granted religious liberty but crushed grassroots democracy. He brought peace and prestige to his country but brutally repressed his opponents. A brilliantly organised and decisive general but was often wracked by self-doubt. Driven but sanctimonious. A man of many contradictions but of great importance.

D

Dampier, William

(1651–1715)

Explorer, pirate, naturalist and writer

Dampier was the son of a tenant farmer in Somerset. By the age of 16, both of his parents had died, and he went on merchant voyages to Newfoundland and Java. He then joined the Royal Navy and took part in the **Third Anglo-Dutch War** in the 1670s. Illness, however, forced him into a long period of recuperation during which time he helped to manage a sugar plantation in Jamaica. After falling out with his employer, he entered the lucrative logging business on the coast of Mexico and it was during this time that he started to record native fauna and natural phenomena. His detailed account of some violent weather in 1676, for instance, is the first accurate description of a hurricane.

In 1679, Dampier got married in England but, soon after, he set sail again and was gone for twelve years. He fell in with a group of pirates (known as buccaneers in the Caribbean) that spent much time plundering Spanish ships and settlements around the Caribbean and on the west coast of South America. The English government merely turned a blind eye, seeing the buccaneers as a cheap way of keeping the Spanish away from its island possessions in the Caribbean. Dampier rested in **Virginia** for a while, where he may have married again, before being hired by another pirate gang as a navigator. Further raiding missions took him to the East Indies and Vietnam and, in 1688, he landed for a while in New Holland (Australia) which had been discovered by Abel Tasman in 1644. Everywhere Dampier went, he wrote detailed observations of the local fauna, flora and local

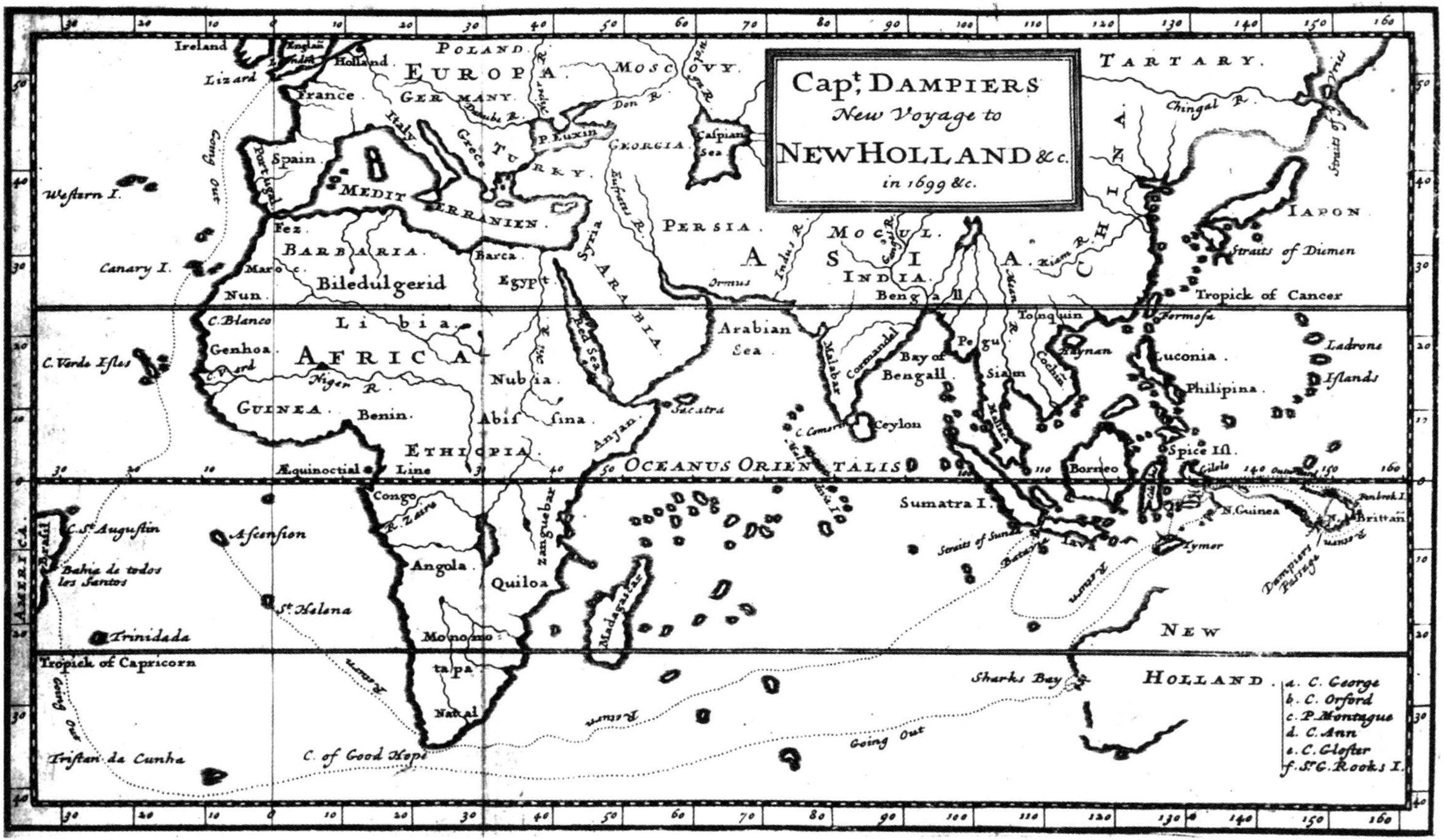

Map of Dampier's 1699–1701 voyage. Dampier used the Lizard as his 0° longitude. Longitude was not accurately calculated until the 1760s. (*Author: W. Dampier, 1703. Princeton University*)

inhabitants and took a great dislike to the aborigines, calling them, 'the miserablest people in the world ... they differ but little from brutes'. He also charted coastlines and noted ocean currents and prevailing winds.

In India, Dampier bought a heavily tattooed man from Sulawesi, named Jeoly, befriended him and took him back to London in 1691, having completed his first circumnavigation of the world. Then he disappears for the next six years although we do know that he sold Jeoly to the Blue Boar Inn on Fleet Street where he was exhibited as a foreign 'prince' before dying of smallpox a few months later. In 1697, Dampier re-emerges as the author of *A New Voyage Round the World*, which was based on his journals. It became a bestseller, and his celebrity status made him a popular dinner guest with people such as **Samuel Pepys**. All the while, he denied any acts of piracy, stating that he was merely an observer and that his only interest was making new discoveries – a claim that does not stand up to scrutiny. The admiralty also became interested in him and decided to employ his skills in the English navy.

In 1699, Dampier was given command of the twenty-six-gun HMS *Roebuck* with a mission, the first of its kind, to explore the east coast of New Holland. En route, he made detailed notes of the flora and fauna on the north-west coast of Australia, including the discovery of a dugong inside the stomach of a shark caught in Shark's Bay. After mapping the northern coast of New Guinea, he decided that the hull was too worm-eaten to go any further and so returned home westward. The *Roebuck* had to be abandoned on Ascension Island – where it was rediscovered in 2001 – and the crew were eventually picked up after five weeks and returned to England in 1701. Upon Dampier's return, he was court-martialled for cruelty to one of his officers during the outward voyage and, after being found guilty, he was docked his pay and dismissed from the navy.

Nevertheless, the War of the Spanish Succession had just broken out, and the government encouraged privateers to maul Spanish and French shipping around the Americas. Dampier commanded two ships and rounded Cape Horn, but he quarrelled with his officers and met with little success, often finding himself outgunned by the enemy. During this voyage, one Alexander Selkirk complained about the seaworthiness of his vessel and marooned himself on an island off Chile. Sure enough, the ship sank soon after and the surviving crew became prisoners of the Spanish. With no possibility of success, Dampier finally managed to return home, westwards, in 1707.

On his final voyage (1708–11), serving as pilot this time, he was far more successful. Sailing northward, after rounding Cape Horn, Dampier remembered Selkirk and was amazed to see him alive and well after a five-year solitary existence. Selkirk was put to work as second mate but became the inspiration for Daniel Defoe's *Robinson Crusoe* (1719). Off the coast of Mexico, a valuable Spanish galleon was plundered, its cargo of spices, porcelain, silver and jewels being worth the equivalent of £25 million. After crossing the Pacific, the ships returned home but disputes over how to share the treasure meant that Dampier died in debt four years later.

William Dampier – part explorer, part pirate, part scientist – was the most important English sailor of the seventeenth century and bridged the eras of Drake and Cook. He was the first person to circumnavigate the world three times and, although a poor leader, his discoveries of weather, currents, coasts and different species were of great importance to those who came after him such as James Cook and Joseph Banks. He introduced the term 'sub-species' and his books were kept on board *The Beagle* by Charles Darwin. His seven books started a new craze in travel writing and brought words such as 'barbecue', 'chopsticks' and 'avocado' into the English language as well as the recipes for guacamole and mango chutney.

Diet

The Stuart period saw some dramatic changes in the diet of the wealthiest although the fare of the poorer sections of **society** did not change radically from that of the previous century. The most common meal for labourers was pottage – a thick stew usually comprising of beans, onions, cabbage, carrots (usually the sweeter orange variety instead of purple, white or black) turnips and grains such as oats. If they were lucky, bacon or fish might be added. This would be accompanied by dark rye bread, cheese and weak beer, which was seen as being more nutritious than water (or even a substitute in areas where the water was not safe). Potatoes only gradually became part of the staple diet. Originally brought to Ireland by Basque fishermen, they were imported from there and became mostly grown in Lancashire and around London but usually used as animal feed.

Meat was generally scarce for the poor in the first decades of the seventeenth century and so poaching was common although this was a **crime** that carried a heavy punishment. In **Scotland**, salmon poaching was done on horseback – horses galloping along rivers would cause the terrified fish to leap ashore where they could be easily speared. As the population flatlined from the 1650s, however, labourers found some disposable income to buy meat more frequently. By the end of the century, around half of them were eating meat daily and the rest, once or twice a week.

The wealthiest in society had a much more varied diet and were less vulnerable to poor harvests as they could afford the associated price increases. What they ate, though, tended to be much less healthy. A predominance of rich, meaty, sugary food with little fibre led to many ailments such as haemorrhoids. Almost every meal included meat of which there was a great variety, ranging from venison, veal and capon (a castrated chicken, especially fattened) to pigeons, pheasants and larks. Turkey – from North America but mistakenly thought to be like the guineafowl

A family dining. (*Artist: unknown, from the Roxburghe Ballads, early seventeenth century via Wikimedia Commons*)

that was imported via Turkey – was also becoming increasingly popular. These meats were often served in pies and flavoured with expensive spices, such as mace and nutmeg, from the Far East. Pepper, by now, had become far more ubiquitous and too 'rustic' for the richest. As for the pies, the thick pastry crust, or 'coffin', was seen as a container, or plate, which would be thrown away after a meal. Bread was eaten, too, but usually made of the finer, white wheat flour.

A final course, known as a banquet, was usually held in a private room away from the servants and was devoted to sweetmeats and fruit. This was a great opportunity to show off the new food that was appearing due to the growth in world trade such as pineapples and bananas. Sugar, too, became increasingly available and came in dark loaves from the Caribbean. The resulting cakes, pastries, marzipan, sugared fruit and jumbals (biscuits resembling shortbread) became very popular as were 'English puddings', which were sweet ingredients squeezed into animal gut and then either boiled or steamed.

Wine, usually from France, Spain or Portugal was often spiced and sherry, port and brandy were also available for the wealthy. In the late seventeenth century, gin – invented in Holland – became popular and affordable for the poorer sections of society. At around the same time, bubbly champagne was 'invented' by the English after the fermentation process was accidentally disrupted in some imported bottles of non-bubbly champagne. Non-alcoholic drinks became available too. **Coffee**

houses sprang up from the 1650s, soon followed by chocolate houses where rich men would socialise and smoke tobacco in their clay pipes over a cup of hot cocoa. Tea, known as 'tay' or 'chaa', was made fashionable by Queen **Catherine of Braganza** in the 1660s. Initially very expensive, it gradually became more popular as the East India Company increased its imports from China.

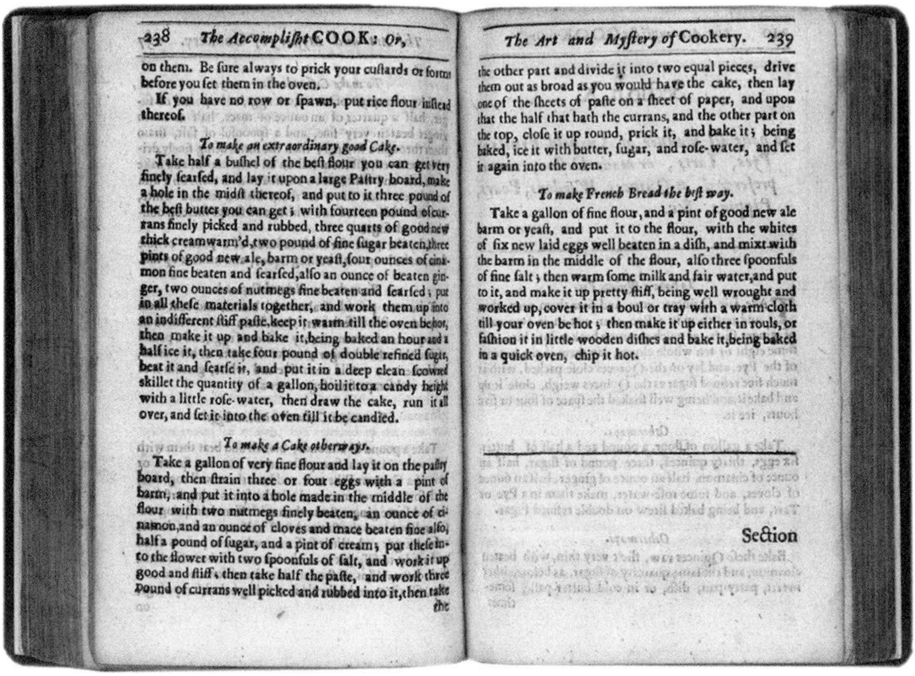

238 *The Accomplisht* COOK: *Or,*

on them. Be ſure always to prick your cuſtards or forms before you ſet them in the oven.

If you have no row or ſpawn, put rice flour inſtead thereof.

To make an extraordinary good Cake.

Take half a buſhel of the beſt flour you can get very finely ſearſed, and lay it upon a large Paſtry board, make a hole in the midſt thereof, and put to it three pound of the beſt butter you can get; with fourteen pound of currans finely picked and rubbed, three quarts of good new thick cream warm'd, two pound of fine ſugar beaten, three pints of good new ale, barm or yeaſt, four ounces of cinamon fine beaten and ſearſed, alſo an ounce of beaten ginger, two ounces of nutmegs fine beaten and ſearſed; put in all theſe materials together, and work them up into an indifferent ſtiff paſte, keep it warm till the oven be hot, then make it up and bake it, being baked an hour and a half ice it, then take four pound of double refined ſugar, beat it and ſearſe it, and put it in a deep clean ſcowred skillet the quantity of a gallon, boil it to a candy height with a little roſe-water, then draw the cake, run it all over, and ſet it into the oven till it be candied.

To make a Cake otherways.

Take a gallon of very fine flour and lay it on the paſtry board, then ſtrain three or four eggs with a pint of barm, and put it into a hole made in the middle of the flour with two nutmegs finely beaten, an ounce of cinamon, and an ounce of cloves and mace beaten fine alſo, half a pound of ſugar, and a pint of cream; put theſe into the flower with two ſpoonfuls of ſalt, and work it up good and ſtiff, then take half the paſte, and work three pound of currans well picked and rubbed into it, then take the

The Art and Myſtery of Cookery. 239

the other part and divide it into two equal pieces, drive them out as broad as you would have the cake, then lay one of the ſheets of paſte on a ſheet of paper, and upon that the half that hath the currans, and the other part on the top, cloſe it up round, prick it, and bake it; being baked, ice it with butter, ſugar, and roſe-water, and ſet it again into the oven.

To make French Bread the beſt way.

Take a gallon of fine flour, and a pint of good new ale barm or yeaſt, and put it to the flour, with the whites of ſix new laid eggs well beaten in a diſh, and mixt with the barm in the middle of the flour, alſo three ſpoonfuls of fine ſalt; then warm ſome milk and fair water, and put to it, and make it up pretty ſtiff, being well wrought and worked up, cover it in a boul or tray with a warm cloth till your oven be hot; then make it up either in rouls, or faſhion it in little wooden diſhes and bake it, being baked in a quick oven, chip it hot.

Section

The Accomplish't Cook showing recipes for cakes and French bread. (*Author: R. May, 1660. Wellcome Collection)*

The growing middle-class section of society increasingly emulated the eating habits of the wealthiest and this was facilitated by the advent of cookery books. Gervase Markham's *The English Hus-wife* (1615) included recipes but was more of a guide for housekeeping. Robert May's *The Accomplish't Cook or the Art and Mystery of Cookery* (1660), however, is considered the first English cookbook and, late in the Stuart period, the pastry chef, Edward Kidder, opened the first cookery schools for male students (women were expected to be educated at home). The middle classes also ate from plates and bowls made of pewter (a malleable tin alloy); only the very rich could afford silver crockery which could be melted down into money during times of emergency. On the other hand, nearly everybody only used knives and spoons. Fingers were preferred to forks which were considered foreign, dangerous and unhygienic.

Dryden, John

(1631–1700)

Poet, playwright, translator and satirist

Dryden was born into Northamptonshire landowning gentry. In 1644, he went, as a scholar, to Westminster School which was run by the charismatic disciplinarian, Richard Busby. A strong royalist, Busby locked the school doors to prevent his boys from witnessing the nearby execution of **Charles I** in 1649. Before he left, though, Dryden had received a good grounding in the arts of rhetoric and translation. He then studied classics, rhetoric and mathematics at Trinity College, Cambridge before graduating in 1654.

Despite a **Puritan** upbringing, Dryden became increasingly royalist and **Anglican** in his views. This, however, did not prevent him from accepting employment as a clerk during the republican Commonwealth and writing his first important poem – *Heroic Stanzas* – in praise of **Oliver Cromwell** in 1659. Following the Restoration, he performed a volte face by writing more gushing praise of **Charles II** in *Astraea Redux* in which he welcomed the king as a restorer of stability after years of chaos.

Now as a professional writer, Dryden produced a critical treatise, *Of Dramatick Poesie* (1666) – a discursive and witty piece of prose that debated different styles of drama. Further monarchist verses were followed up by *Annus Mirabilis* (1667), an epic poem that celebrated the naval victories of 1666 in the **Second Anglo-Dutch War** and the defiant spirit of citizens after the **Fire of London**. Uplifting and patriotic and written in 304 quatrains with an a-b-a-b rhyming pattern, it contrasted sharply with **Milton**'s *Paradise Lost* that came out in the same year. Undoubtedly, it led to him being appointed the first official Poet Laureate in 1668. The following two quatrains, written in iambic pentameter, reveal his skilful use of language and poignant treatment of the Fire's victims.

Those who have homes, when home they do repair
To a last lodging call their wand'ring friends.
Their short uneasie sleeps are broke with care,
To look how near their own destruction tends.
Those who have none sit round where once it was,
And with full eyes each wonted room require:
Haunting the yet warm ashes of the place,
As murder'd men walk where they did expire.

Dryden spent most of the 1660s and 1670s, however, as a playwright writing both tragedies and comedies. The tragicomedy, *The Royal Martyr* (1669), was loved by Charles II and starred his soon-to-be mistress, **Nell Gwyn**. His most successful, however, was *All for Love* (1678) which was written in blank verse (non-rhyming) and is considered the greatest tragedy in English after Shakespeare's work.

It is, however, his satirical verse that earned Dryden the most fame. From 1679, he took aim at many high establishment figures. *An Essay Upon Satire* (1679) attacked several courtiers, mistresses and even the king himself. Soon after, one of the aforementioned's hired thugs beat him up badly on his way home from Will's **Coffee House**. Undeterred, Dryden's influential *Absalom and Achitophel* (1681) flayed **Shaftesbury** and the **Whigs** in the aftermath of the **Popish Plot** and *Mac Flecknoe* (1682) made great fun of his literary rival, Thomas Shadwell.

Upon **James II**'s accession to the throne in 1685, Dryden declared himself a **Catholic**, an act that has led many to accuse him of blatant opportunism. His subsequent poems praised the new king and Catholicism but cost him his official positions after the **Glorious Revolution** three years later. Much to his chagrin, Shadwell replaced him as Poet Laureate, but Dryden turned to translations to maintain an income. Most famous of these was *The Works of Virgil* (1697) which included a translation of the *Aeneid* into rhyming couplets. As a result, many classical works now became available to English speakers.

Long afflicted by gout, Dryden died from gangrene in 1700 and was later put to rest in Westminster Abbey. A writer of tremendous versatility and output, he was the colossus of English literature in the last four decades of the seventeenth century; some literary historians have even referred to the Restoration period as 'The Age of Dryden'. He established the heroic couplet (rhyming iambic pentameter much used in long, epic poems) as the main form of English poetry and was an influence on the later greats – Pope, Scott, Byron and Keats. The writer, Samuel Johnson, later stated that 'he refined the language, improved the sentiments, and tuned the numbers of English poetry'.

John Dryden. (*Artist: J. Richardson, 1730s. Folger Shakespeare Library*)

E

Education

The Stuart education system, like those before it, was one that very much favoured the wealthy male section of **society**. Sons of the gentry usually started their education at home while the middle classes would send their five-year-old sons to the local 'petty school' – usually the home of an educated part-time teacher – where the rudiments of reading, writing and the Christian faith were taught. Phrases such as 'I will renounce the Devil' would be learned alongside behaviour skills and table manners. Aged seven, boys could then move up to grammar schools. Many of these had been set up in the previous century with endowments from wealthy trade guilds or local gentry. Then, after about seven years, boys could go to one of the colleges at Cambridge and Oxford universities. Many would just stay for a year before attending one of the Inns of Court in London to gain some legal training while others would seek a 'wider education' by embarking on a Grand Tour of Europe.

Some historians regard the early Stuart period as a golden age for education with 142 new grammar schools established in the first half of the seventeenth century. Literacy rates rose to around 30 per cent of men by 1650 (if the number of signatures on documents instead of crosses can be relied upon), schoolteachers became better qualified and entries to universities peaked at 1,200 a year in the 1630s. These increases can be attributed to the growing number of middle-class families and parents' desires for their children to be equally successful in business. At the same time, the growth of printing presses greatly increased the number of available books which reduced their price and made them accessible to more people.

Within the grammar schools, little had changed since mid-Tudor times. The long school day ran from 6 a.m. to 5 p.m. (7 a.m. to 4 p.m. in the winter) with a two-hour lunch break; lessons focused on Latin grammar and the study of religious texts and learning was done by rote. Corporal punishment was common for a plethora of offences including being caught speaking English! There were some attempts to broaden the curriculum with subjects such as arithmetic, but these relied upon travelling specialists known as scriveners. Entry was still theoretically free but costs often exceeded the original endowments and so fees were often charged. Even the free schools, however, failed to attract many boys from the poorer sections of society. In most of the country's households, children were seen as an economic asset. Why bother learning Latin when a child could be learning a trade as an apprentice? After buying an apprenticeship, parents would send their son or daughter to live with a master for seven years. Afterwards, they could start earning money as journeymen with the aim of becoming a master (or mistress) themselves. A few grammar school endowments were aimed at helping the poor though. In 1624, for example, Sir William Borlase set up a free school in Marlow to teach reading, writing and arithmetic to twenty-four local poor boys.

Girls, too, lacked an education although not from choice. Predominantly, the accepted view within the wealthier families was that girls should be taught how to run a household and be obedient to make them more marriageable. Even the liberal-minded Czech philosopher, John Comenius (widely regarded as the father of modern education), wrote in 1657 that female education should aim to increase a woman's contentedness and ability to serve her family rather than encourage her 'tendency to curiosity'. However, a few boarding schools for girls did open and merchants among the growing middle class sought more private tutors to provide an education that would allow their daughters to inherit or help run a business.

A golden opportunity to improve the education system arose in the aftermath of the **Civil Wars**. A common belief held by the various sects that sprang up during and after the conflict was millenarianism – the idea that the second coming of Christ was imminent and that it was necessary to prepare by creating the perfect society. There was much debating of the ideas of philosophers such as

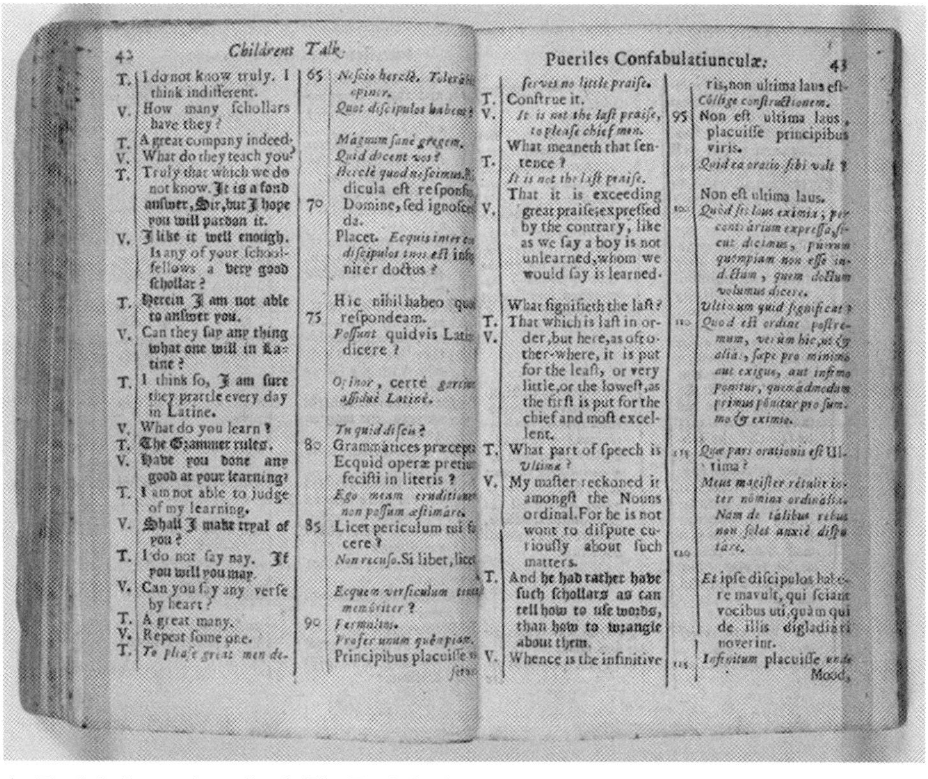

42 *Childrens Talk.*

T. I do not know truly. I think indifferent.
V. How many ſchollars have they?
T. A great company indeed.
V. What do they teach you?
T. Truly that which we do not know. It is a fond anſwer, Sir, but I hope you will pardon it.
V. I like it well enough. Is any of your ſchool-fellows a very good ſchollar?
T. Herein I am not able to anſwer you.
V. Can they ſay any thing what one will in Latine?
T. I think ſo, I am ſure they prattle every day in Latine.
V. What do you learn?
T. The Grammer rules.
V. Have you done any good at your learning?
T. I am not able to judge of my learning.
V. Shall I make tryal of you?
T. I do not ſay nay. If you will you may.
V. Can you ſay any verſe by heart?
T. A great many.
V. Repeat ſome one.
T. *To pleaſe great men de-*

65 *Neſcio herclè. Tolerabi[liter] opinor.*
Quot diſcipulos habent?
Mágnum ſanè gregem.
Quid docent vos?
Herclè quod neſcimus. Ridicula eſt reſponſio,
70 Domine, ſed ignoſcenda.
Placet. *Ecquis inter eos diſcipulos tuos eſt insigniter doctus?*
Hic nihil habeo quod
75 reſpondeam.
Poſſunt quidvis Latinè dicere?
Opinor, certè *garriunt aſſiduè Latinè.*
Tu quid diſcis?
80 Grammátices præcepta.
Ecquid operæ pretium feciſti in literis?
Ego meam eruditionem non poſſum æſtimáre.
85 Licet periculum tui facere?
Non recuſo. Si libet, licet.
Ecquem verſiculum tenes memóriter?
90 *Permultos.*
Profer unum quémpiam.
Principibus placuiſſe viris...

Pueriles Confabulatiunculæ: 43

ſerves no little praiſe.
T. Conſtrue it.
V. *It is not the laſt praiſe, to pleaſe chief men.*
What meaneth that ſentence?
T. *It is not the laſt praiſe.*
That it is exceeding
V. great praiſe; expreſſed by the contrary, like as we ſay a boy is not unlearned, whom we would ſay is learned.
What ſignifieth the laſt?
T. That which is laſt in or-
V. der, but here, as oft o-ther-where, it is put for the leaſt, or very little, or the loweſt, as the firſt is put for the chief and moſt excellent.
T. What part of ſpeech is *Ultima*?
V. My maſter reckoned it amongſt the Nouns ordinal. For he is not wont to diſpute curiouſly about ſuch matters.
T. And he had rather have ſuch ſchollars as can tell how to uſe words, than how to wrangle about them.
V. Whence is the infinitive

ris, non ultima laus eſt.
Cóllige conſtructionem.
95 Non eſt ultima laus, placuiſſe principibus viris.
Quid ea oratio ſibi vult?
Non eſt ultima laus.
100 *Quòd ſit laus eximia; per contrárium expreſſa, ſicut dicimus, púerum quempiam non eſſe indoctum, quem doctum volumus dicere.*
Ultimum quid ſignificat?
110 *Quod eſt ordine poſtremum, verùm hic, ut & aliàs, ſæpe pro minimo aut exiguo, aut infimo ponitur, quemádmodum primus pónitur pro ſummo & eximio.*
115 *Quæ pars orationis eſt* Ultima?
Meus magiſter rétulit inter nómina ordinália. Nam de tálibus rebus non ſolet anxiè diſputáre.
120
Et ipſe diſcipulos habere mavult, qui ſciant vocibus uti, quàm qui de illis digladiari noverint.
125 *Infinitum* placuiſſe unde Mood,

An English–Latin phrase book. The English phrases give us a clue about how people spoke in seventeenth-century England. (*Author: C. Hoole, 1673. Beinecke Library*)

Comenius and Francis Bacon who called for a broader curriculum and an education based on reasoning and use of the senses. Compulsory, free education for all was demanded by the **Levellers** and the leader of the Diggers, Gerrard Winstanley, and they were supported by respected merchants in their calls for a more realistic education that addressed languages, arithmetic, science and more vocational skills. Universities were attacked for hindering reform, accentuating class divisions and being backward. At the same time, demands were made for better training of teachers and more use of praise instead of corporal punishment to get the best out of children. Unfortunately, **Oliver Cromwell** and the **parliament**s of the 1650s, while sympathetic, considered such ideas too radical and destabilising to society and so took little action.

After the **Restoration**, the push for educational reform was associated with republican **Puritan**s and therefore rejected. A great opportunity had been lost but, despite this, there were progressive developments after 1660. The **Clarendon** Code banned non-**Anglican**s from teaching, but this did not prevent reforming Puritans from setting up dissenting academies that challenged Oxford and Cambridge by providing a modern curriculum and allowing greater freedom of discussion and tuition in the vernacular. It can be argued that these dissenting academies were the forerunners of modern-day higher education in Britain and, although were constantly threatened by government legal action, they proliferated after the 1689 Toleration Act. Grammar schools continued but several struggled to survive on their original endowments and had to adapt to the growing demands for the teaching of English and French now that Latin was no longer considered obligatory for many professions. They also faced competition from a multitude of private, unendowed schools, especially in London, that provided the more modern curricula favoured by the business classes. Fees tended to range from £20 to £30 per year (equivalent of a year's wages for a skilled labourer). More girls' boarding schools were opened outside London, too, and the first coeducational schools appeared in the 1680s.

School classroom. Note the quills, inkpots and the master's long disciplinary stick. (*Artist: unknown, from the Roxburghe Ballads, early seventeenth century via Wikimedia Commons*)

At the other end of the social scale, greater urbanisation and the decline of traditional apprenticeships towards the end of the seventeenth century meant greater poverty so several local committees set up charity schools for poor children funded by subscription. Basic literacy and numeracy were taught but the main aim appeared to be the indoctrination of Anglican Christianity. Also, in the 1690s, many workhouses were established for the increasing number of pauper children. The idea behind these was to provide children with manual skills and a basic education and reduce the rates people had to pay for local poor relief. Conditions varied wildly though, and many children suffered from being poorly housed, clothed and fed.

Eliot, Sir John

(1592–1632)

Politician and member of **Parliament**

Eliot was born into landed gentry in south-east Cornwall and attended Exeter College, Oxford in 1607. After just one year, he acquired some legal training at London's Inns of Court and then, as was customary for the wealthy, completed his **education** by travelling around Europe for several months. In 1609, after his father's death, he became financially independent by way of his inheritance and through his **marriage** to the Cornish heiress, Radigund Gedy.

It seems likely that he met **George Villiers**, later the Duke of Buckingham, while on the continent and their subsequent relationship proved to be very lucrative for Eliot. He became a member of Parliament in 1614, was knighted four years later and then Buckingham, now a court favourite, made him Vice-Admiral of Devon in 1622. He carried out his new duties vigorously and managed to capture the infamous pirate, John Nutt. However, Nutt had friends in high places, and it was Eliot who was thrown into prison for refusing to return the pirate's ship. After four months, Buckingham managed to procure his release (December 1623).

It was in the Parliament of 1624 that Eliot first drew attention to himself. Showing fine oratory skills, he called on **James I** to confirm parliamentary liberties and attacked the use of monopolies and 'tonnage and poundage' (import duties) as a way of raising money. At the same time, quite naively perhaps given the Crown's need for money, he gave full support to war with Spain probably to curry further favour with Buckingham who was arguing for this. The same motive was probably behind his stinging verbal attacks on Buckingham's enemies too. However, Eliot himself faced accusations of financial irregularities in his role of Vice-Admiral and was never quite able to disprove them.

War with Spain did break out in the following year but the disastrous attack on Cadiz created a fundamental shift in Eliot's thinking. In Plymouth, he heard first-hand about how the fiasco had unfolded, witnessed the shocking state of the surviving soldiers and realised that Buckingham's poor organisational abilities were to blame. In the Parliament of 1626, he attacked his former patron, stating, 'Our honour is ruined, our ships are sunk, our men perished, not by the sword, not by an enemy, not by chance, but … by those we trust,' and then leading calls for his impeachment. The new king, **Charles I**, protected his favourite by dissolving Parliament and briefly imprisoning Eliot in the Tower of London.

With insufficient money for the war, Charles introduced forced loans on his wealthier subjects. As these lacked parliamentary approval and were never likely to be repaid, Eliot refused to pay claiming, 'Upon this dispute not alone our lands and goods are engaged, but all that we call ours. These rights, these privileges, which made our fathers freemen, are in question.' Along with seventy-four other refuseniks, he was imprisoned again in 1627. After his release he attended his fifth Parliament in March 1628, this time representing the whole of Cornwall. Bristling with energy now, Eliot led further attacks on Buckingham following his disastrous attack on La Rochelle and denounced 'illegal' taxes, arbitrary imprisonments and the forced billeting of soldiers upon people's homes (introduced by the government to reduce expenses). Refusing to agree to subsidies until Charles had accepted their grievances, Parliament forced the king to accept the Petition of Right – a bill, drafted by **Sir Edward Coke** – that set out the above complaints.

Afterwards, Eliot focused his attacks upon Charles's ministers, the continued collection of import duties and the king's encouragement of Arminianism – a High Church form of **Anglican**ism – that many feared would presage the return of **Catholic**ism. With Charles about to dissolve Parliament in February 1629, Eliot and eight others staged a dramatic protest. With the Speaker pinned down in his chair and unable to adjourn the session, Eliot read out his protest against Charles's taxation and religious polices. An infuriated king immediately ordered their imprisonment. The others were eventually released after admitting their guilt and paying a fine, but Eliot refused and claimed parliamentary privilege. A vindictive Charles ensured an uncomfortable incarceration in the Tower where he wrote a few articles on politics and ethics before eventually dying from tuberculosis in 1632. Eliot's son asked for his body to be brought back to Cornwall, but Charles refused.

There had been nothing particularly commendable or extraordinary about the first half of Eliot's career but, in the eyes of many, he more than redeemed himself after 1625. A courageous, principled and eloquent speaker, he became a martyr for the parliamentary cause and only in 1667 were the official charges against him repealed.

Elizabeth Stuart

(1596–1662)

The 'Winter Queen' and Electress of the Palatinate

The only daughter of James VI of Scotland (**James I** of England) and **Anne of Denmark** to survive infancy, Elizabeth was born in Dunfermline Palace and named after her godmother, Queen Elizabeth I of England. In 1603, her father inherited the English throne and, after travelling south with him, was put into the care of Lord and Lady Harrington at Coombe Abbey near Coventry. While there, she developed a great love of nature as shown by the 'fairy farm' she kept in the park which comprised of an aviary, small menagerie and little buildings for stuffed animals. Her **education** was a relatively broad one, including natural history, geography, languages, music, dancing and horse riding but James banned any instruction in Latin as he believed it 'had the unfortunate effect of making women more cunning'.

The hand in **marriage** of the English king's daughter was much sought after on the continent with suitors including Gustavus Adolphus of Sweden and Philip III of Spain. James preferred a Protestant husband for Elizabeth and a **Catholic** wife for his oldest son, Prince Henry. With familial ties to both rival blocs, he hoped to be able to mediate peace between them. Subsequently, he eventually chose for his daughter Frederick V, the Elector Palatine – an important Protestant prince in Germany. Despite her mother's disapproval (he was not a king), the couple got on very well with each other after his arrival in England in October 1612. The following month, Elizabeth was heart-broken when Henry died from typhoid. The two had had a very close bond and her name was the last word he uttered on his deathbed. Despite this, the marriage went ahead in February 1613 amid extravagantly lavish celebrations. These were repeated when the couple later arrived in Heidelberg where the charismatic Electress proved to be very popular with her new subjects.

Elizabeth Stuart. (*Artist: after M. van Mierevelt, 1623. Rijksmuseum*)

Despite a rather frosty relationship with her mother-in-law, Elizabeth led a happy life until Frederick's fateful decision to accept the crown of Bohemia in 1619. This was a dangerous snub to the Catholic Holy Roman Emperor, whose son had been deposed by the Bohemian nobles, and sparked off the cataclysmic Thirty

Years' War. Elizabeth had supported Frederick's decision, but imperial armies soon ejected them from Bohemia and forced them to flee to the Dutch Republic as the Palatinate, too, had been conquered. Her reign as Queen of Bohemia was so short-lived she became known as 'The Winter Queen'.

The next forty years of Elizabeth's life were spent in The Hague where she campaigned tirelessly for the complete restoration of her husband's German lands and became a powerbroker for the Protestant cause. She was grief-stricken after Frederick's death from the **plague** in 1632; their relationship had been a loving one and had produced thirteen children for whom she worked hard to secure advantageous marriages. Becoming increasingly autocratic and voluble, she often fell out with them though. After her eldest son accidentally drowned, his brother angered her by accepting the Emperor's offer of half the Palatine lands and three of her children became Catholics. Her younger brother, **Charles I**, invited her back to England but she refused, regarding such a move as defeatist. Her sons, **Rupert** and Maurice, however, went off to fight for him during the **Civil Wars** and continued to do so after Charles's execution in 1649.

After the Restoration in 1660, Elizabeth finally returned to England but, soon after, she died after catching pneumonia and was buried next to her beloved elder brother in Westminster Abbey. Before her death, the knowledge that one of her grandchildren would later become King George I of Great Britain may have been of some comfort to her.

F

Fairfax, Sir Thomas

(1612–71)

General and politician

Fairfax was born into a wealthy, landowning, **Anglican** family in north Yorkshire, his father being Lord Fairfax of Cameron (a Scottish peer). He studied at St John's College, Cambridge before attending the Inns of Court in London. Afterwards, he gained military experience with an Anglo-Dutch army fighting imperialist forces in the Netherlands during the Thirty Years' War. In 1639–40, he led a troop of dragoons during the Bishops' War against **Scotland** and, although he was forced to retreat along with the rest of the English army, he was rewarded with a knighthood by **Charles I** for his efforts.

Fairfax reluctantly joined the parliamentary side when the **Civil Wars** broke out in 1642 but always maintained his belief in the monarchy albeit supported by a strong **Parliament**. Fighting under his father's command in Yorkshire, he met with some success but was badly defeated at Adwalton Moor (June 1643) and forced to retreat to Hull. Despite this, 'Black Tom' – so called due to his dark complexion – gained a reputation for his reckless courage and decisiveness. Always in the thick of fighting, Fairfax received several wounds during the wars, the most life-threatening being a musket shot to his shoulder at the siege of Helmsley Castle. This occurred after the Battle of Marston Moor (July 1644) in which he commanded parliamentary cavalry on the right wing. Despite suffering a reverse, he continued to fight and contribute to the royalist defeat. In the following year, the **New Model Army** was formed and Fairfax, due to his military reputation, integrity and political moderation, was made its Lord General. Another rising star, **Oliver Cromwell**, was made his lieutenant-general and cavalry commander. Together, they crushed the royalist army at **Naseby** (June 1645) before Fairfax defeated the remaining royalist forces in the south-west.

After Charles finally surrendered, Fairfax had the unenviable task of trying to position himself among the different competing groups during the prolonged negotiations with the king. In war, the heat of battle and clarity of who the enemy was were more preferable to the political machinations of 1647–48. Fairfax soon found himself out of his depth and senior officers began to gravitate towards the more radical and politically adept Cromwell as their leader. He campaigned for the payment of arrears of his soldiers' wages though and brutally repressed royalist revolts in Maidstone and Colchester during the Second Civil War. He also appears to have approved of Pride's Purge of Parliament although he generally disapproved of the army's involvement in politics. It was only very late in the day that he comprehended the army leadership's determination to execute the king. This, Fairfax could never accept, and he personally appealed for clemency. He was named as one of the commissioners at Charles's trial but refused to attend. After his name was called out as one of the judges, his wife, Lady Fairfax, apparently cried out, 'He has more wit than to be here!'

Thomas Fairfax. Note the blocks of pikemen interspersed with those of well-drilled cavalry in the distance. (*Artist: after E. Bower, mid-seventeenth century. Printed 1808. Emmet Collection of Manuscripts*)

Always conservative by nature, Fairfax took part in suppressing the **Leveller** mutiny within the army (May 1649) but, in the following year, resigned after refusing to lead an invasion of Scotland. Such an action would have also cost him his Scottish peerage which he had since inherited.

Thereafter, he retired to Yorkshire where he looked after his estate, wrote poetry and collected books. He was elected to Parliament in 1654 but after Cromwell's death he feared the country's descent into anarchy. Subsequently, he assisted General **Monck**'s march on London in 1659 and the creation of a parliament that restored the Stuart monarchy. Fairfax, himself, headed the delegation to The Hague to formally offer Prince Charles the throne. His support and political inactivity during the Commonwealth meant that he escaped the fate of the regicides although he was deeply angered by the treatment of Cromwell's corpse. After 1660, he retired again, spending much of his remaining life in a wheelchair due to his numerous war wounds. A widely respected and popular general, Thomas Fairfax's reputation avoided political blemishes and, ironically, his most appropriate epithet was uttered by Charles I – 'The general is a man of honour and keeps his word'.

Fiennes, Celia

(1662–1741)

Traveller and writer

Fiennes was the daughter of Nathaniel Fiennes, a Parliamentarian colonel during the **Civil Wars**, and ancestor of the explorer, Ranulph Fiennes, and the actors, Ralph and Joseph Fiennes. She never married, preferring to maintain her financial independence, and lived in the family manor house in Wiltshire until her mother died in 1691 at which point she moved to London to be near relatives. Soon after, she developed an urge to travel around the country, partly to benefit her health and see relatives but mostly because she had an insatiable desire to discover how people lived.

In an age when domestic tourism was unheard of and long before the arrival of stagecoaches, Fiennes rode side-saddle with one or two servants and visited every county of England along with parts of Wales and **Scotland**. Being a woman (in a strongly patriarchal **society**) made this feat even more remarkable, and she wrote a memoir of her travels in 1702 although she continued to make journeys until 1712. This memoir was only intended for family viewing but was finally published in its entirety in 1888 – *Through England on a Side Saddle*. Fiennes wrote plainly, with little punctuation and odd spellings but, although patronising in places, her account is invaluable for economic and social historians of the late seventeenth century.

From the newly fashionable spa towns of Harrogate and Bath to the dockyards of Plymouth, from glass-spinning in Nottingham to the paper mills of Canterbury, from coal mining in Newcastle to salmon fishing in Lancaster, from great mansions to tumbledown cottages, Fiennes noted it all with avid interest. She liked to sample

Map of England and Wales showing distances between towns. Possibly used by Celia Fiennes. (*Published by J. Overton, 1695. Bibliothèque nationale de France*)

the local food and drink such as the clotted cream of Cornwall, the strong ale of Yorkshire (which she enjoyed!) and the oat clap bread of Kendall. Observing different architecture and crops, riding over the Cumbrian Fells, clambering over rocks at Land's End and even counting the stones at Stonehenge (91), she noted everything. Often giving her opinions, Fiennes was critical of the state of many inns and roads although she welcomed the first signposts – as required by a new act of Parliament – and only once, near Whitchurch, did she encounter highwaymen before escaping into the town.

This remarkable person, who created a window into the past, eventually died in Hackney aged 78. Few memorials commemorate her – a plaque in the church of

Newton Toney, the village where she was born, and a waymark near Whitchurch. Possibly, also, she inspired the nursery rhyme, *Ride a Cock-Horse to Banbury Cross, to see a fine lady upon a white horse*. Is there a play on the words 'fine' and Fiennes?

Fire of London

(1666)

A disaster that destroyed much of London

In the summer of 1666, London was a disaster waiting to happen and, by all accounts, most contemporaries realised this. The use of wood and thatch for construction had long been banned but these cheap materials were still used along with pitch for waterproofing. The overhanging upper stories, known as jetties, almost touched and would facilitate the spread of any fire. King **Charles II** had forbidden these in 1661 and, four years later, he had threatened with imprisonment those who built dangerous houses. The proudly independent city ignored such warnings, however. Moreover, although the River Thames provided water and a means of escape, it was lined with warehouses containing flammable materials such as tar, hemp and gunpowder. Furthermore, the city was surrounded by an old Roman wall with only eight gates. During the disaster, panicked citizens with carts full of goods clogged up these exits, as well as the narrow streets, thereby hindering the fire-fighting teams.

In the very early hours of Sunday, 2 September, a fire broke out in Thomas Farriner's bakery in Pudding Lane. He and his family escaped through an upper storey window, but their maid lost her nerve, refused to do so and became the first victim of the Fire. The London Mayor, Sir Thomas Bloodworth, was woken and informed of the spreading blaze. Fires were common occurrences, however, and he showed little concern. 'Pish! A woman might piss it out,' he muttered before returning to bed. Furthermore, he refused to create firebreaks by pulling down adjoining houses because most of them were rented and their owners could not be contacted to receive their permission.

Unfortunately, the imminent catastrophe was facilitated by bone-dry houses after the hot summer and a strong easterly breeze. Also, the creation of firebreaks was hampered by people's reluctance to leave their homes until the last minute; not surprising, perhaps, given the absence of any house insurance. Very quickly, the flames spread and, by later that morning, had engulfed three hundred houses. Amid the early damage was a building next to the river that housed the only pump for extinguishing fires. By Sunday afternoon, the conflagration had developed into a firestorm which sucked in air, giving the flames further impetus as they marched west and north and the intense heat drove away the primitive fire engines and

Map of London after the Fire. The white area was razed. The map was used to help rebuild the city. (*Artist: W. Hollar, 1667. Royal Collection Trust*)

human bucket chains. On Monday, the financial centre of the city, including the Royal Exchange, was destroyed and the fire threatened to cross London Bridge but a gap on the bridge from a previous fire saved Southwark.

Panic gripped the capital's inhabitants as rumours spread that the blaze had been started by foreign agents (the **Second Anglo-Dutch War** was happening) so several foreigners became victims of mob violence. At the same time, people fled west or attempted to cross the river but the sudden demand for carts and boats caused prices to rocket. The cost of hiring a cart, for instance, shot up from 2 shillings to £40 (several thousand pounds today). With Bloodworth seemingly absent, the king ordered his brother, **James Duke of York**, to take command.

His organised response, using soldiers and gunpowder to create larger firebreaks, had some effect but Tuesday was the worst day. The luxury shopping street of Cheapside was engulfed followed by St Paul's Cathedral as the flames shot up the wooden scaffolding and set fire to the roof. As the molten lead poured down the sides it resembled some ghastly volcano and even previously rescued goods, stored in the crypt, were destroyed. The Tower of London, itself, and its stocks of gunpowder were threatened, too, until its nearby houses were blown up. By Wednesday, the combination of the firebreaks and the wind dropping stopped the fire from spreading further.

Samuel Pepys vividly described the events in his diary and, straight after the catastrophe, he climbed a steeple and observed, 'the saddest sight of desolation that I ever saw.' Four-fifths of the city had been laid waste, including 13,000 private homes, eighty-nine churches, several markets and jails and a host of public buildings such as the Guildhall and the General Letter Office (centre of postal deliveries). The material cost amounted to £10 million (about £2 billion in 2025). Although only around half a dozen people were killed, more probably died from hunger and exposure in the following months and about 100,000 were made homeless. The wealthy went to stay with relatives while the poor suffered in makeshift homes in the fields outside the city.

Abroad, the disaster was seen as divine retribution, which only fuelled the belief that it had been a foreign plot. A French watchmaker called Robert Hubert soon confessed to being part of a gang that started the fire. Despite his dubious mental state and inconsistent evidence, the authorities provided the people with the scapegoat they wanted and convicted him. After the hanging, his body was seized by the crowd and torn apart. Only later, did a Swedish captain prove that Hubert was on his ship when the fire started.

Several new designs for the rebuilding of London were put forward by architects such as **Christopher Wren**. His, however, with its open plazas connected by straight, broad streets in a grid pattern – like Manhattan Island today – was considered too radical. Most people wanted their houses to be rebuilt on their previous sites, but Wren was allowed to redesign St Paul's Cathedral, fifty-one new churches and the Monument, a memorial which, when laid on its side reaches the site of Farriner's old bakery. Some streets were widened, houses were not allowed to block access to the Thames and, most importantly, brick and stone had to be used for construction. After London's reconstruction, which took fifty years, far fewer people lived within the city walls as the population density of the surrounding suburbs grew. Significant too was the establishment of the first insurance company – the Fire Office (1667) – which also hired firemen. In 1833, the different insurance companies combined their forces to create the London Fire Brigade.

Frith, Mary (Moll Cutpurse)

(1584/89–1659)

Notorious criminal, cross-dresser and subverter of social norms

Patchy and conflicting evidence means that some of the following may be exaggerated or even untrue, but the story of Mary Frith is so fascinating that it cannot be omitted.

The daughter of a cobbler in north London, Frith refused to be pigeon-holed into a girl's upbringing and much preferred boisterous play with the boys on the streets. Before long she had become a 'cutpurse' – equivalent of a pickpocket – and became known as Moll Cutpurse (a moll was a criminal girl and slang for Mary). After her parents died, her uncle, seeing no hope for her, tricked her into boarding a vessel bound for America in 1609 but she managed to jump ship and get back ashore. From then on, Frith made her own way in London's criminal underworld and soon gained quite a reputation.

Often seen singing bawdy songs, dancing and playing a lute in taverns, she shocked many people by permanently dressing as a man and smoking a pipe. Smoking had been condemned as a bad habit by King **James I**, especially for women, so Frith was making a rebellious statement as well as becoming the first known female smoker. Before long, her tall figure, armed with a sword and accompanied by mastiffs that she bred herself, became instantly recognisable as she strode through the streets of London. Such was her fame that two plays were written about her in 1610–11 – *The Madde Pranckes of Mery Mall of the Bankside* and *The Roaring Girl* (rowdy young men were known as 'roaring boys'). For the latter, Frith even appeared on stage herself (illegal for women) at the Fortune Theatre sharing obscene songs and banter with the audience.

At the same time, Frith showed her entrepreneurial side by moving away from theft to setting up her own fencing business in which she bought stolen goods and sold them on at a profit. This became so well known that victims would often come straight to her to buy back their own property, a process much quicker than going through the law courts. Even the authorities turned a blind eye – she was seen as a regulating influence who was partly solving crimes! According to her biography, *The Life and Death of Mrs. Mary Frith* (1662), she branched out into the prostitution business in the 1620s by providing men with young women and wealthy wives with young men.

Mary Frith. (*After unknown artist, printed late eighteenth/early nineteenth century. Wellcome Collection*)

Once, she was offered a £20 wager daring her not to ride through the middle of London dressed in men's clothes. Not only did she accept but, despite upsetting many in the crowds, she also flew a banner and blew a trumpet to announce her presence. It was actions such as these, not her criminal activities, that often led to incarceration at Newgate Prison. The Bishop of London once interrogated her and accused her of being a prostitute and a social deviant who wore men's clothes, swore, got drunk and hung out with thieves. Frith admitted to all but the first accusation and was subsequently forced to commit a public penance in St Paul's churchyard. There, she wept bitterly and begged for forgiveness, but it turned out to be a sham; she had, in fact, been completely inebriated on fortified wine.

Although Frith claimed to have no interest in sex, despite the assumption that she was promiscuous, she did marry Lewknor Markham in 1614. This was likely a **marriage** of convenience, however, as the elevated status of being a married woman gave her some protection from the law. Certainly, there is no record that the two ever lived together and her later years are shrouded in even more mystery. It is claimed that she was a royalist and, during the **Civil Wars**, she indulged in highway robbery and even shot the Parliamentarian general, **Thomas Fairfax**, in the arm before robbing him on Hounslow Heath. She then avoided being hanged by paying a £2,000 bribe. Another account states that she was released from Bedlam mental asylum in 1644 after being cured of madness. What is more certain is that she eventually finally died of oedema in Fleet Street, London in 1659. A criminal she may have been, but Mary Frith was undoubtedly a brave and spirited woman who demonstrated financial independence, happily broke all social barriers and stuck two fingers up at a misogynistic **society**.

G

The Gabbard, Battle of

(2–3 June 1653)

Decisive battle fought during the **First Anglo-Dutch War**

War had broken out in the previous year, and the Dutch had successfully gained effective control over their trade routes through the English Channel and North Sea. For them, the destruction of the enemy's fleet would allow their commercial ships to continue their trade unimpeded. For the English, the Dutch navy needed to be eliminated so that Holland could be blockaded and forced to accept the imposition of peace terms.

At noon on 1 June, English reconnaissance vessels spotted the Dutch navy near the Gabbard shoal off the coast of Suffolk but by the time battle was joined the following day, the two fleets were 12 miles off North Foreland in Kent. The Dutch, led by Maarten Tromp, were divided into five squadrons and had ninety-eight ships.

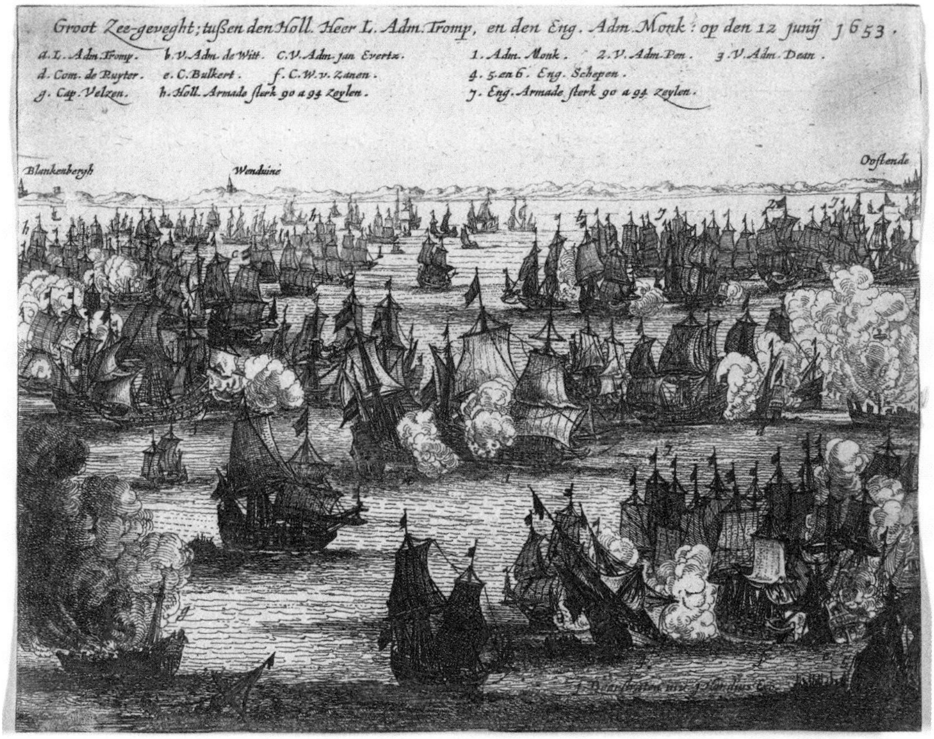

Battle of the Gabbard or Battle of Nieupoort. Dutch ships on the left and English on the right. The English line of battle is not obvious but the Dutch fire ships are. (*Artist: after J. Beerstraten, 1654–56. Rijksmuseum*)

The English had a similar number and were divided into three squadrons – Red, White and Blue. Their overall commanders were **George Monck** and Richard Deane, both on board *Resolution* in the main division (centre) of Red squadron.

At around 11 a.m. on 2 June, the two fleets came within range of each other – about 400 yards – and in the ensuing artillery duel, Deane was cut in two leaving Monck in sole charge. As the Dutch gained the weather gauge (upwind of the English), Tromp ordered a general attack. The favoured tactic of the Dutch at this time was melee fighting, the aim being to surround enemy ships and board them with their superior numbers of soldiers. They also employed more fireships to finish off any crippled vessels. The English, meanwhile, had just put into force new 'Fighting Instructions' which ordered enemy ships not to be boarded unless crippled and squadrons to fight in lines of battle, one ship behind the other. This allowed ships to maximise their firepower in deadly broadsides and prevented friendly ships obstructing each others' line of fire. Strict adherence to line of battle also prevented any captain from holding back or charging off into battle alone. A system of flag signalling was also introduced to help maintain order.

The English line came under pressure in a couple of places. At one point, William Penn's flagship, the *James*, was boarded but the attack was repulsed, and Tromp's own *Brederode* was then briefly taken until he ordered its upper deck to be blown up, and it escaped. Overall, though, the Dutch struggled to get close enough to employ their grappling irons due to the larger and more powerful English ships. The Dutch navy had largely been neglected since the end of the war of independence against Spain in 1648 and it had the added disadvantage of having to operate out of shallower waters. This meant that its warships either had to be smaller or carry fewer guns. By 1652, the English had at least eighteen ships that were larger than anything the Dutch possessed. Attempts to remedy this after the war could still only produce first-rate ships that matched English fourth rates.

As a result, the English could pack in three gun decks and heavier, 42-pound (the weight of the iron ball) cannon at the expense of a lower freeboard – distance between water line and main deck – and so had less speed and manoeuvrability. The Dutch ships only had two gun decks with, at most, 24-pounders. With a subsequent higher freeboard, they were much nimbler in the water, but their broadsides made less impact.

This contrast in tactics, ships and armaments inevitably led to a one-sided affair. At around 6 p.m., the Dutch withdrew but on the following morning, Tromp decided to attack again even though his fleet was running low on ammunition. Monck, on the other hand, had been reinforced by the late arrival of **Blake**'s squadron which persuaded Tromp to make a fighting retreat to the safety of the Dutch coast. Disastrously, however, the wind dropped and his ships became sitting ducks to the longer-range English artillery. Eventually, the remains of his battered fleet staggered into harbour.

The final toll made The Gabbard one of the worst defeats in Dutch naval history: nine ships sunk, eleven captured, 1,000 prisoners and 800 casualties (most deaths and injuries were caused by splinters and musket fire). In contrast, the English had won their greatest naval victory since the Armada, suffering 400 casualties with no ships lost. Now that they controlled the North Sea, they went on to blockade the Dutch coast to cripple their enemy's economy. The following month, out of desperation, Tromp led out another fleet. At the subsequent Battle of Scheveningen, this too was badly damaged, and Tromp was killed by a sharpshooter. Both defeats, allied with their freefalling economy, precipitated Dutch calls for peace and the end of the war in 1654.

Glorious Revolution

(1688–89)

A dramatic coup within the monarchy that led to major constitutional change

By 1688, King **James II** had alienated most sections of **society** in England and **Scotland**. His attempts to promote **Catholic**ism, pack **Parliament** with supporters and use arbitrary power backed up by a standing army even made his traditional **Tory** supporters uneasy. There was also a widespread fear that the persecution of Protestants in France would spread across the Channel despite only around 1 per cent of the English population being Catholic. This fear began to materialise in the form of anti-Catholic demonstrations and riots across the country and rumblings of discontent within the army and navy over the appointment of Catholic officers. When James stationed troops on Hounslow Heath, it was assumed that the motive was to intimidate London and Parliament. Matters came to a head on 10 June 1688 when the king's Catholic wife, Mary of Modena, gave birth to a boy. James's heirs had been the Protestant daughters from his previous marriage – **Mary** and **Anne**. Now, however, the country was faced with the prospect of an unlimited period of Catholic rule.

Within days, several politicians secretly gathered to avert a possible return to civil war. Seven of them, representing **Whigs**, Tories, the Church, the army and the navy, sent a formal letter to the Stadtholder of Holland – Prince **William of Orange** – asking him to invade and rescue them from an unpopular king. The letter also reassured William of the support he would find in England and, to increase the legitimacy of any regime-change, declared that the new baby boy did not belong to the queen. William himself was a nephew of James and was married to his eldest daughter, Mary, which provided more legitimacy although, at this stage, it was claimed that the intention was never to remove James from power but merely to force him to change his ways. Of greatest concern to William, at that time, was the balance of power within Europe. France was encroaching east into the Netherlands and Germany, and he desperately wanted England's commercial and naval power to aid the alliance that he had formed to resist this expansion. Despite James's assurances, he even feared an Anglo-French alliance which would have put the Dutch in a very difficult position.

William's chance came in September 1688 when the French launched their main assault into Germany and left him free to divert half of the Dutch army to England. At first, he was thwarted by earlier than expected south-westerly storms which kept his armada in port. By now, of course, the huge scale of the planned invasion had destroyed any secrecy. James, for his part, was confident that the notorious autumn storms along with the outbreak of war with France would prevent any Dutch invasion. He also had faith in his army and navy; this was misplaced, however. The former had low morale and resented its Catholic officers; the latter was outnumbered two to one and underresourced.

On 14 October, the 'popish wind' became the 'Protestant wind' by veering to the east and William's fleet set sail on 1 November. The largest armada ever seen in Europe consisted of over 450 ships carrying artillery and 20,000 soldiers (a quarter were British exiles and French Protestant volunteers) but everyone knew the great risks of attempted seaborne invasions. However, the same easterly that propelled William also trapped the English fleet in the Thames estuary, further storms did not materialise, and supporters had secured a landing spot near Torbay in Devon. After successfully landing on 5 November – an auspicious date for those celebrating the defeat of the **Gunpowder Plot** – William captured Exeter where he issued a proclamation supporting Parliament's rights and his wife's inheritance. Meanwhile, James gathered 19,000 men at Salisbury.

William's preference was for James's regime to inwardly collapse, thereby averting the need to shed English blood and appear as a foreign invader. Despite a couple

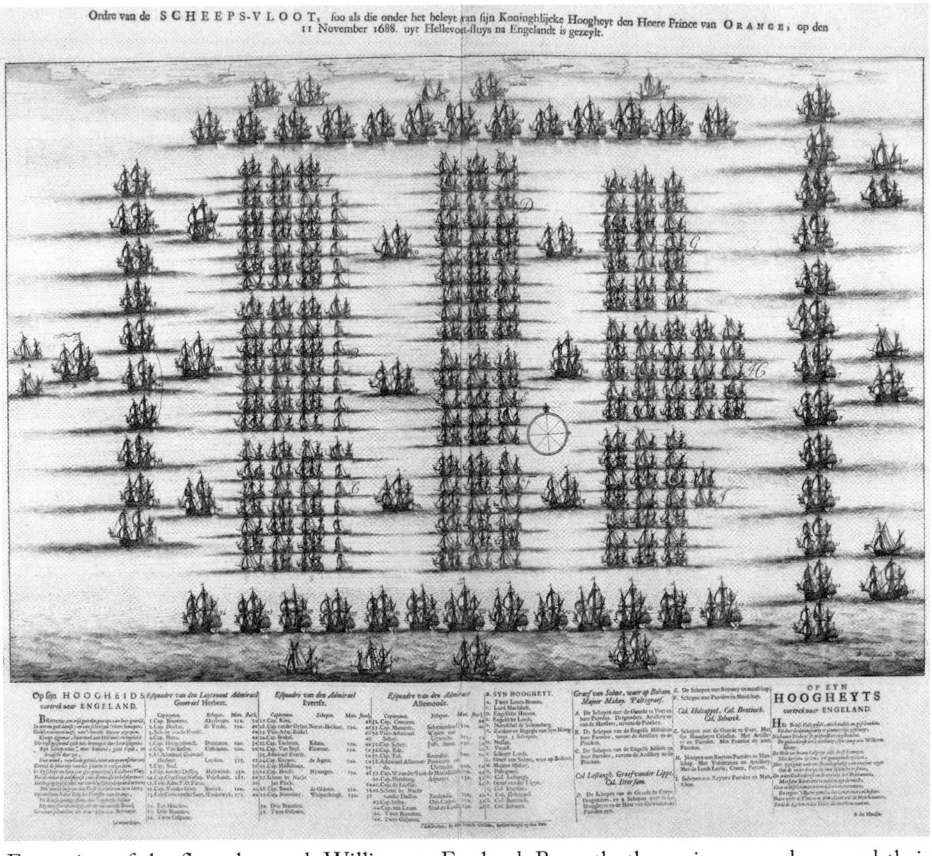

Formation of the fleet that took William to England. Beneath, the various squadrons and their captains are listed. (*Authors: L. Bake & A. du Moulijn, 1688. Rijksmuseum*)

of skirmishes, this is exactly what happened. Low morale in the English army was exacerbated by the defection of a few key officers such as **John Churchill** and news came in of Protestant rebels capturing York and Hull in the north. James, suffering from debilitating nose bleeds and lack of sleep, decided to make an ignominious retreat towards London. Even at this stage, though, it would have been possible for him to keep his throne as his Tory support base, while desiring reform, believed in allegiance to the divine monarchy. However, on 11 December, James left his supporters without a cause when he fled London for France and threw the Royal Seal (needed for conducting all royal business) into the Thames. Abandoning his country was considered an act of abdication and most Tories now sided with the Whigs in supporting William. James was captured by fishermen in Faversham and returned to London but William, not wanting him on his hands, allowed him to escape again, this time successfully.

After Mary refused to rule alone, a new Parliament finally offered the throne jointly to William and Mary in February 1689 once the new monarchs had been read the Declaration of Right – a document that listed Parliament's grievances against James II and thirteen clauses that limited royal power. This then became enacted into law by the famous **Bill of Rights** in December. At their coronation in April, William and Mary were also made to swear to 'govern the people of this kingdom of England ... according to the statutes in Parliament agreed on, and the laws and customs of the same'. The Glorious Revolution is of great significance; for one thing, it brought England (and later, Britain) into William's protracted war against France but also the divine right of kings had been replaced by a constitutional monarchy in which the power of the Crown was more clearly defined and limited. Just as remarkable is the fact that it came about so peacefully. Therefore, it is sometimes called the Bloodless Revolution although its consequences were far more violent in **Ireland** and Scotland.

Grand Remonstrance

(1641)

A list of Parliamentary grievances presented to the king

1641 was a year of continuous disputes and rising tension between King **Charles I** and **Parliament**. The Long Parliament had initially been summoned (November 1640) to raise money to pay off the victorious Scots after the Bishop Wars. However, after eleven years of personal, arbitrary rule by Charles, the majority of MPs now saw the opportunity to impose reforms that would limit royal power. As a result, acts were passed that demanded regular parliaments, abolished Crown courts such as the Star Chamber and declared non-parliamentary taxes illegal.

A bill was also introduced to remove bishops and bring about a Church along **Presbyterian** lines. Charles was even forced into allowing the execution of his ablest advisor, **Thomas Strafford**.

By agreeing to these, Charles was playing for time, waiting for his opponents to overreach themselves and lose their majority within the Commons. This may well have happened but, in late October, news of a **Catholic** revolt in **Ireland** and massacres of Protestant settlers created hysteria in England. The **Puritan** core of Charles's opposition in Parliament – a junto led by **John Pym** – took advantage and spread rumours of a Catholic plot which even involved the queen, **Henrietta Maria**. 1641 saw the first involvement of ordinary people in politics – there had already been public petitions, demonstrations, riots and vandalism of churches – and the junto, by aligning itself with the London mob, was dangerously raising the stakes.

Pym then poured oil over the fire by producing the Grand Remonstrance in mid-November. This was a long list – 204 points – of complaints about Charles's policies since the start of his reign. Carefully worded to avoid direct criticism of the king, it attacked his ministers and the bishops and demanded more parliamentary control over the military, finances and religious matters. The implied criticism of Charles and attacks on the royal prerogative caused such heated debates in the Commons that swords were drawn at one point. In the early hours of 23 November, it was finally passed by eleven votes and the radicals then demanded its publication and distribution. Moderates, such as **Edward Hyde**, considered 'King Pym' had gone too far and joined the royalist side; restricting royal power was one thing but inflaming further unrest by hanging out the king's dirty washing was another. However, when the king refused to accept it, the junto had it published anyway and the political crisis became public knowledge to all within the realm.

The Grand Remonstrance did not make the **Civil Wars** inevitable, but it did make a peaceful resolution much harder to attain. Its effect was to radicalise and polarise opinion in both Parliament and **society** while the moderates were squeezed out. Charles, feeling backed into a corner, now adopted a more offensive strategy which further raised the prospect of civil war.

Great Storm of 1703

One of the worst natural disasters in British recorded history

On the evening of 26 November 1703, the most brutal storm in living memory hit southern Britain. Weather forecasts were non-existent so there was little time to prepare or seek safety although an Essex barometer did record an extreme low of 973 millibars. Winds of 75 mph, gusting to 120 mph, have since led the storm to be classed as a Category 2 hurricane.

The tempest unfortunately coincided with the recent outbreak of the War of Spanish Succession so many warships were out and about at the time. Around 20 per cent of the Royal Navy's sailors (8,000) were killed and the entire Channel squadron of thirteen ships foundered on Goodwin Sands 6 miles off the Kentish coast. The residents of Deal, however, preferred to loot wrecked vessels than to launch attempts to rescue sailors on their disintegrating ships although the mayor did organise the recovery of 200 men. On the Thames, 1,700 sailing craft were forced into a big heap by huge waves and dozens were lost while sheltering in Milford Haven. One ship, HMS *Association*, was blown from Harwich to Sweden and another was found 15 miles inland on the Somerset Levels. The first offshore lighthouse, on Eddystone Rocks near Plymouth, was destroyed and all six occupants, including its visiting architect, perished.

There was widespread destruction on land too. Four thousand oak trees in the New Forest alone were toppled and 2,000 chimney stacks were knocked over. Around 400 windmills were also destroyed with some even catching fire as their wooden gears went so fast that they overheated. Two tornadoes were spotted with one even lifting a cow into the branches of a tree. Roof tiles and wooden beams were ripped out of buildings and killed several people while the lead roofing of Westminster Abbey peeled off and flew away. Queen **Anne** had to hide in the cellar of St James's Palace to avoid a collapsing roof but, in Wells, Bishop Kidder and his wife were killed in bed when the chimney stacks inwardly collapsed on top

Destruction on Goodwin Sands. (*Artist: unknown. 18th century via Wikimedia Commons*)

of them. Flooding was extensive with 5,000 homes in London alone swept away by the Thames, the Severn rose by eight feet and several towns such as Plymouth, Bristol, Hull and Portsmouth were devastated. Thousands of livestock were lost, crops and orchards were flattened, and much land was deemed unusable for years due to salt contamination from sea spray.

It was not until 2 December that the storm started to abate, leaving a death toll of possibly 10,000 lives and property damage worse than that which occurred in the **Fire of London**. An even worse tempest may have happened nine years earlier, but the Great Storm of 1703 was the first natural event in British history to be recorded in any detail and become 'national news' as special editions of newspapers were printed to report it. It was also made famous by the novelist, Daniel Defoe (of later *Robinson Crusoe* fame), who wrote his first book – *The Storm* (1704) – based upon the many eyewitness accounts that he gathered. As people viewed the disaster as divine retribution for the nation's sins, the government ordered a day of fasting and special prayers, to prevent a similar catastrophe, were uttered in sermons well into the nineteenth century.

Gunpowder Plot

(1605)

A conspiracy to alter the monarchy and the country's religion

Soon after becoming king of England (1603), **James I** announced his desire for religious toleration, saying he would not persecute **Catholic**s who were law abiding and worshipped in private. The collection of recusancy fines for non-attendance of **Anglican** church services had become very inconsistent and Catholics' hopes were further raised by rumours that his wife, **Anne of Denmark**, had converted to their faith. **Parliament**, however, was fiercely anti-Catholic and, after the discovery of two minor Catholic plots in 1603, James's attitude also hardened. The recusancy laws now became more strictly enforced with fines as much as £20 per month for the wealthiest (approximately £5,000 in 2025). In the eyes of some Catholics, James had betrayed them.

The mastermind behind the plot was the charismatic Robert Catesby, a man well known to the authorities after his involvement in the abortive Essex Rebellion against Elizabeth I (1601). Initially, he sought support from abroad, but the Spanish had only just made peace with England, and the pope did not want to risk further persecution of English Catholics. Catesby then decided on more extreme measures. His plan was to blow up James, his ministers and MPs at the next opening of Parliament, initiate a rebellion in the Midlands, kidnap the king's 9-year-old daughter, **Elizabeth**, and make her a puppet sovereign who would restore Catholicism. In early 1604, he recruited Thomas Winter (a cousin) and

Gunpowder Plot conspirators. It is unlikely the Dutch artist ever saw them. (*Artist: C. van de Passe the elder, c. 1606 via Wikimedia Commons*)

John Wright, who had also taken part in the Essex Revolt. Afterwards, Winter introduced an English soldier who had fought for the Spanish army in the Netherlands – Guido (Guy) Fawkes – a man known for his courage and expertise with gunpowder. The last of the initial recruits was Thomas Percy, a man with connections to nobility who was able to provide much of the funding. By October 1605, seven more men were recruited, the last being another of Catesby's cousins, Francis Tresham.

At first the conspirators aimed to tunnel underneath Parliament, but this difficult task was made unnecessary by discovering a cellar that lay directly beneath the House of Lords where James would be opening Parliament on 5 November. Grateful for their luck, Percy immediately hired the room, and thirty-six barrels of gunpowder were brought over the Thames at night and stored under piles of wood in the cellar. Fawkes, under the alias John Johnson, was left behind to guard the room and light the fuse. After the explosion, he was to cross the Channel and try to gather support from abroad.

The plot, however, began to unravel on 26 October when Lord Monteagle received an anonymous letter warning him not to attend Parliament as it will receive 'a terrible blow'. Monteagle was one of a group of Catholic peers and, previously, a few conspirators had questioned the morality of killing fellow Catholics. The letter was quite possibly written by Tresham, Monteagle's brother-in-law; certainly, that is what Catesby later suspected. Monteagle immediately took the letter to the king's first minister, **Robert Cecil**, and he then showed it to James who suspected a planned explosion like that which had preceded the death of his father (Lord Darnley). A search of all buildings around Parliament was then ordered. This would have been time consuming as the chambers were surrounded by a myriad of homes, inns and shops within the precincts of the old palace of Westminster many of which adjoined the palace itself. The conspirators' 'cellar', in fact, was on the ground floor but beneath the Lords' chamber which was on the first floor; possibly it used to be a royal kitchen.

Fawkes was discovered but he coolly stated that his name was Johnson and he was merely guarding the property of his master, Thomas Percy. The soldiers left him but, given that Percy was a well-known Catholic agitator, a more thorough search was ordered late on 4 November. This time, the gunpowder was discovered, and Fawkes was arrested and sent to the Tower. Torture was rarely used and permission from the king or Privy Council had to be obtained but assent was given as Fawkes refused to give the names and details behind the plot. News of his arrest spread, and the other plotters fled north-west to raise rebellion. On 7 November, Fawkes was finally broken on the rack and started providing information.

With the authorities now in pursuit, Catesby and his band made it as far as the manor of Holbeche House in Staffordshire. Unfortunately, that evening, an attempt to dry out the rain-soaked gunpowder in front of the fire caused an explosion and several injuries. Meanwhile, efforts to incite a general uprising had failed so it was decided to make a final stand as 200 men, led by the Sheriff of Worcestershire, closed in. In the shootout the following morning, five of the conspirators were killed including Catesby and Percy (by a single bullet). The rest were taken to London to await their fate. A show trial declared them guilty and, on 30 and 31 January 1606, they were hanged, drawn and quartered outside St Paul's Cathedral in front of a baying crowd. Fawkes was relatively lucky. His torture meant that he had to be helped up the scaffold, but he managed to break his neck in the noose and thereby avoid the agony of being disembowelled. Catesby's and Percy's bodies were disinterred and decapitated and their heads placed on spikes outside the House of Lords. As for Tresham, he died in the Tower on 23 December possibly from cancer of the bladder.

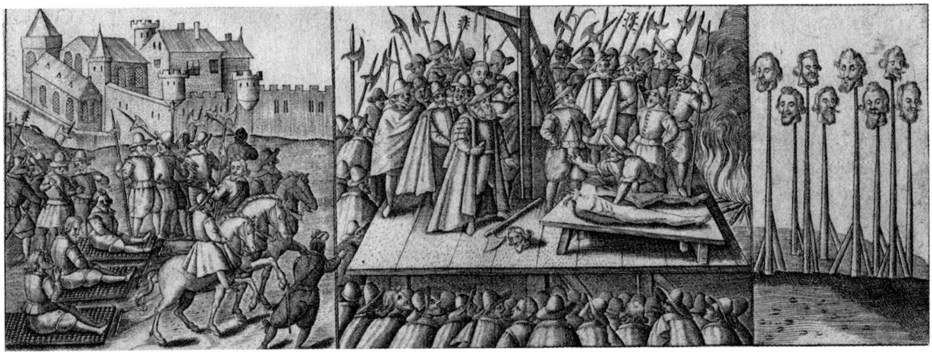

Executions of the surviving conspirators. The victims are being hanged, drawn and quartered. 'Drawn' either meant being dragged on hurdles to the scaffold or having one's insides drawn out. (*Artist: C. van de Passe the elder, c. 1606. Osterreichische NationalBibliothek*)

The failure of the Gunpowder Plot prompted many celebrations and Bonfire Night has been celebrated on 5 November ever since. For a long time, effigies of the pope were burned before they became 'guys'. Also, the ritual of searching the cellars below Parliament before it opens continues. More importantly, hatred and suspicion of Catholics (even though only a small minority) increased, they had to swear an oath of allegiance to the Crown and recusancy laws were more strictly enforced. James could have acted more severely (a degree of leniency was necessary to appease Spain) but fear of Catholics would bubble away beneath the English political landscape for many more decades. Not until 1829 were they largely emancipated.

Conspiracy theories about the plot soon became popular as some suspected Cecil of encouraging the scheme or even inventing it to gain favour with the king or enable greater persecution of Catholics. He possibly suspected that some plot was underway but, other than that, historians have found no evidence to incriminate him.

Gwyn, Nell

(1642/50–87)

Actress and mistress

Little is certain about Eleanor Gwyn's early life. Worcester, St Martin in the Fields (London) and Oxford all claim to be her place of birth and there is an eight-year disparity between the dates she was born. Her father may have been a Welsh soldier, and her mother was an alcoholic who ran a brothel in Covent Garden. Young Gwyn acted as a serving girl there and may even have been a child prostitute. The theatres reopened upon **Charles II**'s accession (1660) and, three years later, Gwyn was selling fruit and sweetmeats inside the Theatre Royal in Drury Lane with her elder sister, Rose. These scantily clad 'orange girls' would also have delivered messages backstage to the actresses from admiring male members of the audience.

Soon after, Gwyn's looks, wit and strong voice caught the attention of the theatre manager, Thomas Killigrew. Now that women were allowed to act, he decided to risk training her for the stage. By 1665, she had become a celebrity actress and, despite being illiterate, was able to learn the lines of lead roles in many plays. In that year, she performed as Montezuma's daughter in **Dryden**'s *The Indian Emperor* and, among her many admirers, was **Samuel Pepys** who called her, 'pretty, witty Nell'. Gwyn took to comedic roles best of all and often played one of the 'gay couple' opposite Charles Hart (a lover in real life). Typically, this involved a couple of witty lovers both pretending not to be interested in any serious relationship. One of her greatest performances was in Dryden's *The Maiden Queen* in which, according to Pepys, she stole the show

In 1667, Gwyn had a brief affair with Charles Buckhurst, a charming but dissolute member of the royal court's 'Merry Gang'. A few months later, she became the king's mistress (according to contemporary stories, she and her friend, **Aphra Behn**, put a strong laxative into a rival's cake before she entered Charles's bedchamber). From 1668, Gwyn was the king's long-term mistress, and she jokingly called him her 'Charles III' in a nod to her previous two lovers. She had few rivals as she supplanted the **Countess of Castlemaine** and, by now, Queen **Catherine of Braganza** had accepted her situation. Louise de Kérouaille (Duchess of Portsmouth), became the chief mistress in the 1670s but Gwyn, with her charisma and native wit, provided a sharp contrast with the proud, French, **Catholic** noblewoman and she was always held high in Charles's esteem. On one occasion, believing her to be Portsmouth, a mob start throwing insults as her coach passed by. Gwyn put her head out of the window and called out, 'Good people, you are mistaken; I am the *Protestant* whore.'

Gwyn had two sons by the king, and a story goes that she threatened to drop the eldest out of a window unless he gave him a peerage. In great haste, Charles cried out, 'God save the Earl of Burford!' and so saved his life. She briefly returned to acting in 1670–71 but spent most of her time entertaining friends at 79 Pall Mall, a property that she was eventually allowed to own after making numerous requests. As far as we know, Gwyn remained faithful to the king and, possibly being the mistress he loved the most, Charles never forgot her. As he lay dying in 1685, he told his brother and successor, 'Let not poor Nelly starve.' **James II** kept his promise and paid off Gwyn's considerable debts. Two years later, she died at her home after suffering two strokes that had probably been caused by syphilis.

Gwyn was certainly the most popular of the royal mistresses and hers is very much a story of rags to riches. Not forgetting her roots, she generously donated money from her will to the poor of St. Martin in the Fields.

H

Halley, Edmond

(1656–1742)

Astronomer, physicist and mathematician

Halley was the son of a Shoreditch soapmaker. As soap was becoming a popular item, his father was a wealthy man who, despite losing much in the **Fire of London**, could afford to privately tutor his son, send him to St Paul's School and thence to St John's College, Oxford. At school, he developed a fascination in the stars and, by 17, was an expert astronomer. In 1676, Halley left university early to sail to St Helena to build an observatory there and map the constellations of the southern hemisphere. At the same time, he observed the transit of Mercury across the Sun to provide the distances between the Earth and the Sun and the size of the solar system. Later, he realised that recording the transit of Venus would be more accurate and he urged future astronomers to do so at its next occurrence (1761). Upon his return in 1678, he was elected a member of the Royal Society – a prestigious group of leading scientists.

While travelling through Europe, in 1682, Halley noticed a comet and, having learnt that comets may be orbital, began to study it. In 1705, he published the results of his calculations and predicted that this comet would return every seventy-six years. He was proved correct in 1758 and, thereafter, the comet was named after him. For the first time, astronomy was recognised as a predictive science and, along with his friend **Isaac Newton**, had proved that gravity held the solar system together. Halley was much interested in the theory of gravity and, in 1684, went to Cambridge to discuss it with Newton only to find that Newton had already written a treatise discussing the concept of gravity and laws of motion. It was Halley who finally persuaded him to publish and provided the funding. As a result, one of the most important pieces of scientific work ever produced – *Philosophiæ Naturalis Principia Mathematica* (prefaced and edited by Halley) – appeared in 1687.

By the mid-1680s, Halley was famous around Europe and even entertained the visiting Czar of Russia, Peter the Great. Apparently, while both were drunk, Halley was seen pushing the Czar around in a wheelbarrow through the streets of Deptford! After the mysterious disappearance and death of his father, however, his financial support dried up and so he sought an academic post. In 1691, he applied for the vacant Savilian Chair of Astronomy at Oxford. However, he was thwarted by the Astronomer Royal, John Flamsteed, and the **Anglican** Church, both of whom opposed his doubts about the age of the Earth according to the Bible. Halley continued to work, though, and in 1693 published a study comparing age and mortality rates in the city of Breslau. As a result, the British government was able to sell life insurance more accurately.

In the late 1690s, **William III** sent Halley on the first ever purely scientific voyage – to discover variations in terrestrial magnetism in the Atlantic. From this, he was able to produce a chart of magnetic variation that would aid sailors in their use of the compass and help solve the great problem of calculating longitude (not achieved until the Harrison Clock of 1759). This complemented his earlier map of the world showing oceanic prevailing winds which he correctly deduced were due to solar heating. In 1703, he finally gained an academic position, the Savilian Chair of Geometry in Oxford, where he published a paper on comets and learned Arabic to translate the works of ancient scientists. He later made the first attempt at scientific dating of ancient monuments when he studied Stonehenge (he was out by over 2,000 years!) and, finally, in 1720 he succeeded his old opponent, Flamsteed,

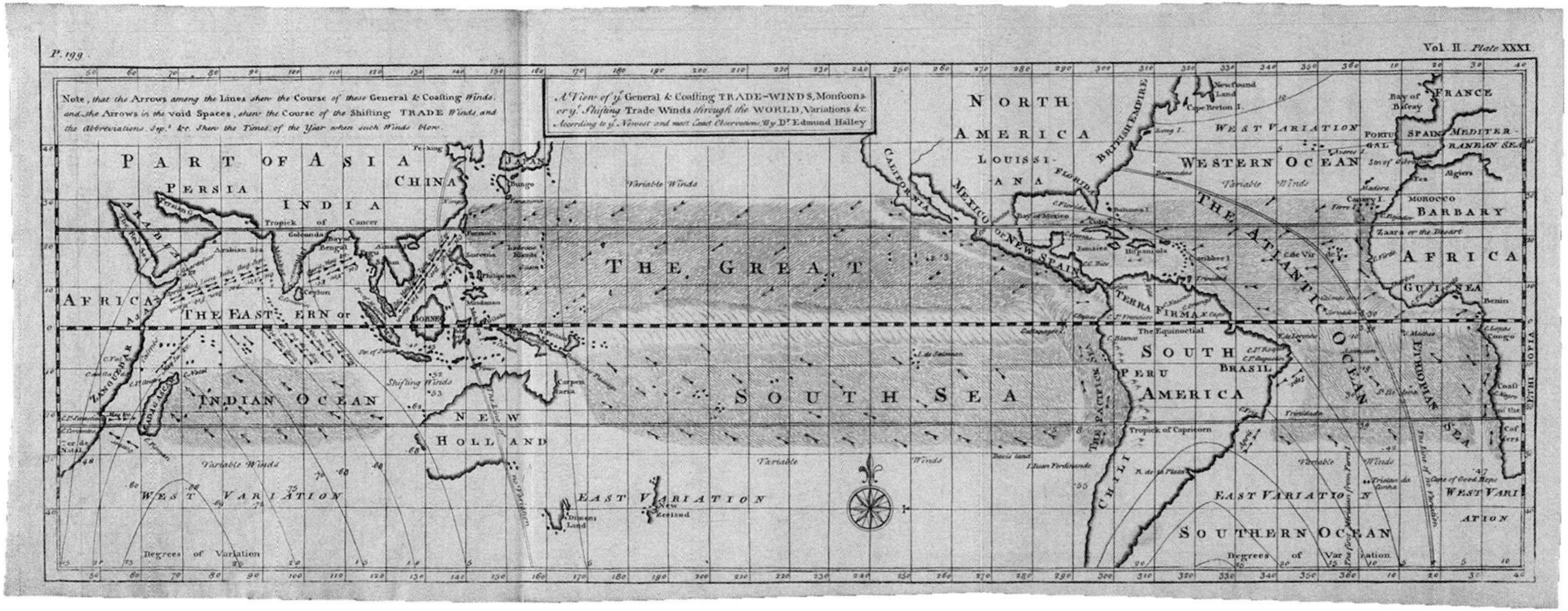

Halley's map of prevailing winds. (*Author: E. Halley, 1686. National Library of Israel*)

as Astronomer Royal – a post he held until his death. An incredibly versatile scientist, who also worked on diving bells, evaporation, tides in the Channel and the height of Mt Snowdon, Halley was an integral part of the Scientific Revolution.

Hampton Court Conference

(1604)

A meeting to discuss reform of the Church of England

Early in his reign, **James I** responded to the Millenary Petition of 1,000 **Puritan** ministers, by agreeing to discuss possible reform of the Church of England at a meeting in January 1604. With **plague** present in London, Hampton Court was chosen as the venue; eight bishops headed the **Anglican** party while four moderate Puritans were also invited. James, himself a keen scholar of theology, relished the prospect of imparting his wisdom. He had previously called Puritans 'pests' but later said he was only referring to the extreme ones.

Three meetings were held over five days to discuss the Puritans' requests which included:

1. Changes to the Prayer Book and the thirty-nine articles of faith (from 1569).
2. A new translation of the Bible.
3. Abolition of private baptisms, especially by women.
4. The Church to have a more preaching and sermonising nature.
5. Abolition of certain practices and ceremonies such as using a ring for **marriage** and wearing surplices.
6. Reform of Church government.

During the meetings, the king would happily give both sides a tongue-lashing. When the bishops stated that a church settlement that had lasted for forty years needed no alteration he asked if a man suffering from the pox for forty years should receive no cure. When he believed the Puritans were asking for a **Presbyterian** Church, he supposedly raged, 'No bishops, no king!' James, however, adeptly used his mediating skills and agreed to elements of the above demands; the most important and long-lasting effect was the creation of the **King James Bible**.

Administrative laziness and Church opposition meant that James failed to carry out the other reforms that he agreed to and he banned further petitions, but the Hampton Court Conference did have a placating affect. Combined with his tolerant religious policy (relative to that of his predecessor), he successfully managed to broaden his base of support while maintaining the status quo and religious disputes rarely surfaced during his reign. It has been argued, however, that he merely succeeded in brushing under the carpet religious tension that would raise its ugly head in his son's reign.

Harvey, William

(1578–1657)

Physician and anatomist

Harvey was the eldest of nine children and son of Thomas Harvey, a wealthy landowner and Mayor of Folkestone. He entered Caius College, Cambridge in 1593 followed by Padua University in 1599. The university there was the leading medical school in Europe and Harvey was much influenced by the teachings of Hieronymous Fabricius who had discovered one-way valves within human blood vessels. He returned from Italy in 1602 and, soon after, married Elizabeth Browne, daughter of Elizabeth I's physician. This helped him to become a lecturer at the Royal College of Physicians (1607) before taking charge of St Bartholomew's hospital.

By 1618, Harvey had attained such eminence that he was appointed **James I**'s Physician Extraordinary, but he also tended to other aristocrats including the statesman/philosopher, **Francis Bacon**. In 1625, he provided important evidence in the trial of the **Duke of Buckingham** which exonerated him from poisoning the king. Thereafter, he continued in his role as a loyal physician to **Charles I** who, in the 1630s, asked Harvey to examine some women accused of **witchcraft**. Always a sceptic, though, he could find no evidence. The king also encouraged his study of how blood circulated by allowing him to dissect dying deer during his hunts.

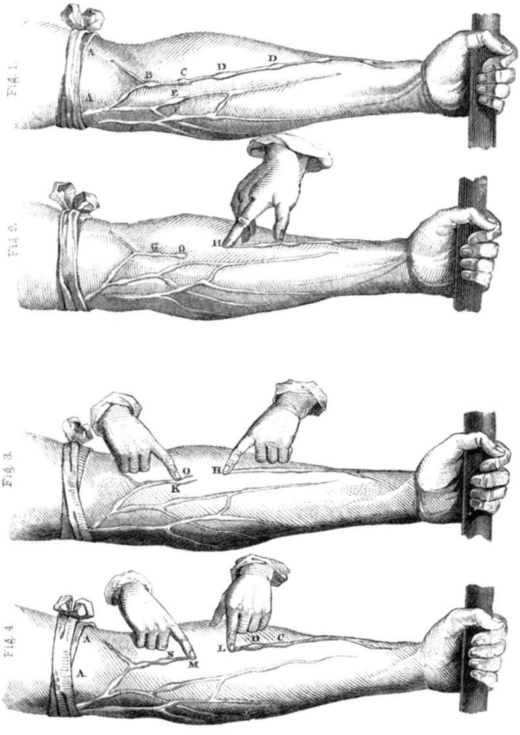

Diagrams from *De Motu Cordis*. (*Author: W. Harvey, 1628 via Wikimedia Commons*)

By 1628, he had gathered enough evidence to publish the book that was to bring him fame – *De Motu Cordis* (*On The Motion of the Heart*) – in which he clearly demonstrated that blood was continuously pumped to all parts of the body by the heart in a circulatory system. He also showed that the purpose of blood vessels' valves was to ensure the correct direction of blood flow. Contemporary thought asserted that blood, carrying nutrients from digested food, was continuously created in the liver then passed through the heart before being consumed by parts of the body. Another, separate blood system, carried blood from the lungs to the organs and the purpose of the heart was to provide heat and was connected to personality and spirituality. It is not surprising, therefore, that Harvey's downgrading of the heart to a mere pump brought about much derision, especially from abroad. His theory also brought him into conflict with the medical profession whose practice of using leeches to draw out bad blood would have been made redundant if he was correct. It took over twenty years before his theories were generally accepted.

Harvey remained a royalist throughout his life. At the Battle of Edgehill (1642), he looked after the king's two young sons from a relatively safe distance. In the same year he was devastated to hear that Parliamentarian troops had ransacked his London home and destroyed the results of much of his research. He remained with Charles at Oxford until the last days of the First **Civil War** and, while there, he made use of the university's facilities to continue his studies while trying to ignore the noisy soldiers around him. After the war, Harvey went into semi-retirement, enjoying books, walks, conversations, sitting in the dark (for contemplative purposes) and drinking **coffee**. He had long been fascinated with the nature of reproduction in animals, though, and 1651 saw the publication of *On Animal Generation*. His investigations into the development of chicken eggs and the role of semen and menstrual blood in the formation of deer embryos made useful contributions to this poorly understood branch of science. Using just a magnifying glass – effective microscopes appeared in 1674 – much hampered his studies, though, and he could prove nothing.

Harvey, described as a 'humorous but precise man', was a traditionalist by heart, often drawing on the thoughts of Aristotle, but he was the first in England to use the scientific method propounded by Bacon – to carefully experiment, observe and record. So, he represents the crossover from the traditional methods of deductive science to the more mechanical and inductive nature of the scientific revolution.

Health and Medicine

In Stuart England, as in previous centuries, death was never far away. Life expectancy at birth was around thirty-seven years although if you survived your childhood then you could reasonably hope to reach your sixties or beyond. The growing number of crowded towns saw the highest mortality rates and, being weaker and having less immunity, children were particularly exposed to the plethora of fatal diseases that abounded. The ringing of church funeral bells – nine tolls for men, six for women, three for children – must have been a constant reminder of the fragility of life. With by far the biggest population, London suffered most; it devoured its people faster than its birth rate. Had it not been for its 8,000 immigrants per year, it would have simply ceased to function.

Predictably, the most dangerous locations were the crowded, dirty slums where diseases could spread easily. Smallpox, for instance, had becomc a major killer by 1700 and wiped out around 10 per cent of each generation. Its most notable victims included Queen **Mary II**, **John** and **Sarah Churchill**'s only son and **Charles I**'s eldest daughter. Survivors could be severely pockmarked, and fashionable ladies would wear dark beauty spots to cover the scars on their faces. Typhoid travelled through infected food and water and killed Prince Henry (**James I**'s eldest son) and Elizabeth **Pepys**. Typhus fever – known as jail fever – was spread by lice and was common in armies and crowded prisons. **Plague** had a high mortality rate. The epidemics of 1625 and 1665 wiped out one-fifth of London's population while over a third of the people of Newcastle and Colchester died in 1636 and 1666 respectively. There was also dysentery, with its debilitating attacks of diarrhoea, malaria for those living near stagnant water and lung-destroying tuberculosis and influenza. The list goes on. Scrofula, a type of tuberculosis that caused neck swellings, also known as 'king's evil', was supposedly cured by a touch from the king. **William III**, however, refused to take part in such a superstition probably because, having been chosen by **Parliament**, he could not claim divine right. Venereal disease – known as the French Disease – was widespread, socially embarrassing and caused impotence. Injection of mercury into the nose or genitals seemed to work but it merely masked the symptoms, thus allowing men to infect more women. Even simple cuts and broken limbs were life-threatening due to the risk of septicaemia and gangrene.

Curing syphilis by inhaling mercury vapours. The 'beneficial' effects of mercury more likely coincided with dormant phases of the disease. (*Author: J. Lagniet, c. 1650s. Digital Library of Gallica*)

Mortality rates were considerably lower in the countryside. Life expectancy at birth in the parish of Hartland in Devon, for example, was over fifty-five years (not until 1920 was that the national average) with a correlating infant mortality rate of under 10 per cent compared to 16 per cent nationwide. Hartland's isolation, widely spaced homes and distance from trade routes were undoubtedly the contributory factors. Observers at the time knew that towns had higher death rates and with the outbreak of any epidemic those who could afford it would flee to the countryside. Ignorance of the causes and the lack of personal, food and water hygiene was the problem, however. Cesspits, providing a constant foul stench, often seeped into the water supply with fatal consequences. They often leaked into neighbours' cellars too. Pepys once received a nasty shock when he opened his cellar door and stepped into 'a great heap of turds'.

The world of micro-organisms appeared to the human eye when the first effective microscope was invented in 1675 (Anton van Leeuwenhoek in the Netherlands), but it was not until the nineteenth century that it was generally accepted that germs caused illness. In the meantime, it was believed that epidemics were caused by foul vapours sent as divine punishment. The perceived link between death and God strengthened the role of religion in **society** and the need for spiritual guidance and soul-searching. Superstitious practices were rife too such as holding a child up to be stroked by a criminal on the gallows to bring good health.

Medical care, if we can call it that, was provided by physicians, barber-surgeons and apothecaries. The university-trained physicians still based their care on the beliefs of Hippocrates and Galen from ancient Greece. Illness, they stated, was caused by an imbalance of the four humours, or substances, that comprised the body – blood, phlegm, black bile and yellow bile. To rebalance the humours, physicians would induce vomiting, use laxatives or perform bloodletting (either through leeches or opening a vein). Affordable only to the wealthy, they tended to flee the towns on the outbreak of an epidemic, to remain close to their clients. Barber-surgeons, who qualified after a period of apprenticeship, were mainly used for broken limbs, internal ruptures and tooth-removal but would also offer services ranging from plastic surgery and mastectomies to ear-waxing and sexual advice. They had a better understanding than most of anatomy as they were allowed to dissect ten bodies a year. Dissection was considered a disgrace for the deceased, so the bodies belonged to executed criminals. The barbers also performed excruciatingly painful lithotomies – the three- to five-minute surgical removal of bladder stones (common at the time due to poor **diet**). With alcohol being the most effective anaesthetic, they hoped that the patients would simply pass out from the pain. Samuel Pepys was lucky to survive the removal of a tennis ball-sized stone in 1662; the mortality rate for the operation was 30 per cent with most deaths caused by the unsterilized surgical instruments. The third main provider of medical treatment were the apothecaries – seventeenth-century chemists. They tended to be cheaper and some of their herbal medicines may even have done some good but one must question the

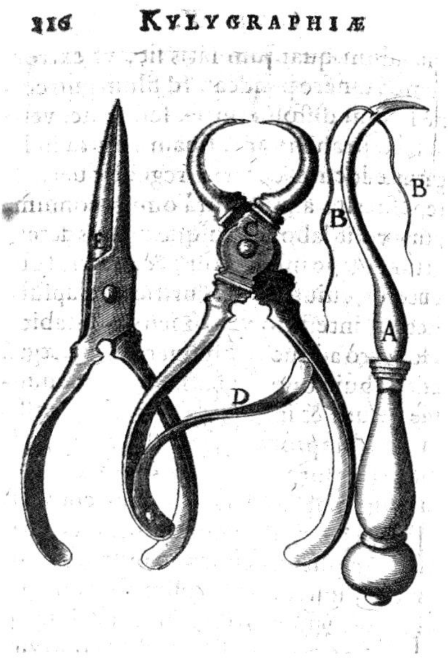

Forceps used for hernia surgery. Cleanliness was judged by appearance. Blood stains were usually rinsed off with water or wine. (*Author: M. Geiger from The Description of Hernias, 1631. Wellcome Collection*)

reasoning behind many of the ingredients that they used. These included the turds of a goose, penises of bulls, frogs' lungs, swallows' brains, castrated cats, discarded nail-clippings and the skulls of those who had died a violent death. Cannabis was available too but often caused impotence.

The impression is of a healthcare system that was haphazard, largely unregulated and dependant on local providers. The poor majority tended to be treated at home by females in the family or local community using homemade medical recipes and itinerant 'quacks' would also offer their services. Residential care was limited to two types of accommodation. Privately run asylums such as Bethlem (or Bedlam) took in the mentally ill. The care and treatment inside these institutions was often inhumane and people could pay for public viewings as a form of entertainment. Men were even known to install troublesome wives as a way of getting rid of them. More often however, a mentally ill person was looked after at home or became a beggar (nicknamed 'Tom O'Bedlam'). The only free residential care was given to the aged deserving poor who could stay in nursing homes financed by the local parish's poor relief fund. Those far from home such as sailors and travellers could also be given beds there as well as women convalescing from difficult pregnancies.

Giving birth, in fact, was another major cause of death. On average, a woman gave birth to seven children and had a 6 per cent chance of dying each time. Midwives, in theory, could only work with a bishop's licence but their quality varied enormously. Some were experienced and skilled but the malpractice of others, along with their unwashed hands, caused many deaths during childbirth. Among upper class women, in particular, annual pregnancies were common as they did not breastfeed, and poorer women were usually forced back to work by their husbands straight after giving birth to maintain the family income. The resultant strains and stresses on women's bodies can only have made them more susceptible to illness.

During the great revolutionary forum of the 1650s, some radical **Puritan**s demanded change and mocked the university **education** of the physicians who, clearly, were powerless in the face of recurring epidemics and only cared for the rich (a claim seemingly verified when they fled the **Plague** of London in 1665). They called for more doctors with up-to-date training and for English to replace

Midwives assisting at birth. Left: midwife with a woman on a birthing chair. Right: midwives washing a baby and caring for the mother. (*Artist and date unknown. Wellcome Collection*)

Latin as the language of their profession. Some also proposed state-funded medical research centres and free or cheaper medical facilities for the poor. Unfortunately, these ideas behind an embryonic National Health Service were swept aside by the Restoration. Hope did lie on the horizon, however. Suffering and death caused by famine ended after 1624 as farmers no longer relied upon one grain crop or one sowing and the work of pioneers such as Thomas Sydenham, **William Harvey** and **Robert Hooke** would open the way for huge medical improvements in the future.

Henrietta Maria

(1609–69)

Wife of **Charles I** and Queen of England,
Scotland and **Ireland** from 1625 to 1649

Henrietta Maria was the youngest daughter of Henry IV of France and Marie de Medici and was born at the Louvre Palace in Paris. Her father was assassinated before she was 1, her mother exiled when she was 8 and she herself was raised by a royal governess. Aged 13, she first met her future husband – Prince Charles of England – as he was travelling through to woo the Spanish Infanta. After that fiasco, it was agreed that Henrietta Maria would marry him to strengthen Anglo-French relations against the powerful Hapsburg threat. After a proxy wedding in Paris (May 1625), the 15-year-old princess travelled to England with a huge entourage and trunk loads of diamonds and pearls and spent the first night with her husband, now king, at St Augustine's Abbey, Canterbury.

The first three years of their **marriage** were very rocky. She clashed with the king's favourite – the **Duke of Buckingham** – and was upset by Charles going to war with France to help French Protestants and his refusal to keep a secret marriage promise of granting toleration to English **Catholic**s. When Charles expelled most of her French retinue in 1626, Henrietta Maria publicly threatened to go home and, in her anger, smashed a window with her bare fist. She was not a popular choice with her new subjects either. The **Gunpowder Plot** was only twenty years previously and many feared that this Catholic queen would become a malign influence in court, a fear that was increased by her non-participation in Charles's **Anglican** coronation ceremony. She was also, like her husband, quite a remote figure and spoke almost no English although people who knew her described a vivacious woman with a great sense of humour.

Henrietta Maria with Charles. With Prince Charles (left) and Princess Mary (right). Known as 'The Greate Peece' at the time, van Dyke was able to convey informal family domesticity. (*Artist: van Dyke, 1632. National Library of Poland via Wikimedia Commons*)

After Buckingham's assassination in 1628, the royal couple's relationship improved significantly. The queen later wrote that during the 1630s, 'I was the happiest and most fortunate of queens … I had a husband who adored me.' Charles increasingly turned to his wife for comfort and support and they hated to be apart; between 1629 and 1644, they had nine children of whom five reached adulthood. The 1630s was also an opportunity for Henrietta Maria to indulge her extravagant passion for the arts. She collected a vast number of paintings, employing some of Europe's finest artists such as **Anthony van Dyck**, was a patron of music, theatre, poetry and sculpture and employed the architect, **Inigo Jones**. She loved to host masques too and, sometimes, even performed in them. This period, however, also saw an increasing degree of mistrust of the queen particularly in **Puritan** London. Combined with the High Church reforms of Archbishop **Laud**, Henrietta Maria's founding of a Catholic chapel, flagrant practising of her religion and conversion of several courtiers along with the emulation of her fashion by noble ladies caused many to fear the creeping spread of Catholicism at court. When the Puritan lawyer, William Prynne, wrote an attack on female actors and compared them to whores it was considered an insult to the queen. His harsh punishment – imprisonment, fine and cropping of his ears in the pillory – in 1634 roused much anger.

There is much dispute about how much influence Henrietta Maria had over the king but by 1641 it seems likely that she was becoming more directly involved in politics. As tensions mounted between Charles and **Parliament**, she was accused of advocating military force against the latter and of inviting French assistance. Even more dangerous were the accusations that she had fomented rebellion in Ireland, and this was followed by MPs' indirect accusations, in the **Grand Remonstrance**, that she was part of a Catholic conspiracy. Fears that she was about to be impeached may have caused her to advise Charles to arrest his five main opponents in Parliament (January 1642). The ensuing fiasco angered the London mob and forced the royal family to flee London. As civil war looked more likely, Henrietta Maria sailed to The Hague to raise funds and support for her husband.

After the outbreak of the **Civil Wars**, she took a very active role in supporting the king. In February 1643, after selling much of her jewellery to buy arms and hire troops, she managed to evade the Parliamentary navy and land safely at Bridlington. That night, however, enemy ships bombarded the town forcing her to dodge bullets and hide in a ditch. She and her supplies eventually reached Charles in Oxford but not before she oversaw the capture of Burton-on-Trent. While in Oxford, Henrietta Maria was a key influence on the king, constantly urging him to take decisive action against his enemies and seeking support from factions in Scotland, Ireland and France. By now, she was nicknaming herself 'the She Majesty Generalissima' and Parliament was seeing her as a key obstacle to peace negotiations. By the spring of 1644, the royalist position in Oxford was becoming less secure and so the queen, now pregnant, was asked to leave for her own safety. After seeing Charles for the last time, she managed to avoid capture and sail to France from Falmouth in July.

Henrietta Maria settled in Paris and formed a royalist court-in-exile. Her constant calls for foreign aid, however, fell on deaf ears and she became quite depressed when she heard of Charles's defeat in 1646. News of his execution in early 1649 sent her into shock and in the following years she found solace in her religion and the company of her children and loyal courtiers. She fell out with her eldest son, **Charles**, over her attempts to convert his youngest brother, Henry, to Catholicism and when he and his court moved to Cologne in 1654, her influence was much diminished. Following the Restoration in 1660, she returned to England largely to prevent the marriage of her second son, **James**, to the daughter of **Edward Hyde** whom she deeply disliked. This failed and, following the deaths of both Henry and her eldest daughter, Mary, from smallpox in London, she returned to France. Another stay in England was shortened by an attack of bronchitis which she blamed on the damp weather, and she eventually died in Paris after the French king's physician gave her too many opiates.

Henrietta Maria was probably the most important of the Stuart queens and the American state of Maryland was named in her honour by Charles I. However, Parliamentary propaganda, influenced perhaps by contemporary dislike of strong, opinionated women, has created the image of an evil, conspiring seductress who brought civil war to England. Certainly, she was not a mediating force, and she made no effort to endear herself to her English subjects but one cannot help but admire her determination and loyalty to her husband and his cause.

Hobbes, Thomas

(1588–1679)

Political philosopher

According to Hobbes, 'my mother gave birth to twins: myself and fear' as he was born prematurely when she took fright over news of the Spanish Armada. His father was a short-tempered parson who had to abandon his family after getting involved in a brawl but, fortunately, Hobbes and his two siblings were taken in by his uncle, a wealthy glover in Wiltshire. This allowed him to receive a private **education** followed by a degree at Magdalen Hall, Oxford. Following this, he began his lifelong connection with various branches of the wealthy Cavendish family, first serving as a tutor and then performed other roles for them such as translator, keeper of accounts and business agent.

Much of the 1630s were spent abroad, particularly in Paris. There, Hobbes joined philosophic debating groups and met René Descartes (of 'I think therefore I am' fame) and started to display a great interest in human nature. He already had a good understanding of the workings of English politics due to his association with the Cavendish family and so he began to consider how societies should be governed from a philosophical point of view. Hobbes also developed a love of geometry inspired by the works of Euclid and, perhaps, by a meeting with

Frontispiece to *Leviathan*. (*Author: T. Hobbes, 1651. British Museum*)

the great astronomer Galileo Galilei in Florence. Branching deeper into the field of mathematics, he carried out much research into optics and ballistics too. With a mind that was constantly busy, he carried an inkwell and pen in his walking stick so that he could jot thoughts down in a notebook and was known to draw lines on his thighs and bed sheets.

The production of various treatises brought Hobbes much attention and respect, but it was 1651's *Leviathan* for which he is chiefly remembered. The death and destruction caused by the **Civil Wars** impelled him to write a book that would help to prevent another, similar outbreak of violence. Its memorable front cover – a giant, made up of hundreds of humans, holding a sword and crozier – gave a clue about its chief message. In a clear rebuttal to the established view of Aristotle, Hobbes stated that mankind, in its natural state, was anarchic – 'The condition of man … is a condition of war of everyone against everyone.' To maintain peace, citizens had created a hypothetical contract with a ruler who could protect them from conflict. In return, he argued, the citizens had given up their natural rights to decide on all political, religious and legal affairs. A sovereign was not bound by any laws, and he could only be deposed if the citizens felt safer without him. The leviathan monster represented **society** with the monarch at its head.

It is hard for us today to understand the impact of such a book. In a period of political and social uncertainty, *Leviathan* caused much discussion, approval, anger and confusion in equal measures. Nearly all who read it found passages which supported their views but later read parts that caused them discomfort and, for decades, it was a book that courted controversy and divided opinion. Although he was a royalist himself, supporters of **Charles II** were angered by Hobbes's suggestion that a monarch ruled, not by divine right, but by the people's consent. **Anglican**s, **Presbyterian**s and **Catholic**s were all indignant about his subordination of the Church to secular authority and his belief that God is immaterial and therefore incomprehensible to humans brought him accusations of atheism which he was forced to deny.

Fears for his own safety forced Hobbes to flee the threats of royalists and Catholics in Paris and return to England where **Puritan** Independents found his work more compatible with their way of thinking. The Restoration brought his enemies closer but Charles II, a former pupil, enjoyed his company and gave him protection and, although 'Hobbism' became a term of disrespect, he was highly regarded in academic circles abroad. An anti-atheism act of **Parliament**, however, banned further publications of his work in 1666 and second-hand copies of *Leviathan* became hard to acquire. Two years later, **Samuel Pepys** had to pay 24 shillings for a book which had previously been a third of that price.

Hobbes continued to write until the last years of his life. His works included an autobiography in Latin verse and translations of *Iliad* and *Odyssey* into rhyming English. *Leviathan*, however, remained banned until long after his death, aged 91, from a stroke and bladder disorder. Hobbes's work is hugely important. He was the first to articulate social contract theory and influenced the likes of **Locke**, Rousseau and Kant and his writings triggered discussions of human rights, political systems and power being based on the consent of the people.

Hooke, Robert

(1635–1703)

Polymath

Hooke was born at Freshwater on the Isle of Wight, the youngest child of a local parson. He was a sickly child, prone to headaches and dizziness and suffering a spinal deformity that became more pronounced with age and so was not expected to reach adulthood. Subsequently, his **education** was largely neglected, thus allowing him to pursue his own interests. Mechanical objects fascinated him and he spent much time building mechanical toys and even produced a working wooden clock, aged 10. Possibly from this young age, Hooke began to see the natural world around him as one big, complicated machine.

He was 13 when his father died and, as he had shown much talent at drawing, Hooke was sent with his £40 inheritance (around £4,000 in 2025) to London to become a painter's apprentice. The smell of oil paints, however, aggravated his headaches so he decided, instead, to broaden his education by going to Westminster School. There, the renowned headmaster, Richard Busby, soon recognised Hooke's prodigious talents and encouraged him to study independently in the school's library. Aged 18, later than was normal, he entered Christ Church College, Oxford as a servitor, meaning he received free tuition in return for various domestic duties and being a chorister. While there, he met members of the 'Invisible College' (many of whom became founder members of the Royal Society) such as **Christopher Wren** and **Robert Boyle** and his fascination with science began. In 1655, Hooke became Boyle's assistant and constructed the air pump for Boyle's experiments on gas pressures. At the same time, he assisted in dissections and the construction of flying machines. Such was his talent and breadth of interests that the Royal Society appointed him as their curator of experiments in 1662. His salary was inconsistent, but this was solved when he became Professor of Geometry at Gresham College in 1665. In this role he had to provide one lecture, in Latin, each week and remain unmarried.

Under pressure to produce regular experiments for the Royal Society, Hooke's bustling mind branched out into all fields of science and the subsequent list of his inventions and new ideas is quite astonishing. In astronomy, he noticed that Jupiter revolved on its axis, built an improved telescope, made drawings of Mars and the Moon and attempted to calculate distances to the stars. There was a long and bitter dispute with **Isaac Newton** about who came up with the theory of gravity when applied to planetary motion. It is hard to ascertain who first suggested the inverse square law of gravitation, but it appears that Newton was the first to mathematically prove it.

In the field of physics, Hooke produced a formula to measure the relationship between force and the elasticity of an object (Hooke's Law), built a universal joint for the smooth movement of machinery, designed a balance spring to improve the accuracy of watches and analysed capillary action in different-sized tubes. In optics, he discovered light diffraction and suggested that light travels in waves and his study of fossils led him to propose theories of tectonic uplift and evolution (150 years before Darwin). Hooke even had time to work with Wren on surveying London and designing new buildings after the **Fire of London**.

Hooke also designed a new type of microscope and was the first to see micro-fungi and use the word 'cell' when describing the structure of objects. Detailed sketches of these, along with the celestial bodies he had seen through his telescope, appeared in *Micrographia* (1665) – a bestseller that instantly brought him fame. The science historian, Richard Westfall, described it as 'one of the masterpieces of seventeenth century science' and contemporaries were fascinated by their introduction to 'invisible worlds'. **Samuel Pepys** called it 'the most ingenious book that ever I read in my life'.

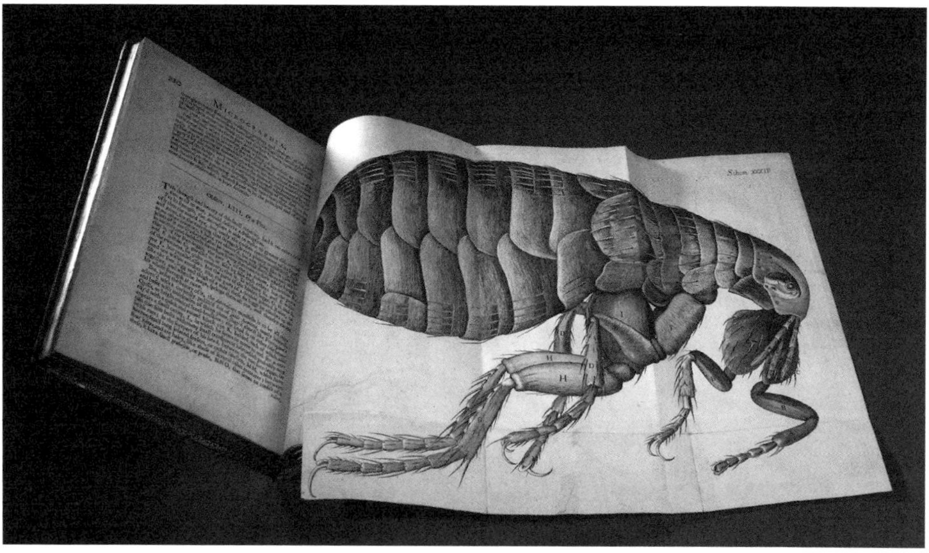

Pull-out picture of a flea from *Micrographia*. (*Author: R. Hooke, 1665. Wellcome Collection*)

Hooke's diaries reveal a man who loved to socialise with friends such as Wren, Boyle and the diarist, John Aubrey, in **coffee houses** and taverns. There is no confirmed portrait of him, however; possibly he perceived himself too ugly to sit for an artist. He certainly seemed to lack the confidence to court women of similar social standing, never married and only admitted to sexual relations with his servants and a teenage niece whom he took into his care after his brother's suicide. Towards the end of his life, Hooke suffered from worsening headaches and the effects of the opiates he took for them and became more cynical and bitter about ideas that others had 'stolen' from him. Unlike Newton or Boyle, he was a more creative scientist whose mind seemed incapable of focusing on one theory for long, so it was inevitably left to others to follow through on his half-ideas. He eventually died, bedridden and blind but Hooke had been the epitome of a seventeenth-century polymath – a genius who could never be constrained by any one field of study.

Hudson, Jeffrey

(1619–c. 1682)

Court dwarf

Hudson was born into a poor family in Rutland where his father was a keeper of baiting bulls for the **Duke of Buckingham**. His parents and siblings were all average sized but, even aged 30, he was a mere 18 inches tall although perfectly proportioned. Contemporaries thought his mother had choked on a gherkin when she was pregnant but, more likely, he had a pituitary gland disorder. In 1626, he was presented to Buckingham's wife as a 'rarity of nature' who, in turn, gifted him to the queen, **Henrietta Maria**. At a sumptuous banquet, provided for by the Buckinghams, a large pie was brought before the queen and, to her astonished delight, a hand poked through the crust before Hudson, clothed in armour, jumped out and started marching up and down the table.

Hudson then lived a life of luxury at the queen's residence at Denmark House along with two disproportionate dwarves, a monkey called Pug and a 7½-foot-tall porter called William Evans. He became known as 'Lord Minimus' and formed a close bond with Henrietta Maria, was given fine costumes and paid the handsome sum of £50 a year. Hudson was often seen riding a horse with the queen while sitting on a specially designed saddle and performed in her masques. One scene drew huge roars of laughter when Evans pulled him out of a pocket along with a loaf of bread.

This comfortable existence, however, was disrupted by the outbreak of the **Civil Wars** (1642). Hudson accompanied the queen abroad to raise money for the royalist cause and returned with her the following year. He may have seen action with **Prince Rupert** and, while in Oxford, Henrietta Maria appointed him a Captain of Horse. As the military situation deteriorated, however, they both had to flee to France where a court-in-exile was established. While there, Hudson took offence at one of her courtiers' mockery and challenged him to a dual. His laughing opponent appeared with a water pistol but Hudson, tired of being the butt of people's jokes, promptly shot him through the head with a real gun. As dualling was a capital offence in France, the queen had to beg for mercy before having to send him back to England in late 1644.

While crossing the Channel, however, his ship was captured by Barbary pirates (this was the second time, after being captured by Dunkirk pirates and released in 1630). Hudson disappeared into North Africa where he was enslaved for around twenty-five years before being ransomed back. By now, he had apparently grown to 45 inches which he said was due to the ill treatment he had suffered. From 1669 he settled back in Rutland, drawing a pension from Buckingham's son, before travelling to London. Unfortunately, his arrival coincided with the **Popish Plot** and being a well-known **Catholic**, was imprisoned. After his release in 1680, he received a couple of mysterious payments from **Charles II** before dying of an unknown cause on an unknown date and buried in an unknown location. England's smallest recorded man, from England's smallest county.

Hyde, Edward (First Earl of Clarendon)

(1609–74)

Statesman and historian

The only surviving son of a lawyer, Hyde was born near Salisbury and educated at home by the local parson. At 13, he went to Magdalen Hall (now Hertford College), Oxford and then attended the Inns of Court to receive a legal **education**. His first wife died from smallpox in 1629 after just six months of **marriage** but his second, Frances Aylesbury, was to provide him with useful socio-political connections as well as six children who survived infancy. In the 1630s, Hyde was a member of the Great Tew Circle – a discussion group of writers and clerics with humanist/royalist leanings, which met at Great Tew, Oxfordshire – and befriended eminent writers such as **Ben Jonson** and John Selden and the archbishop, **William Laud**, despite disapproving of the latter's religious policies.

Elected as an MP for the Short and Long **Parliament**s in 1640, Hyde joined the demands to restrict the Crown's arbitrary powers that **Charles I** had displayed during his eleven years of personal rule. In the following year, however, he moved to the royalist side believing that the radical opposition in Parliament had gone too far, especially disagreeing with the execution of **Strafford**, attempts to ban bishops from the Lords and the **Grand Remonstrance**. Hyde, always an advocate of the rule of law, particularly disliked the radicals' use of the London mob as a political force. After becoming the king's behind-the-scenes advisor, he urged compromise but that became far more difficult after Charles's attempt to arrest five MPs.

As **civil war** approached in the summer of 1642, Hyde joined the king's privy council in Oxford and constantly urged for a peaceful solution based on a constitutional monarchy. The hawks in Charles's war camp, however, distrusted a former parliamentarian and eventually succeeded in side-lining him to the West Country where he joined the council of Prince Charles. After defeat in 1646, he followed the royalist exiles to France but, being a devout **Anglican**, Hyde despaired of Charles's search for support from **Catholic** powers and **Presbyterian** Scotland. Final defeat and a narrow escape from England in 1651 put a brake on Charles's immediate ambitions, however, and the prince seemed happy to appoint him as his chief advisor in his nomadic court. During the 1650s, Hyde's watchwords were caution and patience, confident in the belief that **Cromwell**'s republican experiment in England would fail – this, despite the death of his sister, Susan, at the hands of Cromwell's men in 1656. Susan had been a royalist spy and member of the Sealed Knot – a secret organisation aimed at overthrowing the republic – but suffered psychological and possibly physical torture after being arrested.

Earl of Clarendon. (*Artist: after P. Lely, late seventeenth century. National Trust*)

Hyde's approach paid off when the Commonwealth collapsed in 1660, and Charles was invited to take the throne as **Charles II**, and he had much input in the conciliatory Declaration of Breda which allowed the Restoration. He continued as the king's principal secretary for the next seven years and was created Earl of Clarendon in 1661 but was beset by problems throughout his time in office. He objected to most of Parliament's laws that persecuted non-Anglicans (ironically called the Clarendon Code) and his attempts to bypass MPs by use of the king's council only heightened their sense that he was a turncoat. At the same time, Clarendon was blamed for any setback that occurred. Many royalists blamed him for not having their old lands returned to them and he was accused of seeking familial power when his daughter, Anne, married the king's heir, **James, Duke of York**. In fact, such was his dislike of James that he allegedly told her that he would rather see her dead than to so disgrace the family. He was even accused of arranging the king's marriage to **Catherine of Braganza**, knowing that she was infertile and thereby ensuring that the throne would go to his heirs. It is true that Clarendon was partly responsible for his own downfall, however. Aloof, overbearing and prudish, he appeared unaware of his weak position, a position that was further eroded by being increasingly incapacitated by obesity and gout. A fish out of water among the king's young, vivacious and promiscuous courtiers, his public criticisms of the mistress-in-chief – the **Countess of Castlemaine** – also created a resolute enemy who turned others against him. The final straw was the humiliating Dutch **Raid on the Medway** (1667) even though he had always been against the **Second Anglo-Dutch War**.

Charles realised that he had the perfect scapegoat for his problems. He had tired of Clarendon's constant criticisms of his morality anyway and unfairly blamed him for the Crown's lack of money and so, with no sign of gratitude for his long service, dismissed him. The simultaneous death of his beloved wife was a further blow to him and, under the threat of impeachment by Parliament, he fled to France. Soon after, an act of Parliament officially banished him from England and made any correspondence with him or visits from his children illegal. Clarendon spent most of his time in exile writing *The History of the Rebellion and Civil Wars in England* (published 1702). Although it contains royalist bias and attempts to vindicate his own actions it has become an invaluable resource for historians studying the events and characters of the Civil Wars. After his death in Rouen, his body was returned to England and buried in a private ceremony in Westminster Abbey.

I

Ireland

Since the 1540s, when Henry VIII appointed himself King of Ireland, the Tudor monarchs had attempted to assert their control over the island by enforcing English laws, customs and religion upon the native **Catholic** population and colonising the land with English and Scottish settlers in a system known as plantations. In response, several uprisings occurred, the most serious being the eight-year conflict known as Tyrone's Rebellion which was concluded in 1603 a few days after the death of Elizabeth I.

The treaty signed in Mellifont Manor, near Drogheda, had been lenient. Tyrone and others were allowed to keep the core of their lands and sit in the Irish Parliament in return for swearing their loyalty and accepting English laws, customs and language. Further encroachments on their authority, however, caused them to flee the island in 1607 and seek assistance from Spain (the Flight of the

Earls). Their abscondment, however, simply facilitated the spread of plantations in Ulster with **Presbyterian** Scots and **Anglican** English settlers and the creation of new towns such as Belfast and Derry. At the same time, hopes that the new king, **James I**, would allow more freedoms for Catholics were dashed when he demanded religious uniformity in the wake of the **Gunpowder Plot** (1605).

The first few decades of the seventeenth century were defined by continued persecution on religious grounds. For centuries, the traditional Gaelic clans and the descendants of the Anglo-Norman settlers had been rivals but intermarriage and the widespread adoption of Gaelic customs and language had softened their animosity and now, with their shared faith under sustained attack, they became more united. In 1628, their representatives appealed to the new king, **Charles I**, for more religious freedom and protection from settlers encroaching on their lands. The king accepted their requests – known as the Graces – in return for three annual lump sums of money. Delay and blocking tactics, however, meant that the Crown received its money, but the Graces were never enacted in the Irish Parliament. Acrimony towards the English overlords increased further after 1632 when **Sir Thomas Wentworth** was appointed Lord Deputy. He merely saw Ireland as a source of revenue and his arbitrary, heavy-handed tactics only further inflamed passions and united his enemies.

Slaughter of Protestant settlers. While atrocities did occur, propaganda such as this fuelled anti-Catholic hysteria. (*Artist: W. Hollar, c. 1642–46. National Library of Ireland via Wikimedia Commons*)

This powder keg of repression, anger and frustration was ignited in October 1641 by fears that the **Puritan** English **Parliament** would win its quarrels with the king and enact harsher measures against the Irish. The rebellion started in Ulster and news of massacres of Protestant settlers horrified people in England. Contemporary accounts of civilian deaths were wildly exaggerated but as many as 12,000 may have lost their lives (10 per cent of the settler population). The uprising soon spread to the entire island but arguments between Charles and Parliament over who should control an English expeditionary force caused serious delays in its creation. Meanwhile, **Scotland** sent troops to protect its settlers in Ulster where retaliatory atrocities against Catholics occurred. By May 1642, Irish forces controlled the entire island bar the largest towns and the area around Dublin. In the same month, a Confederation of Ireland was proclaimed at Kilkenny, and this was followed by the establishment of a provisional government, supreme council, a national treasury and a mint. The outbreak of the **Civil Wars** in England later that year, prevented the arrival of loyalist reinforcements and the defeat of a Scottish/settler army at Benburb (1646) meant that a stalemate ensued.

Parliament's victory in the Civil Wars would prove to be catastrophic for Ireland's newfound autonomy. In August 1649, **Oliver Cromwell**'s well-trained and well-equipped **New Model Army** landed in Dublin and began a reconquest of the island which included the massacring of soldiers and civilians in Drogheda and Wexford. In 1652, the Confederation's last forces at Galway surrendered and brutal guerrilla warfare was finally ended by English use of scorched-earth tactics including the forced removal of entire civilian populations. The war brought untold misery and destruction to the island. Many thousands of Irish and English troops were killed by disease alone, but civilians suffered more from the accompanying scourge of famine that further weakened their resistance to disease. It has been estimated that the fighting of 1641–53 wiped out around 20 per cent of the Irish population or 420,000 people.

The Act of Settlement (1652) ordered the largest confiscation of lands ever seen in Ireland; land owned by Catholics fell from 60 per cent to 8 per cent. Even those who had remained neutral either had to become tenants on their old lands or resettle in less fertile western parts. Most of the available estates were then either given to London merchants who had financed the reconquest or New Model soldiers in lieu of unpaid wages. On top of this, those involved in the 1641 rebellion, along with any Catholic priests that were found, were to be executed and no Catholics could enter Parliament or live in towns. Thousands of ex-soldiers were allowed to leave and serve in other countries, but many were also sold as indentured servants to sugarcane and tobacco plantations in the West Indies and America. The owners put little trust in these 'papist' arrivals, but their labour was sorely needed, a point highlighted by the practice of 'spiriting' whereby huge numbers of Irish men, women and children were, in effect, kidnapped and transported illegally to the New World.

Hope for many came in the form of the Restoration in 1660 when **Charles II** promised religious toleration. A new Act of Settlement (1662) attempted to return the lands of Catholics who had always remained loyal to the Crown but strong opposition from settlers and the Protestant-dominated Irish Parliament meant that only the wealthiest and those best connected benefited. Religious uniformity became more laxly enforced though and some Catholics were even admitted to office. Their lot improved significantly in **James II**'s reign (1685–88) however. Increasing numbers of Catholics were appointed to the Lord Deputy's council, became judges and sheriffs and were allowed into the army. Catholic clergy were given protection and started to influence **education** and plans were made to re-examine the land issue.

The Protestant population was therefore much relieved when James was deposed during the **Glorious Revolution** and replaced by William of Orange (**William III**).

The Earl of Tyrconnell (the Lord Deputy appointed by James), however, was quick to raise an army of 45,000 men and seize all the strongholds bar Derry in the name of his king and James himself landed in Ireland with French troops in March 1689 – the first English king to do so since 1399. William, who was already at war with France, could ill-afford to allow Ireland into becoming a launching pad for a French invasion of England. He therefore sent troops to relieve Derry, but another, larger force succumbed to typhus amid the bogs and heavy rains near Dundalk. William himself then crossed over with an international force of English, Dutch and Danes and defeated the Jacobite forces at the Battle of the Boyne (July 1690), a significant victory in the sense that James then fled to France and effectively conceded defeat. Another victory at Aughrim followed by the capture of Limerick in the following year handed the Williamite forces control of the whole island. The war had not been as destructive as previous conflicts but the harsh strictures of the 1650s were reimposed, Irish soldiers were exiled and new restrictions on inheritance brought Catholic land ownership down to 5 per cent of the island over the following decades. From 1704, even the Presbyterians in the north, who had helped William, were barred from holding public office or bearing arms such was the belief that only Anglicans could be trusted. For the remainder of the Stuart period and beyond, Irish Jacobites continued to look to

James II embarks at Waterford for France. (*Artist: P. Pickaert or L. Scherm, 1691. Rijksmuseum*)

the Stuarts and the Irish regiments serving abroad to return and reverse the penal laws but, in 1715 and 1745, it was Scotland that they chose as their launch pad to regain the throne.

The suffering brought upon Irish **society** in the Tudor period had merely been a preamble to the disaster of the Stuart era. Their island became the victim of a more powerful neighbour that discriminated ruthlessly on the grounds of race and religion. A centralised government was, for the first time, established but this was only to facilitate the repression and economic exploitation by the English. Beef, cheese and timber, for example, were cheaply exported to Britain and its colonies, Irish cloth exports were suppressed to prevent competition with English cloth merchants while high tariffs on imports were imposed to raise more funds for the Exchequer. By 1700, most Irish people, now second-class citizens, were forced to survive as subsistence farmers while 90 per cent of the land was owned by the Protestant 25 per cent of the population. Their Catholic faith, however, was reinforced by brave missionaries trained on the continent and remained a unifying banner against the hated oppressors. The persecution of the Irish was to continue for centuries but the events of 1641, Drogheda and the Orangist victory of 1691 seared themselves into the collective Irish memory and sowed the seeds of the ugly sectarian violence that was to follow.

Ireton, Henry

(1611–51)

Soldier and politician

Ireton's parents were minor **Puritan** gentry from Nottinghamshire and, after completing his **education** at Trinity College, Oxford, and the Inns of Court, he returned to help manage his parents' estate. Contemporaries described him as 'a grave, serious, religious person' who was 'very active, industrious and stiff in his ways and purposes' and when the **Civil Wars** broke out in 1642, he had no doubts about joining **Parliament**'s side against King **Charles I**.

Appointed as captain of a troop of horse from Nottingham, he fought at Edgehill and, in 1643, met **Oliver Cromwell** while campaigning in Lincolnshire. Cromwell soon realised that Ireton was a man he could trust and gave him the responsibility of organising the defences around Ely. In 1644, he fought at Marston Moor and, afterwards, joined Cromwell in denouncing the half-hearted leadership of the Earls of Manchester and Essex which, in turn, led to the Self-denying Ordinance later that year. The night before the decisive Battle of **Naseby** (1645) Ireton led a daring raid into the royalist camp and captured some prisoners and, the following day, was given the command of the cavalry on the **New Model Army**'s left wing.

His forces, however, were shattered by **Prince Rupert**'s cavalry charge and he himself was wounded and captured but he managed to escape as Parliament's forces closed in on victory. Upon recovering from his wound, he fought in the campaigns to destroy the remaining royalist forces in the south-west and took a leading role in the successful siege of Oxford. A few days before its surrender, he even managed to find time to marry Cromwell's daughter, Bridget, at Cromwell's headquarters (June 1646).

1646–48 witnessed the complicated political manoeuvrings and negotiations that involved Charles, Parliament and the Army and Ireton was to play a key role. At first, like Cromwell, he believed in a constitutional monarchy in which Charles would keep his throne, with more limited powers, and religious liberty for all forms of Protestantism was allowed. Fearing that Charles and Parliament were about to make a deal that would enforce a **Presbyterian** Church, it was probably Ireton who ordered the king to be seized and become the army's captive. He was then largely responsible for drawing up the Heads of Proposals which were presented to Charles in July 1647. These offered Charles his throne in return for regular Parliaments, religious toleration, reduced power of bishops and Parliamentary appointments of all officials and officers for ten years.

While the king procrastinated, trouble broke out within the army. 'Agitators' within several regiments were angry about many months of unreceived pay and denounced Ireton for betraying his men while dealing with Charles. To defuse the situation, Ireton arranged the Putney Debates (October) in which the Agitators could present their grievances to the senior army officers known as the Grandees. Of all the Agitators' demands the most radical was that of universal male suffrage which Ireton refused, eloquently arguing that it would lead to anarchy. The Grandees did, however, calm the situation by promising to amend the Heads of Proposals and arrange the payment of owed wages.

Ireton's thinking regarding the king was radicalised by Charles's flight to the Isle of Wight (November) and the subsequent Second Civil War in 1648. He realised, earlier than Cromwell, that no deal with the king was possible and, after suppressing the royalist revolts in Kent and Essex, focused on bringing Charles to account. In November, he was the principal drafter of the *Remonstrance of the Army* which condemned Parliament's continuing negotiations with the king and justified the need to bring him to justice (possibly Ireton was among the first to desire his execution). This was soon followed by him ordering Colonel Pride to purge Parliament of all moderate MPs which left a 'Rump' that voted to put Charles on trial. Ever-present as one of the court's commissioners, Ireton signed the death warrant that led to the king's execution in January 1649.

That summer, he was promoted to major-general and was second-in-command to Cromwell in the expedition to reconquer **Ireland**. He was present at the massacres in Drogheda and Wexford and, after being appointed Lord Deputy, he revealed his plans to extend English colonisation (he took 14,000 acres for himself) and suppress the

Catholic religion. Ireton took charge of the military operation after Cromwell's recall the following year and showed much skill and brutality in completing the conquest. He did petition Parliament to offer lenient peace terms to bring the war to a swift conclusion but, after this was rejected, he resorted to scorched-earth tactics to combat the guerrillas (known as 'tories') that threatened his lines of communication. He made a strategic error by not attacking Limerick while its defences were weak and then suffered heavy casualties before finally starving it into surrender in October 1651. Exhausted by months of energetic campaigning, Ireton was killed soon after by the **plague** that had been rampaging through the town.

Pride's Purge. Soldiers block Presbyterian MPs' entrance to Parliament. (*Artist: unknown, from T. Roosevelt's Oliver Cromwell, 1900 via Project Gutenberg*)

Cromwell mourned the loss of his right-hand man and ordered a state funeral in Westminster Abbey. In 1661, though, both their bodies were disinterred by the restored monarchy, gibbetted at Tyburn and their heads displayed at Westminster. Henry Ireton has often been regarded as Cromwell's mere shadow, but he was much more than that. He may have lacked Cromwell's broad range of mind but neither did he share Cromwell's hesitancy, and it was he that provided the driving force that led to the creation of the English republic.

J

James I

(1566–1625)

King James VI of **Scotland** (1567–1625) and
King James I of England and **Ireland** (1603–25)

James was born in Edinburgh Castle, his parents being Mary, Queen of Scots and Henry Stuart, Lord Darnley, both great-grandchildren of King Henry VII of England. At the christening, his mother refused to let the Archbishop of

St Andrew's spit into the baby's mouth as was customary, but she was to have little other effect on his life. In 1567, her **marriage** to her husband's suspected murderer sparked off a rebellion that deposed her and she never saw her son again. Scotland was ruled by a series of regents while James was given a strictly Protestant upbringing (and regular beatings by one of his tutors) until 1583 when he assumed effective control of the country.

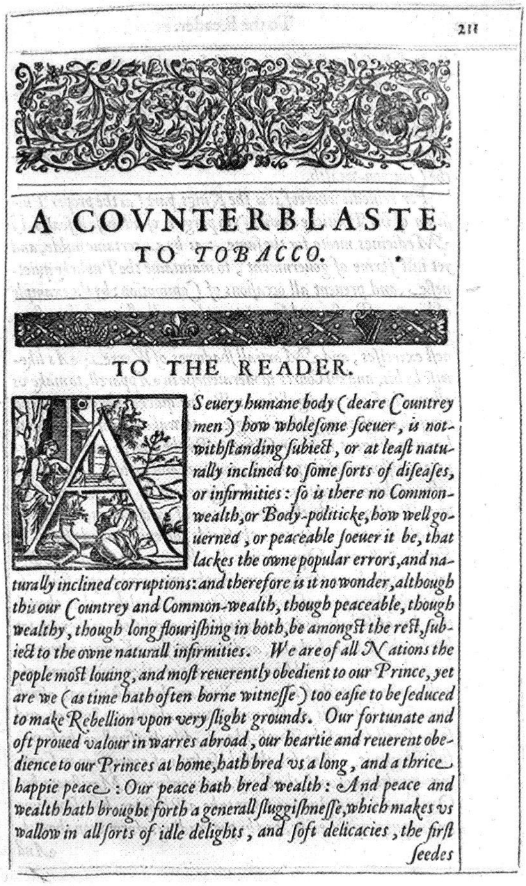
211

A COVNTERBLASTE TO TOBACCO.

TO THE READER.

AS euery humane body (deare Countrey men) how wholesome soeuer, is notwithstanding subiect, or at least naturally inclined to some sorts of diseases, or infirmities: so is there no Common-wealth, or Body-politicke, how well gouerned, or peaceable soeuer it be, that lackes the owne popular errors, and naturally inclined corruptions: and therefore is it no wonder, although this our Countrey and Common-wealth, though peaceable, though wealthy, though long flourishing in both, be amongst the rest, subiect to the owne naturall infirmities. We are of all Nations the people most louing, and most reuerently obedient to our Prince, yet are we (as time hath often borne witnesse) too easie to be seduced to make Rebellion vpon very slight grounds. Our fortunate and oft proued valour in warres abroad, our heartie and reuerent obedience to our Princes at home, hath bred vs a long, and a thrice happie peace: Our peace hath bred wealth: And peace and wealth hath brought forth a generall sluggishnesse, which makes vs wallow in all sorts of idle delights, and soft delicacies, the first

seedes

A counterblast to tobacco. James tells readers that peace and wealth have brought sluggishness and idle delights to citizenry. (*Author: James I, 1604. Wellcome Collection*)

For the next twenty years, he showed himself to be a very effective monarch. He successfully negotiated his way through the notorious factionalism among the lords and asserted greater royal control over Scotland including the imposition of his authority over the Kirk (Church of Scotland) by appointing bishops despite its **Presbyterian** nature. James's marriage, in 1589, to **Anne of Denmark** was initially a very loving one and produced three heirs (Henry, **Elizabeth** and **Charles**) who survived childhood. James also revealed himself to be a very enthusiastic scholar. His *The True Law of Free Monarchies* (1598) set out his belief in the divine right of kings and *Basilikon Doron* (1599) was an instruction book for his son, Henry, on how to rule and included the advice that parliaments should seldom be summoned. *Daemonologie* (1597) revealed his great interest in **witchcraft**, which he considered to be a branch of theology (he would personally supervise the torture of 'witches') and his *Counter-Blaste to Tobacco* (1604) denounced the new habit of smoking which he said was 'dangerous to the Lungs'.

For most of his reign, however, James's primary aim was to acquire the English throne for which he was the most obvious heir after the childless Elizabeth. His cultivation of her goodwill (he only made a token protest after the English queen beheaded his mother, for example) and behind-the-scenes work by her chief minister, **Robert Cecil**, allowed for his smooth accession to the English throne when she died in 1603. Despite possessing an innate dislike of the Scots, the English welcomed their new king jubilantly. Elizabeth's last years had been marred by economic hardships, but the pervading sense of gloom was lifted by the arrival of a new monarch whose healthy children dispelled the prevailing uncertainties about the royal succession.

Indeed, the contrast with his predecessor could not have been starker. Whereas the queen had projected a godlike image to her awestruck people, James took little care in public relations. When told that an adoring crowd had come to glimpse him, he cried, 'God's wounds! I will pull down my breeches and they shall also see my arse!' His court was more open and accessible but became seedier and known for sex scandals and, at its centre, was a king with spindly legs (he often had to lean on a courtier) and an over-large tongue (he appeared to slobber as he ate and drank) who became known for his coarse language (when he could be understood through his thick Scottish accent) and bouts of drunkenness. More shocking (to us, not then) were his interviews with couples requesting the intimate details of their post-wedding nights. Moreover, despite sodomy being a crime, he almost certainly had homosexual affairs with his two main favourites – Robert Carr (until 1616) followed by **George Villiers**. James, however, was clever at creating rival factions in court and, by acting as their arbiter, prevented others from gaining too much power. As for day-to-day business, for which he showed little interest, he delegated this to able ministers such as Cecil and (afterwards) Lionel Cranfield.

Religion

The Church of England was less than fifty years old when James became its head and there were two main groups who resented their enforced membership – **Catholics** and **Puritans**. By 1603, only around a fifth of the population was Catholic and the vast majority of these had displayed their loyalty to the Crown. They did, however, appeal to the king to remove the fines for non-attendance of **Anglican** services. James had to tread a thin line though. On the one hand, he had a natural tendency to religious toleration and wanted to keep on good terms with Catholic Spain. On the other, he was fully aware of the anti-Catholic mood in the country, a mood that flared up in the wake of the minor Main and Bye Plots (1603) and more serious **Gunpowder Plot** of 1605. These were therefore followed by harsher anti-Catholic laws but, over the course of his reign, James allowed the lax enforcement of these laws and Catholics were allowed to worship privately.

At the other end of the spectrum were the Puritans. They had lost the militancy they had once had but still desired a more strictly Protestant Church with no traces of Catholicism and James agreed to hear their views at the **Hampton Court Conference** (1604). The king enjoyed showing off his theological knowledge and making it clear that he was the ultimate Church authority, but he agreed to implement some of their main requests. Due to his natural indolence, perhaps, these reforms never happened other than the creation of the hugely important **King James Bible** in 1611. Afterwards, James made it clear that he wanted no more discussion of religious reform and some Puritan clergy were sacked but, as with Catholics, he showed a high degree of tolerance and even permitted Puritans' prophesying meetings (discussion groups that Elizabeth had banned).

The spectre of religious strife kept its head down during James's reign partly because he successfully displayed a willingness to compromise and be tolerant and because he acted as an impartial arbiter who took no sides (other than the established Church). Only near the end of his reign, did he reveal a leaning towards High Church (Arminianism), a doctrine to which his son critically attached himself.

Foreign Affairs

The principle behind James's foreign policy was that of pacifism. The Treaty of London (1604) ended the ruinously expensive, nineteen-year war with Spain but was condemned by many contemporaries as a betrayal of their fellow Protestants fighting for independence in the Dutch Republic. James, however, ensured that the treaty did not ban any unofficial aid while the Spanish agreed to end their

Sack of Magdeburg (1631). The destruction of this German city and slaughter of 20,000 inhabitants by a Catholic army horrified Protestant Europe. (*Artist: D. Manasser, 1632. Ludwig-Maximilians-Universität München*)

interference in Ireland. This, in turn, ended any lingering hopes that Irish Catholics had of outside assistance and facilitated further land acquisitions by English and Scottish colonists.

The king then turned to his dream of uniting the realms of England and Scotland to prevent any more conflicts between the two. He declared himself to be King of Great Britain, planned a new union currency starting with a 20-shilling coin called a 'unite' and decreed the design of the first union jack flag (1606). Parliament, however, considered Scotland a barbaric place which would only have a detrimental effect on England. The Scottish Parliament too, fearing domination by a more powerful neighbour, rejected the idea. In the end, much to James's disappointment, all that was agreed was the repeal of mutually hostile laws and an extradition treaty.

In his role as *Rex Pacifica*, James aimed to be the non-aligned mediator of international relations by marrying his children into Europe's opposing religious camps. As a result, Elizabeth was wedded to the Protestant Frederick, Elector of the Palatinate in Germany, and efforts were made to marry Henry into the Catholic Hapsburg royal family of Spain. More active and outgoing than his brother and more popular and dignified than his father, Henry's death from typhoid in 1612 came as a terrible shock to everyone. James then sought a Spanish match for Charles but events in Europe made this perceived pro-Spanish policy unpopular. The outbreak of the Thirty Years' War and the loss of his son-in-law's lands to invading Catholic Hapsburg forces (1620) created a war party at home that demanded hostilities against Spain but James, ever the pacifist, only condoned a volunteer force that was eventually forced to surrender in Germany. The humiliation that followed Charles's and Buckingham's 'secret' trip to woo the Spanish Infanta in 1623 heightened calls for a declaration of war and James's refusal led some to believe that he was involved in a 'Popish Plot' to subvert the English Church and Parliament. War inevitably followed soon after his death.

Finance

James had a prickly relationship with Parliament for which a large part of the blame was his. Not inserting enough of his privy councillors into the Commons meant that he had less control over the debates and his tendency to lecture MPs about divine right and his royal prerogative caused much alarm especially given the trend of growing monarchist absolutism on the continent. In private discussions, however, he was adept at negotiation and compromise and thereby allaying most MPs' fears. The main sticking point between the two, though, was the subject of royal revenue. In 1603, the crown debt was £400,000; five years later it had risen by 50 per cent. This was partly because, unlike Elizabeth, he had the extra expenses of a royal family, but the problem was magnified by his extravagance. Elizabeth had become particularly parsimonious, but James was overly generous in giving away money and lands in the belief that this was the best way of maintaining loyal courtiers although accusations of favouring his Scottish retinue, such as Carr,

A James I shilling. The use of soft silver allowed it to be clipped. The practice of coin clipping led to mistrust in the currency and ended when grooved edges were introduced in 1696. (*Artist: Tower Mint, 1603–25. Portable Antiquities Scheme*)

were unfair as he was equally benevolent to his English courtiers. Less defensible, however, were the huge outgoings in private expenditure. Designed by **Inigo Jones**, the Banqueting House at Whitehall Palace alone cost a huge £15,600 while the queen was also criticised for her lavish masques and commissioning of the Queen's House at Greenwich.

Insufficient grants from Parliament meant that James sought other sources of revenue such as the sale of crown lands (which led to reduced annual income), wardships (income from lands inherited by minors), impositions (import duties) and monopolies (selling the right to sole control of trade in any item, which inevitably raised its price). A particularly derided scheme was the selling of titles. Anyone with enough money could buy a knighthood from one of the king's courtiers and James created a new title – baronet – which was sold for £1,000. Inevitably, the value of both titles quickly became devalued amid concerns about the damage done to a **society** that valued respect and deference to the upper class. In his role as Lord Treasurer, Cecil made futile efforts to persuade James to be more frugal and, in 1610, he came up with an innovative plan called the Great Contract. In return for the king giving up some of his feudal revenues such as the unpopular wardships, Parliament would grant an annual sum of £200,000. After initial agreement, however, both sides dragged their feet then raised their terms which led to a collapse in negotiations and James dissolving Parliament early the next year.

For the next ten years, the king ruled without Parliament and continued to struggle financially while the royal debt increased. For two months in 1614, there was the 'Addled Parliament', but this was quickly dissolved after its complaints about impositions. In 1618, the merchant, Lionel Cranfield, was employed to investigate ways of making each government department more cost-efficient and was very successful in reducing royal expenditure. His solutions were only short term, though, the main problem being that too many courtiers, such as Buckingham, had too much self-interest in maintaining a system in which they profited very nicely. Increasingly short of money, James finally summoned his third Parliament in 1621 but was met, inevitably, by complaints about his attempts to circumvent Parliament as the sole provider of the Crown's finances.

* * *

In the final year of his life, James cut an increasingly isolated figure as he suffered from arthritis, gout, kidney stones and fainting fits, thereby giving Buckingham the opportunity to consolidate his control over the heir. A stroke followed by a violent attack of dysentery finally finished him off in March 1625. James I's reign has traditionally attracted negative views from historians and usually been seen as the precursor to, and even the cause of, all the troubles of his son's reign. However, this is not a fair judgement. It is true that James hindered all attempts by competent ministers to improve the Crown's solvency, a crucial factor that led to the outbreak of the **Civil Wars**. Towards the end of his reign, he also eased

James I and his family. Adults from left: Henrietta Maria, Charles I, Anne of Denmark, James I, Henry, Frederick, Elizabeth. Skulls on laps represent death. (*Artist: J. Webster, 1625 and 1634. British Museum*)

open the religious fault line by obstinately pursuing the Spanish Match – despite contrary public opinion – and promoting Arminianism, which alarmed Puritan elements within society. It was the fracturing of this fissure in 1641 that precipitated the ensuing violence.

Despite this, as well as his pomposity, laziness and sordid court, there is much in James that deserves praise. His pacifism gave England a long period of peace and averted all the expense, risk and hardship of war and, for the most part, his leniency and non-alignment smoothed over all religious differences. His handling of Parliament could have been better, but he was a shrewd operator who was willing to negotiate and compromise. Such flexibility would have done his son many favours. Indeed, it is fascinating, if somewhat pointless, to consider the 'what might have beens' had Prince Henry – a very different character to Charles – not caught typhoid.

James II

(1633–1701)

King of England, **Scotland** (as James VII) and **Ireland** from 1685 to 1688

As Duke of York

James was born in St James's Palace, the second son of **Charles I** and **Henrietta Maria**. His upbringing, in a loving household, was disrupted, aged 9, when the royal family had to flee London during the prelude to the **Civil Wars**. He was a spectator at the Battle of Edgehill (1642) and for the next four years, he lived in Oxford – the royalist capital. His mother and elder siblings (Charles and Mary) had already fled when **Parliament**'s forces captured the city, and James, along with his father and younger siblings (Elizabeth, Henry and Henrietta) were captured and held at the place of his birth. Soon after, Parliament toyed with the idea of making James king to fill the power vacuum but, in April 1648, he dressed as a girl and made a daring escape to the Dutch Republic.

After hearing of his father's execution (1649) and the founding of the republican Commonwealth, James embarked on a military career by joining the army of his cousin, the French king, Louis XIV. Serving under the great general, Turenne, he gained a reputation for bravery but when Louis decided to ally with the English republic he was forced to serve in the Spanish army instead. His new employers gave him command of six regiments of British royalist volunteers that fought on the right wing in the Battle of the Dunes (1658) where, despite personally leading several charges himself, James and his allies were defeated. Afterwards, he considered serving in the Spanish navy as an admiral, but everything changed in 1660 with the Restoration and proclamation of his brother as King **Charles II**.

Upon his return to England, James was restored to his title of Duke of York and was also appointed Duke of Albany and Lord High Admiral. Later, in the same year, both Mary and Henry died from smallpox but, by that time, he had scandalously seduced Anne Hyde, the daughter of Charles's chief minister, **Edward Hyde**. Possibly ordered by his brother to fulfil an earlier promise to Anne, James secretly married her when she became pregnant despite the shock caused by this **marriage** to a commoner. Anne went on to have seven children, all of whom died in infancy except for the future queens, **Mary II** and **Anne** with whom James displayed a loving and playful nature. Anne was a strong character but there was little she could do about her husband's string of mistresses such as Arabella Churchill (sister of **John Churchill**). Indeed, **Samuel Pepys** called him 'the most unguarded ogler of his time' after he spent one evening eyeing up Mrs Pepys. Anne bitterly complained and even retaliated by having her own affair but nonetheless she is thought to have been a strong influence on James and, herself being a converted **Catholic**, probably persuaded him to adopt the same faith in the late 1660s. Weakened by a quick succession of multiple births, she died from breast cancer in 1671.

James was a prominent figure in Charles's reign. He gained much popularity for his decisive action during the **Fire of London**, and his prestige was further raised when he led the English fleet during the **Second** and **Third Anglo-Dutch Wars**, showing sang-froid during the Battle of Lowestoft (1665) when a courtier standing next to him was decapitated. Earlier, Charles had granted his brother lands in America and when the fleet captured New Amsterdam (1664), it was renamed New York in James's honour. James also profited as the governor of the Royal African Company which traded in gold, silver and **slaves** (branded 'DY' on their chests for 'Duke of York') from West Africa.

However, his change of religion was to be the source of much trouble later in Charles's reign. Parliament's Test Act of 1673 banned anyone refusing to take the **Anglican** communion from holding public office and James felt compelled to resign as Lord High Admiral, thereby revealing his new faith. Later that year, he married the 15-year-old Italian Catholic, Mary of Modena, who many people suspected

Mary of Modena. The cockatoo is depicted as a symbol of luxury. (*Artist: W. Wissing, 1687. Scottish National Gallery*)

of being a papist agent aiming to restore England to the Catholic fold. Charles denounced his brother's conversion, but the problem was all too clear to see: the king's wife, **Catherine of Braganza**, had still not produced any children, which made James the most likely heir to the throne. Opponents to James's accession – the **Whigs** – coalesced around **Anthony Ashley Cooper** while those who supported the principle of hereditary succession were called **Tories**. Matters came to a head in 1678 when the **Popish Plot** claimed there was a Catholic conspiracy to overthrow the government. Amid the ensuing hysteria, Charles urged James to adopt a low profile by moving to Brussels and then to Edinburgh to oversee the Scottish government. The king then fought hard to preserve his brother's inheritance as Whigs tried to exclude him from the succession but, by 1682, the crisis had died down, and James returned to London. In the following year, news spread of a Whig conspiracy to assassinate Charles and James – the **Rye House Plot**. The subsequent wave of sympathy for the brothers and purge of Whigs from Parliament and the judiciary enabled the Crown to put itself in a position of strength not seen since 1641.

As King

The man who ascended the throne upon Charles's death in February 1685 was very different to his brother. Although similar in their large stature, James was fairer with blue eyes and lacked his brother's wit and warmth. Certainly, he was a harder worker who people considered more serious and trustworthy, but his fatal flaw was his obstinacy. Whereas Charles had always been shrewdly expedient, James lacked both flexibility and an understanding of the English psyche. Charles realised this when he uttered, '*la sottise de mon frère*' ('the stupidity of my brother') and predicted that James would not last more than four years as king – a prophecy that turned out to be uncannily accurate. Arguably, however, no monarch had enjoyed such an advantageous start to a reign since 1509. Basking in a glow of loyalty, James had no active political opponents, and his Catholicism was largely ignored as Mary had produced no children, and both of his daughters had been raised as Protestants. He was also in a great position of solvency – crown revenue had increased dramatically due to a boom in trade; this was further increased when the 'Loyal Parliament' voted the king a generous, perennial annual income. James's position was further strengthened that summer when Protestant revolts in the south-west (**Monmouth's Rebellion**) and Scotland were both crushed having received little popular support.

The mood changed, however, in the autumn of 1685. With characteristic lack of tact, James announced to Parliament that he wanted to repeal the Test Act and maintain a standing army (not seen since the 1650s and considered a tool of political repression) and had already promoted Catholic officers within the army. Parliament was then prorogued and did not meet again for the rest of his reign. News from France further poisoned the atmosphere. Louis XIV's Revocation of the

Edict of Nantes reignited the persecution of the Huguenots (French Protestants) there. Waves of Huguenot refugees brought with them horror stories that only strengthened the belief that Catholicism and despotism were one and the same.

Far from placating Anglicans' fears, James stoked them. In the test case of *Godden vs Hales* (1686), a rigged court of judges ruled that the monarch could overrule Parliament and ignore the Test Act by appointing Catholics to positions of authority. At the same time, James funded missionary campaigns, encouraged the building of Catholic chapels and schools, created more Catholic officers in the armed forces and stationed his standing army of 16,000 men on Hounslow Heath to overawe the capital. He then suspended the Bishop of London for refusing to clamp down on anti-Catholic sermons and began to insert Catholics into important posts in various Oxford colleges. In Ireland, all the tools of persecution of Catholics were removed and when similar attempts were rebuffed by the Scottish Parliament, James resorted to the royal prerogative.

By 1687, it was clear to the king that the Anglican Church would be the main opponent to his reforms and so attempted to ally with the Protestant dissenters (such as **Presbyterians**, Baptists and Quakers) by issuing a Declaration of Indulgence which granted toleration to all religions. A campaign was then launched to purge municipal authorities and justices of the peace to provide majorities of Catholics and dissenters who could provide compliant members for the next Parliament. It is doubtful that the dissenters would have lent their support to creating a packed Commons but two incidents in mid-1688 precipitated a chain of events that would prevent James from summoning another Parliament anyway.

The first was the refusal by the Archbishop of Canterbury and six bishops to endorse the king's Declaration of Indulgence to be read out in all churches. In fact, it was only read out in 200 of the country's 9,000 churches with many congregations walking out upon hearing it. James then made the catastrophic mistake of suspending the bishops and incarcerating them in the Tower of London, thereby creating popular figureheads of opposition. Public anger then turned to scenes of joy when, on 30 June, the bishops were acquitted in court, the seven celebratory candles that were lit in people's windows showing the king just how widespread the opposition to his policies had become. In the same month, came news that Queen Mary had given birth to a boy. James had been tolerated while his heirs were Protestants but now an unlimited period of Catholic rule loomed. Attempts were made to discredit the royal birth, including claims that another's baby had been smuggled into the palace in a warming pan, but many now realised that drastic action was required to save the country from the kind of events that were unfolding in France.

On the same day that the seven bishops were acquitted, seven leading politicians – both Tory and Whig – invited the Protestant Stadtholder of Holland, **William of Orange**, to save them from their tyrannical monarch. William was keen to bring England into his alliance against France and probably hoped to safeguard his wife's

The Seven Bishops in the Tower. (*Artist: P. Schenck, 1688 via Wikimedia Commons*)

inheritance (he was married to James's eldest daughter, Mary) and so launched an invasion fleet in November 1688. James attempted some last-minute concessions, but it was all in vain as William slowly marched on London from Devon and popular uprisings occurred in Cheshire and Yorkshire. Suffering from insomnia and persistent nose bleeds as well as a string of desertions among senior officers, James lost his nerve and ordered his forces to retreat. Upon hearing that his own daughter, Anne, had fled the court he lamented 'God help me ... my own children have forsaken me', but even at this stage, he could have retained his throne. Most Tories did not support a coup, and William had never been asked to replace him. James, however, possibly feared the same fate as his father and, after botching his first escape attempt, fled to France after dropping the Great Seal into the Thames as a final act of sabotage. In effect, this abdication of power enabled the **Glorious Revolution** and accession of William and Mary.

Three months later, James landed in Ireland with French troops to win back his crown. There, his loyal supporters gathered an army for him, but this was defeated at the Battle of the Boyne (1690) and he hastily fled back to France again. For this reason, some of his erstwhile Irish supporters referred to him as *Séamus an Chaca* or 'James the Shit' but they continued to fight on in his name until defeated the following year. Thereafter, he spent the rest of his life in exile in a small chateau near Paris spending more time in devotional prayers and hunting than making any effort to regain his throne. Louis XIV once offered to have him crowned King of Poland, but James refused, persistent in his belief that the English would eventually accept him. He finally died from a brain haemorrhage, aged 67, and the Jacobite cause was taken up by his son, James, and his grandson, Charles. Both led abortive uprisings in Scotland (1715 and 1745 respectively) after which Jacobitism was effectively finished.

Some efforts have been made to portray James II as an enlightened monarch who promoted religious toleration. Some state that he may not have sought absolutism and merely believed that, with time, Catholicism would have gradually been embraced by the English again. It is very difficult, however, to get past his narrow-minded, political blindness. With all the initial advantages that he enjoyed, one feels that even with half of his brother's wits he would have accomplished a great deal more but his determination to promote a faith that was shared by only 3 per cent of the population was doomed to failure. Even Louis XIV and the pope recognised that no good would come of it and vainly urged him to backtrack. Just as bizarre was his belief that the dissenters, themselves only 5 per cent of the population, would help bring his reforms to fruition. Like his father, James paid the price for being completely out of touch with the nation.

James, Duke of York

see James II

Jones, Inigo

(1573–1652)

Designer and architect

Little is known of Jones's early life. The son of a Smithfield cloth-worker, he came from a humble background; some claim that he had Welsh origins and had been baptised Ynyr Jones. Around the turn of the seventeenth century, he appeared as an apprentice joiner, and it seems that a wealthy patron was so impressed with his sketches that he sent him to Italy to study drawing. While there, his work impressed King Christian IV of Denmark who decided to employ Jones on the design of a couple of palaces in his home country.

After Jones returned to England in 1605, Christian probably recommended him to his sister – **Anne of Denmark** – and wife of **James I**. Anne employed Jones as the designer of sets and costumes for her masques. These were a fashionable form of entertainment in the royal court that combined acting, singing and dancing by performers wearing elaborate costumes and masks. Performances, based on mythological gods and English history, were allegorical and hinted at the divine right of the Stuarts; 'anti-masques', performed by wild, drunken dancers, would symbolise the chaos before the Stuarts. Jones is the first producer to maximise stage space, use curtains for scene changes, create moveable scenery and experiment with lighting and, in the *Masque of Blacknesse*, he astonished the audience with his sea monsters and realistic waves. For many years, he collaborated with the playwright, **Ben Jonson**, who created the scripts but eventually the two fell out over which was more important – the spoken word or visual effects.

Inigo Jones. (*Artist: W. Hollar after van Dyck, 1655. Thomas Fisher Rare Book Library*)

Jones continued to work on royal masques right up until 1640, but he had also started to show an interest in architecture. In 1613, he was invited to join the Earl of Arundel's touring party of Italy and, while there, he explored the ancient Roman ruins and studied the works of the great Renaissance architect, Andrea Palladio, himself greatly influenced by ancient Greek and Roman architecture. Upon his return, in 1615, Jones was appointed Surveyor of the King's Works and went on to benefit from the extravagant largesse of the first two Stuart monarchs by implementing a new style that the English had never seen in their buildings. Only a few of his creations still survive, one of the most notable being the Queen's House in Greenwich. Commissioned first by Anne in 1616 and later by Queen **Henrietta Maria**, it was revolutionary for its time and incorporated classical features such as the long portico of columns, vertical motifs and mathematical symmetry. His other famous project was the rebuilding of the Banqueting House, in Whitehall Palace, after it had burned down in 1619. Based on the basilica design of ancient Rome, it included a ceiling painted by Paul Rubens that glorified the Stuart dynasty. Ironically, it was under this very painting that **Charles I** walked before being beheaded on a scaffold outside the Banqueting House.

Jones also built the Queen's Chapel in St James's Palace (completed 1625) and was commissioned by the Earl of Bedford to design a residential square on his land at Covent Garden. This was the first planned town square in England and was based on the piazza in Livorno, Italy. Its arcaded houses have since disappeared but St Paul's Church and its impressive portico, on the west side, still survives. For much of the 1630s, Jones was employed in redesigning St Paul's Cathedral. Tragically, his work was destroyed by the **Fire of London** (1666) but was a major influence on **Christopher Wren** when he rebuilt the cathedral and many other churches.

Being so closely linked with the monarchy, Jones felt compelled to leave London when the **Civil Wars** broke out in 1642. Three years later, he was captured by Parliamentary forces at the third siege of Basing House and, having had his clothes ripped off him by soldiers, was carried out wearing only a blanket. He was heavily fined but then pardoned in the following year and, for the rest of his life lived, unmarried, at Somerset House. Inigo Jones was England's first important architect who showed that it was possible, given enough talent and the right connections, to rise from humble origins and, more importantly, he left a lasting mark on English architecture and theatre.

Jonson, Ben

(1572–1637)

Poet and playwright

Jonson's father was of Scottish ancestry and joined the clergy after losing his lands under Mary I. He died a month before the birth of his son who later joined his stepfather's trade as a bricklayer before a family friend's generosity allowed him to attend Westminster School. Guided by the headmaster and famous scholar,

William Camden, Jonson soon developed a love of classical literature and poetry, but his **education** was cut short against his will when he returned to bricklaying instead of attending university. Soon afterwards, he joined the English army that was fighting the Spanish in the Netherlands and then, upon his return to England, married (1594) and began working as an actor for the Admiral's Men at the Swan Theatre. The company's producer, Philip Henslowe, started to employ him as a playwright but this new career was briefly threatened when Jonson was imprisoned for co-writing *The Isle of Dogs* which the authorities considered seditious.

Ben Jonson. (*Artist: G. Vertue after G. van Honthorst, 1711. Library of Congress*)

1598 marked the beginning of Jonson's rise to fame when he wrote the comedy, *Every Man in His Humour*, which included William Shakespeare among the cast. Later that year, however, he was jailed again for killing an actor in a duel but avoided the hangman's rope by claiming benefit of clergy. By reciting *Psalms 51:3* (known as the 'neck verse' as it saved one's neck!) an ecclesiastical court gave him the more lenient punishment of loss of goods and being branded with the Tyburn 'T' on his thumb. While in prison, Jonson came under the influence of a Jesuit inmate and converted to **Catholic**ism (in 1610, he reverted to the **Anglican** faith in protest at the murder of the religiously tolerant Henry IV of France by a Catholic). In the last years of Queen Elizabeth's reign, he took part in the 'War of the Theatres' in which his plays satirised the work of his rivals who, in turn, mocked him on stage for being boastful and attention-seeking.

It was during the reign of **James I** that Jonson's career became more prestigious despite attending a supper with conspirators in the **Gunpowder Plot** in October 1605. It was he, along with the designer **Inigo Jones**, who produced the fashionable and highly successful masques for the royal family. He wrote around twenty-five scripts and invented the riotous anti-masque – seen as a forerunner to pantomimes – but the different tastes of the new king in 1625 (**Charles I**) and a fallout with Jones led to this source of work drying up.

Concurrently, Jonson was writing the plays for which he is most famous. His satirical comedies were particularly popular – *Volpone* (1605), *The Silent Woman* (1609), *The Alchemist* (1610), *Bartholomew Fair* (1614) and *The Devil Is an Ass* (1616) – while his tragedies and later works were less favourably viewed. In these plays, he popularised and perfected the comedy of humours – comedies that focused on people's characters (humours). The pacey and sharp-witted *The*

Alchemist, for example, attacked mankind's vices, vanities and follies, especially greed and gullibility, poked fun at all levels of **society** and gives a valuable insight into life in early Stuart London. The poet, Samuel Coleridge, later stated that it had one of the three most perfect plots in English literature and it continues to be performed on stage.

In 1616, King James hired Jonson as the court's official poet with an annual pension, leading many to regard him as England's first Poet Laureate. He became particularly well known for his epigrams and country house poems. The former, written in rhyming couplets, were short verses that usually summed up his thoughts about various people of the time. Most were cynical but the poignant *On My First Son* summed up his feelings after the death of his 7-year-old child and starts with:

Farewell, thou child of my right hand, and joy;
My sin was too much hope of thee, lov'd boy.

The latter were written in praise of various aristocratic patrons by describing their stately homes; *To Penshurst*, for example, was written as a gift to Robert Sidney of Penshurst Place.

There is no doubt that Jonson was an immense figure in English renaissance literature. At his peak, in 1618, he embarked on a ten-week walk from London to Edinburgh and was lavishly welcomed in every town and country house along the way. Upon his arrival, he was made an honorary burgess of Edinburgh and, after his return, was given a rare honorary Master of Arts degree from Oxford University. Despite his decline in the 1620s, he enjoyed adulation by many aspiring writers, and some formed the 'Sons of Ben' who would regularly meet with Jonson in various London taverns where they hung onto his every word. In the early years of the seventeenth century, he rivalled Shakespeare himself and the two would engage in a combat of wits during literary meetings at the Mermaid Tavern. He had much praise (and some criticism) for the famous bard, and later critics, while praising Jonson, placed him second to Shakespeare who was considered a more natural genius with a broader range of ability.

Jonson must have been a difficult man to know. He spent most of his married life living apart from his wife and, although generous, was described as a quarrelsome man, much given to drinking, who loved himself and was contemptuous of others. After suffering the first of several strokes in 1628, he became increasingly bedridden but continued to write plays although none was successful. Upon his death, huge numbers, including nobility, turned out for his funeral. It appears, however, that he had become relatively poor and his estate could only afford a small space for his burial at Westminster Abbey and, consequently, Jonson is the only person there who was buried standing up. The inscription on his plaque simply reads 'O Rare Ben Jonson'.

K

Kidd, William

(1654–1701)

Privateer/pirate

Little is known of Kidd's early life, but he was probably the son of a sailor and born in Dundee. In the 1680s he was working in pirate crews operating in the Caribbean but by the end of the decade he had become a successful privateer who made a living attacking French vessels in the West Indies. The distinction between pirate and privateer could be quite blurred but, officially, it meant that Kidd had permission to use his own vessel to plunder designated enemies so long as a share of the profits went to the Admiralty in London. By 1691 he had become a respected member of New York **society**, living in Wall Street, and married to the city's wealthiest widow, Sarah Oort.

In 1695, Kidd was in London where he was asked by Lord Bellomont, the designated Governor of New York, to attack pirates and French shipping in the Indian Ocean and Red Sea. Four wealthy **Whig** politicians donated money to the scheme and, as England was at war with France, **William III** himself issued a royal commission to 'My trusty and well-beloved Captain Kidd' which included a warning not to attack shipping that was friendly to the Crown.

Kidd's new ship, *Adventure Galley*, loaded with thirty-four cannon along with 150 hand-picked crew and officers, left Deptford in early 1696. For some reason, near Greenwich, he failed to salute a passing Royal Navy ship and then his men added insult to injury by turning and slapping their backsides. The irate navy officer retaliated by pressing many of the privateers into the navy which forced Kidd to sail for New York to find replacements. Unfortunately, most of these were hardened criminals and ex-pirates.

Most of 1697 was spent fruitlessly searching for targets in the Indian Ocean. Many of his crew died from cholera or deserted and the others increasingly pressurised Kidd to capture any ship that would provide them with bounty. In one argument, over a Dutch vessel that he refused to attack, Kidd accidentally fractured a mutinous crewman's head with a bucket and killed him. His luck finally turned in January 1698 when they captured an Armenian vessel, *Quedagh Merchant*, sailing under French protection and laden with valuable satins, silks, gold and silver.

However, it was events back in England that were to seal Kidd's fate. Political infighting led to him being denounced as a pirate to bring down his Whig backers. The 1698 Act of Grace pardoned all pirates, but Kidd was specifically made exempt and, upon discovering this on his way home, he decided to sell off the

Quedagh Merchant's goods in the Caribbean and bury the proceeds in secret locations. Bellomont, meanwhile, was concerned about being implicated in Kidd's 'piratical' actions and wanted to clear his name. So, he lured him to Boston under the pretensions of clemency then promptly arrested him and sent him to London. Sarah, too, was imprisoned and never saw her husband again.

Kidd burying his treasure. (*Author: H. Pyle from his Book of Pirates, 1921 via Wikimedia Commons*)

In London, Kidd was held in the notoriously awful conditions of Newgate Prison. The **Tories** were now in power and hoped he would provide evidence to discredit their leading Whig opponents, but Kidd refused to talk. His erstwhile supporters, however, eagerly distanced themselves from him and even deprived him of the money necessary for a proper legal defence. At a rigged trial, in May 1700, he was accused of murder, piracy and, while in Madagascar, consorting with a very pirate he had been sent to capture. Testimonies were provided by former crewmates who had deserted him while his own evidence – French passes which proved that the *Quedagh Merchant* was a legitimate target – went 'missing'. Unsurprisingly, Kidd was found guilty and, in May 1701, was hanged at Tilbury. The rope snapped on the first attempt but, despite spectators' calls for his release due to this 'act of God', he was hanged a second time, and his body was left to rot for three years as a warning to any would-be pirates.

The exploits of Captain Kidd are said to have inspired Robert Louis Stevenson's *Treasure Island* and attempts to discover his hidden treasure continue. To date though, only one cache has been found (near Long Island), some of which went to pay for **Christopher Wren**'s Royal Naval College in Greenwich. The Golden Age of Piracy (1650–1730) with its legends of buried treasure has been romanticised but the shoddy treatment of Kidd merely revealed the murky side of England's political and legal systems.

King James Bible

(1611)

By the time **James I** acceded to the English throne in 1603, the Elizabethan Church of England was forty-five years old but there was no one authorised Bible in use. The official Bishops' Bible (1568) was largely based on Tyndale's

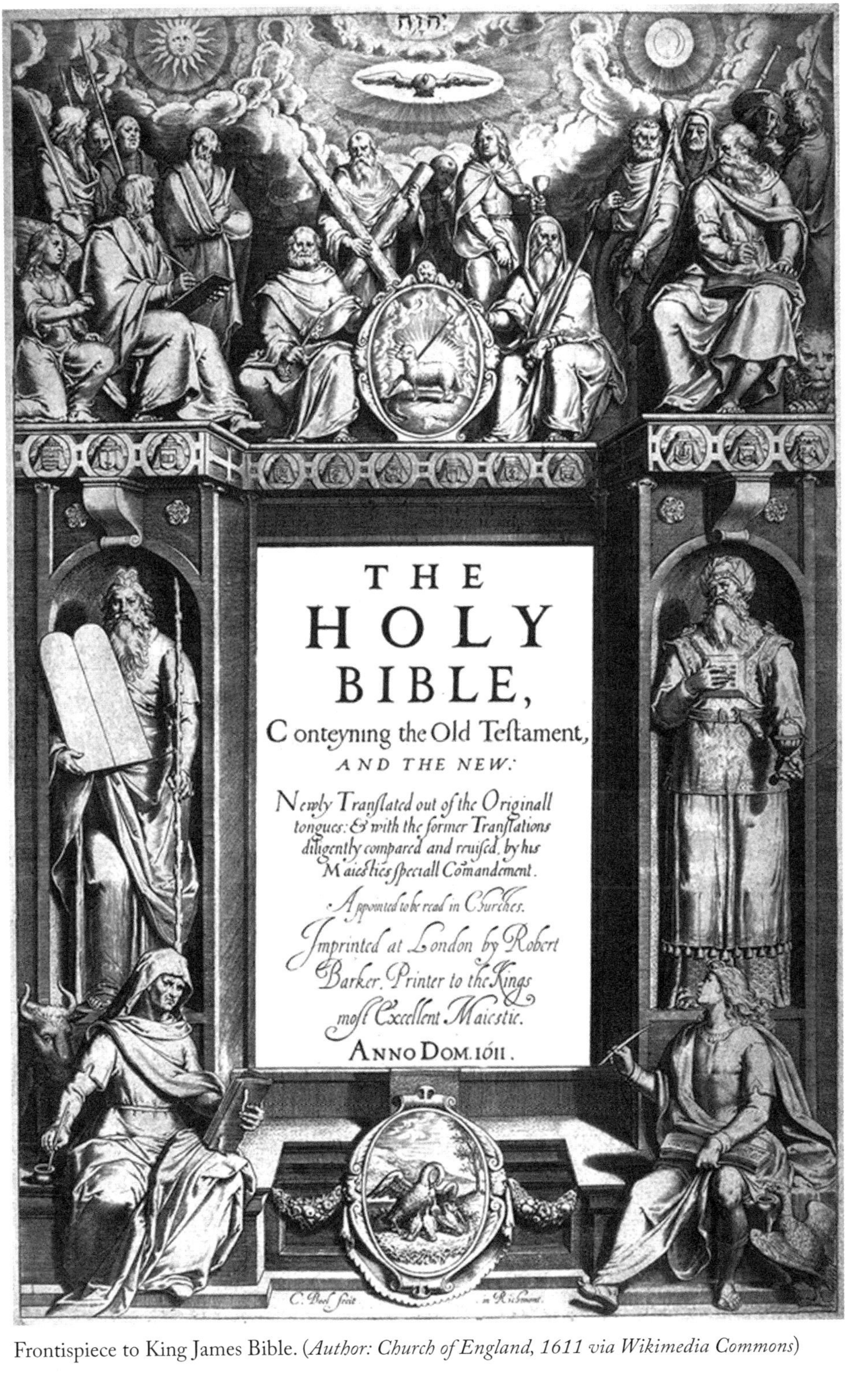

Frontispiece to King James Bible. (*Author: Church of England, 1611 via Wikimedia Commons*)

and Coverdale's earlier Great Bible but its attempts to translate from the original Hebrew were inconsistent and uninspiring. Alongside it was the Geneva Bible, originally produced in Switzerland by Protestant exiles during the reign of Mary I. Its smaller size, greater affordability and more powerful language made it more popular than its rival. However, it also included Calvinistic annotations that questioned the authority of the king and his bishops.

When, at the **Hampton Court Conference** (1604), leading theologians requested a new and more accurate edition of the Bible, James was only too happy to oblige and thereby rid himself of the Calvinistic references. Forty-seven scholars worked in three teams based in Cambridge, Oxford and Westminster, and were overseen by Archbishop Bancroft. Their attempts to faithfully translate from the original Hebrew and Greek combined with instructions to write in a simple and attractive form of English created a poetic masterpiece of the English language. Predominantly written in iambic pentameter and with much emphasis on imagery, the new Bible seemed to reach out to people in a way it had never done before.

Spellings were yet to be standardised, and printers often contracted or expanded words to create even columns of text. 'V' was used for capital 'u', 'u' replaced 'v' elsewhere and a long 's' (ſ) replaced any non-final 's'. Punctuation was overly heavy and some of the language was rather archaic even for contemporaries. For instance, *thou/thee* were used instead of *you*, *his* instead of *its* and *–eth* instead of *–s* at the end of verbs. Nevertheless, the translators also created a rich bank of idioms, 257 in all; twice as many as Shakespeare did. *A fly in the ointment, fight the good fight, let there be light, thorn in the side, we see eye to eye* and *kiss of death*, for example, all originate in the Bible.

The first two editions were finally printed in 1611 by the King's Printer, Robert Barker. They were popularly known as the 'He' and 'She' Bibles as the first stated '*he went into the city*' in Ruth 3:15 and the second had '*she went into the city*'. The King James Bible (KJB), also known as the Authorised Version (AV), gradually became accepted by all although the Geneva Bible remained popular in **Scotland** for a while and was the only version acceptable to **Oliver Cromwell** and the **New Model Army**. As language and knowledge of the ancient texts developed, the KJB underwent several editions over the following centuries, the most notorious being the Wicked Bible of 1631, so called because the word 'not' was omitted from the seventh commandment – 'Thou shalt not commit adultery'. For this, the printers were fined £300.

The twentieth century saw several updated editions, but the KJB is still the most popular version in the US, especially among Christian fundamentalists. More importantly, it is seen as the most influential book in the English-speaking world. With mass-printing now available, it entered almost every home and became the heart of American religious culture after it travelled across the Atlantic with the **Pilgrim Fathers**. Later, it followed the spread of the British Empire with its words translated by missionaries into native languages, and, in popular culture, its influence can be seen in Handel's *Messiah*, the works of Hemingway and Melville and Martin Luther King's *I Have a Dream* speech. The beauty of its language is such that even the famous atheist, Richard Dawkins, said, 'A native speaker of English who has never read a word of the King James Bible is verging on the barbarian.'

L

Lambe, John

(c. 1546–1628)

Astrologer and occultist

Almost nothing is known of Lambe's early life but by 1600 he had gained a reputation as a 'cunning man' – one who could provide helpful magic and repel **witchcraft**. Accusations of invoking evil spirits, however, got him into trouble with the Worcestershire authorities who sent him to the King's Bench prison in London. Lambe lived comfortably there for fifteen years and continued to practise the dark arts. Claiming to be a physician, he charged visitors exorbitant sums of money for 'healing' their maladies, doing harm to their enemies and using a crystal ball to find lost property.

John Lambe. (*From J. Caulfield's Biographical sketches, 1823. Wellcome Collection*)

By 1625, Lambe had been released and become a close advisor to the **Duke of Buckingham**. As Buckingham's power and influence over the new king, **Charles I**, increased so did his unpopularity and whilst some dismissed Lambe as a charlatan, others considered him to be a malign influence at the centre of power. A rhyme soon went around:

Who rules the Kingdom? The King.
Who rules the King? The Duke.
Who rules the Duke? The Devil!

Stories went around that he had summoned a violent whirlwind up the Thames that unearthed corpses from a churchyard and that he had conjured up a miniature tree out of thin air and three miniature woodmen to chop it down.

Many Londoners became terrified of him and thought their chance to get rid of him had finally come in 1626 when Lambe was accused of raping an 11-year-old girl. To their dismay, however, he was given a royal pardon and released. Nevertheless, by 1628, Buckingham had become so loathed that a mob decided to take justice into their own hands. On Friday 13 June, Lambe was spotted coming out of a theatre and pursued. The octogenarian made it to the safety of a tavern but was then ejected and beaten to death by the baying crowd. According to one eyewitness, his skull was broken and an eye was left hanging out of its socket.

Whilst Londoners rejoiced, a furious Buckingham fined the city for not seeking the culprits and imprisoned several constables. He himself, however, would be dead within two months.

Laud, William

(1573–1645)

Archbishop of Canterbury

Laud was born in Reading, the son of a wealthy cloth merchant and graduated from Oxford University in 1594. He was ordained a priest in 1601 before becoming a Doctor of Divinity and a don at St John's College. By now, it was clear that he supported Arminianism – a High Church form of **Anglican**ism that favoured an episcopal hierarchy and a return to various pre-Reformation forms of worship. Indeed, he caused controversy as Dean of Gloucester, by converting the wooden communion table into a stone altar and moving it to the choir. Clerical promotions came slowly largely because **James I** regarded him as a troublemaker: 'he hath a restless spirit and cannot see when matters are well.'

This, however, changed upon the accession of **Charles I** who saw Laud as a kindred spirit in religion. Being the chaplain to the king's favourite – the **Duke of Buckingham** – further oiled the wheels of promotion so that, by 1628, he was Bishop of London and privy councillor. It was Laud, along with **Thomas Wentworth**, who became the king's chief advisor when Charles

William Laud. (*Artist: W. Hollar after van Dyck, date unknown. Thomas Fisher Rare Book Library*)

embarked on his personal rule the following year and pursued his programme of 'Thorough' – strict implementation of royal policies.

In 1633, Laud was promoted to Archbishop of Canterbury. Now aged 60, he embarked on a programme of restoring the Church of England to its former pomp and glory by removing all traces of Calvinism (much favoured by **Puritans**), thereby fomenting the religious tensions that contributed to the **Civil Wars**. In line with his Arminian ideals, he ordered the beautifying of churches, the wearing of surplices by priests, the creation of altars with rails separating them from the congregation and more singing and bowing at the mention of Jesus's name during services as well as strict enforcement of the Book of Common Prayer. Laud saw the Puritans as a threat to the Church and rejected their key belief in predestination, banned them from preaching and used censors to stamp out their literature.

Intrusive visitations to each diocese ensured that his reforms were enforced while his harshest critics could expect to receive arbitrary justice in the Star Chamber and Court of High Commission. Most famous were the cases of William Prynne, Henry Burton and John Bastwick who were charged with seditious literature and speeches. For this, they were fined, imprisoned and had their ears cut off in the pillory (1637). The severity of the penalties caused popular unrest and many Puritans decided to escape persecution by emigrating to America. He even alienated much of the Anglican gentry by trying to restore to the clergy some of the land lost a hundred years previously. The overriding suspicion was that Laud was aiming to bring back **Catholic**ism (never his intention).

The archbishop's desire for uniformity finally went too far when he and Charles tried to enforce the English prayer book upon **Scotland** in 1637. This led to the Bishops' Wars, the summoning of **Parliament** and the slide towards civil war. By late 1640, Laud had become such a hated figure that there was little the king could do as Parliament ordered his arrest and confinement within the Tower of London. There he remained for most of the war. At his trial, prosecuted by Prynne in 1644, Laud was described as 'the roote and ground of all our miseries and calamities ... the sty of all pestilential filth that hath infected the State and Government', and accused of tyranny, causing the Bishops' Wars and subverting 'the true religion'. It ended with no verdict due to the lack of evidence, but nevertheless, a bill of attainder was later passed which declared him guilty of treason and led to his decapitation early the following year.

A diminutive, red-faced man who was renowned for being bad tempered, humourless and fastidious, Laud's passing was mourned by few. Even Charles later admitted that he had put too much trust in him by allowing him to exacerbate divisions within the Church. William Laud's actions were not the predominant cause of the Civil Wars, but he entangled religion with politics so that people associated his Arminianism, or Laudianism, with the concurrent political and fiscal absolutism of the Crown. He also engendered much sympathy for the Puritans, thereby allowing them to pack a political punch far greater than their minority status.

Levellers

A political movement that grew out of the **Civil Wars**

Political and economic uncertainties during the war, along with the relaxation of Church censorship, allowed for the growth of radical ideas, especially in London where there was less respect for traditional hierarchy. One ex-army officer, John Lilburne, agitated for more 'natural' human rights and when his supporters campaigned to free him from prison in mid-1646, their opponents called them 'Levellers'. This was a pejorative term meaning that they wanted to bring everyone down to the same level; Lilburne disliked the term, but the name stuck. A trio of leaders – Lilburne, Richard Overton and William Walwyn – organised a campaign of pamphleteering and petitioning that demanded a radical overhaul of the political and social system now that **Charles I** had been defeated. Their supporters wore sea-green ribbons and sprigs of rosemary in their hair, held meetings in taverns, raised funds and later produced a newspaper called *The Moderate*.

In the following year, this movement was given some muscle by various regiments of the **New Model Army** which were unhappy at the prospect of being disbanded by **Parliament** despite being owed several weeks of pay. There were also concerns that soldiers could be prosecuted for some of their actions during the war. 'Agitators' were elected to put forward their complaints and were initially supported by army leaders such as **Thomas Fairfax**.

The Levellers' ideals appealed to the Agitators and the two groups came together to discuss their views with the army's senior officers (the Grandees) at St Mary's Church, Putney in late October 1647 – the Putney Debates. The radicals put forward *An Agreement of the People* whose main tenets (including later editions) were:

1. Abolition of the monarchy and House of Lords.
2. Freedom of religion (except for Catholics).
3. Biennial elections for Parliament.
4. Reorganisation of constituencies according to the number of inhabitants.
5. Equality before the law.
6. All men from the age of 21 to vote except for servants and those paid wages (it was feared that these men would simply be told how to vote by their masters just as women were considered subservient to the 'masters' of the house).

The Grandees, including **Cromwell**, **Ireton** and Fairfax, were never that keen on such societal upheaval and, realising that the discussions were jeopardising the unity of the army, ended the debates. Moreover, the Levellers' proposals went counter to their own peace terms with the king – *The Heads of Proposals*. Days later, perhaps fortuitously for the Grandees, news arrived that Charles had escaped from captivity. The army closed ranks to deal with the new royalist threat and subsequent Second Civil War, and, for the Levellers, the moment was lost. Most discontent among the soldiers evaporated with only minor trouble in some regiments, the most serious being the Leveller-inspired mutiny of 400 troops at Banbury in May 1649 which was brutally crushed with several being killed in a skirmish or summarily executed afterwards. The Leveller movement in London, particularly among apprentices and women (unusually), continued to campaign but Parliament and the Grandees would brook no more discussion and by mid-1649 its leaders were in prison.

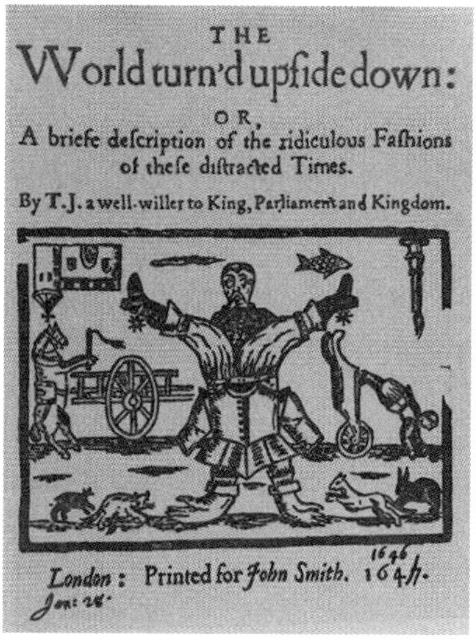

'The World Turned Upside Down'. Flying fish, cats chasing dogs, a cart set before a horse and upside-down clothes; this picture was originally a protest against Parliament banning Christmas but also reflected the perceived chaos of the mid-1640s. (*Artist: unknown, 1646 via Wikimedia Commons*)

The True Levellers or 'Diggers' were another post-war group that sought radical reform. Their leader, Gerard Winstanley, envisioned an egalitarian, land-based **society** that worked closely with nature, even provided a nascent form of health insurance and is recognisable as an early form of communism. In 1649–50, various communes sprang up around London and started to farm on common land. However, local mobs, evictions and legal action extinguished the movement. Another group that arose were the Ranters who believed that God was inside all creatures and therefore humans could ignore all manmade laws and moral constraints. Accused of being amoral extremists, the disorganised and leaderless Ranters were a short-lived phenomenon.

The vacuum created by the defeat of the monarchy in the late 1640s created the opportunity for idealists to seek ways of bettering their society. The Levellers, it can be argued, were the first English political party – well organised and with a clear manifesto. Their progressive values inspired the American Declaration of Independence (1776), and the Chartists' demands of 1838. England in the 1640s, however, was not ready for such radical change; proof, perhaps, that democracy cannot be imposed but must evolve.

Locke, John

(1632–1704)

Philosopher and physician

Locke was born in a small Somerset cottage, the son of a lawyer with **Puritan** sympathies who fought for **Parliament** in the **Civil Wars**. His father's commanding officer sponsored him to attend Westminster School where the headmaster was the formidable disciplinarian and monarchist, Richard Busby, who once boasted that he had birched sixteen of the bishops in the House of Lords (Locke did not enjoy his time there and later attacked the use of corporal punishment). Afterwards, at the late age of 20, Locke attended Christ Church College, Oxford, but was dissatisfied with its continued emphasis on the knowledge of the Ancient Greeks. Instead, he became increasingly influenced by modern philosophers such as Descartes. He also liked to spend time with members of the 'Invisible College' – natural philosophers of later renown such as **Boyle** and **Hooke** – and developed much interest in medicine and science.

In 1666, Locke met the politician, **Anthony Ashley Cooper** (later Lord Shaftesbury) who was so impressed by the younger man that he invited him to live with him, as his personal physician, in London. As he was seeking a career, Locke agreed even though he lacked a medical degree (achieved in 1675). He learnt much under the guidance of the great physician, Thomas Sydenham, however and probably saved his patron's life by carrying out pioneering surgery which involved the insertion of a silver tube that could regularly drain a tumour on Ashley Cooper's liver. A constitutional monarchist and founder of the **Whigs**, Ashley Cooper was a great influence on Locke, who as his secretary and friend, now became closely involved in the politics of the 1670s. In the aftermath of the Exclusion Crisis and the **Popish Plot**, Ashley Cooper fled to Holland in 1682. After discovery of the Whigs' **Rye House Plot** the following year, Locke fled there too although his

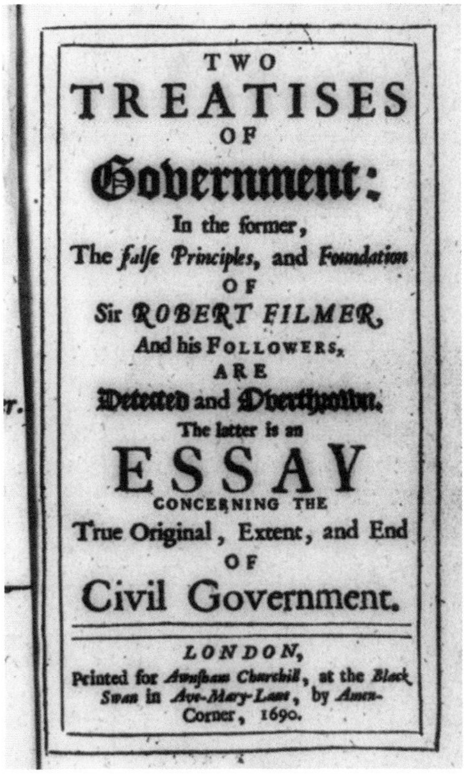
TWO
TREATISES
OF
Government:
In the former,
The *false* Principles, and Foundation
OF
Sir ROBERT FILMER,
And his FOLLOWERS,
ARE
Detected and Overthrown.
The latter is an
ESSAY
CONCERNING THE
True Original, Extent, and End
OF
Civil Government.

LONDON,
Printed for *Awnsham Churchill*, at the *Black Swan* in *Ave-Mary-Lane*, by *Amen-Corner*, 1690.

Title page of *Two Treatises of Government.* (*Author: J. Locke, 1690. Library of Congress*)

patron had already died. It was while in exile that he redrafted several treatises that were to establish his fame and importance, most importantly perhaps *An Essay Concerning Human Understanding* (1689), *Two Treatises of Government* (1689) and *Some Thoughts Concerning Education* (1693). Locke considered ways of improving many facets of **society**, but these are probably the most significant:

1. Unlike Descartes, he believed that humans start off in life with minds that are empty slates or '*tabula rasa*', rather than the prevailing view that babies are born with innate ideas. Instead, we develop our own ideas through our individual experiences and reflections. Therefore, it was vital that parents and schools provide positive experiences for children so that they later become caring, confident adults.
2. Locke believed in overhauling the curriculum in schools. He thought subjects such as Greek, music and poetry were pointless. Instead, children should learn more practical subjects which would help them later in life such as science, ethics and psychology (the latter so that we can calm ourselves and be kind to others).
3. Locke urged religious toleration and the separation of Church from State. He believed that people cannot be forced to worship in a different way and that trying to do so could only cause social disruption. He excluded atheists though as he considered religious morals vital for knitting society together.
4. Like **Hobbes**, he believed in a social contract between the people and the government. However, Locke disagreed with Hobbes's view in a preexisting violent state of nature and that absolutist monarchs, chosen by divine right, were needed to maintain order. Instead, he believed that humans lived in a largely peaceful natural state and allowed governments to rule for them but only to protect their natural rights to life, liberty and property. Locke continued to state that society had every right to overthrow any authoritarian government that impinged on these rights.

Locke returned to England soon after the **Glorious Revolution** (1688) which, along with the **Bill of Rights** (which he helped to draft), seemed to vindicate his beliefs although he had hoped for greater religious toleration. He tried to become involved in more political projects, but London's air exacerbated his asthma, and he retired to the Essex home of his great friend and philosopher, Lady Masham. There, he entertained friends such as **Newton** and **Dryden** before his death in 1704.

Along with Descartes, John Locke can be considered the founding father of liberalism and the European Enlightenment, and his thoughts had a great influence upon the likes of Voltaire, Rousseau, Hume and Kant. He was highly respected in his own lifetime, but his ideas had their greatest impact in the late eighteenth century with the French Revolution and American Declaration of Independence. Today, Locke's thoughts provide the basis of much of what we take for granted.

M

Marlborough, Duke of

see Churchill, John

Marriage

As expected, marriage was only permitted between men and women. Sodomy (the term homosexuality was only coined in 1869) was a capital offence despite **James I** being strongly suspected of bisexual behaviour. Homosexual relationships undoubtedly existed such as within the Church, armed services and between masters and servants but discretion was vital. Only a handful of men in the seventeenth century were hanged for the offence but accusations of sodomy, such as those levelled against **Francis Bacon**, could ruin a career.

'The Scales of Marriage'. A man and woman are being weighed with their coins to see what they can bring to a marriage. Their families pull down on the scales, a moneylender looks on while Cupid flees the scene. (*Artist: N. Braeu after K. van Mander, c. 1592. National Gallery of Art*)

The minimum legal age to marry was 12 for women and 14 for men and it was still possible – until 1753 – for a couple to marry privately and outside a church – a scenario favoured by those wishing to elude their families' wishes. However, a church ceremony, along with the reading of the banns (often read out in marketplaces too), was becoming increasingly common although marriage was not permitted during the periods of Lent, Trinity and Advent. The usual habit among the middle classes was for the man's father to write a formal introduction to the woman's father before his son visited his intended three times. On the third occasion, he would offer some money and a pair of gloves and, if she accepted, a wedding would take place about six months later. A new pair of shoes and jacket, along with many ribbons, were more common than wedding dresses and the preferred colours varied – a 'fertile' pale green for teenage girls, brown for those in their twenties and older women wore black. Only the poor wore white, which symbolised that they brought nothing to the marriage.

People could marry without their parents' consent from the age of 21 and, generally, the wealthier married younger and had less choice in their spouse. It was important for a family to maintain its social status and much time and effort was expended arranging a marriage contract that would include the value of the dowry (payment by bride's father) and jointure (payment by groom's father should the daughter-in-law become a widow). The poorer majority, though, could ignore these considerations, tended to marry later when a couple had earned enough money to raise a family and were more likely to marry out of love. Among the rich, it was hoped that love would develop after marriage. This certainly happened for **Oliver Cromwell** and his wife, Elizabeth, judging by the affectionate letters they wrote to each other.

For men, marriage meant more career opportunities such as becoming a reeve (supervisor of a landowner's estate). It also gave women greater respectability in **society** although, once wedded, they had no legal rights, and their assets became the property of their husbands. Their main responsibilities lay within the home and family and to ensure their husbands' wishes were carried out. Moreover, it was considered acceptable for a man to beat his wife and children for disobedience but not excessively so; no stick thicker than a finger was condoned. Any accidental deaths resulting from such beatings were generally considered unfortunate. Only with widowhood could a woman expect any financial and social independence. Women were not completely submissive, however. Many could negotiate greater power through their roles as household managers and economic co-workers and through the support of female networks outside the home.

Although domestic violence was common, public disapproval was increasing during this period. **Edward Coke** spoke out against it in the early part of the century, and the pervasive influence of **Puritan**ism probably had an impact. Puritans regarded the relationship between husband and wife as analogous to that between God and mankind: the husband should be dominant but loving, not violent. Law courts would punish serious cruelty, but it was common for local communities to step in beforehand to protect the natural order of society. Abusive or unfaithful husbands, nagging wives and rowing couples could expect 'rough music' outside their homes when neighbours would yell and loudly bash their pots and pans. Or they would go on a 'skimmington ride' by which offenders would be forced to ride a horse backwards, wear humiliating costumes and be mocked before being dunked in the local pond. The promiscuous infidelities of Restoration England very much went against the grain and were confined to London's elite.

A skimmington ride. A shrewish wife and henpecked husband are the victims in this procession. (*Artist: W. Hogarth, 1726. British Museum*)

The main purpose of marriage was to have children who could inherit the family's business or estate and care for their parents in old age. Having children was also a sign of social respectability. Passionate love was generally considered undesirable so it may come as a surprise that it was common for a bride to be already pregnant at her wedding. This, however, reflected the fact that marriage was a process that began with the betrothal, after which couples lived together; the church ceremony was merely its conclusion. On average, a woman gave birth to around seven children of whom five might survive their first year. Given the high infant mortality rate, little attention was given to birth control by the majority. Nevertheless, those in illicit relationships or poverty could not rely purely on abstinence and coitus interruptus. In apothecaries and marketplaces one could buy herbal potions to prevent pregnancies or cause abortions (bay leaves were considered particularly effective) or condoms made of animal gut. Bloodletting from the foot was also believed to induce abortions.

Marriage was no longer considered a holy sacrament as it had been pre-Reformation, but it was still regarded as a vital mainstay of society and blessed in the eyes of God. So, to escape an unhappy marriage was not easy. Divorce was impossible unless through an expensive and protracted application to **Parliament**. By 1857, only 200 people had attempted this of whom six were women. An annulment, granted by the local bishop, was more feasible and this required proof of impotence, being too closely related or having been minors when initially married. Both partners could then remarry but any children were declared illegitimate. Alternatively, a legal separation was possible in cases of proven infidelity and extreme cruelty. This did not bastardise any heirs but prevented both husband and wife from remarrying.

The institution of marriage remained an important, and patriarchal, cornerstone of seventeenth-century England but its traditional bonds were starting to loosen. A higher proportion than ever – around 20 per cent of adults – never married and the average age of first marriage had reached a high of the mid- to late twenties, a fact that may be explained by the weakening influence of the Church and the growing size of the middle classes which put more emphasis on economic well-being. The shackles of same-status marriage were also starting to loosen. **Clarendon** blamed the chaos caused by the **Civil Wars** for some noblemen's daughters marrying mere clergymen, **Pepys** married into a poor, immigrant family purely out of physical attraction and **Monck** married his laundress. The campaign for gender equality was still a long way off (the first feminist literature – Mary Wollstonecraft's *A Vindication of the Rights of Women* came out in 1792) but growing individualism and literacy, greater emphasis on love within marriage and females marrying later allowed the position of women to gradually improve in Stuart England. It is hard to imagine the likes of **Mary Frith**, **Aphra Behn** or **Celia Fiennes** existing in any previous century.

Mary II

(1662–94)

Wife of **William III** and Queen of England,
Scotland and **Ireland** from 1689 to 1694

Mary was the eldest daughter of **James, Duke of York** and his first wife, Anne Hyde – daughter of the **Earl of Clarendon**. She was born in St James's Palace and named after her great-great-grandmother, Mary, Queen of Scots. Despite both of her parents converting to **Catholic**ism, both she and her sister, **Anne**, were brought up as **Anglican**s under orders from her uncle, King **Charles II**. To facilitate this, the girls were moved to their own lodgings at Richmond Palace and only occasionally visited their parents. Mary's **education** was typically quite limited for girls of her position at that time and revolved around music, dance, drawing, French and religious studies. For several years, from the age of 9, she idolised a maid of honour almost ten years her senior – Frances Apsley – and demonstrated an obsessive attachment through the passionate letters that she wrote her.

Two years after her mother's death (1671), her father married Mary of Modena who was only four years older than herself. By this stage, it was clear that Charles was unlikely to father a legitimate heir. This made Mary second in line to the throne after her father and so the choice of her husband became a politically charged subject. In 1677, to defuse the building Exclusion Crisis and under pressure from **Parliament** and the **Whigs**, Charles agreed that she should marry the Protestant

William of Orange – her 27-year-old cousin. Upon receiving this news, Mary apparently wept for two days as well as during the wedding. Afterwards, the royal family attended her bedding ceremony to confirm consummation with the king himself drawing the bed curtains before leaving.

Bedding ceremony. A bishop sprinkles holy water on the couple's bed. Such ceremonies had largely died out by the eighteenth century. (*Artist: unknown, fifteenth century via Wikimedia Commons*)

On their journey to Holland, ice around Rotterdam forced the couple to make a detour and land on a remote part of the coast. From there they had to walk through the icy countryside before coaches finally took them to The Hague where they were welcomed in a formal procession. The statuesque Mary (five feet, eleven inches) had a friendly and vivacious nature which quickly endeared her to her new Dutch subjects, but her **marriage** was not a happy one at first. William was often away coordinating campaigns against the French and allegedly had an affair with one of her ladies-in-waiting, Elizabeth Villiers. Her first pregnancy (1678) ended in a miscarriage which was followed by three more.

In England, meanwhile, matters were becoming more politically and religiously fraught. Her father had acceded to the throne in 1685 but his policies soon aroused fears that he wanted to create a Catholic, absolutist state. This was tolerated while he had no children and Mary was his heir but after his wife gave birth to a son in 1688, leading politicians invited William to invade England to rescue their rights and religion. This he did in November and, during the ensuing **Glorious Revolution**, James fled the country. Mary followed in January with the leading **Tories** wanting to offer the throne solely to her. They both rejected this, however, with Mary happy to defer to her husband and so Parliament agreed on a joint monarchy, and they were crowned together in April 1689. Later that year, they put their seals to that hugely important democratic milestone – the **Bill of Rights**, that henceforward restricted monarchical power.

Continued warfare often called William away to Ireland and the Netherlands, leaving Mary, aided by a regency council (can be considered England's first cabinet), to rule the country. It is not clear just how much she contributed to government although we know that she preferred to consult her absentee husband, sometimes at the council's impatience. She showed herself capable of making urgent decisions though such as ordering the arrest of her maternal uncle for plotting to restore

James II and took a particular interest in religious reform such as reducing pluralism (holding more than one office) within the Church. On a personal level, not only was she saddened by her miscarriages, but she had a permanent falling-out with Anne over her friendship with **Sarah Churchill** and often felt remorse over her role in deposing her father. Her devout Protestantism was of great comfort to her, though, and she took much interest in garden design and oriental porcelain. Also, her marriage became a warm and loving one with both monarchs finding support and strength in each other.

William's distraught behaviour in response to Mary's death from smallpox in 1694 was uncharacteristic and genuine. Many Englishmen, too, felt unsettled about being ruled solely by a foreign king. Mary, however, had successfully bridged the gap between her father and her husband. Always a reluctant queen, she had grown into her role, taken her responsibilities seriously and became, possibly, the most relatable and popular of the Stuart monarchs.

Milton, John

(1608–74)

Poet, pamphleteer and civil servant

The son of a legal scribe and accomplished composer, Milton was born in the City of London. Little is known of his mother, Sara Jeffrey, other than she was a generous local almsgiver. Between 12 and 16, he attended the prestigious St Paul's School where he began his studies of Latin and Greek and from there he went to Christ's College, Cambridge with a view to a career in the Church. He studied there for seven years despite finding the **education** unimaginative and not fitting in with his fellow students. They called him the 'Lady of Christ College' due to his pale, androgynous features and dislike of physical activities. By now, he had developed **Puritan** beliefs which were repelled by the increasingly Arminian nature of the Church of England and so he decided to deploy his linguistic skills and become a poet instead of a priest.

After leaving Cambridge in 1632, Milton spent the next six years absorbed in private study at his father's new home on the outskirts of London, first in Hammersmith then Horton. By researching subjects ranging from theology, philosophy and history to science, politics and various languages, Milton probably made himself the most educated poet in England's history. He had already written much poetry but 1634's *Comus* and 1637's *Lycidas* made people stand up and take notice of his ability. *Comus* was a philosophical poem written for a masque, an allegory concerning the battle between vice and virtue. *Lycidas* took the form of a pastoral elegy that beautifully memorialised a close friend who had drowned in the Irish Sea.

In 1638–39 Milton continued his education by travelling around Europe and meeting many of its greatest intellectuals such as Galileo (then under house arrest for believing the Earth revolved around the Sun). Upon his return to England, the worsening political crisis, ensuing **Civil Wars** and the resulting possibilities for change kindled a desire in Milton to write pamphlets instead of poetry. These included eloquent assaults against Archbishop **Laud** and the episcopal hierarchy of the Church and the renowned *Areopagitica* (1644) which attacked state censorship of printing – 'Give me the liberty to know, to utter, and to argue freely, according to conscience, above all liberties.' More controversial were his tracts arguing for divorce based on incompatibility and lack of love rather than just infidelity. This may or may not have reflected the initial failure of his first **marriage** – to Mary Powell, 1642 – when she left him and returned to her royalist-supporting family upon the outbreak of war (she returned three years later, and they had four children).

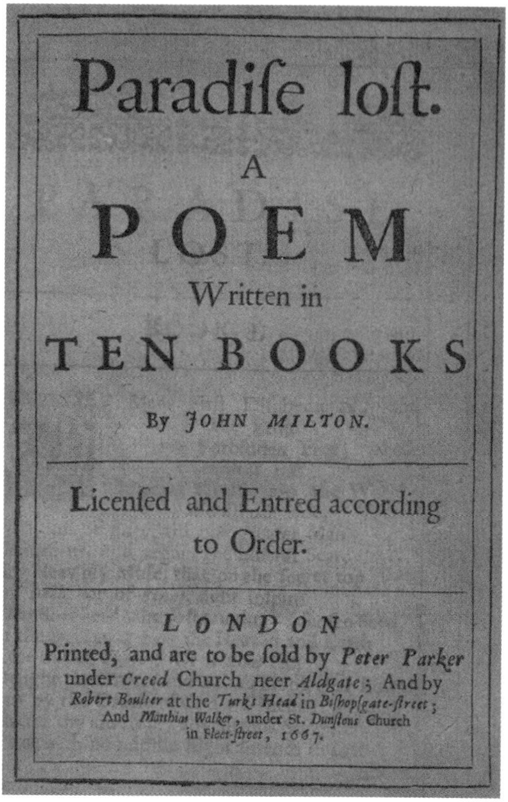
Paradiſe loſt.
A
POEM
Written in
TEN BOOKS
By *JOHN MILTON.*

Licenſed and Entred according
to Order.

LONDON
Printed, and are to be ſold by *Peter Parker*
under *Creed* Church neer *Aldgate*; And by
Robert Boulter at the *Turks Head* in *Biſhopſgate-ſtreet*;
And *Matthias Walker*, under St. *Dunſtons* Church
in *Fleet-ſtreet*, 1667.

Title page of *Paradise Lost*. (*Author: J. Milton, 1667. Houghton Library*)

In 1649, Milton wrote a tract arguing for the downfall of tyrannical monarchs, thereby showing his support for **Charles I**'s execution. Thereafter, he was employed by the government as the Secretary for Foreign Tongues – a role in which he used his linguistic skills to handle all foreign correspondence and write defences of England's new republic. Although totally blind by 1652 Milton carried on working by dictating to secretaries and, after the death of **Cromwell** (1658), he continued to argue against the return of a monarchy despite the ensuing chaos. Being such a prominent supporter of regicide, the restoration of the monarchy two years later immediately put his life in great danger. The intervention of influential friends and relatives, however, allowed him to escape with a fine and brief imprisonment.

Milton retired from public life, married again and returned to writing poetry. It was not until 1667 that his masterpiece, for which he is most famous, was published – *Paradise Lost*. Inspired by Homer, Virgil and Spenser, *Paradise Lost* is an epic poem of over 10,000 lines, written in unrhyming iambic pentameter. It describes the war between God and Satan, the latter's expulsion to Hell and his revenge on God's creation in Eden which ultimately leads to Jesus's sacrifice to redeem the sins of humankind. Due to its sheer scope, vivid descriptions using epic similes, sonorous rhythms and powerful messages of courage and independence, *Paradise Lost* is generally considered to be the best poem in English literature. It made little impact after its publication due to Milton's unpopularity (being a Puritan and a republican) but was later revered by the likes of Pope, Voltaire and Wordsworth. It also inspired Blake, Shelley and Byron who regarded Milton's Satan as an anti-hero who suffered and wept after bravely fighting an all-powerful God.

Paradise Regained followed (1671), which concerned Satan's failure to tempt Jesus, and some tracts calling for religious toleration and an elective monarchy. Milton died peacefully, possibly from gout, and was buried in St Giles, Cripplegate. He may have been a serious and austere man (and had a very difficult relationship with his daughters) but he is second only to Shakespeare as England's most important writer. Also, although not a democrat or liberal in the modern sense, Milton stands alongside **Locke** as an early campaigner for freedom and independent thought.

Monck, George (Duke of Albemarle)

(1608–70)

General, admiral and statesman

George Monck. (*Artist: D. Loggan, 1661. S. C. Dickson via Wikimedia Commons*)

Monck was the younger son of an impoverished landowning family in Devon. As such, a career in the army was one of the few opportunities open to him and so he joined **Buckingham**'s disastrous expeditions to Cadiz (1625) and La Rochelle (1627). For Monck, the latter may have been an escape from arrest after he stabbed an under-sheriff who had arrived to arrest his father for debt. For most of the 1630s, he gained further military experience fighting for the Dutch in their war against Spain and distinguished himself at the successful siege of Breda (1637).

Monck returned to England during the Bishops' Wars and, despite coming out on the losing side at the Battle of Newburn (1640), he gained credit for rescuing the English artillery. The following year, he was given command of a regiment to suppress the Irish Rebellion but was unhappy when **Charles I** ordered a truce with the rebels so that soldiers could return to England to aid him in the **Civil Wars**. Initially, he refused to swear allegiance to the king, but the threat of imprisonment changed his mind, and he was sent north to meet his former troops who had landed in Cheshire. However, this force was defeated by **Fairfax** at Nantwich (early 1644) and Monck was captured and sent to the Tower of London for two years.

While there, he started an affair with his laundress, Anne Clarges, the daughter of a farrier. Her husband had absconded some years earlier and his whereabouts were unknown, but this did not stop Monck from marrying beneath his social class in 1653 amid accusations of bigamy (only in the following year was evidence found that Anne's first husband had already died). The **marriage**, however, proved to be a very loving one.

With the first civil war over, **Parliament** sent Monck back to northern **Ireland** to suppress the continuing revolt. However, outnumbered and ill-supplied, he was forced to make a secret truce with a rebel faction. For this, he was recalled to London and reprimanded but the parliamentary general, **Oliver Cromwell**, recognised Monck's qualities and experience, particularly in siege warfare and artillery, and gave him a command in the army that invaded **Scotland** during the third civil war. Some officers mistrusted this former royalist, but he fought bravely in the centre of the **New Model Army** at Dunbar (1650).

Afterwards, Cromwell gave him the responsibility of conquering the rest of Scotland and then its governorship. Monck repaid this trust with absolute loyalty and ruthless efficiency. At Dundee, he allowed a massacre to be perpetrated by his troops with the town being so badly ransacked that it took over a century for it to economically recover. By mid-1652, using scorched-earth tactics and transportation to the West Indies, the whole of Scotland had been conquered for the first time in British history.

Upon the outbreak of the **First Anglo-Dutch War** in 1652, Cromwell appointed him as a General at Sea of the English fleet, an unusual decision given Monck's complete lack of naval experience. However, his knowledge of artillery and understanding of the importance of coordinated military manoeuvres made him an ideal choice for implementing Admiral **Blake**'s recent 'Fighting Instructions' that required a line-of-battle formation and a flag-signalling system. The result was the decisive English victory at the **Battle of the Gabbard**, which Monck followed up with further success off Scheveningen. The end of the war in 1654 then allowed him to return to Scotland to suppress a royalist revolt. There he remained for the rest of the decade.

If that had been that, then Monck would simply be remembered as one of Cromwell's abler generals, one who planned meticulously, looked after the welfare of his troops and was able to learn from his experiences and adapt to different circumstances. Ironically, given that he was someone who shunned the limelight, the events of 1660 propelled Monck to centre stage in English history. After

Cromwell's death in 1658, political chaos ensued as no one person or group had enough support to rule. Fearing a breakdown in law and order, Monck gathered 7,000 men at Coldstream (including a regiment later named the Coldstream Guards) and crossed the border on January 1, 1660. English troops, led by General Lambert, went north to confront him and the possibility of a new civil war loomed. This was not the New Model Army of old, however; outnumbered, cold and unpaid, Lambert's men melted away, and Monck was able to march unmolested into London a month later. His intentions, at this stage were still not clear. The exiled **Charles II** had sent messages asking for his support, but Monck never committed himself this way or that. One thing was clear to him though: the prospect of continued military rule was widely unpopular. So, he ordered new parliamentary elections and would back whatever new form of government was chosen.

The resulting Convention Parliament returned a majority of royalist MPs who called for the return of the monarchy. Again, Monck bent with the wind, and it was his recommendations that formed the basis of Charles's conciliatory Declaration of Breda in April. It was Monck who then greeted the new king at Dover and, in return for his actions, was richly rewarded with money and a peerage – the Duke of Albemarle. He continued to command the English army and serve the new government and became known for his opulent lifestyle. An increasingly large man, he once drank a whole dinner party under the table and walked away!

1665 saw him in charge of maintaining order in London during the **Plague** and in the following year he commanded the English fleet again during the **Second Anglo-Dutch War**. Despite showing courage and tenacity during the Four Days' Fight, Monck was outnumbered and came off worse. He was then appointed First Lord of the Treasury (1667) but, suffering from oedema, he remained largely inactive for the last years of his life. When he died, he was held in such esteem that he was buried in Westminster Abbey.

Inscrutable, taciturn, uncultured, volatile and fond of alcohol and bawdy jokes, one would have had a poor impression of Monck upon meeting him. He commanded respect, however, and proved himself loyal to whoever ruled. He never craved political power but believed strongly in its existence. So, when the power vacuum appeared in the late 1650s, it was his decisive action that pivoted England away from a military republic and towards a constitutional monarchy.

Monmouth's Rebellion

(1685)

An attempt to depose **James II**

During the reign of **Charles II**, there had been concerted efforts by the **Whigs** and **Lord Shaftesbury** to exclude the king's brother, **James, Duke of York**, from the throne due to his **Catholic**ism. However, as Charles had no legitimate children, he fought for his brother's right to succeed him and thereby ensured James's smooth accession to the throne in February 1685. The two brothers' success was largely because the Whigs had been severely discredited after the **Popish** and **Rye House Plots**. Also, James's heirs were his Protestant daughters (**Mary** and **Anne**) and so most people were prepared to tolerate his religion while he was king.

Some Whigs, however, feared the worst and embarked on an attempt to depose James and replace him with the Protestant James Scott, the Duke of Monmouth. Monmouth (born 1649) was the illegitimate son of Charles II and his first mistress, Lucy Walter, although the Whigs tried to boost his claim to the throne by spreading rumours that Charles and Lucy had secretly married before his birth and that proof of this lay inside a mysterious black box. Neither proof nor box was ever found. Previously, Monmouth had been feted and rewarded during his father's reign, promoted to the privy council and had commanded English land forces during the **Third Anglo-Dutch War**. However, after the Rye House Plot fiasco (1683), he had fled to Holland and thrown himself under the protection of his cousin, **William of Orange**.

In Amsterdam, Monmouth met the Earl of Argyll and other exiles and planned coordinated risings in **Scotland** and south-west England – an area known for its large numbers of Protestant dissenters. Funding for the enterprise was provided by selling his own belongings and donations from various sympathisers such as Ann Smith, the wealthy widow of a London sugar-baker who had owned a sugar refinery in London.

Three ships transported Monmouth's four cannons, 1,500 muskets and eighty-one men and landed them at Lyme Regis on 11 June 1685. Over the next couple of weeks around 6,000 men flocked to his support, the majority being farmers and skilled cloth workers. One was a young merchant named Daniel Defoe who later became famous for writing *Robinson Crusoe* (1719). James II, meanwhile, had already received intelligence about the invasion and sent forces led by the Earl of Feversham and **John Churchill** to intercept the rebels.

Monmouth marched north, denounced the king at Chard and underwent a coronation ceremony in Yeovil. He then aimed his swelling ranks at Bristol – England's second-most important city – which he might have taken had he been more decisive after winning a skirmish against local militia. Instead, he turned

Execution of Monmouth. Ketch finishes the job with a knife to the horror of those assembled. (*Artist: J. Luyken, 1689. Rijksmuseum*)

east towards London, but royalist regular troops were beginning to mass and assemble artillery. At the same time, came the news that Argyll had been defeated and captured in Scotland. Amid worsening weather and a host of desertions, Monmouth retreated west to Bridgwater on the edge of the Somerset marshes.

On 5 July, Monmouth decided on a night attack before further royalist forces arrived. Led by a local servant, the rebels reached a deep drainage ditch but the noise they made while crossing it alerted pickets and the royalist forces made a flanking counterattack. Their superior training and weapons allowed them to rout the rebels, many of whom were armed with just pitchforks. This was the Battle of Sedgemoor, arguably the last pitched battle fought on English soil, and from it fled Monmouth disguised as a peasant. Three days later, he was captured cowering in a Dorset ditch and taken to London where he was beheaded by the infamous Jack Ketch. After several blows of the axe, Ketch had to finish the job with a butcher's knife.

The aftermath in the West Country was brutal too. James sent Judge Jeffreys on a series of trials – the Bloody Assizes – which led to around 300 people being executed and 850 deported to the West Indies to work on sugar plantations. Indecisive leadership combined with a ragtag army meant that the rebellion was never likely to succeed and it was noticeable that Monmouth received little support from the local gentry. Had he gambled a couple of years later, after James's tactless moves towards Catholicism and absolutism, the result may well have been different.

N

Naseby, Battle of

(14 June 1645)

Decisive battle in the **Civil Wars**

After the usual lull in fighting during the winter months, when there was insufficient fodder for horses, King **Charles I** convened a council of war meeting with his senior officers to discuss the best strategy for winning the war. His nephew, **Prince Rupert**, advocated marching north from the king's capital at Oxford to recapture those lands lost after his defeat at Marston Moor the previous year. A subsequent link-up with the Scottish royalist, the Earl of Montrose, was certainly a possibility that appealed to Charles. Lord Goring, however, preferred to capture Taunton and consolidate control in the southwest. Charles, aware of the animosity between the two and seeking a compromise, allowed Goring to take 3,000 cavalry and 1,500 infantry west while he and Rupert took the bulk of the army north (Goring later ignored a command to rejoin the main army).

On 31 May 1645, the king's troops stormed the key parliamentarian town of Leicester where, in brutal street fighting, they suffered heavy casualties and massacred several hundred inhabitants. **Sir Thomas Fairfax**, leading the **New Model Army**, decided to lift his siege of Oxford and head north to confront the royalist threat to **Parliament**'s heartlands. Then, almost by accident, the two armies blundered into each other near the village of Naseby, Northamptonshire. Rupert advised retreat but George Digby and other close advisors had nothing but scorn for Parliament's new army; their argument that retreat would be bad for morale won the day.

The two armies drew up on opposite sides of a shallow valley on a front that was just over a mile wide. Parliament's forces numbered around 13,000; the king's 10,500 with the shortfall mainly in cavalry (a relatively small-scale affair compared to continental armies which were three or four times larger). They adopted the usual formation of cavalry on the wings and infantry in the centre. Several officers had gained experience in the Swedish army and applied the 'Swedish pattern' to their infantry regiments. This involved blocks of musketmen, armed with slow-loading matchlocks, formed up in rows. The front row would fire and then the rows behind would step forward allowing the first row to reload at the back. In close combat, these troops would fight with swords and the butts of their muskets.

Interspersed with these were blocks of pikemen with sixteen-foot pikes whose job would be to defend the musketmen (only in the 1680s did the introduction of the bayonet make pikemen obsolete). Both sides had artillery pieces too with a large array of calibres – the biggest being 12-pounders – but they were inaccurate and were only used at the start of a battle to avoid hitting their own men. It was the cavalry, armed with three-foot swords and carbines (shortened flintlock muskets),

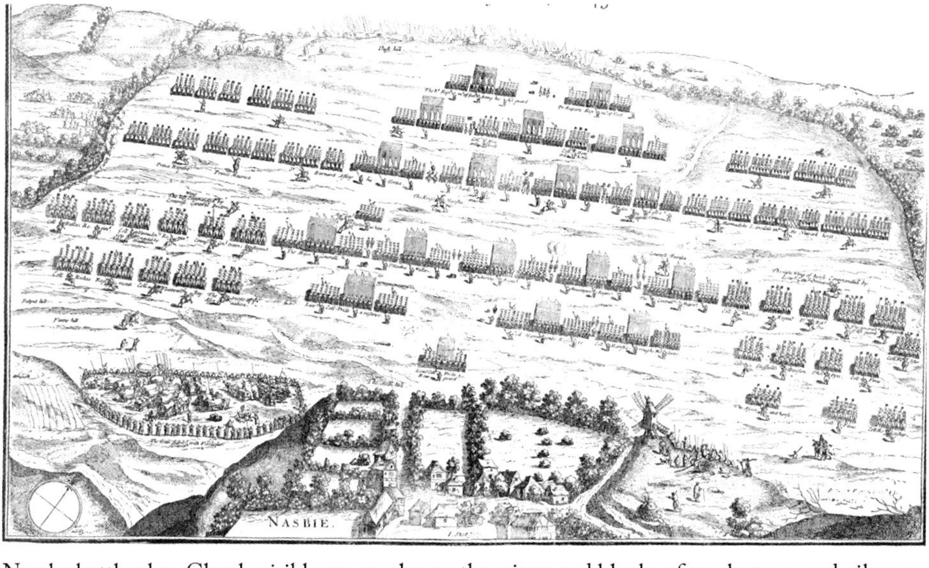

Naseby battle plan. Clearly visible are cavalry on the wings and blocks of musketmen and pikemen in the centre. Cromwell can be seen on the right with Rupert and Ireton on the left and dragoons hiding behind the hedge beyond them. (*Artist: R. Streeter, 1647 via Wikimedia Commons*)

who were expected to decide the outcome of a battle if they could get behind the enemy infantry's rear.

The action started in the morning when Rupert, on the royalist right, attacked **Henry Ireton**'s cavalry. Despite being harassed by parliamentarian dragoons (mounted musketmen) hidden behind a hedge, Rupert succeeded in driving off most of Ireton's regiments. As at Edgehill (1642), however, Rupert's wild charge was difficult to control, and he ended up attacking the baggage train far behind Parliament's rear.

Meanwhile, Lord Astley's royalist infantry had advanced, locked with their opponents and started to drive them back. At this point, the parliamentary commander, Major-General Skippon, was wounded by a musket ball that pierced his breast plate. To relieve the pressure, a couple of Fairfax's regiments, previously hidden behind the crest of a hill, advanced on Astley's left flank and, at the same time, Ireton's two surviving regiments of cavalry and the hidden dragoons attacked Astley's right.

The most consequential events were happening on the royalist left, however. On this flank were Lieutenant-General **Cromwell**'s 'Ironsides'. The nickname had originally been given by Rupert to Cromwell after Marston Moor as a reference to his durability and strength but was then applied to Cromwell's cavalry. Unlike Rupert's men, the 'Ironsides' were trained to charge, regroup and charge again. Using their discipline and superior numbers, they drove off the king's Northern Horse and then proceeded to wheel round behind the doomed royalist infantry.

At this point, Charles wanted to lead his reserves into the fray, but the situation had become hopeless and one of his courtiers grabbed his horse's bridle and urged him to flee. Rupert, meanwhile, had returned but it was too late as Astley's troops were already making a fighting retreat. Only Rupert's private infantry regiment – the Bluecoats – stood firm until terrible losses finally made them surrender. The final bloodshed occurred at the royalist baggage train. Believing the female camp followers to be Irish, **Catholic** 'whores' (most were just some of the soldiers' Welsh wives), parliamentary troops slaughtered or disfigured around a hundred of them. Of greater significance though, was the discovery of secret correspondence between the king and his wife which revealed plans to use Irish and French troops to assist his cause. This damning evidence was later used at his trial as proof that Charles had treasonably plotted against his own country.

Naseby was a small affair that lasted for just two hours and had relatively few casualties (700 royalists and 150 parliamentarians killed) but it can be counted among the most important battles fought in Britain. It saw the defeat of the king's last major field army and allowed the New Model Army to conduct mopping-up operations in the south and west. After Naseby, parliamentary victory was inevitable. However, had Goring's troops been present and had Rupert's cavalry stayed on the field the result may have been very different. It is easy to see how a royalist victory would have led to Cromwell, whose reputation was closely aligned with the fortunes of his New Model Army, being discredited and replaced by the aristocratic generals he had usurped a few weeks previously. It is easy to see, too, how such generals after such a defeat would have come to terms with Charles. The republic may never have happened and England's transition to a parliamentary democracy would have been much delayed.

New Model Army

(1645–61)

England's first standing army

Lobster-tail helmet. (*Author: unknown, seventeenth century. Royal Armoury*)

The New Model Army – or New Modelled Army, as it was then known – was created during the First **Civil War** and arose out of **Parliament**'s military setbacks in 1644. A chastising defeat at Lostwithiel and a desultory performance at Newbury convinced many that the war could not be won. One of its generals, the Earl of Manchester, moaned, 'If we fight 100 times and beat him 99 he will be King still, but if he beats us but once, … we shall be hanged, we shall lose our estates.' The cavalry commander, **Oliver Cromwell**, then famously replied, 'If this be so, why did we take up arms at first?'

It had become clear to Cromwell that a major reorganisation of Parliament's forces was required to win the war. First, he persuaded Parliament to sanction the New Model Ordinance (February 1645) which established the founding of a new, national army. Soon after, it passed the Self-Denying Ordinance which banned anyone from holding both military and parliamentary office at the same time. This forced half-hearted generals such as the earls of Manchester and Essex to leave the army as, being nobility, they were automatically in the House of Lords. Cromwell stayed in the Commons but, given his military ability, was allowed to remain in the army under a series of three-month commissions.

Previously, regional forces were based on local trained bands (irregular troops with variable levels of training and equipment) and they would only operate within their areas as this would allow them, if necessary, to defend their homes. The New Model, however, had a centralised command and supply structure that allowed it to fight anywhere in the country and officers were appointed on merit rather than social position. Overall command was given to **Sir Thomas Fairfax**, while Cromwell and Sir Philip Skippon led the cavalry and infantry respectively. Initially envisaged to be an army of 22,000 men (there were 68,000 at its peak) the soldiers were organised into regiments and sub-divided into troops (cavalry) and companies (dragoons and infantry).

Proper training and uniforms were provided. The cavalry wore buff leather coats, back-and-front breastplates and lobster-tailed helmets while the infantry were issued with red coats (Venetian red was the cheapest dye). There were two musketmen for every pikeman. The latter were heavily armoured with sixteen-foot pikes and swords, and it was their pace that largely dictated the speed of an army on the march. Musketeers had no armour and wore a bandolier with twelve wooden containers – known as the 'Twelve Apostles' – each containing powder and a lead musket ball for their matchlock guns.

Regular pay was another feature with foot soldiers receiving 8 pence per day and the cavalry troopers 2 shillings although they had to provide their own horses. Instead of camps, soldiers were billeted in people's houses with the owners, in theory, being compensated later. Some looting and poaching were inevitable as the rations of bread and cheese were quite meagre but the New Model was renowned for its harsh discipline. Those caught stealing or shortening their pikes, for instance, were severely whipped while deserters were summarily executed. Their royalist counterparts, however, were far less disciplined as the supply of food and pay was very inconsistent. Therefore, it was the royalist forces that citizens came to fear and detest the most especially in the later years when Charles ran out of money. Another contrast was ideology. The majority in the New Model were **Puritan**s who volunteered in the belief that they were fighting in God's true cause and went into battle with Bibles or the 'Soldier's catechism'. Royalist troops, on the other hand, may have had a sense of loyalty to the king, but were conscripted by their landowners.

Despite being in its infancy and not fully formed, the New Model won a decisive victory at **Naseby** in June 1645. As with later battles, its success was largely built upon its extremely disciplined cavalry which grew out of the core of Cromwell's 'Ironsides' – two regiments of horse that Cromwell had previously built up. Within a year, it had mopped up the last areas of royalist resistance and then, thinking the war was finished, the New Model started looking to the future and became politicised. Parliament, to lower the heavy tax burden, wanted to disband several regiments even though soldiers' pay was several weeks in arrears. It also refused to grant them an amnesty for any crimes, such as theft, committed during the war. Discontented men now latched on to the ideas of the **Levellers** and began to demand more democratic and religious freedoms. Two elected 'Agitators' per regiment, along with officers, formed the Army Council and drew up a new constitution known as the Agreement of the People. Matters worsened when it

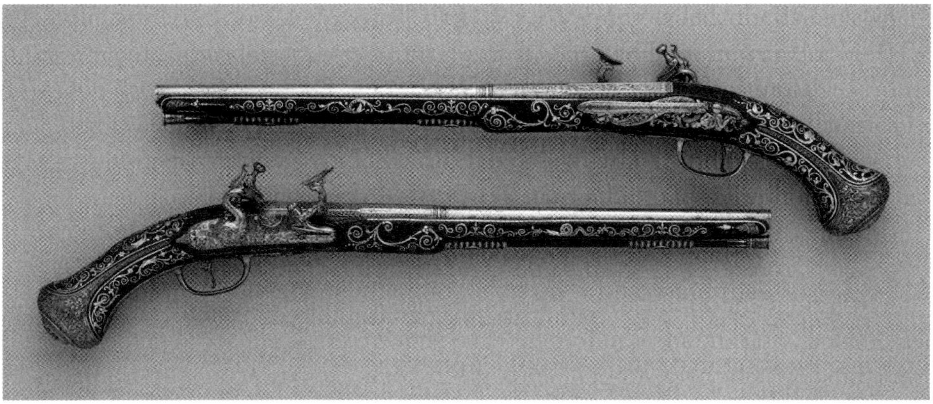

A pair of snaphaunce pistols. An early form of flintlock, the snaphaunce was technologically superior to the matchlock guns but its expense meant it was only available to cavalry. (*Artist: Matteo Cecchi – gunsmith, c. 1690. Metropolitan Museum of Art*)

became clear that the **Presbyterian**-dominated Parliament was about to make a deal with the king, a deal which clearly would have ignored all their demands. Subsequently, in the late summer of 1647, the army started to slowly march on London to intimidate its new opponent. For the first time in English history, the army was trying to bring about political change

To defuse this tense situation and to win the New Model over to their own deal – the Heads of Proposals – the senior officers (the Grandees) invited the Agitators to the Putney Debates. With the Grandees unhappy with the Agitators' more radical demands, the debates were inconclusive, but army unity was rescued by the king's escape from captivity and the opening of the second civil war. After putting down royalist revolts and destroying the Scottish army at Preston, the New Model and Grandees agreed that there could be no lasting peace as long as Charles lived. Subsequently, Colonel Pride and his troops purged Parliament of all moderate Presbyterians (December 1648), leaving a 'Rump' that voted to put the king on trial. This then led to his execution the following month. Discontent in some units continued to simmer but a few minor mutinies were rapidly crushed.

Between 1649 and 1653, the army suppressed the long-running rebellion in **Ireland** and brought the whole island under English control. On occasions, it acted with brutality such as the attacks on Drogheda and Wexford and used scorched-earth tactics to combat guerrilla warfare. At the siege of Clonmel (August 1650), the New Model suffered its single biggest loss – 2,000 men – as it tried to storm the town's deadly defences. Simultaneously, other regiments were battling the Scots after they formally recognised the dead king's son, **Charles II**, as their new monarch. Despite being in a poor condition, the army managed to rout their enemy at Dunbar (September 1650) and, exactly a year later, finished the civil wars with a victory at Worcester. By mid-1652, General **Monck** had completed England's first conquest of **Scotland**.

The New Model also saw action abroad. Once the **First Anglo-Dutch War** was over, Cromwell initiated a war against Spain, for religious and commercial reasons, in 1655. In that year, it saw its only-ever defeat in the West Indies when its disease-ridden troops suffered a bloody reverse in Hispaniola, a defeat that Cromwell saw as an agonising sign from God that England was still not a godly nation. Three years later, Cromwell's French allies were amazed at the New Model's courage and discipline as it stormed Spanish defences on a fifty-metre sandhill to gain victory in the Battle of the Dunes.

After the defeat in Hispaniola and the failure of various parliamentary experiments, Cromwell resorted to military rule to improve the moral fibre of the nation. Twelve military districts, each run by a major-general, experienced differing degrees of puritanical rule which was so unpopular that the project was abandoned after ten months but it was the army, not Parliament, that continued to rule the country. After Cromwell's death in 1658, the New Model lacked a strong leader who could unite the various factions and drive forward policy and so the republic, politically, began to fall apart. Military rule had become so unpopular that people increasingly called for the restoration of the monarchy. Another civil war threatened as General Monck marched his regiments south to resurrect parliamentary supremacy but, fortunately, opposing forces melted away. Therefore, ironically perhaps, it was the New Model Army that enabled the return of the monarchy in 1660 but its role in the defeat and death of Charles I meant that Charles II had no choice but to disband it the following year.

Newton, Sir Isaac

(1642–1727)

Physicist and mathematician

Newton was born at Woolsthorpe Manor, Lincolnshire, on Christmas Day 1642, premature and so underweight that few expected him to live more than a few days. His father, a wealthy landowner, had died a few months earlier and, three years later, his mother remarried and had another family, leaving her son in the care of his maternal grandmother. She returned after her second husband's death nine years later, but the separation had a marked effect on Newton and may well explain his later tendencies to be overanxious, hypersensitive and temperamental. Certainly, he later admitted to threatening arson against his stepfather's home.

Instead of school, his mother wanted him to manage the estate, but Newton had no interest in farming and, despite being bullied, preferred the more intellectual atmosphere of Grantham grammar school where he impressed teachers with his model windmills and accurate sun dials. At 19, quite late, Newton attended Trinity

College, Cambridge, as a sizar (one who received funding in return for doing some menial jobs). On paper, he was an average student, but this was because he was sidetracked by his fascination with the concept of science interacting with nature. This was the period when he devoured the works of ancient and modern philosophers such as Aristotle, Descartes and Galileo.

The threat of **plague** in 1665 caused the university to temporarily close so Newton returned home and the next two years, at Woolsthorpe, represent the most productive time of his life. In isolated, self-directed study, Newton developed the infinitesimal theory of calculus – the study of rates of change. This enabled him to model the trajectory of a cannon ball, for instance, the Moon's orbit around the Earth or the growth pattern of a spiral shell. By the time his tract on the subject was finally published in 1669, he was Europe's leading mathematician.

The plague years also witnessed Newton's revelations in optics. He discovered that white light was, in fact, composed of different colours which could be seen after refraction through a prism. Such was his belief that all theories should be vigorously tested, he once inserted a blunt needle into his eye which led him to believe that we see things 'upside-down'. Incorrectly, however, he believed that light travelled as particles rather than waves. Newton's work then led him to create the first reflecting telescope (1668) that used mirrors instead of lenses which made it far more powerful. His studies in the field of light – *Opticks* – were finally published in 1704. Remarkably, in this book, he was the first to consider electrical force and later hypothesised that electricity conducted messages in the nervous system.

Newton's greatest work, though, came out in 1687 – *Philosophiæ Naturalis Principia Mathematica* – or *Principia*. In this, he stated the Three Laws of Motion:

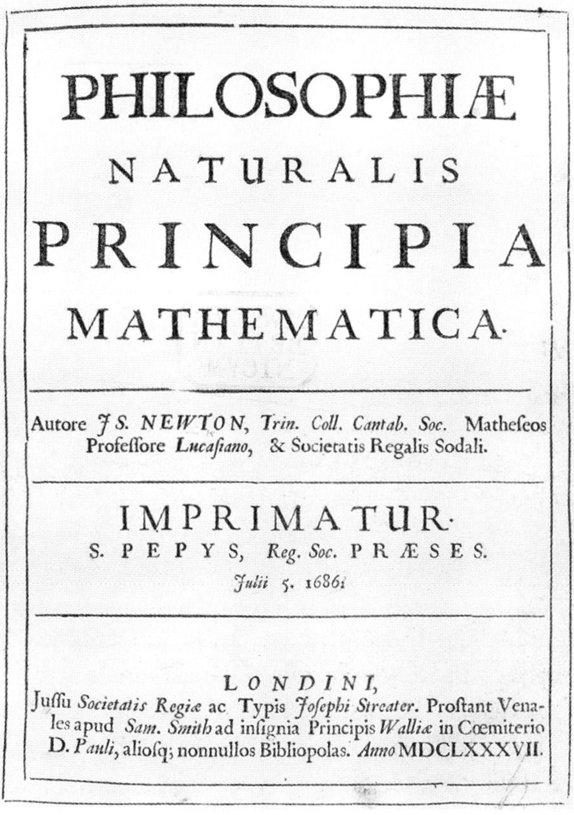

PHILOSOPHIÆ

NATURALIS

PRINCIPIA

MATHEMATICA.

Autore *J S.* NEWTON, *Trin. Coll. Cantab. Soc.* Matheſeos Profeſſore *Lucaſiano*, & Societatis Regalis Sodali.

IMPRIMATUR.

S. PEPYS, *Reg. Soc.* PRÆSES.

Julii 5. 1686.

LONDINI,

Juſſu *Societatis Regiæ* ac Typis *Joſephi Streater*. Proſtant Venales apud *Sam. Smith* ad inſignia Principis *Walliæ* in Cœmiterio *D. Pauli*, alioſq; nonnullos Bibliopolas. *Anno* MDCLXXXVII.

Title page of *Principia*. (*Author: I. Newton, 1686 – Book 1. Wellcome Collection*)

1. An object remains at rest or in constant motion unless an outside force acts upon it.
2. Force equals mass times acceleration.
3. For every action, there is an opposite and equal reaction.

In the same work he identified gravity (a concept inspired by witnessing a falling apple) as a force that acted upon all objects and kept planetary objects within elliptical orbits, determined the speed of sound, reasoned that the Earth is not perfectly spherical and much more. Some elements of his studies, such as the motion of the Moon, were so complex that Newton became ill due to lack of sleep and food.

In 1672, he was invited to be a Fellow of the Royal Society – a forum for debating and sharing scientific ideas. However, when **Robert Hooke** made some condescending criticism about his work on light, Newton's response was entirely disproportionate. His intermittent rages, nervous breakdowns and attempts to publicly humiliate Hooke showed that he could not cope with honest discussion. 'Forgive and forget' was certainly not Newton's mantra and he refused to accept the presidency of the Royal Society until Hooke's death in 1703. To avoid further criticism, he withdrew into private study and wrote many pieces on alchemy and religion (to some, his rejection of the concept of the Holy Trinity made him a heretic). He also embarked on a long, bitter row with the German polymath, Gottfried Leibniz, over who first developed the theory of calculus (it is now recognised that both developed the idea independently, using different mathematical notations, but Newton was first). A difficult man who was obsessed with his studies, it is perhaps not surprising that he never developed any romantic relationships. During one nervous breakdown, he even attacked his friend, **John Locke**, for trying to involve him with a woman.

A **Whig** by nature, Newton represented Cambridge University in the **parliament**s of 1689 and 1701 but showed little interest in his duties. He was far more conscientious, though, when working for the Royal Mint (from 1696). After moving to London, he oversaw the Great Recoinage of 1696 which attempted to restore the value of silver coins which had been repeatedly clipped or counterfeited. Newton improved minting technology and estimated that 10 per cent of England's coins were forgeries. He himself would visit taverns to acquire evidence with which he could prosecute and sometimes hang counterfeiters.

Near the end of his life, Newton lived with his niece and her husband near Winchester, and he died in his sleep. A wealthy and revered man, his funeral at Westminster Abbey was attended by an array of eminent scientists, nobles and philosophers. In his hair were found traces of mercury (possibly a result of his extensive experiments in alchemy), a substance that may have caused his eccentricity in later life.

Isaac Newton's achievements represent the apogee of the Scientific Revolution. His breakthroughs in maths and physics brought all the physical phenomena of the universe into one, mathematical system and enabled the Industrial Revolution and the technologies that we have today. Plaudits from a multitude of experts show that Newton's importance cannot be overstated: 'the greatest genius that ever existed' (LaGrange), 'a shining spirit ... who deserves our veneration' (Einstein), 'the Christmas of the modern age' (Goethe on Newton's birth). In his home, Thomas Jefferson kept portraits of 'the three greatest men that have ever lived' – **Bacon**, Locke and Newton. The list is endless. Newton himself, an introvert of simple tastes, veered between egotism and modesty. Referring to the work of predecessors such as Bacon, Descartes, Galileo, Kepler and **Boyle**, he once wrote, 'If I have seen further than others, it is by standing on the shoulders of giants,' and in a late memoir he wrote, 'I do not know what I may appear to the world, but to myself I seem to have been only like a boy playing on the sea-shore, and diverting myself in ... finding a smoother pebble or a prettier shell than ordinary, while the great ocean of truth lay all undiscovered before me.'

P

Palmer, Barbara (Countess of Castlemaine)

(1640–1709)

Courtesan

Born into a rich and powerful family, Barbara Villiers was a granddaughter of the **First Duke of Buckingham**'s older half-brother. Her father, however, spent a fortune raising a regiment for the king during the **Civil Wars** and died from a wound received at Bristol in 1643. This created much financial hardship for the family which was compounded by persecution during the Interregnum. Such was her impoverishment that her first love, the Earl of Chesterfield, was not allowed to marry her and she eventually wedded Roger Palmer, the son of a **Catholic** landowner, in 1659. That year, the Palmers were part of the entourage that travelled to Holland with the aim of escorting the king-in-exile, **Charles II**, back to England.

The young king instantly became infatuated with Barbara Palmer. Charming and voluptuous with slanting, heavy-lidded, violet eyes and pale skin, Palmer oozed sexual magnetism and was soon regarded as the most beautiful of the new, royalist women. The birth of their first child (although some were to claim that it resembled Chesterfield) cemented her place as the king's chief mistress and led to her separation from her husband whom Charles had already made Earl of Castlemaine, thereby making her a countess.

In the 1660s, Palmer dominated the English court much to the chagrin of the queen, **Catherine of Braganza**, whom Charles married in 1662. With supreme arrogance, Palmer happily humiliated Catherine by insisting on giving birth to their second child at Hampton Court while the royal couple were honeymooning there and then becoming Lady of the Bedchamber – the queen's chief lady-in-waiting. When Charles became besotted with a beautiful, new arrival – Lady Frances Stuart – Palmer attempted to undermine her by leading him to her bedchamber where she was found naked with her future husband (Frances was one of the few women who refused Charles's advances). Assertive and demanding, Palmer was known for her violent outbursts and dislike of certain courtiers and probably influenced politics. She viewed the **Earl of Clarendon**, for example, as a rival and so constantly undermined him and rejoiced at his downfall in 1667. She also profited from selling audiences with the king.

Palmer was known to be an entertaining and generous host for her numerous social events and **Pepys** (a self-confessed admirer) once noted that she was the only lady present who went to check on the welfare of a child after some scaffolding collapsed at the king's coronation. Her influence, open promiscuity and extravagance, however, led the other diarist of the period, John Evelyn, to call her 'the curse of the nation' and her notoriety was often the subject of satirical plays. There are numerous portraits of Palmer too which often show her in relaxed poses with loose clothing and bedroom eyes. These were then copied onto engravings and printed for a public thirsty for salacious gossip making her the most recognisable woman in England.

Lady Frances Stuart. The face that became the model for Britannia on the reverse of copper coins from 1672. (*Artist: P. Lely, c. 1662. Royal Collection*)

By the end of the 1660s, Palmer was beginning to lose her dominance as Charles took more interest in others such as **Nell Gwyn** and Louise de Kerouaille. She, too, had other lovers such as an acrobat (Jacob Hall), a courtier (Henry Jermyn) and a soldier (**John Churchill**). The latter was probably the father of her sixth child although Palmer insisted it was the king's to earn the baby a titled inheritance, like its siblings. In 1670, Charles made her Duchess of Cleveland and gave her the old Tudor mansion, Nonsuch Palace, but, after the 1673 Test Act banned Catholics from holding positions of power, Palmer left court (she had converted in 1663).

From 1676 to 1682, Palmer spent most of her time living a life of luxury in France with her four youngest children and continued to have lovers on whom she spent extravagantly. In particular, she lost huge sums of money gambling on card tables. Unsurprisingly, therefore, Palmer had the dilapidated Nonsuch Palace torn down in 1683 and sold its building materials to help pay off her debts. By now, she and Charles had become reconciled, and they spent time together a week before his death.

Soon after, aged 45, Palmer had a child fathered by Cardonell Goodman, an actor with a reputation for violence who tried to poison two of her children. He later became a gamester and a Jacobite who plotted against **William III**. After Lord Castlemaine's death in 1705, she married General Robert Fielding, an unscrupulous rogue who, only two weeks earlier had been tricked into marrying a commoner whom he thought was a wealthy heiress. After prosecuting him for bigamy, Palmer had to seek protection from his physical assaults and, after the discovery of his affair with her granddaughter, annulled the **marriage**.

Bloated from the effects of oedema, Palmer died from heart failure at her home in Chiswick where she had been looking after her illegitimate grandson. Undoubtedly, she represents the worst excesses of the Restoration court and the risks of exercising power without responsibility. At the same time, though, Barbara Palmer had successfully used her looks and personality to carve out the kind of career and independence that most seventeenth-century women could have only dreamed about.

Parliament

The first Stuart parliament assembled in March 1604, and it was comprised, as it had been for centuries, of the Lords, the Commons and the Crown. The former was made up of twenty-six bishops and archbishops and 277 peers while the Commons had 462 members – all unpaid – who represented towns (boroughs) and counties. These 'commoners' tended to be landed, male gentry and wealthy merchants. Chosen by election, only those with property worth more than 40 shillings had the franchise (around one-third of the male population). In effect, though, elections were rarely contested as candidates were usually chosen through 'back-room deals'. Nor were the various constituencies fairly distributed. Migration had emptied many of those in Cornwall, but it still returned forty-four MPs while the notorious 'rotten borough' of Dunwich, in Suffolk, had once matched London's population but coastal erosion had reduced it to around fifty households by 1700 when it was still sending two MPs to Parliament. The growing town of Manchester with around 10,000 people, meanwhile, had no representation.

This first parliament must have been disappointing for the new king. **James I** had been used to working with a Scottish parliament that was accustomed to royal authority. In London, though, he found a parliament that was less easily influenced by royal patronage and members who were well-grounded in their rights and the law. Thus began a century of almost continual conflict between parliamentary privilege and royal prerogative. Previous monarchs had been prepared to compromise as some sort of working relationship with the MPs was vital if they were to obtain extra funds, carry out religious reform and have their laws enforced (many who sat in the Commons also acted as justices of the peace in their constituencies). James I and **Charles II** understood this; much less so, **Charles I** and **James II**. In the background, too, was the growing trend towards absolutism on the continent which caused much concern among MPs.

Not often, however, was Parliament united – MPs spent much time aiming to further their own interests and campaigning for bills that affected their localities. Dominant factions did sometimes arise though – the **Puritan** junto of 1640–42 and the **Whig** junto of 1694–99, for example. One of the great ironies of the seventeenth century, perhaps, is the series of failed parliaments in the 1650s. Free of the shackles of interference from the Crown or Lords, this was the Commons' opportunity to really assert itself. Internal divisions and disputes with the army, however, led to its failure and the return of the monarchy in 1660.

Parliament in 1640. (*Artist: unknown, c. 1640. British Museum via Wikimedia Commons*)

The Cavalier Parliament (1661–79) is the longest to sit in British history and it passed a host of important bills most of which were initiated by the Lords. These included those that promoted trade, enforced **Anglican** uniformity, imposed an unpopular and intrusive hearth tax, reformed provision for the poor and created toll gates on the Great North Road to finance repairs to that important transport artery. It also weakened the 1640 Triennial Bill by merely suggesting that elections should be held every three years. From the early 1670s, though, the Commons rediscovered its assertiveness mainly over fears about the royal succession and the Exclusion Crisis. It was only in 1681, after the pro-exclusion Whigs had been discredited by the farcical **Popish Plot**, that Charles II felt strong enough to dissolve Parliament and rule alone.

The **Glorious Revolution** (1688) and its aftermath marked a huge shift in England's political development. Although the **Bill of Rights** was not exactly radical, it was a formal declaration of Parliament's demands which both **William of Orange** and **Mary** agreed to before being crowned. English government was now more contractual with a recognition that responsibility for running the country was shared between Crown and Parliament, but it was the latter who, in effect, now pulled the strings. The last Stuart monarchs could still appoint and dismiss ministers and veto bills, but the threat of non-cooperation usually forced their hand. More telling are the Triennial Act (1694) which requested parliamentary elections at least every three years (later deemed so disruptive to the running of the country that it was replaced by the Septennial Act of 1716) and the Act of Settlement (1701) which set out **Anne**'s heirs. For the first time, it was Parliament, not the monarch, that established the royal succession.

The nature and power of Parliament changed dramatically in the Stuart period. In the first decades of the seventeenth century, it had had a working, if somewhat brittle, relationship with the monarch with the Lords still considered the dominant chamber. With its bishops and aristocracy owing their positions and titles to the king, this created a counterbalance to the more strident Commons although the Lords was not always compliant. By the end of the century, however, there had been a sea change. During the long wars with France in the last twenty-five years, its role as the initiator of tax bills gave the Commons a crucial voice. Parliament had shown itself to be indispensable, most significantly during three pivotal points of the century – 1649, 1660 and 1689 – when it, not the Crown, had taken control.

Penn, William

(1644–1718)

Theologian, writer and founder of Pennsylvania

Penn was born near the Tower of London, the son of a naval officer who later became the distinguished Admiral Penn who fought for both **Cromwell** and **Charles II** in England's naval wars against Spain and Holland; his mother was Margaret Jasper, the daughter of a rich Dutch merchant. Aged 4, he contracted smallpox which caused his hair to fall out (and the subsequent necessity for wigs) and his family to move to the Essex countryside. From 1660, he attended Christ Church College in Oxford but was expelled for his association with the highly respected **Puritan** dean and theologian, John Owen and for refusing to attend **Anglican** services.

His despairing father then sent him to Paris in the hope that this would reform his character. Instead, his son conveyed a dislike for the extravagance and privilege he witnessed and was far more interested in attending the lectures of the French theologian, Moise Amyraut, who argued for religious toleration. After his return, he began to study law at Lincoln's Inn but his **education** there was interrupted by the **Plague** of 1665. During this catastrophe he noticed a group of people – the Quakers – defying orders by smuggling food and drink to those quarantined, helping to bury the dead and taking in orphaned children. Penn was sent to manage his father's Irish estate the following year; and it was in Cork that he met his final influencer, the Quaker missionary, Thomas Loe, and thereupon decided to join his sect.

This was a dangerous move. The Quakers, or Friends, were one of several religious groups that had sprung up in the aftermath of the **Civil Wars**. They believed in an inner light, meaning God was in everyone, and that there was no need for churches or rituals. Instead, they would meet regularly, often in silence, and anyone could speak. As individualists, they rejected authority by refusing to pay tithes to the Church, swear oaths or remove their hats in front of social superiors and regarded women as equals. Pacifism, tolerance and equality were the cornerstones of their faith. In 1660, there were an estimated 35,000 Quakers and this figure almost doubled over the next twenty years. It is no wonder that the Anglican authorities (and Puritans before them) considered the Quakers as a threat to **society** and the established hierarchy. Many were fined, imprisoned and brutally punished. Their leader, George Fox, was incarcerated eight times. Penn was jailed too and, although his family connections obtained his release, his depressed father felt compelled to disown and disinherit him. It was only on his deathbed that the admiral recognised the courage of his son's convictions and agreed to patch up their differences.

Penn spent much of the next twelve years travelling with Fox around Britain and Germany doing missionary work. He also wrote many tracts and treatises which established the theology behind Quakerism, his most famous being *No Cross, No Crown* (1669), which was written during one of his several imprisonments. In the following year, he was arrested for being in breach of the Conventicle Act which banned religious gatherings of more than five non-conformists. After the judge refused to allow him to see a copy of the charges, the jury returned a verdict of not guilty. Incensed, the judge then imprisoned the whole jury for as long as it took to change their minds. One of them, Edward Bushel, then appealed to the Court of Common Pleas from his cell and won. The famous *Bushel Case* established the independence of the jury from the judge.

With the situation for his co-religionists worsening, Penn appealed to the Crown for a grant of land in America where Quakers could settle. To his surprise, in 1681, Charles II gave him 45,000 square miles west of the Delaware River and north of the province of Maryland in return for a debt that he had owed his father.

Penn first called it New Wales then Sylvania (Woods) before the king insisted on the prefix 'Penn' in honour of his father. The next year, Penn travelled to his new lands and negotiated one of the few fair treaties with the indigenous people – the Lenape – which allowed them to cross his territory for hunting and fishing. Some of the new settlers were Quakers already living in the neighbouring province of Delaware, but Penn conducted a vigorous marketing campaign to attract more people from all over Europe with the promise of religious freedom. Within six months, he had parcelled out 300,000 acres to over 250 settlers. Most were Quakers but Huguenots, Amish and Jews also braved the journey across the Atlantic.

To administer his 'Holy Experiment', Penn drew up a 'Framework of Government' based on the ideals of equality and fairness. Inspired by the work of **John Locke**, it set out two elected chambers, a separation of powers, fair taxes and trials, **education** for all, progressive prisons, capital punishment only for treason and murder (there were 200 capital offences in England) and freedom of worship. Unlike the northern, Puritan colonies, **witchcraft** was deemed not an offence although laws against 'morally-corrupting' activities such as cockfighting, drunkenness, gambling and stage plays were introduced. Far more radical was the inclusion of an amendment clause which allowed for a constitution that could 'bend' with the times. This 'Framework' would later form the basis of the American constitution.

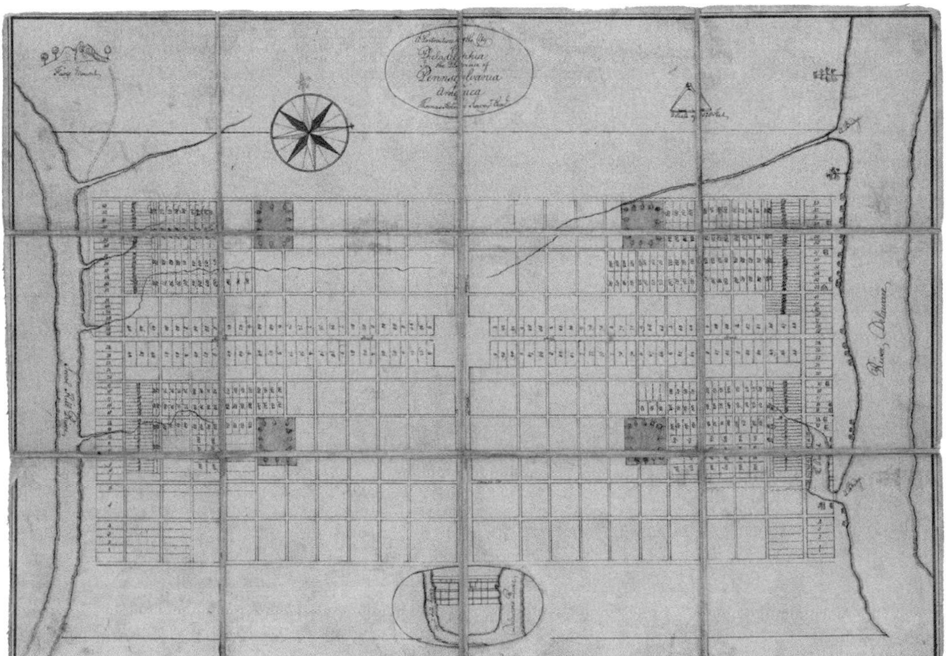

Original plan of Philadelphia. A rectangular grid of 12,000 acres with a large central square and four smaller squares in each quadrant. The main streets were kept wide to prevent the sort of fire that destroyed London. (*Author: T. Holme, 1683. Historical Society of Pennsylvania via Wikimedia Commons*)

Next to the Delaware River, Penn founded the province's chief city, Philadelphia (Brotherly Love), which was planned on a grid system with streets named after trees and numbers.

Penn returned to England in 1684 and only spent a further two years in Pennsylvania (1699–1701). He spent much of this time writing, including tracts recommending a European parliament that would prevent wars and a union of the American colonies. The remaining time was spent fighting court cases. One concerned a boundary dispute with Maryland. Another concerned his business secretary, Philip Ford, who embezzled him into huge debts and tricked him into signing his province away. His eldest son then added to his financial woes by building up huge gambling debts. At one point, Penn even ended up in a debtors' prison. After the **Glorious Revolution**, he also received much criticism for openly supporting **James II** when the king had granted toleration to Quakers. Meanwhile, there was much bickering in Philadelphia about the province's governance. To solve all his problems, Penn attempted to sell Pennsylvania to the Crown but suffered a stroke (1712) before he could succeed. He eventually died penniless at his home in Berkshire after being nursed by his wife, Hannah.

Pennsylvania remained in the Penn family's hands until the American Revolution, but William's heirs lacked his vision, and it gradually became a more secular and commercial colony. Penn himself may come across as a hopeless idealist, a poor judge of character who baulked at administrative detail and whose dreams did not match reality. Hypocritically, perhaps, he even involved himself in the **slave trade** although slaves were better treated on his territory than elsewhere. One could also argue, however, that the world needs idealists and, after all, it was Pennsylvania that became a beacon of tolerance and fairness to many other states and countries.

Pepys, Samuel

(1633–1703)

Naval administrator and diarist

Pepys was born in Fleet Street, London, his father being a tailor who had migrated from Huntingdonshire and his mother the daughter of a Whitechapel butcher. Through connections to his father's wealthier cousins, he was allowed to attend Huntingdon Grammar School, the alma mater of **Oliver Cromwell**, before going to St Paul's in London. As a **Puritan** and a republican, Pepys skipped school in early 1649 to witness **Charles I**'s execution and, in the following year, completed his **education** at Magdalane College, Cambridge. In the mid-1650s, he entered the service of a powerful relative, Admiral Montagu, and married Elisabeth de St Michel, the 14-year-old daughter of a poor Huguenot immigrant.

This **marriage** was quite unusual as he was marrying beneath himself, but he was completely taken by her beauty. Around three years later, Pepys finally decided to have bladder stones removed from his urinary tract – a very risky procedure but the incessant pain had left him with no choice. Although the incision on his bladder opened up later in life, the operation was a success, and Pepys celebrated its anniversary every year.

After Cromwell's death in 1658, Pepys, like many others, believed that a restoration of the monarchy was the best way to avoid anarchy. He was a minor official on the ship that brought **Charles II** back to England and, thereafter, his career took off as he tied his colours to the Stuart mast. That same year (1660), he was appointed Clerk of the Acts to the Navy Board, an important administrative position that oversaw naval contracts. Pepys had had no experience of the navy, but it was typical of him to learn quickly and act with great efficiency.

He successfully defended himself against accusations of failures in his responsibilities in the wake of the disastrous Dutch **Raid on the Medway** and in 1673 became the administrative head of the navy. In this role, he was thorough in dealing with corruption and massively increasing England's shipbuilding programme. Pepys also improved the quality of sailors' rations (although the lack of fruit and vegetables meant that scurvy remained a huge problem), created the first exams for officers (including tests in navigation and mathematics) and set higher standards for ships' surgeons. He demanded a more scientific approach to navigation and so encouraged the building of the Royal Observatory at Greenwich. Pepys's efficiency drives and known association with the former head of the navy and

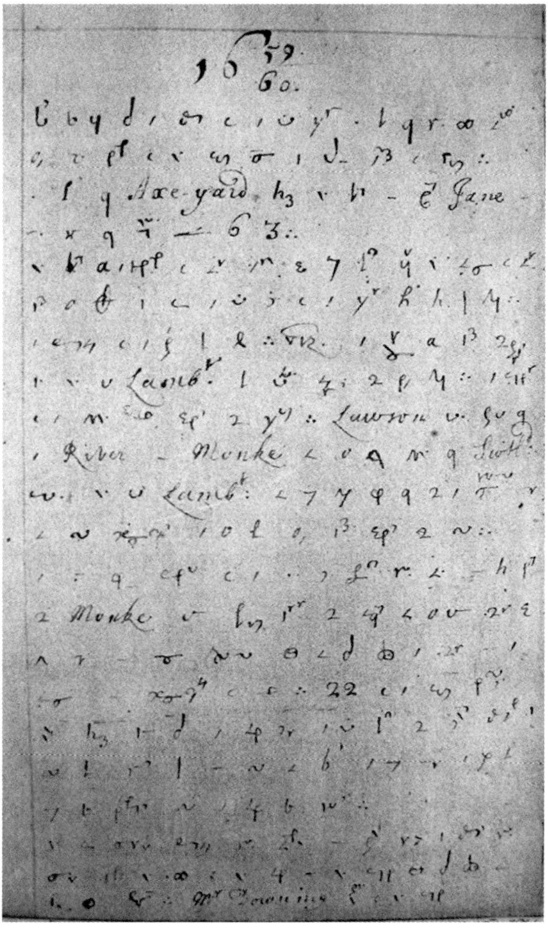

First page of Pepys's diary. Note the date – 1659. In England, the new year began on 25 March. Only in 1752 did 1 January start the new year. (*Author: S. Pepys, 1660 via Wikimedia Commons*)

self-confessed **Catholic, James, Duke of York**, brought him many enemies though, including the **Earl of Shaftesbury**. During the **Popish Plot** crisis, having been accused of being a secret Catholic and selling naval secrets to the French, he was briefly incarcerated in the Tower of London.

Pepys returned to favour in 1684, resumed his post and became MP for Harwich so he could represent the navy in **Parliament**. After **James II**'s flight during the **Glorious Revolution**, he was again imprisoned but no charges were brought against him. He then retired to the village of Clapham and spent the rest of his life amassing a huge library collection which was later donated to Cambridge University. As well as being a book collector, Pepys was passionate about theatre and music, could play several instruments and was a keen singer who liked to perform in **coffee houses**. He was very interested in science too and was president of the Royal Society for four years from 1684. As such, his name appears on the front of **Isaac Newton**'s *Principia*. However, more than anything else, it is his diary that has made Pepys famous.

Over a million words and enclosed in six volumes, the diary was written in shorthand to keep its contents secret. Pepys began it on 1 January 1660 and finished in 1669 when he feared that it was making his eyesight worse. Written in detail and with remarkable candour, it provides a fascinating insight into life in Restoration England and covers major events such as General **Monck** marching into London, the **Plague** and **Fire of London** and the **Second Anglo-Dutch War**. No subject was too trivial for him including the weather and being woken by his cat in the middle of the night. All was included – even court gossip:

> 'I hear that Harry Killigrew is banished … for saying that my **Lady Castlemayne** was a little lecherous girle when she was young.'
>
> frustration with incompetent colleagues, money concerns, his new watch with an alarm, his worries about alcoholism and health, 'Went to bed with my head not well, by my too much drinking today. And I have a boyle under my chin which troubled me greatly.'
>
> his vanity and concerns that Elisabeth was having an affair with her dance teacher, 'This is my devilish jealousy … it makes a very Hell in my mind …'
>
> a passing bell-man crying out, 'Past one of the clock, and a cold, and frosty, windy morning'
>
> and going to the theatre, 'we saw *Midsummer's Night's Dream* … it is the most insipid ridiculous play that ever I saw in my life. I saw, I confess, some good dancing and some handsome women, which was all my pleasure.'

Indeed, Pepys is very frank about his sexual desires and affairs. Elisabeth may have had gynaecological problems which prevented sex, so her husband often sought to relieve his considerable libido elsewhere. There were at least eight married women whom he fondled, flirted or slept with and he even tried to molest one young woman during a church service. He hardly visited prostitutes but records how he paid a shilling to have one 'play' with him in a coach. He seduced the 15-year-old daughter of his neighbour and colleague, Admiral William Penn, but got into terrible trouble after Elisabeth caught him embracing her servant, Deb, with a hand up her skirt. After dismissing the poor girl, she threatened to leave him and slit Deb's nose if he continued to see her. A remorseful Pepys eventually begged for forgiveness. After Elisabeth's death (1669), he remained single and childless although he had a long-term housekeeper who people assumed was his mistress.

A Cambridge student, John Smith, was the first to transcribe the diary into proper English. It took him three years (1819–22) only to be told that Pepys had provided a cypher that lay on a shelf above the diary. So sexually explicit are the diary's contents that it was censored for 150 years, and the full details only emerged in the 1970s. Pepys certainly had his flaws, not least being his objectification of women, but there is no questioning his importance for anyone studying the seventeenth century.

Pilgrim Fathers

(1620)

The founding settlers of New England in America

The Pilgrim Fathers originated around the village of Scrooby in Nottinghamshire and were Separatists. Like the **Puritans**, they wanted a simpler, non-hierarchical form of worship but, unlike the Puritans, they believed that the **Anglican** Church was incapable of reform and wanted to exist outside it. Such a belief was considered dangerously destabilising for **society** and so they suffered repression in the form of fines and imprisonment for non-attendance of church services and general harassment. Led by the local postmaster and manor bailiff, William Brewster, around thirty attempted to flee to the Dutch Netherlands in 1607 but were betrayed by their ship's captain and arrested for attempting to leave the country. They finally succeeded the following year by leaving in small groups.

They and other Separatists settled in Leiden, Holland, where they were allowed religious freedom and attempted to settle down and learn new skills so that they could work in the local textile, printing and brewing trades. This was hard for some as they only knew farming and, with the language barrier, many also struggled in their relations with the Dutch. Fears also developed that they were losing their children to Dutch culture and seeking employment elsewhere. War loomed too as, by 1617, Holland's truce with Spain appeared on the verge of collapse. To save their community from eventual extinction, it was decided to emigrate to America. A successful colony had already been established in **Virginia**, and, at the same time, the Separatists saw an opportunity to spread Christianity to a remote part of the world.

Painstakingly lengthy negotiations began with the London Company, a group of merchants who administered and invested in Virginia. Eventually, it was agreed that the company would provide passage and all necessary supplies for establishing a settlement. In return, the colonists' land would belong to the company for seven years and they would send back any natural resources such as fish and furs. Then, after seven years, all assets would be divided between the company and the settlers. It was decided to locate at the mouth of the Hudson River, on the edge of Virginia, where they could still practise their religion freely. The congregation bought a small ship, the *Speedwell*, to take those who were ready to Southampton. There, they met other settlers – gathered by the investors – and the larger *Mayflower*, a 180-ton, 100-feet-long cargo ship.

The two ships left Southampton on 5 August 1620 but were forced to dock at Plymouth after discovering leaks on the *Speedwell*. After deciding that it was unseaworthy, some families had to be split up with room for only 102 on the *Mayflower* which eventually left on 6 September. After a difficult, stormy voyage in cramped conditions that lasted two months the passengers finally sighted land, now known as Cape Cod, on 9 November. The crew then headed south, aiming

The landing of the Pilgrims. The *Mayflower* is in the distance and, possibly, *Squanto* on the left. (*Artist: after W. Bradford, 1876. Library of Congress*)

for the Hudson River, but shoals and strong currents forced them to turn back. With provisions running low, it was decided to settle in the area (already named New England in 1614 by Captain John Smith who had helped found Jamestown in Virginia). As this was not Virginia, however, the non-Separatists threatened to break away so, to allay fears, the Pilgrims drew up the *Mayflower Compact* by which it was agreed that the settlers would create fair laws that would benefit the whole community while maintaining loyalty to King **James I**. Brewster himself was elected as the community's senior elder (religious leader). Considered by many to be the the world's first written constitution, the *Compact* became a seed of the future American constitution.

Exploratory expeditions, led by their professional soldier, Myles Standish, discovered a suitable site for a settlement on the west side of Cape Cod Bay and was named New Plymouth (the Hudson River location was soon settled by Dutch colonists in 1624 and named New Amsterdam which became New York in 1664). Construction was started on the site of an abandoned Patuxet village where the land had already been cleared. Unburied skeletons in the village revealed the fact that nearly all the local inhabitants had been wiped out by disease, possibly smallpox, brought by earlier European explorers.

Corn for future planting was found in local burial mounds and building work soon began while the settlers continued to live on the *Mayflower*. That first winter, however, almost saw the death of the nascent colony. Scurvy caught during the voyage along with pneumonia brought on by the cold, wet winter decimated the settlers. At one point, only seven of them were well enough to feed the others. By the end of March 1621, almost half of them had died and graves were covered up to conceal their weakness from the Wampanoag (People of the First Light) living further inland. That spring, the surviving Pilgrims made a treaty with their indigenous neighbours by which they agreed not to harm or steal from one other. The help of one man was crucial. Squanto had previously been kidnapped by explorers and had lived in Spain and England before returning home only to find that he was the last of the Patuxets. As an interpreter, Squanto was able to facilitate the treaty and show the Pilgrims how to catch eels, trap for furs and grow crops (the seeds from England had mostly failed). In the autumn of 1621, a three-day Thanksgiving festival, attended by ninety Wampanoag, was arranged to mark the success of the Pilgrims' first harvest. By 1627, over a hundred more settlers arrived, including those who had been left behind in Holland and England, and New Plymouth had become a stable settlement.

Contemporaries gave little thought to the whole event. Having no cargo, the *Mayflower* was not even mentioned in Plymouth's port records of 1620 although the authorities probably considered sailing into an Atlantic winter an act of madness. The event also presaged the mass migration of 20,000 Puritans to New England in the 1630s. Unfortunately, unlike the Pilgrims, they showed little tolerance for others such as migrating Quakers and unleashed much cruelty upon the indigenous people over the next few decades. The story of the Pilgrim Fathers (known as The Forefathers until the 1820s), however, is a key episode in the annals of American history and, quite rightly, is considered one of courage, resilience and collaboration.

Plague

The Black Death of 1348–49 was the first incidence of plague in England and proceeded to wipe out 30 to 50 per cent of the population. From then on, it was endemic in **society** and very rarely was there a year when no one died from it. Periodically, an epidemic would be unleashed with devastating consequences. In 1563, an estimated 25 per cent of London's population perished and the 1625 epidemic, after killing around 35,000 people, became known as the Great Plague. This epithet, however, was transferred to the final, even more disastrous, outbreak that struck in 1665.

Plague (from the Latin '*plaga*' meaning wound or blow) was caused by the bacterium, *Yersinia Pestis*, carried by fleas and lice. These, in turn, lived on the rats that multiplied among the rubbish and sewage that clogged up so many of the streets in England's towns. These were black rats that could climb the wooden walls and nest above people's ceilings. When, invariably, these rats were killed by the bacteria the fleas would jump down to live off a human host. No one at the time, however, seemed to notice that many dead rats would precede an epidemic. Typically, symptoms in humans included red rashes, fever, vomiting, headache and inflamed lymph nodes (buboes) in the armpits, neck and groin; there was about a 50–60 per cent survival rate. Pneumonic (lungs) and septacaemic (blood) varieties were far more fatal but, fortunately, it was largely bubonic plague that devastated London in 1665.

News of rising levels of plague on the continent had reached England by 1663 and so the authorities placed all incoming ships into a period of quarantine. Nevertheless, it is thought that the disease arrived from Amsterdam hidden in bales of cotton. Certainly, the first cases were reported in the docks as well as the parish of St Giles – a slum outside the city. By April 1665, it was clear that incidents of plague were on the rise and the authorities ordered the boarding up and quarantining of those houses with victims inside for forty days. The cleric, Thomas Vincent, wrote, 'it was very dismal to behold the red crosses, and read in great letters "LORD, HAVE MERCY UPON US" on the doors, and watchmen standing before them with halberds.' It was a useless measure anyway that simply reflected the persistent belief that infection spread from human to human. With quarantining showing no effect, more people believed that the disease was caused by foul vapours and so large fires were lit in the streets to purify the air and people held aromatic posies to their faces. There was a certain irony to this as it was London itself, with its coal fires and black smoke belching from soap factories, breweries and iron foundries, that produced foul air.

To record the spread of plague, two searchers per parish were employed to examine bodies to discover the causes of death which were published on weekly bills of mortality. These were usually illiterate, old women who knew little about diseases and were paid a pittance. They lived alone and had to carry a white stick as a warning to others when out and about. Invariably, they were open to bribes as people wanted to avoid quarantine and so the bills often gave other causes of death such as consumption (tuberculosis). With cries of 'Bring out your dead!', corpses were put onto carts at night and, with no ceremony, flung into plague pits around London and covered in lime.

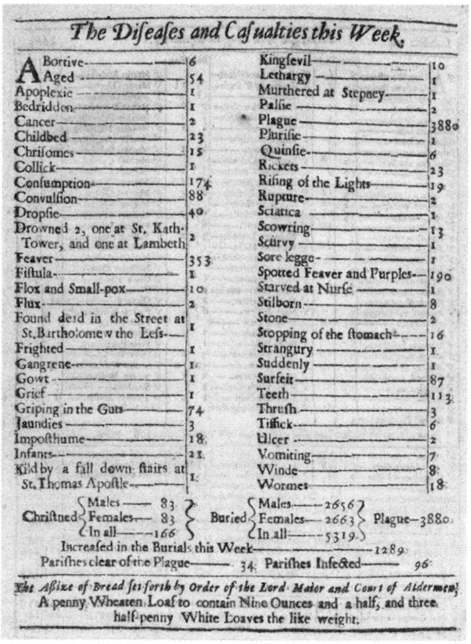

The Diſeaſes and Caſualties this Week.

Abortive	6	Kingſevil	10
Aged	54	Lethargy	1
Apoplexie	1	Murthered at Stepney	1
Bedridden	1	Palſie	2
Cancer	2	Plague	3880
Childbed	23	Pluriſie	1
Chriſomes	15	Quinſie	6
Collick	1	Rickets	23
Conſumption	174	Riſing of the Lights	19
Convulſion	88	Rupture	2
Dropſie	40	Sciatica	1
Drowned 2, one at St. Kath-Tower, and one at Lambeth	2	Scowring	13
Feaver	353	Scurvy	1
Fiſtula	1	Sore legge	1
Flox and Small-pox	10	Spotted Feaver and Purples	190
Flux	2	Starved at Nurſe	1
Found dead in the Street at St. Bartholomew the Leſs	1	Stilborn	8
Frighted	1	Stone	2
Gangrene	1	Stopping of the ſtomach	16
Gowt	1	Strangury	1
Grief	1	Suddenly	1
Griping in the Guts	74	Surfeit	87
Jaundies	3	Teeth	113
Impoſthume	18	Thruſh	3
Infants	21	Tiſſick	6
Kild by a fall down ſtairs at St. Thomas Apoſtle	1	Ulcer	2
		Vomiting	7
		Winde	8
		Wormes	18

Chriſtned: Males 83, Females 83, In all 166. Buried: Males 2656, Females 2663, In all 5319. Plague 3880.

Increaſed in the Burials this Week 1289

Pariſhes clear of the Plague 34 Pariſhes Infected 96

The Aſsize of Bread ſet forth by Order of the Lord Maior and Court of Aldermen; A penny Wheaten Loaf to contain Nine Ounces and a half, and three half-penny White Loaves the like weight.

Bill of Mortality. For the week beginning 12 August. Note the huge plague figure, the increase in burials and the bizarre variety of causes of death. (*Author: unknown, 1665. Wellcome Collection*)

As the weather warmed up, it was clear that London was in the grip of an epidemic. In July, the wealthiest, with their doctors, fled to their country homes. **Charles II** and his retinue migrated to Hampton Court and then Oxford where **Parliament**, too, assembled. Those who stayed were not impressed. The civil servant, Thomas Povey, wrote, 'Death is now become so familiar, and the People soe insensible of danger … neither the richer sort will be brought to contribut, nor the meaner to submit, though to their own apparant good and preservation.' **Samuel Pepys** remained by his post for the most part, however. In August, he wrote 'The people die so, that now it seems they are fain [obliged] to carry the dead to be buried by daylight, the nights not sufficing to do it in.'

Those who were crowded into the unhygienic slums that surrounded the city suffered the most and had nowhere to run. Many tried to flee but were turned back by the nervous inhabitants of surrounding villages and so had to live off the country or die of starvation. Back in London, brave plague doctors – usually young and inexperienced – with their distinctive attire would visit the sick and were often seen as harbingers of death. Some were undoubtedly quacks, but others genuinely had faith in their treatments. These included bloodletting with leeches, the lancing of buboes and putting frogs onto the lumps. Many thought tobacco to be a good prophylactic and a general cull of cats and dogs was ordered as it was thought they were spreading the disease. This, in fact, made matters worse as the fleas were now more likely to jump onto humans.

Plague doctor. The 'beak' contained herbs. (*Author: J. J. Manget, before 1721. Wellcome Collection*)

The plague reached its peak in September when 7,165 Londoners died in one week alone and only gradually abated. On 16 October, Pepys was writing, 'But, Lord! How empty the streets are and melancholy, so many poor sick people in the streets full of sores; and so many sad stories overheard as I walk, everybody talking of this dead, and that man sick.' Only in February was it considered safe for the monarch to return. Other parts of England, such as York and Norwich, were badly hit too. Most famous is the village of Eyam in Derbyshire where the plague apparently arrived in a merchant's bag of cloth. The small population agreed to cut themselves off from the wider world in order not to spread the disease and neighbouring villagers left food on boundary stones in return for coins that were 'sterilised' in running water. Sadly, 74 per cent of these brave and well-meaning villagers died. Far better if they had camped in the open fields and let the fleas die out in the village.

In London alone, the bills recorded a total of 68,596 deaths although 100,000 is probably a more accurate figure. This represented 15 per cent of the capital's population but within two years, masses of migrants, seeking new trading and work opportunities, brought the figure back to pre-plague levels. 1665–66 saw the last plague epidemic in England with a few localised outbreaks over the following two decades (the Suffolk countryside saw the last occurrence in 1918!). The cause of plague was not discovered until 1894 so what stopped it being a scourge of society? Not the **Fire of London** which left the slums untouched. The answer lies in a combination of factors. A decline in the virulence of *Yersinia Pestis* and greater human immunity, perhaps, as well as a change in trade routes. With more goods being transported by sea rather than overland from the Far East, where plague persisted, rats were less likely to survive as long on a ship. Also, from 1730, the larger and more aggressive brown rats crowded out the black ones. The brown variety could still carry fleas but not being a climber, tended to live in sewers and farther from humans. Living conditions in cities became more hygienic too as the cesspits and accumulating filth were gradually replaced by underground sewers and better waste disposal.

Popish Plot

(1678–81)

A fabrication that instigated a crisis

The fuel for this crisis had existed in England since the Reformation. Societal fear and distrust of **Catholic**s had been periodically stoked by events that lived long in the national psyche – the Marian persecutions of the 1550s, the Spanish Armada and various plots in Elizabeth's reign, the **Gunpowder Plot**, the Irish Rebellion of 1641 and the belief that the **Fire of London** was started by Catholic agents. However, Catholics made up, at most, a mere 5 per cent of the population and posed no threat to the country. They lived harmoniously with their Protestant neighbours and paid their fines for non-attendance of **Anglican** services, or they attended but held private masses at home too. Unfortunately, **Charles II** added to the irrational fears. Were not his wife and mother Catholics and what was behind his Declaration of Indulgence (1672) that offered toleration to Catholics? Even more suspiciously, why had he allied with Catholic France against fellow Protestants during the **Third Anglo-Dutch War**? Worrying, too, was the question of the succession. The king's heir was his brother, **James, Duke of York**, who in 1673 had revealed his Catholic faith.

Into this atmosphere appeared two disreputable troublemakers: Titus Oates and Israel Tonge. Oates, only 29 years old in 1678, already had a long history of personal failure and deceit. He had been expelled from St John's College, Cambridge, for refusing to pay a tailor, sacked as a village priest for stealing, drunkenness and lewd behaviour, bound over for perjury after falsely accusing a schoolteacher of sodomy and dismissed as a naval chaplain for homosexuality. By 1677, penniless and desperate, Oates converted to Catholicism later claiming that he was 'seduced by Popish sirens'. Initially, however, he stated that he had wanted to go undercover to discover any nefarious plans in the Jesuit training colleges he attended in Spain and France. After being expelled from these for blasphemy, he had returned to London and teamed up with Tonge, an unhinged and fanatical anti-Catholic priest. Together, they cooked up the Popish Plot.

Oates and Tonge claimed to have found letters (forged by themselves) outlining plans by Jesuits to assassinate the king during his regular walks in St James's Park. One attempt had already failed, apparently, when an assassin's gunpowder was too wet to ignite. A contingency plan involved Sir George Wakeman (physician to Queen **Catherine**) who would poison the king. Charles himself was very sceptical but allowed further investigation. Before the Privy Council, Tonge was derided but Oates impressed everyone with his confident grasp of details which included the names of several conspirators along with five lords, two Irish archbishops, **Samuel Pepys** and **Sir Jeffrey Hudson**. He also made vague claims that thousands

Anti-Catholic propaganda. British innocents being killed by Catholic devils and a monster. Full Catholic emancipation only occurred in 1829. (*Author: B. Harris, 1720. Compositor via Wikimedia Commons*)

of Catholic Irish and Scots, supported by the French, were about to rise to depose the Anglican monarchy. Nevertheless, there were growing inconsistencies in his story and doubtless he would have been uncovered as a charlatan.

However, two events worked in Oates's favour. A search of the home of one of those he accused, a former secretary to the Duke of York's wife, revealed secret correspondence with members of the French royal court that seemed to corroborate what Oates was saying. The second event revolved around the magistrate, Sir Edmund Godfrey, who had received Oates's original depositions. In October, Godfrey went missing and, five days later, his corpse was discovered, looking like he had been strangled and run through with his own sword. To many, it appeared that he had been silenced by Catholic agents and panic, fanned by a multitude of rumour-mongering pamphlets (like that of 1641), ensued. It is quite remarkable how quickly 'fake news' could spread in pre-internet, seventeenth-century **society**.

Amid the hysteria, many Catholics were rounded up and imprisoned or banned from entering a ten-mile radius of London, **Parliament** was searched in expectation of another Gunpowder Plot and thousands of Londoners attended pageants in which effigies of the pope were tipped into fires. London's militia was doubled in size and there were even rumours of a French landing in Dorset. Oates, now in receipt of a Whitehall apartment and an allowance, fanned the flames by producing several 'informers' – usually men of ill repute looking for extra cash – who made increasingly fanciful claims such as assassins' plans to shoot the king with a silver bullet so that the wound would not heal. The **Whigs** in Parliament took advantage of the crisis too. Led by **Lord Shaftesbury** they forced through a Test Act which banned Catholics from high office and attempted, unsuccessfully, to have Catherine removed from court and the Duke of York excluded from the succession. They also used the plot to bring about the downfall of Charles's chief minister, Lord Danby. Many other reputations and livelihoods were ruined; there were around thirty-six fatal victims (executed, died or suicide in prison), largely Catholic priests.

The continual pleas of innocence of those in court, the mounting inconsistencies of Oates's evidence and the attempt to implicate the queen through Wakeman (who was acquitted) gradually produced more level heads and the hysteria waned. The final execution was that of Archbishop Plunkett of Armagh (July 1681) – the last Catholic martyr to die in England. The hanging, drawing and quartering of such a clearly pious man brought about much revulsion and the closure of a particularly ignominious episode in English history.

Politically, the Whigs were discredited by the whole affair. This put their opponents, the **Tories**, in the ascendancy and allowed for the absolutist government of Charles's final years and the smooth accession of James in 1685. As for Oates (Tonge had died in 1680), he was dismissed soon after Plunkett's execution and later imprisoned for perjury. At his trial, Judge Jeffreys described him as 'a shame to mankind' and regretted the fact that perjury was not a capital offence. During **James II**'s reign, he was repeatedly whipped through the streets of London and pilloried and only gained his release and a pardon after the **Glorious Revolution** in 1689. Oates was given a pension, but his reputation was ruined, and he eventually died in obscurity in 1705.

Presbyterian

Presbyterianism had its theological roots in the Protestant Reformation, more specifically in the Calvinism of Geneva in the 1530s. A young, Scottish **Catholic** priest called John Knox studied with Jean Calvin and brought his teachings back to **Scotland**, which adopted the new faith in 1560. Very Protestant in terms of doctrine, it stressed the importance of the scriptures, the sovereignty of God, salvation through faith rather than good works, predestination and the belief in only two sacraments – baptism and communion. The new Church of Scotland (the Kirk), having rejected papal authority, also instituted a more democratic form of governance that comprised an ascending series of elected courts, made up of ministers and elders, with autonomy and decision-making at every level.

It was a fully established Presbyterian Church when **Charles I** and Archbishop **Laud** decided, in 1637, to impose upon it an episcopal hierarchy (top-down governance by bishops, deans, etc.) and the English Prayer Book. Armed rebellion was inevitable followed by Charles's defeat in the Bishops' Wars. By 1643, the **Civil Wars** were underway in England and, militarily, **Parliament** was on the back foot and so it entered a deal with the Scots – the Solemn League and Covenant. The terms of this stated that Scotland would provide military support to defeat the king; in return, Parliament guaranteed to preserve the Scottish Church and vaguely promised to introduce Presbyterianism to the rest of the British Isles.

In 1648, however, English Presbyterians were purged from Parliament and its 'Rump', along with the **New Model Army**, was dominated by Independents who rejected any form of centralised Church governance. Fearful that their Kirk was under threat and shocked by the king's execution, the Scots proclaimed his son **Charles II** and brokered a deal with him. By the terms of the Treaty of Breda (1650), Charles promised to establish Presbyterianism in England in return for their military support for reestablishing the monarchy. **Cromwell**'s victories at Dunbar and Worcester and **Monck**'s conquest of Scotland, however, put an end to this unlikely coalition. During the years of the Commonwealth, English Presbyterians were tolerated but lost all their political influence and in Scotland, too, Presbyterianism was allowed to continue although the power of the Kirk was much reduced.

The Restoration of 1660 represented the return of an episcopal Church of England and one that would brook no opposition. Presbyterians, Independents and all other non-conformist groups were fined for non-attendance of Anglican services, and their ministers were expelled if they refused ordination or to use the Prayer Book. In fact, 2,000 Presbyterian ministers resisted and subsequently lost their livelihoods. It was only after the **Glorious Revolution** of 1688 that all Protestant faiths were tolerated but, by then, Presbyterianism in England was disorganised and never came close to becoming the political force that it had been in the 1640s. It was, however, recognised as the official faith in Scotland in 1690 and episcopacy there was abolished. The 1707 Act of Union further confirmed the Kirk's form of government.

Purcell, Henry

(1659–95)

Composer

Purcell was born in Westminster into a musical family; his father sang at **Charles II**'s coronation, and his uncle was an accomplished musician. He was 5 when his father died and, as his guardian, his uncle sent him to the Chapel Royal to be trained as a chorister. Despite the lack of evidence, he is said to have started composing at the age of 9 although he certainly wrote an ode to the king's birthday when he was 11. After his voice broke in 1673, he continued his **education** at Westminster School and became an assistant organ-builder. In this role, he would also tune the organ at Westminster Abbey and copy the organ parts of anthems. In 1679, Purcell became the abbey's organist by which time he had written several anthems. One of these – *They that go down to the sea in ships* – was particularly challenging as it was written for the king's favourite singer, the Reverend John Gostling, whose booming basso profundo voice was known to have a range of at least two full octaves. At around this time, he married Frances, the daughter of a Flemish immigrant. They went on to have six children, of whom two reached adulthood.

Purcell wrote elegies too, such as those performed at Queen **Mary II**'s funeral in 1694. He also composed music for hymns and psalms and twenty-four odes written to celebrate various events such as **King James II**'s birthdays but the most popular, by far, was *Hail! Bright Cecilia*, a tribute to the patron saint of music which received an encore in 1692. Most famous, however, was his music for plays, semi-operas and his only opera – *Dido and Aeneas*. Performed at a London boarding school for young gentlewomen, this Baroque masterpiece is considered one of England's earliest operas and contains the famous, heart-wrenching aria, *Dido's Lament*.

The semi-opera, or English opera, was popular in the late Stuart period and combined elements of all-singing opera from Italy and the more traditional

Opening bars of Dido's Lament. (*Artist: H. Purcell, 1689 via Wikimedia Commons*)

masques from earlier in the century. The main actors would do all the speaking while other characters would sing and dance often with the accompaniment of spectacular machinery. Purcell composed five semi-operas including *Dioclesian*, *King Arthur* and *The Fairy-Queen*, the latter being an adaptation of Shakespeare's *A Midsummer Night's Dream*. The semi-opera died out in the early eighteenth century due to the growing popularity of Italian opera and English ballad opera which was characterised by cheaper performances involving lower-class and criminal characters with satirical dialogue.

A great deal of Purcell's work was creating music for stage plays, most of which were written in the last five years of his life. On several occasions, he collaborated with **John Dryden**, for example *The Indian Queen*, but his most recognisable piece is the Movement Two rondeau in **Aphra Behn**'s tragedy, *Abdelazer*. His music for these performances was largely incidental, and he skilfully created just the right mood for a great variety of scenes.

Purcell tragically died in his mid-thirties. One given cause of death is tuberculosis; the other is that he caught a chill after returning late from the theatre and having to spend the night outside after Frances had accidentally locked him out. Contemporaries recognised him as 'as a very great master of music' and he was buried, appropriately, next to the organ in Westminster Abbey. Purcell's distinctive style of Baroque music was a blend of continental influences and the work of more traditional English composers such as Byrd. His considerable output covered a wide variety of occasions and instruments, including the organ, harpsichord, bass viol and violin as well as voices. Above all, he was a master of creating emotion in his music. Particularly skilled he was at suspending a note while others changed to a new chord, thereby creating a tension which was only resolved by bringing the note down to the new harmony and he frequently used bass ostinato – a repeating bass line that contributes to the atmosphere. For 200 years, no other English composer could surpass Purcell's abilities and his work influenced the likes of Handel, Elgar and Britten and, more recently, Pete Townshend of The Who.

Puritan

For around a hundred years, Puritanism was an important religious, social and political force in England; its roots lay in 1550s Geneva. It was there, during Queen Mary I's reign, that many English Protestant exiles had gathered and been inspired by the words of Jean Calvin regarding the purest form of religion. When Elizabeth succeeded her sister, she created a Church of England that was essentially Protestant but retained some **Catholic** influences and ambiguities. The exiles returned and campaigned for a 'purer' **Anglican** Church and, as a result, were given the perjorative name 'Puritan', meaning stickler, although they referred to themselves as 'the godly'.

The key tenets of their belief were:

1. Predestination. Human salvation and damnation are decided by God at conception. Good works are irrelevant; only faith is necessary.
2. The Bible is the only source of religious teachings and its use during sermons is central to all church services.
3. Images and decorations in churches violate the Second Commandment and should be banned.
4. Belief in the importance of personal faith. Therefore, ministers should not wear vestments which mark them out as being superior and a top-down prescriptive hierarchy of bishops was unnecessary.
5. Catholicism represents the Antichrist.

During Elizabeth's reign, agitators for reform were suppressed and, by the 1590s, the first wave of Puritan militancy was over.

Puritans continued to live their distinctive lifestyles, however. Much time was spent in prayer, Bible reading and introspection in search of clues that they were part of God's Elect – those chosen for salvation. Inevitably, many suffered agonising doubts which drove some to consider suicide. Each Puritan's home was a centre of prayer and meditation, and, on Sundays, it was common to attend three sermons and then meet afterwards to discuss their contents. They also sought 'a reformation of manners' to create a godly **society** that would receive divine support; this was to be achieved through virtuous behaviour, austerity and a strong work ethic.

By 1603, Anglicans and Puritans were, generally, coexisting well. On a local level, there were cases of the former showing exasperation with their Puritan minister and the latter walking several miles from their parish, or 'gadding', to hear a preferred minister's sermon. On a national level, though, King **James I** showed little inclination to enforce strict uniformity. He had shown clear support for the status quo at the **Hampton Court Conference** (1604) but punishment for non-attendance at church varied greatly from one diocese to another depending upon each bishop's views and energy.

Puritans. Nineteenth-century depiction of Puritans passing cavaliers. (*Artist: unknown, from Cassell's History of England, c. 1865. Internet Archive via Wikimedia Commons*)

This balance worked reasonably well when the Head of the Church (the monarch) acted as an impartial arbiter, but the apple cart was upset after **Charles I**'s accession in 1625. The new king, through his belief in divine right, considered the Church to be an extension of the royal prerogative and saw the necessity to enforce strict uniformity of Anglican rules. Even more alarming for the Puritans was the suspicion that he favoured Arminianism, a Protestant faith that denied predestination, one that was confirmed in 1633 by his appointment of **William Laud** as Archbishop of Canterbury. Laud then embarked on a programme of beautifying churches, installing rails in front of altars, ordering clergy to wear surplices and placing more emphasis on the Prayer Book rather than the Bible. Bishops were given more authority, non-attendance laws were strictly enforced and Church censorship banned undesirable literature. All of this, of course, was anathema to the Puritans and initiated their second wave of militancy although many thousands fled to New England in America to escape persecution.

The brutal treatment of three Puritans – William Prynne, John Bastwicke and Henry Burton – for seditious writings and sermons in 1637 only fanned the flames of outrage. The Star Chamber ordered them to be fined, imprisoned for life and have their ears removed in a pillory (Bastwicke's wife kissed his ears before removal and afterwards kept them by her bosom!). Burton's ears were cropped so close that his temporal artery was cut. After they finally healed, he was transported to Lancaster prison where he was kept in an empty room above a dark cell containing five **witches**. Prynne was also branded 'S.L.', for 'seditious libeller', on both cheeks which he later claimed stood for '*stigmata laudis*' – a pun meaning 'mark of praise' or 'mark of Laud'.

To many, the Church was now associated with tyranny and Puritans gained considerable sympathy. Added to this were Charles's 'illegal' taxes which strongly affected a merchant class that contained many Puritans and members of **Parliament**. So, when the king finally summoned Parliament in 1640 to raise funds to fight their **Presbyterian** brethren in **Scotland**, it is little wonder that a Puritan junto was able to dominate proceedings and attack the power of the bishops and the king's prerogative.

It was during the **Civil Wars**, however, that Puritan MPs split over what a new Church should look like. The more moderate ones favoured a Presbyterian structure while Independents, such as **Oliver Cromwell**, preferred a congregational one with no hierarchy or centralised control. By 1648, it was the latter, backed by the **New Model Army**, that gained the upper hand and brought about the king's trial and execution.

The 1650s saw the zenith of Puritan power in England. Cromwell allowed toleration for most Protestant groups but tried to impose a 'reformation of manners' upon the country. Without popular backing, however, this was doomed to failure and when he tried to enforce it through the army, Puritanism became associated with military dictatorship. So, inevitably, when the monarchy and the Anglican

Church were restored in 1660, Puritans and other non-conformists were labelled 'dissenters' and suffered persecution under the **Clarendon** Code. It was only with the Toleration Act that followed the **Glorious Revolution** (1688) that they were allowed some freedom of worship but, fragmented and sidelined, Puritanism never regained anything like its former influence. It remained a strong force in New England but the growth of secularism, the distraction of economic opportunities and competition from other religious groups meant that, by 1740, its influence there had waned too.

It is easy to mock the Puritans as a bunch of eccentrically naïve killjoys, the followers of a relatively short-lived religious fad. However, they also made a beneficial impact on society in ways that were not obvious at the time. Their work ethic inspired many others in their search for commercial success, for example, and their prioritising of the need to read the Bible encouraged greater literacy. Furthermore, they contributed to gender equality because, although theirs was still a patriarchal community, Puritans believed that male and female souls were equal, that women should receive a better **education** and that **marriage** was all about mutual help between a husband and wife.

Pym, John

(1584–1643)

Politician and member of **Parliament**

Born in London, his father was a Somerset landowner, successful lawyer and member of Parliament who died when Pym was only 7 months old. His mother then married Sir Anthony Rous, a friend of Sir Francis Drake and one of the richest men in Cornwall. Pym was much influenced by his stepfather's **Puritan**ism and hatred of **Catholic**s and married his niece, Anne Hooke in 1604 (aunt of **Robert Hooke**). They went on to have seven children, four of whom survived childhood. He attended Pembroke College, Oxford, furthered his **education** at London's Inns of Court and, in 1605, was employed as a collector of taxes.

In 1621, Pym was elected as an MP and went on to attend seven consecutive parliaments, usually representing Tavistock, Cornwall. Later that year, he was briefly placed under house arrest after criticising royal financial practices and the **Duke of Buckingham** (**James I** described him as 'an ill-tempered spirit'). Throughout the 1620s Pym was a hard-working, vocal critic of royal policies in the Commons although overshadowed by others such as **Coke** and **Eliot**. During the 1630s, under **Charles I**'s personal rule, he busied himself on his Somerset estate and became treasurer to the Providence Island Company. This established Puritan colonies in the Caribbean which were later destroyed by the Spanish.

He invested in other schemes too such as collieries in Coventry and his various business meetings were often a guise for gatherings that planned how to oppose Charles's unpopular policies.

Pym's importance comes to the fore in the period 1640–43. In the wake of failure against the Scots in the Bishops' Wars, the king was forced to summon Parliament in 1640, and Pym soon emerged as the leader of opposition to royal policies. His first target was the Lord Deputy of **Ireland** and Charles's advisor, the **Earl of Strafford**, who he considered to be the embodiment of royal tyranny, a man who could deploy Catholic military forces against Parliament. He may have been acting out of self-defence too, suspecting that Strafford had evidence of Pym colluding with the Scots, which he probably had. So, he organised an impeachment of Strafford followed by a bill of attainder that brought about his execution in May 1641.

Throughout 1641, Pym worked tirelessly to achieve his vision, one in which there was a fair balance of power between Crown and Parliament. To this aim he

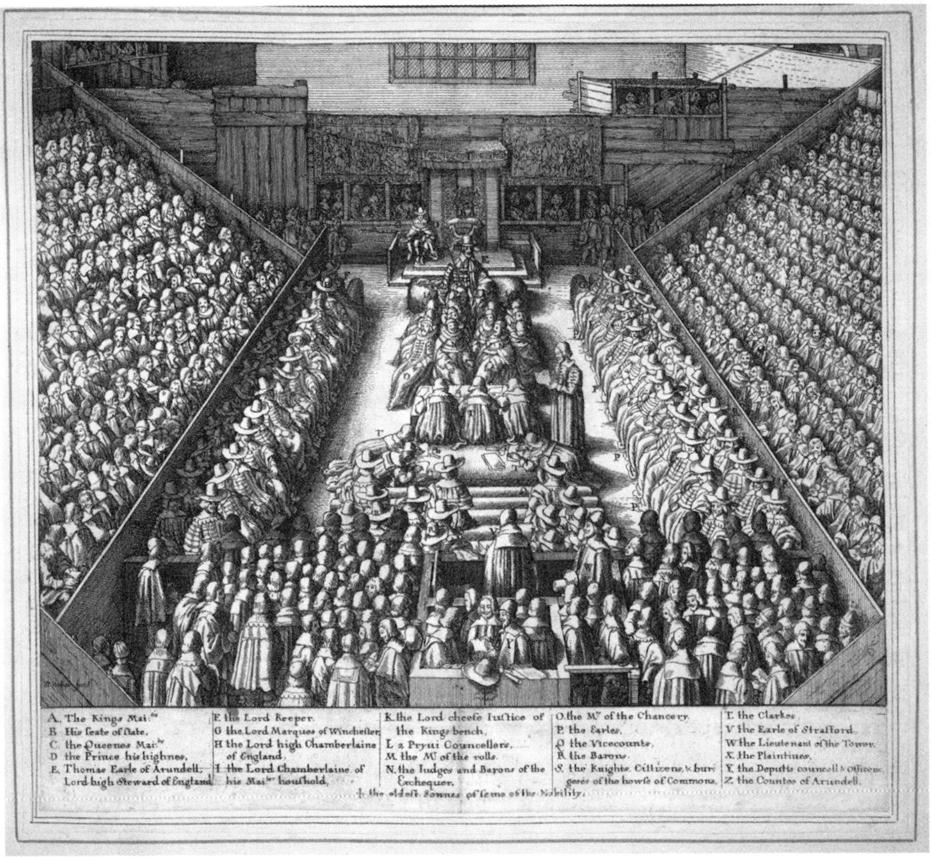

Trial of Strafford. Strafford stands in the dock in the foreground. (*Artist: W. Hollar, 1641. Thomas Fisher Rare Book Library*)

proposed ninety motions in the Commons, sat on 226 committees and attended 191 conferences between the Lords and Commons. As a result, he and his colleagues stripped away much royal power – the abolition of prerogative courts such as the Star Chamber, the prohibition of non-Parliamentary taxes, non-dissolution of Parliament without its approval and Parliament's right to hire and fire royal ministers. Pym's industry and stamina were remarkable but just as important, was his ability to come across as a moderate and thereby bring potentially opposing factions together and coordinate actions between the Commons and the Lords and between Parliament and the City of London.

Nevertheless, opposition to Pym did develop. After Charles left to visit **Scotland** in August 1641, Pym organised the Recess Committee which effectively ran the country during Parliament's adjournment. Several MPs such as **Edward Hyde** believed he had gone too far and started referring to him as 'King Pym'. Dividing lines became even sharper after Pym helped to draft the **Grand Remonstrance** which documented the king's 'wrongdoings'. It seems likely, too, that he used printing presses to inflame the London mob which, subsequently, barred the bishops from attending the Lords where they could have blocked the document's publication. Matters came to a boiling point in January 1642 when Charles came to the Commons to arrest Pym and four others. Forewarned, they had fled to safety of the city and avoided inevitable traitors' deaths.

After the outbreak of the **Civil Wars**, Pym maintained his role as a unifier by placing himself between the 'peace group' and the 'war group'; he supported the latter's demands for total military victory while agreeing with the former's wishes for a return to the 1641 status quo. In August 1643, he supported moves to impress men into the Parliamentary armies, but his greatest war achievement was his negotiation of the Solemn League and Covenant with the **Presbyterian** Scots the following month. Cleverly drafting it so that it could be palatable for Independents in Parliament, it facilitated the destruction of royalist power in northern England.

Pym's death soon after (probably from bowel cancer) was greeted with much joy by the royalists who claimed that he had been killed by flesh-eating creatures. Buried in Westminster Abbey, his body was disinterred in 1661 and flung into a common pit outside St Margaret's nearby. A shadowy character, he left behind few written clues about his personality other than he was a hard worker and eloquent speaker. Had he lived, he quite possibly would have sided with the Presbyterians in their attempts to deal with the king, which gives us the mouth-watering prospect of how he would have dealt with the likes of **Cromwell** and the **New Model Army**. Undoubtedly, his actions contributed to the outbreak of war, but his greatest legacy was his ability to preserve a united Parliament that was able to fight for its rights and lay the basis for its ultimate victory.

R

Raid on the Medway

(1667)

One of England's greatest naval disasters

The **Second Anglo-Dutch War** had broken out in 1665 and within two years had turned into an expensive stalemate. Crown finances had dried up partly because of the economic damage caused by the **Fire of London** and partly due to delays in obtaining revenue from **Parliament**. So, in early 1667, believing the war to be as good as over and to cut costs, the government reduced its active fleet to a few squadrons dotted around the coast, laid off many crews (most of whom were still unpaid) and decommissioned its largest ships at Chatham. There, they had their removable equipment such as guns and sails put into storage in the dockyard, with only a few maintenance men on board. The Dutch, for their part, had suffered much damage to trade during the war and so they too were happy to engage in the peace negotiations that began at Breda in March. King **Charles II**, however, deliberately procrastinated, knowing that a French attack on Holland was imminent which would allow him to gain extra concessions. Aware of this, the Dutch leader, Johan de Witt, decided on a gamble that would force England to conclude the peace talks quickly.

Reports from English spies of a likely Dutch attack were largely ignored. Certainly, there were few concerns regarding the ships at Chatham. Access to them was guarded by shore forts, an iron chain at Gillingham and the treacherous shoals of the Medway estuary. On 6 June, a large Dutch fleet, including sixty-two frigates and twelve fireships, was spotted heading up the Thames estuary. Led by Michiel de Ruyter and Willem van Ghent, it initially chased twenty English merchant ships, but they fled west past Gravesend. Meanwhile, one Dutch squadron appeared off Sheerness where a combined bombardment and marine landing soon captured the unfinished fort. Guided by English pilots who had deserted, the Dutch then entered the Medway.

The naval commissioner at Chatham, Peter Pett, now sent pleas for help to London and complained about the lack of senior officers who could give commands. Charles ordered mobilisation of the local militias and dispatched General **Monck** to take charge. Part of the problem, however, was that the Dutch intentions were still not clear. Extra artillery was sent to Gravesend to defend against a direct attack on the capital and reports of Dutch landings in Essex and on the Isle of Grain added to the confusion. Upon arriving at Chatham, Monck was shocked to see there was no gunpowder, only twelve dockyard men and ten sloops for towing the warships – the other twenty had been requisitioned to evacuate officials' personal possessions such as Pett's model ships.

The Dutch, meanwhile, had broken through the chain and removed the blockships that had been sunk to hamper their advance. The next obstacle, Upnor Castle, was 100 years old, poorly provisioned and had fallen into disrepair. Monck sent cavalry and artillery reinforcements, but de Ruyter was able to sail past towards his prizes at Chatham docks. Various English frigates had been towed south but there were not enough men to save them all. Dutch fireships destroyed several while the flagship, *Royal Charles*, was captured and towed back to Holland. Monck now considered that he had no choice but to scuttle his remaining warships to avoid them being captured too.

The *Royal Charles*. Probably sketched as it was leaving the Dutch coast with Charles as a passenger in 1660. (*Artist: W. van de Velde the Elder, 1660 via Wikimedia Commons*)

Under continued fire from Upnor and other shore batteries and fearful of stiffening resistance, de Ruyter and van Ghent decided to withdraw on 14 June and they returned to heroes' welcomes. The *Royal Charles*'s draft was too deep for Dutch waters and so was dry-docked and became an attraction for tourists and foreign dignitaries. Outraged by this personal attack on his honour (it had been the *Royal Charles* that had brought him to England in 1660), Charles protested and the ship was dismantled in 1672 leaving just the stern transom, which is now displayed in the Rijksmuseum, Amsterdam.

In England, panic spread up the coast to London itself. With rumours that the Dutch were transporting a French invasion force, many people started to pack their belongings and flee. Over the next few days, the scale of the disaster became clear – for the loss of one Dutch ship (excluding fireships), four out of England's five largest ships had been lost (the *Royal Sovereign* was in Portsmouth) along with ten other frigates. The estimated cost for repairs and rebuilding the fleet came to £200,000 (approx. £25 million in 2025). The only silver lining was that the Dutch had not destroyed the Chatham dockyards, and this allowed the navy to return to its former strength by 1670. The general desolation and consternation are revealed in **Pepys**'s diaries:

June 12 – I … fear … that the whole kingdom is undone [meaning the downfall of the monarchy].

June 13 – never were people so dejected as they are in the City … We are betrayed by the Papists.

England quickly signed the Treaty of Breda to end the war, on terms that favoured the Dutch and, inevitably, Pett was made a scapegoat and was sacked and fined. Ironically, though, his rescued model ships came in very useful for the rebuilding of the navy. There were others, higher up the chain of command, who should have borne the brunt of blame for the country's lack of readiness though. Charles himself was particularly anguished by the blow to national prestige and his desire for revenge contributed to the **Third Anglo-Dutch War** five years later. To this day, the Raid on the Medway is considered one of the greatest disasters in England's naval history.

Rochester, Second Earl of

see Wilmot, John

Rupert, Prince

(1619–82)

Soldier, admiral and scientist

Rupert was the third son of Elector Frederick V of the Palatinate and **Elizabeth**, daughter of King **James I**. Born in Prague, he was almost left behind when his family had to flee in haste from the imperial forces that invaded Bohemia at the start of the Thirty Years' War (1618–48). He spent most of his childhood living with his family in exile in the Dutch Republic as the Palatinate too had been conquered. Preferring the company of her pet monkeys and dogs, Elizabeth put her children's **education** in the hands of a pair of French Calvinist governors and Rupert excelled in almost everything, especially maths, science and art. However, he also acquired a reputation for his wild and fiery behaviour and became known as 'Rupert the Devil'.

When his father died in 1632, his older brother, Charles Louis, became Elector Palatine in absentia and Rupert pursued a military career along with his younger brother, Maurice. For much of the next six years, he spent his time fighting Spanish and Imperial forces. Standing at six feet and four inches, Rupert became renowned as a cavalry commander for his reckless courage and enthusiasm. In 1638, though, his audacity led to his capture at the Battle of Vlotho after which he was imprisoned for three years at Linz. As a respected adversary with royal connections, he was treated well and offered his freedom if he became a **Catholic** or a general in Emperor Ferdinand's army. Rupert refused, however, and spent much time etching, hunting, playing tennis and studying military textbooks. He was also gifted two poodles to keep him company, one of which he named **Boy**. Rupert was finally released in late 1641 in return for swearing never to fight against the emperor again.

Prince Rupert with Boy. Roundhead propaganda showing Rupert destroying Birmingham. (*Artist: unknown, 1643 via Wikimedia Commons*)

As soon as the **Civil Wars** broke out in 1642, he and Maurice went to England to assist their uncle, King **Charles I** in his conflict against **Parliament**. Appointed as General of Horse, Rupert soon assembled a force of 3,000 troops and won a minor skirmish at Powick Bridge in September. From that point on, it is probably fair to say that he acquired a reputation that exceeded his ability. Certainly, his heroic courage, openness and determination inspired his men, and his knowledge of up-to-date tactics earned him much respect. However, this mere 23-year-old with his frankness, cutting wit and short temper soon made enemies in Charles's court. His arguments with the established courtier, George Digby in particular, led to his position being repeatedly undermined. Also, Rupert's derring-do in battle was as much a weakness as it was a strength. At Edgehill, for example, his ill-disciplined cavalry charge drove off the enemy's left wing but failed to return and make a decisive impact.

The icon of the royalist cause, Rupert became the bête noire of the roundheads and was accused of atrocities such as destroying Birmingham (probably false) and slaughtering innocents in Leicester (probably true). His greatest victory came in mid-1643 when he captured England's second city – the important port of Bristol. He was at his best, however, when raiding deep into enemy territory as evidenced the following year when Charles ordered him to relieve the besieged city of York. Through speed and secret marches, he first broke the parliamentary siege of Newark and then captured Liverpool and Bolton before surprising the enemy outside York and forcing them to withdraw. Poor communications with his co-commander, the Earl of Newcastle, however, led to defeat at Marston Moor.

Rupert's appointment as general of the entire royalist army in late 1644 sharpened the tensions between him and the king's other advisors. In June 1645, he advised Charles to avoid battle at **Naseby** but the king, instead, listened to Digby. Unfairly, despite yet another ill-disciplined attack by his cavalry, Rupert was blamed for the crucial defeat that followed. Afterwards, short of supplies, men and money, he urged his uncle to make peace but instead was sent to campaign in the south-west.

Facing impossible circumstances, he was forced to surrender Bristol in September for which the king dismissed him from his service. Rupert then fought his way through to Charles at Newark and demanded a court martial which cleared his name of any wrongdoing. 1646 finally saw the royalist surrender and, after their capture at Oxford, both he and Maurice were banished from the kingdom.

Rupert now fought in the service of the French king against Spain and, in one action, was shot in the head. Then, after recuperating, he joined a small fleet of English ships which had mutinied against Parliament in 1648. Lack of money, however, was always a problem and this led to mutinies and desertions among the crews. Rupert, now in charge of a small fleet of seven warships, consequently decided to resort to semi-piracy against parliamentary merchant shipping but after leaving Ireland he was hounded by Admiral **Blake** into the Mediterranean. Regrouping his fleet, he headed back into the Atlantic, captured some ships and explored the west coast of Africa. While there, he acquired a Moorish boy who became his servant for many years and sailed up the Gambia River where he caught malaria. Rupert then crossed to the Caribbean to seek more treasure ships, but his force was scattered by a hurricane in which Maurice was drowned. After realising the futility of this naval campaign, he returned to France in 1653.

Rupert and his warlike stance were unwelcome at the Stuart court-in-exile which was trying to negotiate the return of the **Charles II** to England, so he moved on to the Palatinate. He fell out with Charles Louis, though, over a lack of income that he thought his brother owed him. Worse still, a love letter he wrote to a maid-in-waiting accidentally ended up with the Electress who herself was very keen on Rupert. When she discovered the mistake, she raided her maid's quarters and found love letters from her husband. The couple subsequently divorced, Rupert left, never to return, and sought service with the emperor.

1660 saw the restoration of his cousin to the throne, whereupon Rupert immediately returned to England. There, he was given financial stability, the dukedom of Cumberland and made an of admiral of the navy. In this role, he was typically energetic and aggressive during the **Second** and **Third Anglo-Dutch Wars** in which he particularly distinguished himself in the Battle of Lowestoft (1665); he contributed to improvements in naval communications and flexibility of tactics during a battle.

At the same time, Rupert was on the Privy Council advising on foreign affairs and, in 1668, Charles appointed him Constable of Windsor Castle. He displayed an astonishing range of weaponry in his apartments there and often entertained the king by hunting and playing tennis together. **Pepys** believed him to be one of the best tennis players in the country. Rupert also developed his skills in mezzotint and created a science laboratory at Windsor where he especially loved to dabble in metallurgy. Many of his inventions were military such as a pistol with a revolving chamber, a type of torpedo, more powerful gunpowder and a device for retrieving objects underwater. A founding member of the Royal Society, he demonstrated glass teardrops – Prince Rupert's drops – that withstood hammers and bullets but exploded when their tails were damaged and posed the mathematical problem of how a cube could be passed through a smaller cube – Prince Rupert's Cube. He became renowned for his ability to break cypher codes too. Undeterred by a trepanning operation he underwent to relieve the headaches caused by his head wound, he also sought to improve surgical instruments. Rupert even found time to organise expeditions to Hudson's Bay in North America and become governor of the Hudson Bay Company that profitably traded in furs.

In the flamboyant Restoration court, he became regarded as a relic from a distant age, a man who had certainly matured since his youthful days but one who could appear distant, haughty and stern. Rupert never married but had two mistresses, the second of whom was the actress, Margaret Hughes, whose extravagant lifestyle he happily funded, and it seems that he very much enjoyed spending time with her and their daughter, Ruperta. Complications arising from pleurisy caused his death, after which he was given a state funeral at Westminster Abbey. Rupert of the Rhine, as he was known, is one of the most extraordinary and colourful characters of the Stuart period, a man of such indefatigable energy and talent whose flaws, if anything, seem to have burnished his reputation over time.

Rye House Plot

(1683)

An attempt to assassinate **Charles II** and **James, Duke of York**

Throughout the 1670s there had been increasing fears among many that Charles II would be succeeded by his **Catholic** brother, James, Duke of York. The **Popish Plot** at the end of the decade had heightened these fears and a political group known as the **Whigs** put much pressure on the king to exclude James from the throne. Charles had resisted though and then hit back after it had become clear that the Popish Plot had been a mere fabrication. Firstly, he dissolved **Parliament** in 1681, thereby removing the Whigs' legal mouthpiece, and then set about persecuting and imprisoning some of their leaders such as **Lord Shaftesbury**. At the same time, he attacked the municipal powerbase of the Whigs by replacing town charters with royal charters. This allowed him to appoint his **Tory** supporters as mayors and sheriffs who could ensure the lack of Whig candidates for any future parliamentary elections.

This increasing autocracy added to the feeling that the king himself was a Catholic sympathiser (he had allied with France against the Protestant Dutch and was married to a Catholic) and forced several Whigs to take extreme measures. One faction preferred armed rebellion followed by the coronation of Charles's illegitimate, Protestant son – the Duke of Monmouth. Another aimed to assassinate 'Slavery' (the king) and 'Popery' (James) first, and discussed various locations such as on a river barge and in St James's Park. Finally, an ex-Roundhead from the **Civil Wars** offered his home at Rye House, 18 miles from London. Alongside it ran a narrow lane that the king often used on his way to and from Newmarket where he liked to attend horse races. From an outhouse next to the lane, it would be relatively straightforward to shoot him and any members in his party as they rode past. The date was set for 1 April, but the conspirators were thwarted by a fire that broke out in Newmarket that destroyed half of the town and caused Charles's party to return to London a day earlier than planned.

In June, news of the plot leaked out, leading to arrests, confessions, whistle-blowing and further arrests. Monmouth himself fled to Holland, but others fell victim to seventeenth-century criminal law which was weighted against defendants. They were allowed neither defence counsel nor prior view of the charges or witnesses against them. Even judges could be dismissed if they were seen to be favouring a defendant. A series of brutal executions ensued, the most senior victim being William, Lord Russell who suffered a botched execution at the hands of the notorious Jack Ketch. Despite paying a generous tip beforehand, as was customary, Russell suffered several agonising blows of the axe. At one point, he is reported to have turned his head and said, 'You dog, did I give you ten guineas to use me so inhumanely?'

Eleven others were executed too, usually hanged, drawn and quartered, including Elizabeth Gaunt – the last woman to be executed for a political crime in England. Many others fled or were imprisoned including the Earl of Essex who cut his own throat in the Tower of London. The Whig cause, after such a shocking setback, went underground only to reappear with a vengeance in the **Glorious Revolution** five years later. Even more unsettling, perhaps, is this: although historians agree that there had been secret discussions to put Monmouth on the throne, many believe that the Rye House Plot itself had been completely fabricated by Charles and the Tories to remove their political opponents.

S

Scotland

There were mixed feelings among the Scots as their king, James VI, travelled south to become **James I** of England in 1603. Although this was only a dynastic union and the two countries remained independent of each other, how would it affect their customs, laws, economy and political standing? In the short term, though, there was little perceptible change. Scotland maintained its laws and **Presbyterian** religion and, although customs duties remained between the two countries, the English market gradually replaced established trade routes to the continent. It did lose its independent foreign policy, however, and many Scots must have felt like junior partners in this new relationship with their wealthier and more populous neighbour. James promised to return every three years but only visited once, in 1617. For him, and the many Scottish nobles that followed, London represented power, extravagance and modernity. Why make an uncomfortable twelve-day journey when, as he boasted, he could 'govern Scotland with his pen'? James did keep up a steady correspondence with the royal commissioner who represented him on the Privy Council in Edinburgh, but it seems that he gradually lost touch with a country that he had governed sensibly prior to 1603.

This became clear in 1618 when he demanded that the General Assembly of the Kirk (the governing body of the Church of Scotland) accept the Five Articles of Perth to bring it in line with the **Anglican** Church. These included '**Catholic**-like' measures such as kneeling at communion, giving power to bishops and observance of Christmas and Easter. Only with great reluctance did the assembly accept them but they were quickly repealed twenty years later. James also made great efforts to unite the two countries and become king of 'Great Britain'. In 1606, he even decreed the creation of a uniting flag – the Union Jack ('Jack' being short for 'Jacobus', Latin for James) – but strong opposition in both parliaments scuppered his plan.

The union of the crowns arguably had a greater impact on those who lived furthest from the central Lowlands. Starting in 1609, the English government encouraged Scottish settlers to take confiscated land in northern Ireland. Around 50,000 sailed over and built new towns and brought over their religion and customs, thereby initiating the future troubles that were to plague Ulster. Even further, were the Highlands and Islands in the far north and west. There, small, subsistence farming communities, connected by mud tracks, continued to speak Gaelic and practise the Catholic faith while the various clans intermittently indulged in cattle rustling and warfare. James's attitude to this area was summed up when he said, 'As for the Highlanders, I see two kinds: the ones who live on the mainland are barbaric, but a little bit civilised; the others who live in the islands are totally barbaric.' In the name of uniformity, he ordered the nine Statutes of Iona (1609). These included the requirements that the children of the wealthiest be educated in the Lowlands (in English), all parishes to have Protestant ministers and the outlawing of bards and firearms outside people's homes. Although some clans resolutely stuck to the old ways, others acquiesced; the Statutes signalled the first in a series of attacks on the Highland culture.

If some of James's actions had caused unease, those of **Charles I**, set the alarm bells ringing. Soon after his accession in 1625, the Act of Revocation attempted to relieve his financial pressures by reclaiming monastic land given to the Scots nobles since the 1540s but it failed and only served to sow distrust among the landowners. Charles eventually visited Edinburgh for his Scottish coronation (1633) but continued to show a disconnect with the land of his birth. Widespread alarm was created in 1637 when he and Archbishop **Laud** decided to impose an English-style Prayer Book, an act that set into motion the steps leading to the **Civil Wars**. At St. Giles' Cathedral, Edinburgh, a street-seller named Jenny Geddes threw her stool at the minister when he started to read the new prayer book, shouting, 'False thief! Dare you say the Mass in my lug?' Rioting in the streets ensued but Charles refused to back down. In the following year, a National Covenant was drawn up, signed by members from all sections of **society**, which vowed to protect the Presbyterian religion and all bishops were formally expelled from the Kirk.

The Prayer Book Riots begin. (*Artist: W. Hollar, c. 1637. From F. Maclean's Scotland, a Concise History*)

Charles, in early 1639, then decided to force the issue militarily but the First Bishops' War only saw fighting around Aberdeen where Scottish Royalists were eventually defeated. Arguably, therefore, it is north-east Scotland that saw the first casualties of the Civil Wars which only ended in 1653 in **Ireland**. Near the border, meanwhile, both sides showed a reluctance to fight and so a truce was called. Politically, the impasse continued though, and the summer of 1640 saw the more decisive Second Bishops' War in which the Covenanter army invaded northern England. Led by Alexander Leslie, who had gained experience fighting on the continent, this force was far superior to the disorganised, unmotivated English army that melted away after its defeat at the Battle of Newburn. The Scots then occupied Newcastle where they took control of the valuable coal export trade. In the subsequent truce, they demanded £850 a day for their occupation costs until peace was finally negotiated in August 1641, after which they evacuated England. The king could not possibly cover such a financial burden and so was forced to summon the Long **Parliament** which used the leverage to dismantle the royal prerogative.

With Parliament struggling in the early stages of the Civil Wars, it called upon Scots' aid to defeat the king. In the ensuing Solemn League and Covenant (1643), Parliament guaranteed Presbyterianism in Scotland in return for the assistance of the Covenanter army. This in turn, marched south and provided a crucial role in the royalist defeat at Marston Moor, which handed northern England to Parliament. Some Scots, however, preferred to remain loyal to Charles rather than be ruled by a Presbyterian government. A Scottish civil war therefore broke out in September 1644 in which a small force of Highlanders and Irish, led by the Marquess of Montrose, won a series of brilliant victories against Covenanter troops. This conflict only ended with the king's surrender in 1646 after which Montrose fled to Norway.

By 1648, the **New Model Army**, dominated by Independents, had replaced the English Presbyterians as the dominant political force in England. Fearful that it would never accept Presbyterianism north of the border, a Scottish faction known as the Engagers performed a volte-face by making a secret 'engagement' with Charles in which he promised to accept Presbyterianism in England for a trial period of three years in return for military aid. In the subsequent, poorly coordinated second civil war, the large but poorly trained Scots army was defeated piecemeal at Preston in August. The following month saw brief fighting near Stirling between the Engagers and the Kirk party (radical Presbyterians) after which the latter took control.

Negotiations with Charles's son after the king's execution (1649) led to **Charles II**'s shameful abandonment of Montrose (who had returned to support him but was then captured and executed) and the third civil war. The Scots' catastrophic defeat at Dunbar in 1650 was largely caused by the Kirk party's purge of its best officers and its orders to leave good defensive positions and attack **Cromwell**'s New Model Army. Exactly a year later, another Scots army found itself trapped in Worcester and defeated. Around 3,000 were killed and 10,000 captured. The majority of these were sent to New England and the West Indies as indentured servants or were used as forced labour on drainage in the Fens.

Scottish mercenaries in the Thirty Years' War. The earliest depiction of Highland clothing although the description wrongly calls them Irish. (*Artist: G. Köler, 1631 via Wikimedia Commons*)

Meanwhile, General **Monck** mopped up the final areas of resistance in Scotland. Dundee and Aberdeen were the last major towns to hold out with the latter quickly surrendering after the brutal sacking of the former. Final resistance in the Highlands was crushed in 1652; for the first time in its history, Scotland had been fully conquered. The Honours of Scotland (Scottish Crown Jewels), however, were smuggled out of Dunnottar Castle in May before it fell and hidden under the floor of Kineff Old Church before being returned to Edinburgh in 1660.

Being a Protestant kingdom, Scotland was treated far more leniently than Ireland during the Interregnum. It was incorporated into the Commonwealth of England, Scottish laws were suspended, and its Parliament was abolished with thirty MPs being allowed to attend Westminster instead. The powers of the Kirk Assembly were much reduced too and Presbyterianism was merely tolerated. A pledge was also made to abolish all feudal duties attached to the holding of land (this was only achieved in 2004!). All trade restrictions were lifted too and military rule brought increased law and order throughout the country (although a royalist uprising in the Islands needed to be suppressed in 1653). These benefits were offset, however, by by the higher taxes needed to pay for the military garrisons. A formal Act of Union was finally passed in London in 1657 but, with the collapse of the Commonwealth soon after, its effect was minimal.

The Restoration of 1660 arguably brought greater change to Scotland than the Civil Wars. Its Parliament was restored but was packed with monarchists who sought royal absolutism. Known as the 'Drunken Parliament', it passed the Rescissory Act in 1661. First mentioned as a joke, it was agreed upon at a meeting where few were sober and resulted in the repealing of all Scottish laws since 1633. This meant the return to episcopy, abolition of the 1638 Covenant, the exclusion of Presbyterians from official positions and the sacking of around 400 Presbyterian ministers. Given that he had agreed to protect Presbyterianism in 1650, it is little wonder that many referred to Charles as the 'two-faced monarch'.

Death of Margaret Wilson. (*Artist: J. Swain, 1862 via Wikimedia Commons*)

Opposition was strongest in the south-west where people refused to accept a Kirk run by bishops. Instead, they attended conventicles – illegal gatherings of thousands in any location considered safe such as barns, fields, moors and ravines. Increased repression led to fines for non-attendance of church and the use of torture such as thumb screws and hanging people by their thumbs. The death penalty was also imposed for attending conventicles which were sometimes infiltrated by royalist spies. The billeting of Highland troops on Presbyterian areas in 1678 was the final straw however and violence spiralled out of control. The summer of 1679 saw the assassination of the Archbishop of St Andrews, followed by a Covenanter victory at a pitched battle at Drumclog. This was avenged by royalist forces three weeks later at Bothwell Bridge on the Clyde but, in the following year, the Covenanters made the Sanquar Declaration which renounced any loyalty to the king for those wanting to follow their Presbyterian faith. What followed is known as 'The Killing Time' – a period of eight years in which countless dissenters were transported to colonies or summarily executed. Most shocking was the treatment of the Wigtown Martyrs. Margaret Maclauchlan and Margaret Wilson, aged 18, were staked to the sands of the Solway Firth and drowned by the rising tide despite a last-minute reprieve from Edinburgh. The Catholic **James II** (VII in Scotland) continued the repression and only granted toleration in 1687 to gain political support.

After the **Glorious Revolution** (1688), **William III** and **Mary II** were accepted as joint monarchs of Scotland in return for greater parliamentary independence and a Presbyterian-dominated Kirk. The overthrow of James and the bishops, however, created armed Jacobite resistance. In 1689, a largely Highland army defeated government forces at Killiecrankie (where plug bayonets and hand grenades were first used in Britain), but their heavy casualties and desertions meant the revolt was over within a year. To secure peace in Scotland while resources were needed elsewhere, the government offered £12,000 to Highland clans if they swore an oath of allegiance to William and Mary before 1 January 1692. Disputes over how to share the money and the seeking of permission from James from his court-in-exile in France caused delays but most chiefs swore the oath in time. After being redirected from Fort William, the chief of the Glencoe MacDonalds finally covered the extra 60 miles to Inverary where he swore the oath on 6 January. Other clans were also late but internal politics, combined with the government's desire to make an example in the most lawless part of Scotland, Lochaber, meant that the MacDonalds had already been singled out for punishment. Late that month, government troops, largely drawn from the nearby Campbell clan, arrived in Glencoe where they were quartered and given hospitality. Then, on 13 February, they conducted the infamous Massacre of Glencoe by turning on their hosts

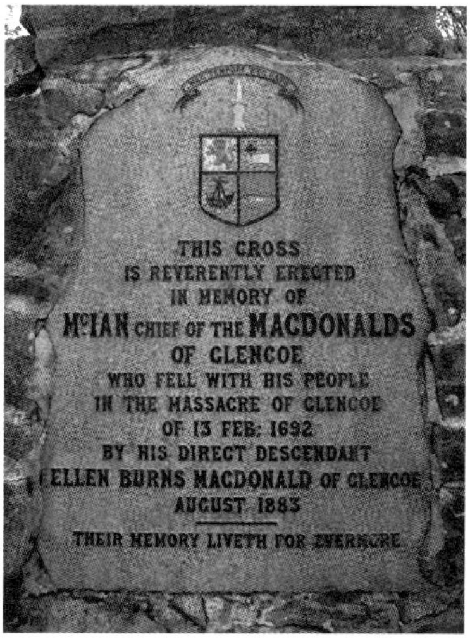

Glencoe Massacre memorial. (*Artist: K. Traynor, 2012 via Wikimedia Commons*)

and slaughtering around thirty men, women and children while others died from exposure afterwards.

The 1690s were, indeed, one of the most brutal decades in Scottish history. The study of tree rings has shown this period to be the coldest of the Little Ice Age that affected Europe, a situation probably exacerbated by huge volcanic eruptions in Iceland and Indonesia. Subsequent shorter growing seasons led to failed harvests, higher prices and a famine that killed around 10 per cent of the population. Scotland was hit particularly hard during 'The Seven Ill Years' due to its greater dependence on subsistence farming and trade with France which was cut by the Nine Years' War. The remoter areas where societies were largely cashless and isolated by poor roads suffered the most. The number of vagrants seeking poor relief doubled and around 8 per cent of the population migrated to Ulster, America and Europe.

To relieve the economic crisis, the government established the Bank of Scotland in 1695 which would lend money to businesses. At the same time, the Company of Scotland was set up to promote international trade. After raising £400,000 (a fifth of Scotland's wealth) it embarked on the Darien Scheme – the establishment of a Scottish colony on the Panama isthmus (in Spanish territory) – which could prosper as a hub of Pacific–Atlantic trade. However, poor planning, disease, difficult terrain, the refusal of natives to trade, attacks from Spain and lack of support from England meant the project was a fiasco. The colony was abandoned in early 1700 with the loss of over 2,000 settlers' lives and huge debts for the many Scots who had invested in the scheme.

With the Scottish economy in freefall, many now saw that their only hope was union with England. The English, for their part, feared their northern neighbour would choose a hostile, Jacobite monarch after the death of the childless Queen **Anne**. In 1707, the MPs in Edinburgh, some lured with English bribes, accepted the Act of Union by a majority of forty-one votes. Among its terms were:

1. The closure of the Scottish Parliament and political union with England (Scotland was allocated forty-five MPs in the Commons – one more than the numerous rotten boroughs in Cornwall! – and sixteen in the Lords).
2. The new country of 'Great Britain' would accept the Hanoverian succession.
3. Scotland would maintain its laws and Presbyterian religion.
4. Economic union and free trade between England and Scotland.
5. £398,000 paid as compensation for sharing England's national debt and the failed Darien Scheme.

Most Scots, however, resented the loss of sovereignty, feared exploitation by their powerful neighbour and felt betrayed by their leaders. Popular demonstrations led to the temporary imposition of martial law and the flames of Jacobitism were rekindled, leading to the rebellions of 1715 and 1745. Increased taxes and the introduction of English weights and measures and coinage also caused resentment. Ultimately, however, Scotland benefited from growing trade and employment opportunities within the expanding British empire and the increased development of its industries and agriculture.

The seventeenth century was very much a transitional period in Scotland's history and, as with most times of change, it was accompanied by strife. For a moment, in the 1640s, it asserted itself as a real force in the British Isles but the Stuart period, ironically, saw its decline as a political entity. A combination of absentee monarchs, the Civil Wars, internal disputes, the loss of its close relationship with France and its relatively remote geopolitical position in an increasingly mercantilist world meant, inevitably perhaps, the loss of its independence. The eighteenth century lay ahead, however, and, for most Scots, that meant political stability, industrial growth and great scientific and intellectual advances.

Shaftesbury, Lord

see Ashley Cooper, Anthony

Slave Trade

In Britain, slavery existed in Roman times but it was not until the early modern period that human trafficking reached an industrial scale, and it was Africa that bore the brunt of the tragedy. As the Portuguese and Spanish conquered the New World in the sixteenth century, they required cheap labour for their mines and plantations. European diseases and dreadful forced labour conditions decimated the native Indian populations and so it was the newly discovered coastlines of Africa that were viewed as the next source of labour. A relative latecomer to the scene, England only started to transport slaves across the Atlantic in the 1560s.

With the establishment of colonies in **Virginia**, New England and Jamaica, England's involvement in the triangular slave trade began to take off (the first Africans arrived in Jamestown in 1619). On the first leg, slavers brought various manufactured goods to African chiefs, such as brass pans, guns, alcohol and textiles, in exchange for slaves captured in tribal raids. Some expeditions attempted to conduct slave raids directly, but these proved to be too costly in time and European lives and so trade with coastal chiefs became the norm. From Africa, the slaves were transported across the Atlantic (Middle Passage) in awful conditions with maybe around 15 per cent dying en route. In North America, they were then sold to plantation owners in return for sugar, molasses (a sweet, syrupy by-product of sugar production), cotton and tobacco. Some of these goods were then sold in New England, where distilleries used molasses to make rum, for example, but the majority

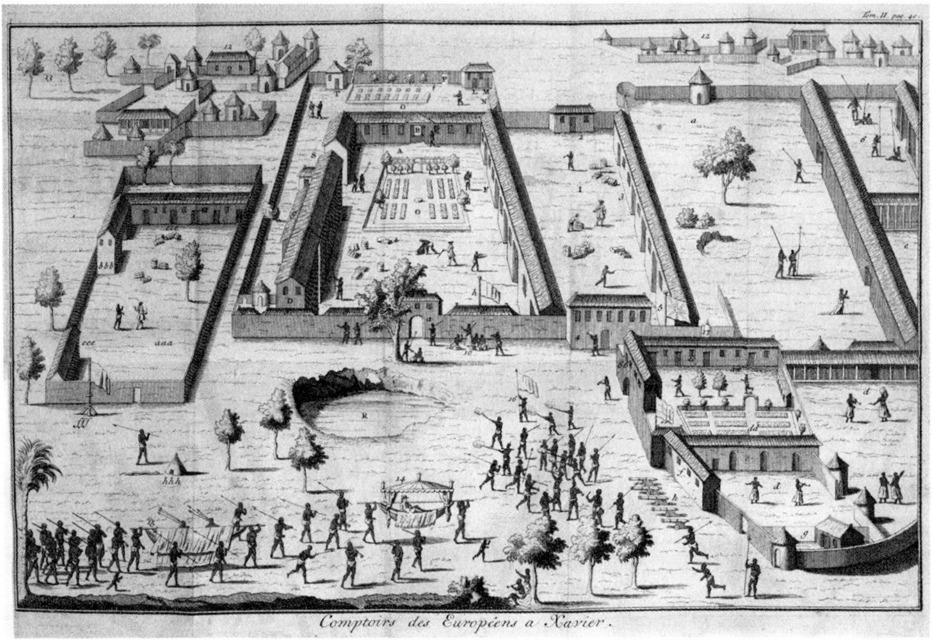

European slave post in Benin. French, Portuguese, English and Dutch compounds are shown. (*Artist: J-B. Labat, 1731. Bibliothèque municipale de Lyon*)

were shipped back to England. The benefits of this hugely lucrative trade were visible in many sections of English **society** – from the bustling ports of Liverpool, Bristol and London and the mansions of the wealthy to increased employment opportunities in cities and the spread of **coffee houses** and tobacco shops.

English common law did not allow ownership of fellow humans, but that principle was put aside for those who were not Christians and were already considered someone else's property when sold to the slavers. Moreover, the profits could not be ignored. As a result, England transported around 430,000 slaves in the seventeenth century and a further 3,100,000 in the following century (by 1730 it was leading the field). While Europeans benefited, the impact on African societies is incalculable. By fuelling warfare and creating labour shortages and coastal kingdoms' dependency on European traders, the slave trade must have had a huge social, economic and political impact. On the plantations, meanwhile, some landowners cared for their workers but, generally, the brutal conditions meant that slaves' life expectancy was almost half that of their white counterparts.

The seventeenth century also saw a steady increase in the number of black people appearing in England. Some were brought directly from Africa and became servants for the wealthy who saw them as fashionable novelties. **Anne of Denmark**, for instance, employed at least one 'Moor'. Many were found by privateers on captured Spanish and Portuguese slave ships and were simply released on English docks while others were the servants of Dutch masters who had fled to England from the Thirty Years' War. By 1700, possibly around 6,000 black people (0.1 per cent of the population) resided in England, the majority living in London and a few other ports. They suffered much discrimination and many became beggars. Their cause was certainly not helped by the Barbary pirates from north Africa who frequently raided the south coast. In 1625, for example, sixty men, women and children were seized from Mount's Bay, Cornwall, and by 1640 there were as many as 5,000 English slaves in Algiers alone.

Portrait of a Black Boy. A servant living in either Holland or England. (*Artist: W. Hollar, 1645. Folger Shakespeare Library*)

Most black people, however, did create livings for themselves. Many were servants but some became skilled craftsmen and a few even prospered. Men were employed as sailors, entertainers or carpenters, for example. A 'negra' called Cattelena set up her own business selling food to travellers near Gloucester and Mary Fillis was a seamstress in east London. Most famous, perhaps, was Lucy Negro – a former dancer in Queen Elizabeth's court who later ran a brothel in Clerkenwell. It is also recorded that black women married white men, black people were baptised and some even fought in the **Civil Wars**. This account of a Scottish soldier captured by a black royalist at Newark, however, reveals just how ingrained racism was: 'A blackamore took a Scottish soldier prisoner upon which the poor Scot, being almost frightened out of his wits, pray'd heartily, saying "O God! O God! O God! have mercy upon me saul, de deel's got my body, de deel's got my body;" and the fellow was so frightened he would not follow the black, so that he was forc'd to kill him.'

Society

English society was predominantly a rural one in 1603 with less than ten per cent of the population living in eleven towns of more than 5,000 people. Of these, London was by far the largest (200,000) followed by Norwich (16,000), Bristol and York (12,000 each). The capital had been growing quickly and continued to do so; by 1650, the number of its inhabitants had doubled, making it the largest city in western Europe. This, despite the frequent ravages of disease that meant its death rate exceeded the birth rate, was enabled by the vast number of immigrants seeking work or escape from religious persecution abroad. The royal court at Westminster, Inns of Court, entertainment centres and prestigious schools such as St Paul's and Westminster also attracted the politically and socially ambitious. The sprawl outside the city's walls had already begun with the wealthiest tending to dwell in the 'West End', upwind of the dense smoke emanating from London's homes and industries such as brick- and glass-making.

The main push factor that drove people to London was rural poverty and this, in turn, was largely caused by the 25 per cent increase in England's population (from four to five million) between 1600 and 1650. With food production unable to keep up, the result was rising inflation in basic commodity prices while landowners were able to charge higher rents and suppress wage growth. Frequent failed harvests – the 1630s and 1690s were particularly bad – only served to tip many more into poverty. Poor relief in the form of alms and workhouses did exist but this varied from parish to parish. Some devoted their energies into driving out the 'sturdy beggars' or 'idle poor' instead of collecting rates to help the deserving poor. For many of these migrants, life was no better in the slums of east and north London, and, in fact, they were far more likely to fall foul of the frequent epidemics such as **plague**. Ship Alley, in Aldgate in 1636, may have had typical poor families. It contained sixteen households, including four couples with children, five childless couples, two households of two 'aged' women living together, and one single man and four single women, two of them widows. Only three households were in employment; the rest were unable to find work or too old to work.

Elsewhere, the two-generation nuclear family with households of four or five people was typical in Stuart England, with the wealthier having cohabiting servants or apprentices. It was also usual for teenage children to migrate up to 20 miles to nearby estates or towns to become maids and apprentices and earn enough to facilitate **marriage** in their mid- to late twenties.

There was a land-based hierarchy comprised of the nobility's great estates followed by the gentry. These were wealthy, non-aristocratic landowners who employed labourers and servants and were usually involved in politics and the law by entering the Commons in **Parliament** or by becoming justices of the peace. Beneath them were the yeomanry – freeholders or leaseholders who typically worked thirty to a hundred acres of land, usually working alongside their labourers and could vote and hold local positions such as constable and bailiff. At the bottom were the labouring poor, maybe around a third of the population, who worked on others' lands and would try to supplement their incomes through cottage industries such as weaving and carpentry.

From the mid-seventeenth century, however, a sea change occurred that was largely brought about by two developments. Population growth started to stagnate, and numbers even declined in the later decades. Simplistically put, this led to higher employment and wage levels and lower prices. Second was the growth and diversification of England's trade based upon its newly acquired overseas colonies. English woollen cloth had been the primary export to the continent for a long time but wars, changes in fashion and increased competition meant sales were

Panorama of London. Clearly visible are old St. Paul's (centre left) and the Tower (right). Heads on spikes decorate the southern end of London Bridge with Southwark Cathedral just to the left. Further left is the Globe Theatre and then the Bear Garden where animal-baiting occurred. (*Artist: C. Visscher, 1616. Library of Congress*)

declining. Many merchants, however, adapted and made huge profits by re-exporting the new, highly sought-after products from America and the East Indies such as cotton, tobacco, tea and sugar. These profits were further augmented as the English replaced the Dutch as the dominant carriers of international trade.

General increased wealth combined with growing demand for new commodities created a much healthier economy than that which existed in the first half of the Stuart period. Entrepreneurs and merchants now had more money to invest in their businesses and new technologies. In 1708, for instance, Thomas Newcomen created a steam engine to pump water out of flooded mines, and, in the following year, Abraham Darby replaced charcoal with coking coal (which gave off more heat) to smelt iron in his blast furnaces. The amount and range of manufacturing increased, leading to more urbanisation as towns grew up around specific industries. Birmingham developed around metal-working, for example, Whitehaven grew around coal exports, Nottingham had the lace industry and north Staffordshire boomed with potteries. By 1714, the number of towns with over 5,000 inhabitants had surged to thirty-two. London, of course, continued to suck in migrants as well as skilled artisans from abroad and grew to 600,000 people. The largest entrepôt in the world, it also hosted a huge range of small-scale manufacturing ranging from glass-making and furniture to textiles and ship-building.

English lady in winter costume, with muffs, scarf, mask and hood. (*Artist: W. Hollar, 1644. Thomas Fisher Rare Book Library*)

Greater production and increased wealth meant that more people could live in brick houses with chimneys and glass windows. Meat and wheat consumption increased and a growth in consumerism caused the retail trade to start shifting from marketplaces to permanent shops. In London, piped water (along elm and lead pipes from a reservoir near present-day Angel tube station) became more available for those who could afford it and experimentation with street oil lamps began. Greater urbanisation and bigger businesses also led to the growth of a professional class of people such as insurers, bankers, surveyors and engineers. People were becoming more politically aware and active too. In the late 1620s, people began posting anonymous political libels upon the outdoor pulpit at St Paul's Cross and, from the 1640s, more printing presses and higher literacy rates contributed to a wide distribution of political pamphlets and treatises. From the 1660s, the new **coffee houses** bubbled with political debates, many of which were printed in new magazines such as *The Tatler* and *The Spectator*. With the expiry of the Licensing Act in 1695, news became more accessible and reading a daily newspaper started to become a habit. Less political was the first women's magazine in 1693 – *the Ladies' Mercury* – which focused on topics such as domesticity, courtship and marriage.

The picture was bleaker in the countryside though. Lower prices, higher wages, migration to the towns, falling cloth sales and the Land Tax (from 1693, raised to fund war with France) meant that many landowners struggled. Forced into making their farms more productive, new crops and techniques were adopted. Planting turnips, for example, created ideal winter fodder for livestock which led to greater manuring of the soil and higher crop yields. A huge breakthrough was the adoption of the four-year 'Norfolk' crop rotation of wheat, turnips, barley (or oats) and clover. The latter was a nitrogen-fixing crop that improved soil health, thereby negating the need to leave a field fallow each year, and was a valuable source of protein for grazing livestock.

This was the start of the Agrarian Revolution which, by feeding the towns, enabled the Industrial Revolution. This was at least sixty years away, however. In 1714, Britain was still very much an agricultural society with only 17 per cent of people living in towns. Huge socio-economic developments took place over the Stuart period, but progress varied from region to region and inequality increased as more wealth became concentrated in the hands of a smaller elite. Social mobility remained limited too. Some successful tenant farmers managed to join the yeomanry by acquiring land from bankrupt farms, but it was the landless labourers arriving in towns who had more hope of climbing the social ladder by seeking apprenticeships.

Sport and Leisure

On 20 July 1607, the people of Lambourn in Berkshire were treated to an astonishing spectacle – a ship that flew to the top of their church spire. With the aid of ropes and pulleys, it then returned to the ground but not before firing off its twelve cannons and fireworks while twenty feet in the air. The ship then travelled overland, followed by around 500 people, using wheels, cranks and pedals before reaching the Thames and sailing to London. This was a stunt of the inventor, William Bush. In 1624, crowds flocked to the riverside to watch King **James I**, no less, purportedly go on an underwater voyage from Westminster to Greenwich. This early submarine – the brainchild of Dutch scientist, Cornelis Drebbel – was wooden, covered in greased leather, powered by oars and contained some mysterious chemical that produced air underwater.

These spectacles were unusual occasions when people of all ilks dropped everything and rubbed shoulders to be entertained. Overall, though, recreational activities in the Stuart period ran along class lines with the better-off having the luxury of more spare time to indulge in leisure pursuits. These included:

Cotswold Games. A variety of sports can be seen such as gymnastics, coursing with hounds, sledgehammer throwing and shin-kicking. The first Cotswold Olympics took place in 1612 and continue to this day. (*Artist: unknown from Annalia Dubrensia, 1636 via Wikimedia Commons*)

Hunting

Falconry and deer hunting, using hounds, on large country estates were still popular but firearms for shooting wildfowl became increasingly common. Not only social occasions, these hunts were often an opportunity to make political deals too. Wild boar were briefly reintroduced before dying out again.

Horse Racing

James I brought 'the sport of kings' back into favour and founded Newmarket as the centre of racing. **Charles II** was a great enthusiast, established his court at Newmarket twice a year and even rode winners in 1671 and 1674. His niece, Queen **Anne**, was a devotee too and founded Ascot racecourse.

Drama

During the first two Stuart monarchs' reigns, masques were de rigueur among **society**'s elite. Performed in private homes, they combined elaborate sets and costumes with singing, dancing and poetry, often with audience participation. From the 1660s, masques evolved into semi-operas which, in turn, were superseded by opera. Tickets were too expensive for the masses who, instead, attended theatres and enjoyed plays by the likes of Shakespeare and **Jonson** and, later, **Dryden** and **Behn**. After the Restoration, popular themes were social satire and sexual intrigue and, for the first time, women were allowed to perform.

Real Tennis

Played in long, narrow indoor courts with sloping ceilings, players used wooden racquets strung with animal gut and balls made of wool, hair or cork wrapped in leather which could be bounced off the walls. **Charles I** and his sons were keen players with Charles II often getting up early to play in his newly constructed court in Whitehall.

Cricket

Originally a children's game, cricket had become an adult sport by James I's reign. After the Restoration, village cricket became very popular, especially as a source of gambling among the rich and the first known county game was played in 1709. The game was played with two stumps and hockey stick-shaped bats, and the ball was rolled along the ground. Cricket's first death occurred in 1624 when a batsman clubbed a fielder while trying to hit the ball a second time to avoid being caught!

For most people, leisure pursuits were only feasible during the various religious festivals and royal celebrations which, when added to any local celebrations, could amount to forty days' holiday per year. Playing sport on the Sabbath (Sundays)

A tavern or brothel. One man plays a violin, another a hurdy-gurdy while another is being robbed by a prostitute. A child watches a couple making out while a woman on the right is keeping track of the drinks consumed. (*Artist: J. M. Molenaer, 1625–68. Rijksmuseum*)

became a politically charged topic in 1618 when James I issued *The King's Book of Sports* which permitted certain activities such as dancing, archery, leaping and the selling of Whitsun ales (to fund local churches) much to the chagrin of many **Puritans**. Popular entertainment for the masses included:

Football

Denounced by many as being violent and a distraction from one's duties, football was the most popular sport of the time. Team sizes were unlimited, games were played over huge areas, the ball could be kicked, thrown and carried, goals could be a pair of gates, tripping was allowed and injuries were common.

Blood sports

The larger towns had special arenas or bear-baiting pits which attracted all classes. In these, tethered bears or bulls were attacked by trained dogs and bets would be placed on which dogs would survive. Bears were rarely killed as they were expensive. Cockfighting, using roosters with blades attached to their feet, was also popular.

Taverns

At the heart of each community lay the tavern, a place where people could drink, eat, sleep, gamble, dance and sing bawdy songs accompanied by a fiddle and fife. Beer was the most common drink, but rum became increasingly popular after the capture of Jamaica and its sugar-cane plantations in 1655. Far more damaging to society was the shift towards cheap and powerful gin after the **Glorious Revolution**. For those seeking quieter confines, **coffee houses** became very popular after the 1650s.

Combat sport

Styles of wrestling varied from region to region. Charles II deemed Cornish wrestlers to be the best in the country after seeing a tournament in Bodmin. The headmaster of Truro Grammar School, Richard Stevens, was a particularly well-known wrestler. Cudgelling was especially popular in rural areas and involved the use of long, blunt wooden clubs with the aim of drawing blood from an opponent's head. Bare-knuckle boxing evolved from street-fighting and involved huge sums of prize money. The first recorded fight was in 1681 when the Duke of Albemarle arranged a fight between his butler and butcher.

Increasing literacy rates and printing presses meant more people enjoyed literature, the best-selling books being Shakespeare's plays and *Don Quixote* by Cervantes. England's first newspapers appeared after the Restoration starting with *The London Gazette* (from 1665) which was essentially a government mouthpiece, but relaxation of censorship laws led to other regular news sources in the following decades. Penny pamphlets were particularly popular. Small and cheap, they spread propaganda during the **Civil Wars** and news from abroad and were often sold by itinerant peddlers. Young men also liked to buy jest books – collections of jokes and humorous stories –which often poked fun at women and thc establishment.

Dice, card and board games were found everywhere in society, usually with a gambling aspect to them. Such games included Whist, Backgammon and Hazard (where bets were placed on the sum of two rolled dice). Chess remained popular too. Charles I was an avid player who allegedly brought a set onto his scaffold and bequeathed it to his personal chaplain.

Fairs were great occasions for all, providing financial boons for traders and entertainers and opportunities to socialise. The most famous occurred upon a river. The fourteenth to the nineteenth centuries experienced the Little Ice Age

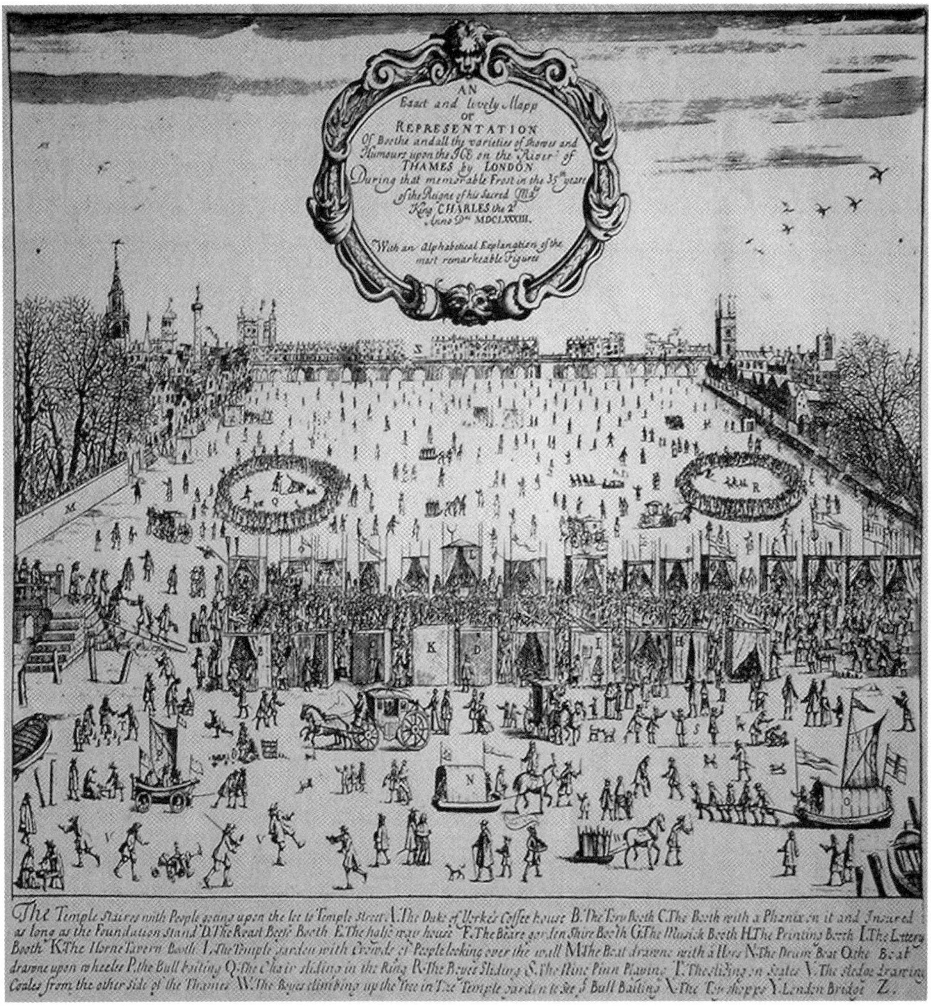

The Frost Fair showing a multitude of activities such as bullbaiting in the centre left. London Bridge is in the distance and Freezeland Street, with all its booths, is in the foreground. (*Artist: probably W. Faithorne, c. 1684 via Wikimedia Commons*)

during which temperature dips caused the Thames to freeze over nine times. This was facilitated by the sluggish water created by the narrow arches of London Bridge and the fact that the river was wider and shallower than it is today. The 'Frost Fair' of 1684, however, was well documented and provides a glimpse of Stuart entertainments: skittles, skating, football, puppet plays, bear baiting, sword swallowing, coach racing, a lottery booth, an ox roast and much more besides. Even a fox hunt was organised. A lane of tented booths was erected too – 'Freezeland-street' – selling all sorts of wares including the provision of women.

In fact, prostitutes were common in every town and military encampment. In 1700, an estimated 20 per cent of women in London were prostitutes; most were escaping poverty or supplementing another income, and all were socially stigmatised. Some were 'six-penny whores' who would walk the streets and hire a room for a night and the luckier ones worked in brothels but all risked violence, venereal diseases and dangerous abortions. Although the authorities usually turned a blind eye, brothels were officially illegal and therefore many congregated in Southwark, just outside the jurisdiction of the City of London. Some of the cheaper, less hygienic establishments were in ports while others catered for the upper end of society such as the luxurious Holland's Leaguer. Owned by the shrewd businesswoman, Bess Holland, it was in an old manor house, replete with walls, moat and portcullis, just south of the Thames. Its clients, such as James I and the **Duke of Buckingham**, could choose a girl from a selection of portraits and rest assured that they were clean and would use contraceptive pessaries. Famously, Holland's Leaguer endured a siege in late 1631 when troops sent to close it were repelled by the raised drawbridge and the girls' chamber pots being emptied upon their heads.

Strafford, Earl of

see Wentworth, Sir Thomas

Stuart, Arbella

(1575–1615)

Noblewoman

By the age of 7, both of Arbella's parents had died and she went into the care of her grandmother, Bess of Hardwick. Only being allowed to visit London occasionally, she was kept in protective semi-isolation as Bess realised that there were many who would seek her hand in **marriage**. This was because Arbella was a great-great-granddaughter of Henry VII and first cousin of James VI of Scotland (later **James I** of England), thereby making her second in line to the throne after James upon Queen Elizabeth's death.

After James's accession, Arbella was well treated largely due to her part in revealing the Main Plot (1604) which aimed to replace the king with herself. Her high rank was displayed during royal ceremonies and she even performed in a royal masque. Arbella got into trouble, however, when she fell in love and secretly married William Seymour (1610) who himself had a claim to the throne. James suspected a conspiracy was underway and had them both imprisoned in the Tower. The following year, they escaped separately, with Arbella disguised as a man (one witness said she reminded him of **Mary Frith**), but they missed their rendezvous which caused delays and her ship was overhauled just before it reached Calais. The stricter confinement that followed led to her mental breakdown, refusal to eat, and eventual death.

T

Tories and Whigs

Political parties

Some may argue that England's first political party were the **Levellers** of the 1640s but they lacked both the necessary formal structure and aim to win an election. The birth of party politics can be more accurately traced to the Exclusion Crisis of 1679–81 when two groups – the Tories and the Whigs – hotly contested **James, Duke of York**'s, right to inherit the Crown. The Whigs, led by **Lord Shaftesbury**, refused to accept the prospect of a **Catholic** monarch and organised a successful propaganda campaign, involving parades and pamphlets, which fanned the flames of the **Popish Plot**. With their headquarters at the King's Head Tavern (named the Green Ribbon Club after its members' habit of wearing green ribbons and bows), the Whigs won three elections in this period and battled to pass an exclusion bill through **Parliament**. They were, however, thwarted by **Charles II** and his supporters – the Tories – and driven to near-extinction after the **Rye House Plot** (1683) and the accession of **James II**.

The name 'Whigs' was a term of abuse derived from the Whigamores – **Presbyterian** rebels in south-west **Scotland** – while their opponents were called 'Tories', named after Catholic outlaws in **Ireland**. After briefly uniting during the **Glorious Revolution**, it becomes very difficult to recognise a party system in the 1690s. With no party whips, members seemed to show just as much loyalty to court and constituents as they did to each other and their views developed with time. Even the names changed. The 'Country' and 'Court' factions, for instance, were broadly Whig and Tory respectively but included members from both groups. Only in Queen **Anne**'s reign, when the matters of the succession, union with Scotland and the war in Europe came to the fore, did more recognisable 'parties' appear with leaders such as Sidney Godolphin (Tory then Whig) and Robert Harley (Whig then Tory!).

Broadly speaking, the Whigs supported religious toleration, union with Scotland, an aggressive land war against France and a Protestant succession. The Tories, on the other hand, were staunch supporters of the **Anglican** Church, opposed union with Scotland and preferred a more limited, maritime conflict with France. Regarding the succession, they favoured divine right and so questioned the legality of the Glorious Revolution, and many refused to cut ties with James II's heirs. The Tories succeeded in bringing the war against France to an end in 1713 but, with many of them supporting the Jacobite succession, they lost power when George I became king and were cast into the political wilderness for decades.

V

Van Dyck, Anthony

(1599–1641)

Court painter

Van Dyck was born in Antwerp, the seventh of twelve children and son of a wealthy silk merchant. A precocious talent, he was recognised as an exceptional artist by the age of 15 and, within a few years, was employed in the workshop of the foremost artist of northern Europe – Peter Paul Rubens. By 1620, some of his works were considered as good as his master's. In that year, to spread his wings and perhaps gain greater recognition, he travelled to England for four months where he worked for King **James I**. Afterwards, he travelled around Italy producing paintings for several aristocrats and came across the works of his second major influence, Titian. Van Dyck returned to Flanders in 1627 and became immersed in creating his renowned *Iconography* – a series of prints showing various prominent people and fellow artists.

From 1632, his main home was in Blackfriars in London. King **Charles I**, an avid art collector, was so impressed with his work that he granted van Dyck a pension of £200 per year, a golden chain, a knighthood and a suite of rooms in Eltham Palace. Previously, much of his work had covered religious and mythological scenes such as the famous paintings of Saint Rosalia in Palermo but now he shifted his focus to portraiture in response to the demands of the English court. Since the great Holbein, English art had become quite formal and stagnant, but van Dyck's Baroque style gave it a new lease of life. Using soft and fluid brushstrokes and clever use of light, he created full-length portraits that combined formality and authority with casualness and elegance. Choosing the most fashionable, graceful costumes for his sitters, his work tended to flatter but, at the same time, revealed something of their personalities and was laden with symbolism.

Van Dyck's workshop in Blackfriars, known as the 'beauty shop' by the wealthiest in **society**, housed a profitable and well-oiled production line of portraits. Sitters would normally pose for an hour as the master drew a sketch which would then be transferred onto canvas and completed by assistants although the heads and finer details were left to van Dyck. While in England, he painted around 400 portraits although his most famous were those of the king (forty portraits) and the royal family, often with an eye to royalist propaganda. He also tried to persuade Charles to decorate the walls of the Banqueting House in Whitehall for which Rubens had painted the ceiling. By 1638, however, the king was too short of money and only a sketch for one wall remains.

Charming, fashionable and vain, van Dyck mixed well in aristocratic circles and was known for his affairs with several women such as the courtesan, Margaret Lemon. In this tumultuous relationship, rife with infidelities, she once threatened to ruin his career by biting off his right thumb. Van Dyck eventually married a lady-in-waiting to the queen, Mary Ruthven, with whom he had one daughter. While travelling in Flanders and France in 1640–41, it appears that he contracted the unknown illness that killed him upon his return to London. He is probably the first painter to be buried in St Paul's Cathedral.

Some criticise van Dyck's work as being blandly flattering and idealistic and lacking emotional depth. However, his paintings were hugely popular, were a major influence on future generations of British artists such as Gainsborough and Reynolds and provide a valuable window into the lives of his aristocratic contemporaries. His importance may possibly be summed up by the fact that, in 2014, the National Portrait Gallery spent £10 million to keep his 1640 self-portrait in the country.

Villiers, George (First Duke of Buckingham)

(1592–1628)

Courtier and statesman

Villiers was born into minor Leicestershire gentry, his father being a prosperous sheep farmer who died in 1606. His mother, ambitious for him to adopt a political career, afforded to send him to Paris to learn courtly skills such as dancing, fencing and speaking French. In 1614, she arranged for him to be at Apethorpe Palace, Northants, where King **James I** was staying during a royal progress. Later described by the Bishop of Gloucester as 'the handsomest-bodied man in all of England', Villiers's dancing in a masque caught the king's eye and he was soon promoted as someone who could replace James's unpopular favourite – Robert Carr. The plan worked. Within two years, he was Gentleman of the Bedchamber, Master of the Horse and had eclipsed Carr.

Villiers's rise continued on a meteoric trajectory. 1619 saw him appointed Lord High Admiral and when he became the Duke of Buckingham (1623), he was the only man with that esteemed title outside the royal family. At the same time, he developed a close friendship with the king's son, **Charles**, whom he tutored in dance. James's own relationship with Buckingham has been one of much conjecture. The king called him 'Steenie' after St Stephen who apparently had an angelic face and correspondence between the two certainly suggests a sexual relationship. The two were noted to exchange 'wanton looks' and 'lascivious kisses' in public and Walter Ralegh jokingly called the king, 'Queen James'. Definitive proof, however, is still lacking. Enigmatically, James once told his privy council, 'Christ had John and I have George.' Buckingham himself was possibly bisexual given his affairs with women and his **marriage** to Katherine Manners (1620) who bore him four children.

As the king's favourite, Buckingham made a fortune for himself and his family by controlling all royal patronage and accepting gifts and bribes. It was he who helped **Francis Bacon** to become Lord Chancellor and later withdrew support when Bacon was accused of corruption (probably to deflect from his own dubious practices). With one of his clients as Lord Deputy of **Ireland**, he also enriched himself by selling Irish titles, owning monopolies and collecting Irish customs duties and income from wardships. Buckingham was also keen to cultivate his own image by commissioning many portraits of himself such as the magnificent 1625 painting by van Mierevelt which showed off his power and wealth.

In 1623, Buckingham made his first foray into foreign affairs when he and Charles travelled overland, as Thomas and John Smith, to Madrid where the prince believed he would amaze everyone with his surprise arrival and win the hand of the Spanish Infanta. However, this poorly conceived plan (made worse by Charles climbing over a wall to surprise the Infanta and Buckingham's crass attempts at womanising) was never going to work while England persecuted **Catholic**s. In fact, it only succeeded in raising the anti-Catholic mood among the English public and in **Parliament** and leaving Charles feeling humiliated and vengeful.

As soon as Charles acceded to the throne (1625), he and Buckingham instigated a chaotic foreign policy that was to profoundly damage England's prestige as well as the king's relationship with Parliament. That same year, Buckingham headed the marriage negotiations for Charles to marry the French king's sister,

Henrietta Maria (an unpopular choice given her Catholicism). He failed, however, to conclude an alliance which would wrest back control of the Palatinate for the king's sister, **Elizabeth**, partly because it seems that he sexually accosted the French queen in her private garden. After war was declared against Spain, Buckingham organised an attempt to capture Cadiz which ended as a fiasco and aided France in its fight against the Huguenots (fellow Protestants) near La Rochelle. An outraged Parliament attempted to impeach a man they saw as being corrupt, incompetent and dangerous but Charles simply sent its members home.

John Felton. (*Artist: R. Sawyer, 1830. Yale Center for British Art*)

After France concluded its own peace with Spain, England completed a volte-face by sending a military expedition to aid the Huguenots in 1627. Buckingham himself bravely led a landing on the Île de Ré but his attempts to capture the fort of Saint Martin were thwarted by having too few men, inadequate cannons and ladders that were too short! Now assaulted by rampant disease and French reinforcements, Buckingham's army of 7,000 men was reduced to 2,000 before it was extracted to safety.

In August 1628, Buckingham went to Portsmouth to arrange another expedition. The town was seething with ill-disciplined, unpaid sailors but he refused to wear any protective mail and, as he was about to leave the Greyhound Inn, an impoverished officer called John Felton stabbed him to death. Embittered by unpaid arrears of wages and lack of promotion, Felton also declared that, by killing Buckingham, he would be doing the country a service. Many sections of **society** rejoiced and acclaimed the assassin a hero; after Felton was hanged, his body was displayed in Portsmouth where it became an object of veneration. Charles, however, was aghast at what had happened and blamed Parliament for the loss of his close confidant.

There are certain parallels between the careers of Buckingham and his grand-niece, **Barbara Palmer**. He took advantage of having power with no accountability and yet he lacked the ability (and resources) to justify his position. Even his mother seemed unsurprised when she heard of his death. In his defence, he was simply using a political system of patronage and favourites that had existed since Elizabeth I's reign; the difference, however, was that there were no 'counter-favourites' to check his power. Buckingham cannot be blamed for the outbreak of the **Civil Wars** fourteen years later, but he certainly helped to set the tone of the relationship between Charles I and Parliament.

Virginia

England's first colony in North America

When Walter Ralegh was granted permission to settle lands north of Florida, the entire region was named Virginia in honour of his queen, Elizabeth – the Virgin Queen. His attempts in the 1580s failed but, in 1606, efforts were revived when merchants created the Virginia Company with the intention of finding gold, spreading Protestantism and establishing a base from which to disrupt Spanish shipping. After a rough, twenty-week voyage, three ships carrying 104 male colonists anchored in the Chesapeake Bay on 26 April 1607. After some exploration, a base was set up on an island on the north bank of the James River – Jamestown – named after King **James I**.

Native American from Virginia. (*Artist: W. Hollar, 1645. Rijksmuseum*)

The settlement only survived the first few years due to periodic supplies (and more settlers including the first women) from England and the strong leadership of John Smith who arranged sporadic trade with the local Powhatan tribe and threatened to starve any settler who did not work. The native Americans, however, having a subsistence culture, resented giving some of their food to the newcomers and occasionally ambushed them. By 1610, 80 per cent of the 500 colonists had died from starvation, attacks and diseases from the surrounding swamps and there is even evidence of cannibalism. The settlement was almost abandoned only to be rescued by last-minute supply ships. Peace with the Powhatan only came in 1614 when the chief's daughter, Pocahontas, married a settler named John Rolfe (Pocahontas had previously saved Smith's life after he had been captured. She converted to Christianity, changed her name to Rebecca and travelled to England where she was fêted as a 'civilised savage' before dying in Gravesend, aged 20).

The settlers' focus on seeking the best land rather than communal security made them vulnerable to any surprise attack. This is exactly what happened in 1622 when the Powhatan wiped out a third of the colony. After the militia combined with native allies to counterattack, the Powhatan sued for an end to hostilities, but their peace party had their wine poisoned before being massacred. Intermittent warfare continued until 1632 and broke out again in the 1640s as the settlers further encroached on indigenous territory upstream on the James River and north of the York River. Overwhelmed by European numbers, along with their diseases, the Powhatan were a broken force by the mid-1640s.

With no gold discoveries, Virginia was economically unviable, and the natives' tobacco had too strong a flavour for English tastes. Rolfe, however, transplanted a milder variety from the West Indies which he called Orinoco tobacco. This new crop was labour-intensive, but it saved the colony as its profits enticed larger numbers of settlers across the Atlantic. Most of these were European indentured servants who were given free passage, board and lodging in return for seven years' labour, after which they gained their freedom and possibly some tools and land to get started independently. The first Africans arrived in 1619; they had been captured from a Portuguese **slave** ship and were sold as indentured servants. One such black person, Anthony Johnson, finished his servitude in around 1635, was legally recognised as a 'free Negro' and became a successful tobacco farmer with his own indentured servants.

Most black servants, however, were treated like slaves and various legal cases were fought over the issue. It was not until 1661 that race-based slavery was formalised by the Virginia government and, in the following year, another law stated that any child was born a slave if their mother was a slave and any fathers of mixed-race children (rapes were common) were absolved of any responsibilities. Codification of these and later laws in 1705 included the right of masters to beat their slaves (and not be prosecuted if a slave subsequently died) and the requirement of slaves to have written passes to leave their plantations. By then, Virginia had become a slave **society** with around 10 per cent of its 60,000 people enslaved.

From 1619, the Virginia government consisted of a House of Burgesses with twenty-two members elected by landowners, the company-appointed governor and his council of six. In 1624, with the colony facing economic and military problems, King James revoked the company's charter and Virginia became a royal colony. Its longest-serving governor was William Berkeley (appointed 1641) who gave greater independence to the Burgesses and promoted diversification of crops so that the colony was not over-reliant on tobacco. From his own plantation, he managed to export silk (by growing mulberry bushes), oilseed rape, flax, fruit and sugar but, with fewer resources, other farmers were reluctant to change. During the **Civil Wars**, Berkeley offered Virginia as a haven for royalists, such as the Washingtons, and so was replaced by **Cromwell** in 1652.

Advert for Virginia tobacco. A slave shades his owner while others hoe the fields. (*Artist: unknown, mid-eighteenth century via Wikimedia Commons*)

After **Charles II** reinstated him in 1660, Berkeley displayed a more authoritarian side. By enforcing acceptance of the **Anglican**

Church, he caused many **Puritan**s and Quakers to move to Maryland; he discouraged schooling and banned printing presses as he considered them subversive. After the Navigation Act (1660) restricted tobacco exports solely to England, the commodity's price dropped, causing economic hardship. At the same time, sustained tobacco cultivation was degrading the soil, causing farmers to seize land further west and north which inevitably brought about native American retaliation in 1675. Berkeley's refusal to conduct a war against the indigenous people confirmed the view of many that he was a self-seeking, corrupt official who was just protecting his investment in the fur trade. One of his councillors, Nathaniel Bacon, decided to take matters into own hands and mistakenly attacked peaceful native tribes. In the ensuing rift between the two men, Berkeley had to flee east in 1676 after Bacon burned down Jamestown and seized control of the colony. In the following year, however, Bacon's Rebellion was suppressed after its leader died from dysentery and Berkeley was recalled to London where he died soon after.

In many ways, Stuart Virginia was a transplantation of England with its political and legal systems, adherence to the Anglican Church and a class structure of landowners and yeomanry. William and Mary College (founded, 1693) and located in Williamsburg (the new capital from 1698) perpetuated this society by being a school for the sons of wealthy and influential Anglican families. While a third of the population was landless and poor, power remained in the hands of the top five per cent who displayed their importance in horse-racing events in which huge sums of money were spent in breeding, training and gambling. Perhaps class conflict was only prevented by a sense of unity created by the existence of a slave underclass.

W

Wentworth, Sir Thomas (Earl of Strafford)

(1593–1641)

Statesman

Wentworth was the son of a wealthy Yorkshire landowner and was educated at St John's College, Cambridge, before studying law at London's Inns of Court. In 1611, he married Margaret Clifford, daughter of the influential Earl of Cumberland; his family connections enabled him to represent Yorkshire in successive **parliament**s from 1614. Up until 1628, Wentworth was primarily an opponent of royal policies such as taxation without parliamentary consent. Indeed, he was briefly imprisoned in 1627 for refusing to pay a forced loan. He also disapproved of the **Duke of Buckingham** and his war plans and became a leading proponent of the Petition of Right (1628) which protected citizens from certain arbitrary actions by the king, **Charles I**.

At heart, however, Wentworth believed in divine right and the importance of a powerful monarchy and thought that king and Parliament could work together. Out of personal ambition and a belief that Parliament had gone far enough after the petition, he sought service with the Crown, much to the disbelief and chagrin of fellow MPs such as **John Eliot** and **Edward Coke**. Seeing Wentworth as a useful ally, Charles appointed him President of the Council of the North in late 1628 and a privy councillor in the following year. In the former role, he began implementing his policy of 'Thorough', by which royal authority was to be enforced efficiently and fairly through the law courts and taxation. Strict application of the law made him particularly unpopular with the wealthier members of **society** who had previously bent the law to their wishes.

In 1632, Charles appointed Wentworth Lord Deputy of **Ireland**. Here was a place where he could implement 'Thorough' with a free hand and less interference from other royal ministers. With great efficiency and single-mindedness, he transformed Ireland from being a drain on the royal coffers to a source of much revenue for the Crown, much to Charles's delight as it granted him more independence from Parliament. By promoting Irish exports, such as a new linen trade, collecting customs duties more rigorously and eliminating piracy, Wentworth more than doubled trade revenue. Through skilful manipulation and browbeating of its members, he also managed to successfully raise subsidies from the Dublin Parliament and, by replacing corrupt officials with his own coterie of servants, he ensured the implementation of his policies, through armed force if necessary.

Wentworth's methods, however, antagonised most sections of Irish society by riding roughshod over all customs and opponents. He used ancient deeds to extend royal lands, imposed some of Archbishop **Laud**'s Arminian reforms upon the Church of Ireland, restored lands lost during the Reformation to the Church which often charged higher rents and used the Court of Castle Chamber to prosecute his opponents. He also alienated the **Catholic** majority by agreeing to implement the Graces (promises to protect their lands and religion) but then reneged on this promise. At the same time, Wentworth enriched himself on the customs farm, wardships and a tobacco monopoly and held court in Dublin like a prince with an entourage including a jester.

Armed rebellion against Laud's reforms in **Scotland** prompted Charles to recall Wentworth to England in 1639 to deal with the crisis and, soon after, elevated him to Earl of Strafford. Feeling that he could tame its members, like he had those in Dublin, Strafford advised the king to recall Parliament to raise the necessary subsidies for prosecuting a war against the Scots. However, he completely misjudged the mood of its MPs who had been rankled by royalist policies since their last

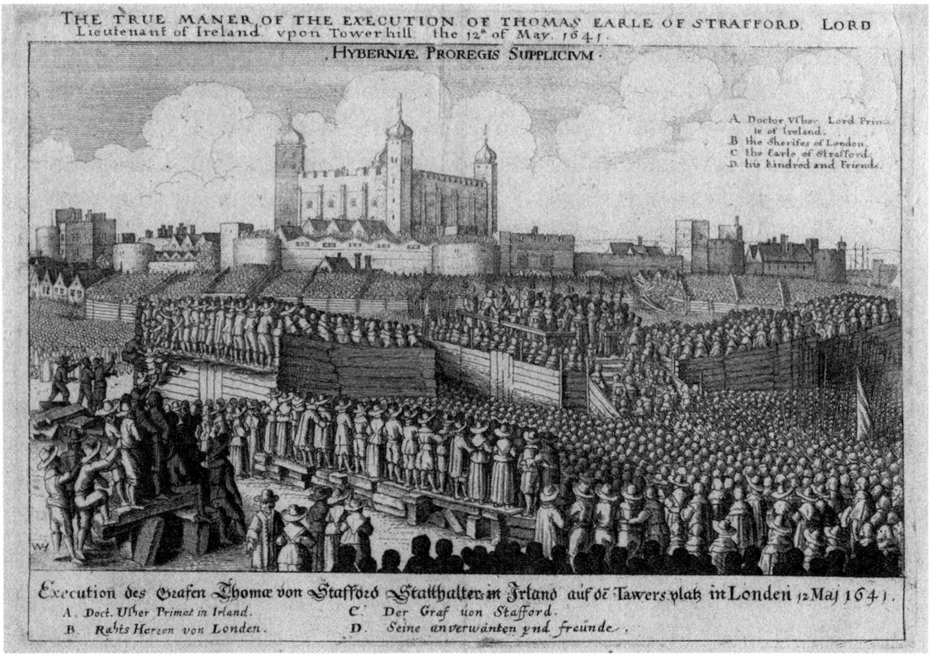

Execution of Strafford. Crowds mass on Tower Hill. (*Artist: W. Hollar, 1641. Metropolitan Museum of Art*)

sitting in 1629 and so the intractable Short Parliament was soon dismissed with no subsidies (May 1640). Strafford still led a force north, but his underpaid and demoralised troops were soon defeated in the Second Bishops' War and Charles had to sue for peace.

Many MPs were alarmed by the king's retention of Strafford as his chief advisor in London. His reputation as an unscrupulous enforcer – Black Tom Tyrant, as he was known – made him the chief target when Parliament was recalled in November. Charles's chief opponent, **John Pym**, was particularly fearful of Strafford unearthing secret negotiations he may have held with the Scots during the Bishops' War. So, later that month, Strafford was impeached and sent to the Tower of London. At his subsequent trial in March, he faced twenty-eight charges of misconduct, most of them from his time in Ireland. Strafford, however, defended himself eloquently and nothing serious could be made to stick. The most serious charge, when he told Charles, 'you have an army in Ireland you may employ here to reduce this kingdom', only had one unconvincing witness and 'this kingdom' may well have referred to Scotland, not England. After the impeachment failed, Pym and his supporters desperately arranged a bill of attainder by which MPs could simply vote for his execution. An army plot in May 1641 to rescue Strafford from the Tower and destroy Parliament with the aid of a French army alienated the support of moderate MPs and the bill was passed and presented to the king. Charles had previously guaranteed his safety but an angry mob outside Whitehall Palace threatened his family and so he reluctantly signed. After reportedly saying, 'Put not your trust in princes', Strafford calmly walked to Tower Hill where he was beheaded in front of a huge crowd on 12 May. Five months later, Ireland rose in rebellion.

An enigmatic character, Strafford displayed a stern countenance but was humorous with his friends and each of his three **marriage**s were evidently very loving. One can draw parallels between Strafford and Thomas Cromwell a hundred years previously. Both were possibly the most effective administrators of their age, both were zealous, hard-working and loyal to the monarchy, both created many enemies and both, in the end, were betrayed by their masters.

William III (William of Orange)

(1650–1702)

King of England, Scotland and Ireland (1689–1702)
and Stadtholder of Holland (1672–1702)

Born in The Hague, William was the only child of Mary – eldest daughter of **Charles I** – and William II, Prince of Orange. His father was the Stadtholder (Lord Protector) of the Dutch Republic, consisting of seven autonomous provinces, but died before William was born. This led to a power struggle between those who believed in a true republic with no princely leader and those who wanted a strong figurehead from the republic's most royal-like family – the House of Orange. It was the former who came out on top, aided as they were by **Oliver Cromwell**'s demand that William should never become Stadtholder after the English victory in the **First Anglo-Dutch War**. Mary showed little interest in her son, often spending long periods in England, and William's Calvinist **education** was controlled by the anti-Orangists who treated him as a ward of the state.

William's personal change of fortune occurred in 1672 during the republic's 'Disaster Year' when it was attacked by England and France and its eastern provinces overrun by French troops. Only the deliberate flooding of central swathes of the country saved it from annihilation but, in the general panic, the republic's leaders – the de Witt brothers – were blamed for the disaster and brutally murdered by an Orangist mob. Now seen as the country's only hope, William was appointed Stadtholder and led an aggressive military campaign. This had mixed results but, after forging alliances with Spain and the Holy Roman Empire, he forced the expulsion of French troops and took the conflict into the Spanish Netherlands. The war dragged on into a stalemate and peace was signed in 1678, but William now decided that his lifelong aim was to prevent French hegemony over Europe.

To achieve this, he understood the necessity of drawing England into the anti-France camp and so readily agreed to marrying **Mary**, his cousin and eldest child of **James, Duke of York** in 1677. With James's brother, King **Charles II**, being childless, William suddenly had a good chance of acquiring the English throne. After James, a **Catholic**, became king in 1685, William maintained secret correspondence with leading English Protestants while, at the same time, trying to persuade James to join the anti-French league. James refused and William could only watch in alarm as the English king embarked on an absolutist, pro-Catholic programme. Matters came to a head in June 1688 when James's wife gave birth to a son whose claim to the throne superseded that of Mary's. Soon after, seven leading **Tories and Whigs** invited William to invade England to rescue the country from a Catholic line of monarchs. Fortunately, Louis XIV of France had sent most of his ships into the Mediterranean and the bulk of his army to the upper Rhine and so he seized the opportunity.

In November, an army of 40,000 men disembarked near Torbay in Devon. The majority were Dutch veterans, considered among the finest in Europe. James, meanwhile, lost his nerve as well as some of his key supporters and fled the country, thus enabling the **Glorious Revolution**. William's accession to the throne was not inevitable, however. The Tories, strong believers in divine succession, would only accept Mary as queen but William refused to merely be his 'wife's gentleman usher' and Mary herself refused to rule alone. The matter was resolved when it was agreed that James had abdicated rather than been expelled and the two were crowned joint monarchs in April 1689. Soon after, they were offered the crown of **Scotland** too.

William and Mary are offered the crown. (*Artist: J. Parker after J. Northcote, 1790. Wellcome Collection*)

Now that he had won his prize, William was careful to be as conciliatory as possible and so tacitly accepted the **Bill of Rights** which restated Parliament's privileges. Regarding religion, the **Anglican**s feared any threat to their control of the Church and so the Toleration Act (1689) did not go as far as William would have liked. Of greater urgency was the matter of **Ireland** where James had landed with French troops in March. William arrived with a multinational, Protestant army and defeated the Jacobite forces at the Battle of the Boyne in July 1690, after which James fled to France and Ireland was eventually conquered. That year, Jacobite resistance in Scotland was quashed too. The Boyne was, in fact, the first victory for the League of Augsburg – a loose coalition of countries which William had assembled to block French expansionism. So, with the British Isles secured, William was able to focus on campaigning on the continent. The king was usually absent from spring to autumn each year but always gave advice to Mary who ruled in his absence, aided by a council. With his taciturn manner, William's **marriage** to Mary had not started off happily, especially after her discovery of his sole mistress – Elizabeth Villiers (cousin of **Barbara Palmer**). The two, however, became dependant on one another and formed a strong attachment and so he deeply mourned her death in 1694.

William's reign is very much defined by his war against France (1688–97). The need to raise sufficient funds for the war effort initiated a financial revolution. This entailed the creation of the national debt that was underwritten by Parliament

1699 bank note. This is a running cash note for £150 8s 8d and is handwritten except for the Britannia medallion and 'promise to pay'. The torn-off corner shows that the balance has been paid. (*Author: Bank of England, 1699. © Bank of England*)

and funded by investments, from an increasingly wealthy merchant class, in the new Bank of England (1694). This replaced the royal debt that had been based on monarchs' unreliable promises to repay their loans. Now, for the first time, the government was able to finance lengthy continental wars and, subsequently, England (and later, Britain) was able to become a major European power. Additionally, to service the debt, annual sittings of Parliament became necessary and a commission of MPs was established to oversee how public finances were spent.

To William's great frustration, Parliament also sought other ways to erode royal power. These he often thwarted by vetoing bills but sometimes he had to give way to receive war funds and acceptance of his foreign policy. The Triennial Act (1694), for example, established elections every three years, the Act of Settlement (1701) defined the independence of the judiciary from the Crown and, after the war finished, Parliament fought bitterly against the king's desire to maintain a standing army. At times, William even had to choose ministers whom he disliked to have his policies accepted and Parliament also criticised his preference for Dutch favourites (contemporary accusations of homosexuality lack any serious evidence). It is little wonder that, privately, he threatened to abdicate.

William's focus was always the war. The attritional campaigns in the Spanish Netherlands were characterised by manoeuvre and lengthy sieges and his aggressive tactics, while revealing much personal courage, led to several defeats and heavy casualties. Although not as skilled or as patient as **Marlborough**, William deserves much credit for assembling and holding together the League of Augsburg coalition and for keeping French power in check. At the Treaty of Ryswick (1697), Louis XIV recognised him as the king of England and promised not to aid the Jacobites, but William knew there was still much to be done as the issue regarding the Spanish succession had still not been resolved. Sure enough, when the Spanish king died in 1701, war broke out again. In the same year, the English succession was resolved after the death of the Duke of Gloucester, the only remaining child of his sister-in-law, **Anne**. The Act of Settlement stipulated that no Catholics could inherit the throne and that, after Anne, the crown would go to Sophia, Electress of Hanover (granddaughter of **James I**) and her heirs.

The following March, William broke his collarbone after being thrown from a horse which had stumbled on a molehill at Hampton Court. Doctors set the bone but, against their advice, he journeyed to Kensington Palace where he caught a chill and died of pneumonia. Aloof, distrustful (many politicians had remained in contact with James) and not one to suffer fools, William had been a hard man to like and courtiers had had to adjust themselves to a court that was far removed from the decadent days of the Restoration. Being a foreigner and abroad for much of the time had reduced his popularity too as did the large increases in taxation such as the 20 per cent Land Tax. Neither had William sought approval; his only **sport** had been hunting, and his asthma had kept him away from any curious onlookers in London. He did gain much sympathy after a Jacobite assassination attempt in 1696 but in Scotland many had blamed him for the Massacre of Glencoe (unfairly, perhaps) and the failure of the Darien Scheme. Although never popular, William's energy, honesty and determination gained him much respect, and his reign can be considered important in two ways: the development of England as a constitutional monarchy and its realisation that it had an important role to play in European politics.

Wilmot, John (Second Earl of Rochester)

(1647–80)

Courtier and poet

Wilmot was born in Oxfordshire, the son of Henry Wilmot who had fought for **Charles I** during the **Civil Wars** and aided Prince Charles in his escape to France after the royalist defeat at Worcester (1651). Aged 13 and now the Earl of Rochester, the younger Wilmot attended Wadham College, Oxford, where he apparently 'grew debauched' and left after a year with an honorary MA conferred upon him by the chancellor and family friend, the **Earl of Clarendon**. Out of eternal gratitude to Wilmot's father, **Charles II** paid for Rochester's tour of France and Italy and provided him with a generous annual pension.

Rochester soon became one of the 'Merry Gang' or 'Rake Hells' whose dissolute behaviour scandalised **society**. He shared mistresses such as **Nell Gwyn** with the king, urinated over a theatre balcony, danced around naked in public and once disguised himself as a gynaecological quack who offered his 'expertise' to various women around Tower Hill. Rochester himself admitted that he was continually drunk for five years. On several occasions, he went too far even for Charles. In 1665, for instance, he abducted the wealthy heiress, Elizabeth Malet, before being caught and imprisoned (he later wedded her, and their **marriage** was a surprisingly happy one and produced four children). A poem of his in 1673 that lampooned the king forced him to flee and, on another occasion, he was involved in a late-night scuffle with members of the night watch in which a man was killed and Rochester fled the scene.

Twice, to redeem himself, he joined the navy and saw action in the **Second Anglo-Dutch War** in which he was noted for his courage under fire. Charles, like a surrogate father, would always let him return and even appointed him Gentleman of the Bedchamber in 1666. Once, the day after Rochester had committed a violent act in court, **Samuel Pepys** saw him walking with the king and commented on Charles's 'everlasting shame to have so idle a rogue his companion'.

Rochester's bawdy behaviour, however, belies his reputation as one of the most skilled poets of the Restoration. Intense, fresh, erotic, witty and disrespectful, many of his poems were satires that attacked societal behaviour, hypocrites, court ladies and even the king. One epigram famously went:

> We have a pretty witty king,
> Whose word no man relies on.
> He never said a foolish thing,
> And never did a wise one.

To which Charles replied, ''Tis true, for my words are my own, but my actions are those of my ministers.' *A Satyr Against Reason and Mankind* criticised the corruption and vanity of ministers while *The Imperfect Enjoyment* described disappointing sexual experiences. Some of his poems were so lewd and explicit (involving mutual masturbation, dildoes and bestiality, for instance) that they were not published until the twentieth century. In fact, Rochester has been called England's first pornographer. His skilled writing was much admired by contemporaries, however, some claiming that he was second only to **Dryden**, and even Voltaire later praised his work.

Rochester wrote for the stage too and even trained Elizabeth Barry, the most famous actress of her age (and another of his mistresses!). His most famous probable piece of work was *Sodom, or the Quintessence of Debauchery*. This was a disguised attack on Charles's willingness to tolerate **Catholic**ism but a quick perusal of the cast's names reveals the obscenity within the performance: Bolloxinion, Cuntigratia and Buggeranthos are to name but a few. It is described as one of the most outrageous works in the English language.

Rochester's writings and behaviour reveal a nihilistic, bisexual atheist, a man who epitomises the bawdy Restoration court but whose artistic abilities could only have blossomed in such an environment. He died, unsurprisingly perhaps, from a venereal disease and apparently converted to Christianity on his deathbed.

Witchcraft

In England, there had been a widespread belief in witches for many centuries. Overall, they were considered harmless and mainly disposed towards good, healing magic. It was not until the mid-sixteenth century (earlier on the continent), amid efforts to impose religious conformity, that witchcraft became a capital offence and the first half of the seventeenth century saw a peak in witchcraft trials.

One reason for this was **James I**'s *Daemonologia* (1597) which set out how to identify witches and protect oneself from them. Among the signs were a devil's mark, the ability to breathe underwater and being unable to shed tears. James's fear of witches stemmed from visions of his mother's violent death and a terrifying storm that almost sank the ship in which he and his new wife, **Anne of Denmark**, were travelling (1589). In the witch hunt and trials that followed, one woman 'confessed' to causing the storm by tying the genitals of a dead man to the legs of a cat and tossing them into the sea. Subsequently, around seventy were executed. Soon after James's accession to the English throne, he introduced the Witchcraft Act (1603) which extended previous laws by making any pact with the Devil a capital offence.

Examination of a witch showing Mary Sutton suffering the ducking test. The misfortune she has 'caused' is shown in the background. (*Author: W. Stansby, 1613. Wellcome Collection*)

Witchcraft cases now became more common, the most famous being that of the Pendle Witches in 1612. The investigation began when a woman caused a black dog to threaten a peddlar, in English, when he refused to hand over some pins and made him suffer a stroke. Based on the evidence of an illegitimate, 9-year-old beggar called Jennet Device, a further ten people were arrested (including her own family) and hanged at Lancaster.

'Witch fever' reached a notorious peak in 1645–47 when a **Puritan** lawyer, named Matthew Hopkins, appointed himself as 'Witchfinder General' and stirred up hysteria in East Anglia. Amid fears that witches were causing untimely deaths and harm to livestock and crops, many parishes paid Hopkins large sums of money to root out as many witches as possible. He claimed that witches could be identified by pricking them with a needle. If there was no blood she was a witch, although clever use of retractable needles raised the number of cases as well as his earnings. Unusual marks on the body where the Devil's familiar, normally a cat, had suckled on her were another sign. Hopkins also liked to tie a person's hands to their feet and dunk them underwater. If they lived, they were a witch; if not, they would be received into Heaven. To gain 'confessions', torture was used and victims were often forced to go days without sleep before submitting. In the end, at least a hundred people, mostly women, were hanged. Many of them had been old spinsters, isolated and on the fringes of **society** and therefore mistrusted. Some cases were the results of family feuds and people settling old scores. The timing was important too: in a world that seemed to have been turned upside down by the **Civil Wars**, confusion, hardship and anxiety prevailed.

Witchcraft trials were to continue for the rest of the century. In 1661–62 alone, 600 witches were 'discovered' and 100 hanged. In 1670, 70-year-old Major Thomas Weir, in **Scotland**, was found guilty of incest, bestiality and of dabbling in the occult and was garrotted and burned. The country was entering the age of science and reason though and judges increasingly refused to convict suspects based on superstition. In 1716, Mary Hicks was probably the last person to be executed for witchcraft in England in a country where around 500, in total, were executed for the crime. In America, the last deaths were at the infamous Salem witchcraft trials of 1692–93 in Massachusetts. Initiated by a few children having fits and making accusations and facilitated by a community feud and a zealous Puritan parson, over 200 people were accused of being witches. Of these, fourteen women and five men were hanged, one man was pressed to death and five died in prison.

Wren, Sir Christopher

(1632–1723)

Architect and polymath

Of fragile health, Wren was the only surviving son of the rector of East Knoyle in Wiltshire and his family became well-off after his mother inherited her landowning father's fortune. His father was appointed Dean of Windsor in 1635 but, having royalist connections during the **Civil Wars** meant they had to flee to his sister's home. There, Wren was taught arithmetic and geometry by his brother-in-law; afterwards, he attended Westminster School followed by Wadham College in Oxford.

From a young age, Wren showed great skill at drawing and an insatiable thirst for knowledge and inventions. He created a language for the deaf, for instance, an instrument for writing in the dark and a pneumatic machine. He also drew an anatomy of the brain and successfully injected fluid into a live dog which, soon after, enabled blood transfusions between dogs. While in Oxford, Wren became a member of the 'Invisible College' – a discussion group of natural philosophers that included **Robert Boyle** and **Robert Hooke**. Astronomy was his greatest interest at this stage and his work on Saturn's rings led to his appointment, in 1657, as Professor of Astronomy at Gresham College where he was expected to give weekly lectures in both English and Latin. It was after one such lecture that a group of twelve men, including Wren, met to discuss how to promote experimental science which led to the founding of the Royal Society (1660).

From 1662, Wren became more focused on architecture after his uncle requested that he design a new chapel for Pembroke College, Cambridge. This was followed by his revolutionary D-shaped Sheldonian Theatre in Oxford. Architecture was not a field of study at the time, but Wren was sought due to his combined knowledge of physics and skill at drawing. He may have thought, too, that this was a field he could dominate since there were no well-regarded English architects since the death of **Inigo Jones** (1652). His interest was further fuelled by a trip to Paris in 1665 where he was stunned by the grand, ornate and dramatic style of Baroque architecture and met the great sculptor and architect, Gian Bernini. Upon his return, he offered **Charles II** a dome design for a new St Paul's Cathedral which needed renovation.

The **Fire of London** (1666) suddenly offered Wren a huge opportunity to showcase his talents and modernise the capital. His plan for the new city – a grid pattern with wide streets and piazzas – was rejected due to the expense and people wanting their properties built on the same locations as before. However, Wren was appointed the King's Surveyor of Works and set about designing fifty-two new churches and a new St. Paul's. Working with Hooke and often delegating to others, Wren's churches had a restrained, English Baroque style with galleries on three sides, domes, steeples and large internal spaces with few obstructions to the view of the altar and pulpit. The magnificent St. Paul's is his most famous achievement though. After two designs were rejected, work was begun in 1675. Over the next thirty-five years, Wren often faced criticism and obstructions to his internal designs but, after completion in 1710, he would often sit inside and reflect on his work. Although generally content, he was unhappy with various details such as the inclusion of a balustrade around the roof line which he thought diluted the building's hard edges.

At the same time, Wren was working on other building projects which are famous today – the Royal Observatory and the Royal Naval College (Greenwich), the Royal Hospital (Chelsea), the Wren Library (Cambridge), the façade of Hampton Court Palace and the Monument to commemorate the Fire. Little is known about Wren the man, however, as few records give any detail. He married twice and had four children and maybe a love letter he wrote to his first wife, a childhood neighbour, reveals something of his nature. He had given her a watch and wrote, 'but have a care for it, for I have put such a spell into it; that every Beating of the Balance will tell you 'tis the Pulse of my Heart.'

Wren continued working into his old age and had time to be a member of **Parliament**. Aged 90, he died in his sleep at his son's house in Piccadilly. The archetypal polymath, his interests had shown no bounds, but his greatest legacy lay in the field of architecture. From the Panthéon in Paris to St. Isaac's Cathedral in St Petersburg and the Capitol in Washington, Wren's work can be seen. Fittingly, the epitaph on his tomb in St Paul's says, 'Reader, if you seek his monument, look around you.'

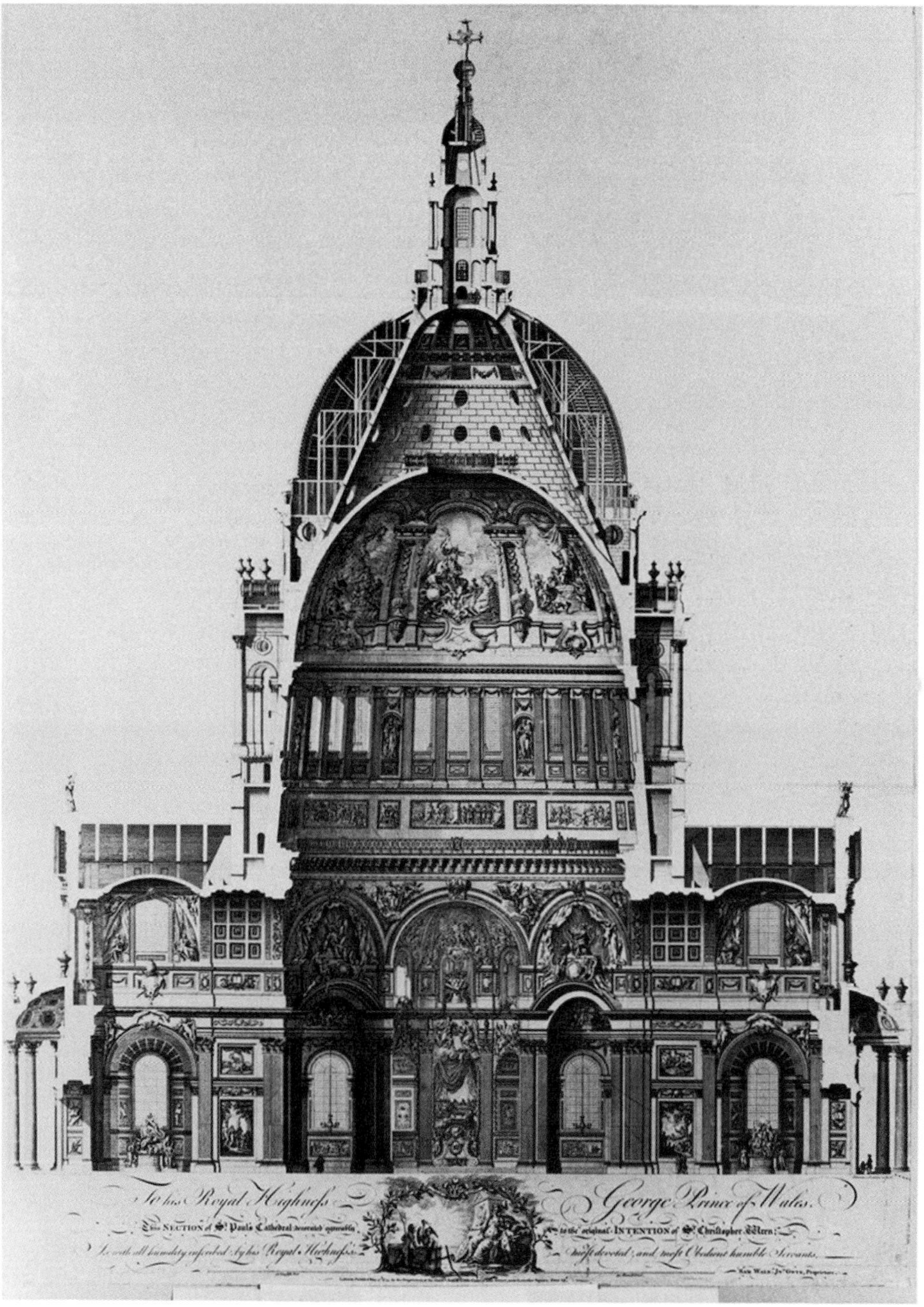

Cross-section of the new St. Paul's. (*Artists: S. Wale & J. Gwynn, 1755 via Wikimedia Commons*)

Sources

AbsoluteHistory
abdn.ac.uk
air-worldwide.com
aisforaphra.org
ajablokov.com
alistairlexden.org.uk
alanmacfarlane.com
allabouthistory.co.uk
andreazuvich.com
anglicancommunion.org
anglican.org
anglicanplanet.net
animato.com.au
anu.edu.au
archive.org
archives.history.ac.uk
artuk.org
atlasobscura.com
avalon.law.yale.edu
battlefieldstrust.com
baus.org.uk
bbc.co.uk – In Our Time
bbk.ac.uk
berkeley.edu
berkshirehistory.com
billofrightsinstitute.org
'Birth control and pregnancy in 17th century England' (C. Scott)
blog.oup.com
bl.uk
brewminate.com
bridgwater-tc.gov.uk
bridlington.net
britannica.com
britishbattles.com
britishfoodandtravel.com
britishfoodhistory.com
britishheritage.com
british-history.ac.uk
buckinghamshire.gov.uk
bushu.ch
cabinet.ox.ac.uk
cam.ac.uk – 'Long-Term Historical Trends in Violent Crime' (M. Eisner)
cambridge.org – 'Last epidemic of plague in England?' (D. van Zwanenberg)
carolana.com
cau.ac.kr
ccel.org
chnm.gmu.edu
christianheritageedinburgh.org.uk
christs.cam.ac.uk
churchillcentral.com
churchofscotland.org.uk
classicfm.com
coffeeaid.co.uk
cornwallforever.co.uk
counterfire.org
cromwellmuseum.org
csun.edu – 'The Rise and Fall of English Coffee Houses' (K. Suter)
davidmhart.com
deadauthorssociety.blogspot.com
delpher.nl
devereuxs.org.uk
dib.ie
dictionary.com
discoverbritain.com
'Disease and Death in Late Stuart London' (M. Waller, Gresham College)
ditext.com
earlofmanchesters.co.uk
earlymodernscribbling.com
ebsco.com
education-uk.org
edwardworthlibrary.ie
eehe.org.uk
eh.net
electricscotland.com
encyclopedia.com
english-heritage.org.uk
englishhistoryauthors.blogspot.com
englishhistory.net
englishmonarchs.co.uk

epa.niif.hu
epoch-magazine.com
eu.theledger.com
explorethearchive.com
familysearch.org
findagrave.com
firefighterfoundation.org.uk
fiveable.me
francisbaconsociety.co.uk
gale.com
geeksforgeeks.org
gethistory.co.uk
gla.ac.uk
goldenhinde.co.uk
goodreads.com
gordons.school
greatfen.org.uk
heritagecalling.com
heritagecollections.parliament.uk
heritagegateway.org.uk
heritage-history.com
historiamag.com
historicengland.co.uk
historic-uk.com
history.blog.gov.uk
history.com
historyextra.com
historyisnowmagazine.com
historylearning.com
historyofparliament.com
historyofparliamentonline.org
historyofwar.org
history.port.ac.uk
historytoday.com
History Roadshow (J. Marshall)
h-net.org
hrp.org.uk
hyperion-records.co.uk
icc-cricket.com
iloi.org
inigo.com
iwhistory.org.uk
johnknifton.com
jstor.org
keithparry.org
'Kings, commoners and homosexuality in the 17th century' (D. Scott)
knebworthhouse.com
'Knowledge and Practice in English Medicine, 1550–1680' (A. Wear)
kronoskaf.com
lancaster.ac.uk
legislation.gov.uk
lenstore.co.uk
libcom.org
libertyfund.org
link.springer.com
livescience.com
localhistories.org
london-fire.gov.uk
lookandlearn.com
lovelymeregis.co.uk
lumenlearning.com
luminarium.org
mapoflondon.uvic.ca
'Marriage in 17th century England' (A. Brabcova)
marryingcultures.eu
mathshistory.st-andrews.ac.uk
mediakron.bc.edu
memorients.com
meredithsweetpea.wordpress.com
merton.ox.ac.uk
mistral.co.uk
monumentoffame.org
moyak.com
museumoflondon.org.uk
nam.ac.uk
naseby.com
nationalarchives.gov.uk
nationalcivilwarcentre.com
ncausa.org
ncbi.nlm.nih.gov
ncpedia.org
nms.ac.uk
nottinghampost.com
nps.gov
oakhamteam.org.uk
olivercromwell.org
ool.co.uk
openbookpublishers.com
openedition.org – 'Another Brick to the Wall' (E. Peyrol-Kleiber)
openedition.org – 'Homicide in Early Modern England 1549–1800' (R. Roth)
ox.ac.uk
oxforddnb.com
oxfordreference.com
ouplaw.com
ourcivilisation.com
ourworldindata.org
parliament.uk

paulinespiratesandprivateers.blogspot.com
pepysdiary.com
philippagregory.com
planbee.com
planethugill.com
plato.stanford.edu
plimouth.org
poetryfoundation.org
portsmouthcathedral.org.uk
princeton.edu
quakersintheworld.org
ranker.com
rcpe.ac.uk
rcplondon.ac.uk
reddit.com
rct.uk
richmond.edu – 'Iron vs gold (W. T. Curtler)
richmond.edu – 'Crime and the common law in England, 1580–1640' (C. Swinden)
rictornorton.co.uk
rmg.co.uk
royalacademy.org.uk
royal.uk
sciencedirect.com
sciencemuseumgroup.org.uk
scotland.org.uk
scottisharchivesforschools.org
scottishhistory.org
scottishhistorysociety.com
spartacus-educational.com
st-andrews.ac.uk
stewartsociety.org
storlann.co.uk
studysmarter.co.uk
tandfonline.com
tastesofhistory.co.uk
theartstory.org
thecharterhouse.org
thecollector.com
theconversation.com
thedockyard.co.uk
thefocusedpastor.org
theguardian.com
thehistoricalfictioncompany.com
thehistoryblog.com
thehistoryofengland.co.uk
thehistoryoflondon.co.uk
thelondonwanderer.co.uk
themonument.org.uk
thenational.scot
thepoetryhour.com
thereformation.info
threedecks.org
'The Stuart Age' (B. Coward & P. Gaunt)
'The use of birth control in early modern Europe' (A. Wiseman)
thingsturnedup.uk
'To Catch a King' (C. Spencer)
traditionalsports.org
Tudors Dynasty Podcast (Dr S. Dunn-Hensley)
tudorplace.com.ar
tudorsociety.com
tudortimes.co.uk
twickenham-museum.org.uk
udel.edu
undiscoveredscotland.co.uk
ushistory.org
uwo.ca
vanityfair.com
virginia-anthology.org
vogue.com
warfarehistorynetwork.com
warhistoryonline.com
warhistory.org
weebly.com
wellcomecollection.org
westminster-abbey.org
whiterose.ac.uk
wikipedia.org
wiley.com
wisemusicclassical.com
worldhistory.org
worldofhorses.co.uk
worldturnedupsidedown.co.uk
womenshistorynetwork.org
writersinspire.org
wrongsideoftheblanket.com
yourirish.com
'Zuvich A'. blog on pen-and-sword.co.uk

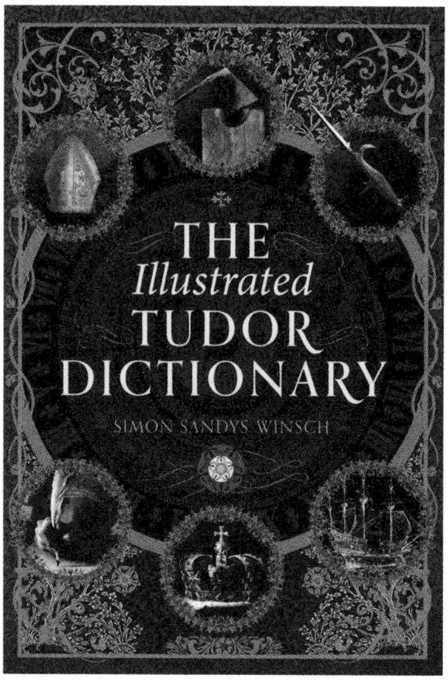

THE ILLUSTRATED TUDOR DICTIONARY

Discover the People, Events and Secrets of Tudor England

By Simon Sandys-Winsch

From Henry VIII and the Battle of Bosworth to Francis Drake, the Reformation and the Spanish Armada, the Tudor age remains one of the most fascinating periods in English history. Now, for the first time, the entire era is brought together in a beautifully illustrated dictionary that makes exploration, learning and discovery effortless.

A Unique Guide to Tudor England
Whether you are a student, teacher, family historian or simply a lover of history, The Illustrated Tudor Dictionary provides a clear, accessible and richly illustrated reference to sixteenth-century England. Cross-referenced entries and striking imagery bring the Tudor world vividly to life.

Inside You'll Discover
The monarchs, nobles, explorers and rebels who shaped the age
Major events including the Battle of Bosworth and the Spanish Armada
Key themes such as education, Parliament, marriage and religion
Lesser-known personalities including court fools, scholars and adventurers
Fascinating stories, mysteries and historical curiosities

Questions Answered Within Its Pages
Which king's head was used as a football?
Who became Europe's first female ambassador?
Which monarch was notorious for cheating at cards?
Why was a renowned scholar kidnapped and forced into a fishing boat?
Which "wizard" claimed to communicate with angels?

Why Readers Will Love It
Unique reference work dedicated to the Tudor period
Clear, detailed and easy-to-use format
Packed with iconic and lesser-known illustrations
Balanced, informative and highly accessible
Perfect for students and history enthusiasts alike

---

288 pages • 130 illustrations • Hardback
ISBN 9781036101985 • £29.00

Dear Reader,

We hope you have enjoyed this book, but why not share your views on social media? You can also follow our pages to see more about our other products: facebook.com/penandswordbooks or follow us on X @penswordbooks

You can also view our products at www.pen-and-sword.co.uk (UK and ROW) or www.penandswordbooks.com (North America).

To keep up to date with our latest releases and online catalogues, please sign up to our newsletter at: www.pen-and-sword.co.uk/newsletter

If you would like a printed catalogue with our latest books, then please email: enquiries@pen-and-sword.co.uk or telephone: 01226 734555 (UK and ROW) or email: uspen-and-sword@casematepublishers.com or telephone: (610) 853-9131 (North America).

We respect your privacy and we will only use personal information to send you information about our products.

Thank you!